TUTANKHAMUN
THE EXODUS
CONSPIRACY

TUTANKHAMUN THE EXODUS CONSPIRACY

The Truth Behind Archaeology's Greatest Mystery

Andrew Collins
and
Chris Ogilvie-Herald

First published in 2002 by

Virgin Books
Thames Wharf Studios
Rainville Rd
London W6 9HA

ISBN 1 85227 972 9

Typesetting by Phoenix Photosetting, Chatham, Kent

Printed and bound by Mackays of Chatham

CONTENTS

LIST OF PLATES

TUTANKHAMUN – THE EXODUS CONSPIRACY

28. The end of the narrow ravine known as the Siq, or Cleft of Moses, at Petra.
29. Al-Madhbah, the High Place, on the summit of Jebel al-Madhbah.
30. The High Place's circular basin.
31. The High Place's carved stone altar.
32. Jebel al-Madhbah, the most holy site in Petra.
33. Carved pair of feet among archaic rock art at the base of a mountain in Wadi Rum.
34. Betyl containing a god-block with twin columns.
35. Hemispherical god-block in a niche within Petra's Siq.
36. Triangular carvings representing the *genius loci*, or spirit, of the Shara mountains.
37. Scarab seal from Tawilan, an Iron Age Edomite settlement near Petra.
38. The Shrine of Aaron.
39. Summit of Jebel Harûn.
40. View from the altar of Petra's High Place across to Jebel Harûn.
41. Michelangelo's statue of Moses in the Vatican.
42. Arthur James Balfour.
43. Chaim Weizmann and Feisal ibn Hussein in June 1918.
44. TE Lawrence, alias 'Lawrence of Arabia'.
45. President Woodrow Wilson with his close aide Col. Mandel House.
46. Howard Carter and Lord Carnarvon.
47. Almina Victoria Marie Alexandra Wombwell, the future Countess of Carnarvon, as a child.
48. Almina, Countess of Carnarvon, wife of the fifth earl of Carnarvon.
49. Lieutenant Colonel Ian Onslow 'Tiger' Dennistoun with Almina, Countess of Carnarvon.

Pictures 10, 11, 12, 13, 17, 18 © The Griffith Institute; picture 33 © panoramaproductions.net; picture 37 © the estate of Crystal-M Bennett; pictures 47, 48 with thanks to Anthony Leadbetter.

LIST OF FIGURES

Figure 9 with thanks to Lisa Adams; figures 13, 14 with thanks to Sue Collins.

This book is dedicated to the achievement of lasting peace in the Middle East. Let us hope that one day this will no longer be simply a distant dream. Also to my wife Sue, for her love and support and our future together.

– Andrew Collins

In memory of Jill (Martin) Ogilvie-Herald whose journey back to the Duat, the stars from whence all life came, began far too soon.

– Chris Ogilvie-Herald

ACKNOWLEDGMENTS

Let me begin by thanking my wife Sue for the wonderful help, drawings, support and patience she has constantly given me during the writing of this book; David Southwell, for his continued help, inspiration and insights; Graham Phillips, for understanding the burdens of being an author and coming to the same conclusions; Amber McCauley and Catherine Hale, for their invaluable translations; Rodney Hale, for his support and aid in the construction of the maps and illustrations; and Richard Ward, for his continued friendship and additional help on book research.

My thanks also go out to Lisa Adams, for her 3D plan of Tutankhamun's Burial Chamber; Dorothy Arnold of the Metropolitan Museum of Art, New York, for answering my queries regarding Arthur C. Mace; Michael Carmichael, for his editorial suggestions and comments on poisons and chemistry in ancient Egypt; Lorraine Evans, for sharing information with us; Nigel Foster, for letting us loose in his cyber café; Jonathan Harris, for his late-night telephone calls; Saleh Hilalat and everyone at Petra's Crowne Plaza Resort, for their hospitality and future support; everyone at Leigh Library, for not running away whenever I enter their establishment; Gareth Medway, for his editorial suggestions; Ahmad Muammar, for providing me with the inner history of Petra, reading the relevant chapters and showing Sue and I the most gracious hospitality; Mu'tasim Nawafleh, for the legend of Aaron's flight to Jebel Harûn; Nigel Skinner Simpson, for his invaluable editorial comments and trips down here to sort out my computer, and Victor Winstone, for providing information on British policy in Egypt and Palestine during the 1920s.

Last, but not least, I would like to thank Matthew Adams; Michael Baigent; Robert Bauval; Todd Borst; Ernie Collins; Storm Constantine; Adrian Gilbert; Clive Harper, Robin Crookshank Hilton; Paul Kyfin; Ian Lawton; Johnny Merron; David Panter; Lynn Picknett; Clive Prince; David Rohl; Ann Smith; Rob Speight; Kathy and Colin Stallard; Pandora Stevens; Greg Taylor at the 'Daily Grail' ('are you getting yours?'); Paul Weston; Marcus Williamson; Caroline Wise; everyone at Peters, Fraser and Dunlop, especially Simon Trewin, for his help in securing publication of this book; and all the staff at Virgin, including Kerri Sharp, Julia Bullock, Fiona McBain and Fiona Wyatt, for the part they have played in the publication of this book.

– Andrew Collins
Leigh-on-Sea
22 July 2002

I would like to take this opportunity of expressing my sincere gratitude to the many people who have helped with this work by answering my requests for information and sharing with us their insights and knowledge. In no particular order they are:

Dr Diana Magee, from the Griffith Institute for her valued assistance during my research into the Howard Carter archives and for responding to various email queries; Mr Chris Naunton, librarian, at the Egypt Exploration Society, for his enthusiastic assistance in locating various periodicals, books and magazines; Ms Lucie Ryzova, temporary archivist, at the Middle East Centre, for her interest in this project, her assistance in locating relevant material and for responding positively to requests for information that fell outside her domain; Mr Anthony Leadbetter, godson to Almina Herbert, the fifth Countess of Carnarvon, for his many communications, recollections of both Almina and a bygone age, and for agreeing to meet the authors for a recorded interview at Highclere Castle in August 2001; Frederick W Bauman, manuscript reference specialist at the Library of Congress, for responding to various email queries and for forwarding photocopies of the Willard Family Papers; Mr Thomas Hoving, former head of the Metropolitan Museum of Art in New York, for responding to a number of our email queries; Dr TGH James for a two-page copy of Lee Keedick's notes on Howard Carter, which became crucial to our understanding of the 'missing papyri' and Carter's threat to use its content; Mr Ted Keedick, the grandson of Lee Keedick, for various communications and his permission to quote from his grandfather's notes on Howard Carter; Mr Eamon Dyas, group records manager at the News International and Times Newspapers archive office, for his kind assistance and for permission to quote the memo from Robbins to Dawson, regarding Carnarvon's offer of an exclusivity deal; Aayko Eyma, for forwarding my messages to his EEF forum and his contacts in our attempt to track down the rings Carter bequeathed to his niece Phyllis Walker; Janet Powell and Martin Argles, for permission to quote from the diary of Mervyn Herbert, and Dr Nicholas Reeves, for responding to our query regarding the whereabouts of two letters written by Lord Carnarvon.

I would also like to thank the following persons and organisations for their assistance: Ahmed Osman, Iain Ogilvie, Barbara Keller, Amargi Hillier, Joseph S Myers, Philip Gould, Chris Townsend, Marcus Allen, Ben Weider, Eugene Rogan and Samir Raafat, the staff at the British Library, the staff at the Egypt Exploration Society and the staff at the British Newspaper Library. If I have omitted anyone who should have been mentioned above, then I humbly apologise for my oversight. Finally, I would like to express my sincere gratitude to my wife Malathi, my mother Elizabeth and my brother Richard for their love and support.

– Chris Ogilvie-Herald
London
22 July 2002

How shall we sing the Lord's song in a strange land?

If I forget thee, O Jerusalem, let my right hand forget her cunning.

If I do not remember thee, let my tongue cleave to the roof of my mouth;

If I prefer not Jerusalem above my chief joy.

— Psalm 137

PRELUDE
SECRETS IN DEATH

THE CONTINENTAL HOTEL, CAIRO, 5 APRIL 1923, 1.55 A.M.
Lord Porchester, the eldest son and heir to the fifth Earl of Carnarvon, became aware that his light slumber was being rudely interrupted. The repeated knocking on the door of his hotel room pulled him to his senses, as he lay half conscious in the semidarkness. Only then did he realise that the nurse was calling his name.

Attempting to regain his composure, 'Porchey' recalled the dire circumstances that had led to his departing for Cairo just two days earlier.[1] He had been taking part in an inter-regimental polo match against the 11th Hussars at the Wheeler Polo Ground, in Meerut, India. After the scorching-hot sun lowered sufficiently, they had played before an audience that included the Viceroy of India, Lord Reading, and his group of guests. The scores were level, and, with just a few seconds of the match to go, Porchey, playing for his own regiment, the 7th Hussars, broke through the opposition's defence, and, with rather a little bit of luck, managed to hit the ball towards the goal. When it caught the wicker of the goalpost, he had let out a cry of frustration. Yet, on looking again, he saw that the ball had managed somehow to trickle past the goal line! God only knows how! The captain, Field, received the cup from the Viceroy, after which the whole team stepped up to receive their medals; it had been one of those glorious days he would remember for a long time to come.

Then the mood had suddenly changed with the arrival of the Viceroy's bodyguard, a Sikh, dressed in white and sporting a scarlet Viceregal sash. He bowed his head respectfully before handing him an urgent telegram from Egypt. After asking the Viceroy if he could open the cable, his heart sank as he read its contents:

FROM SIR JOHN MAXWELL COMMANDER-IN-CHIEF EGYPT TO SIR CHARLES MUNROE C-IN-C INDIA URGENT PLEASE EXPEDIATE AN IMMEDIATE PASSAGE FOR LORD PORCHESTER TO CAIRO WHERE HIS FATHER IS VERY DANGEROUSLY ILL.[2]

It was bad news that he had not wanted to hear. His dear father was seriously ill, and he should be by his side, as would his mother and sister.

After he had ordered his wife Catherine to pack their belongings, sell the polo ponies and make plans to meet him in either Egypt or England, arrangements were made for him to leave right away. She took it badly, the poor girl, knowing full well that there was little chance of seeing him again for some while. More than this, he knew instinctively that his military career was over, and that very soon he would have to take on the responsibilities that came with being the sixth Earl of Carnarvon.

The Viceroy had pulled out all the stops to ensure that his journey to Egypt via Aden would be in the quickest possible time. He had departed on a vessel named the *Narkunda* and disembarked eventually at Suez, where a launch was waiting to whisk him across the harbour to the rail sidings. Here he joined a private train belonging to Sir John Maxwell, who warned him that it might already be too late since his father was very poorly indeed.

He had arrived at the Grand Continental Hotel around 2 p.m. on Wednesday 4 April to be greeted by a nurse, who informed him that his mother, Almina Herbert, the fifth Countess of Carnarvon, was already at her husband's side. His sister, Lady Evelyn Herbert, who had become their father's constant travelling companion in his latter years and most recently had devoted her time to tending him during his illness, was also with their mother.

On climbing the stairs Porchey had found everyone asleep, and, although the nurse said that his mother would take him to see his father when she awoke, he insisted on visiting him immediately. She led the way, explaining as they moved that the earl was incoherent, and so was unlikely to recognise him. On entering the room, Porchey found his father lying in bed unshaven, his eyes bloodshot and traces of yellow foam lining his lips. He looked in a bad way.

The son held his father's hand and told him that he had come to make him better, even though he knew that his condition was surely terminal. In response, his lordship simply began spouting some gibberish about killing Italians like rabbits, even though he had never even fought in the war. He was quite delirious, the poor fellow.

Porchey looked down on him, full of sadness, in the knowledge that he would never be able to make up the lost years when they had known so little of each other. Yet he reminisced over what a remarkable man his father had been. Despite his ailing health, he had achieved so much during his life, as a sportsman, a breeder of racehorses, a motorcar driver, an accomplished photographer and as a man with a thirst for mystery and adventure. Yet by far his greatest accomplishment had been as an amateur Egyptologist, collecting antiquities and acting as patron to Mr Howard Carter, whose five-year search to find the tomb of the pharaoh Tutankhamun culminated with its discovery in the Valley of the Kings the previous November. Now his father was a celebratory, known throughout the world. His present state of health was a tragedy, not just on a personal level, but to everyone who had become transfixed by the mystery of Tutankhamun, and the wonderful treasures that awaited removal inside the burial chamber.

According to Lady Evelyn it had been a mosquito bite nicked by the blade of a razor that had brought about their father's deterioration in health. Even though he had applied iodine and some cotton wool to the small cut on his right cheek, his temperature had soared to a hundred and one. Yet by the next morning it had returned to normal. But that night he had taken a turn for the worse, and, when Eve found that his temperature was once more a hundred and one, she had called in the best doctors in Cairo. Here at the hotel he had been given all possible care and attention, but was later diagnosed as having succumbed to blood poisoning.

After ten days the fifth earl had seemed to be over the worst of it, and even sat up in bed. However, he then suffered a relapse and was diagnosed as having contracted viral pneumonia. There had been no change in his condition since that time, and upon seeing him the previous afternoon Porchey knew his fears that his father was dying seemed agonisingly confirmed. He had visited him again before retiring to bed that night, but there was no change in his condition.

The knocking on the door continued as he glanced at his watch. It was 1.55 in the morning.[3] Having asked the nurse to enter, the door opened as she said, regretfully, 'Lord Porchester, you had better come quickly. It is your father, he has died.' The reaction was one of shock, even though he had known it was inevitable. 'Your mother is with him now. Please come quickly,' she added.

Having put on a dressing gown, Porchey combed his hair, picked up a torch from the bedroom table and made his way along the passage towards his father's room. Suddenly, the electric lights extinguished in the hotel and, from what he could see, across Cairo as a whole, plunging everything into darkness. Quickly he switched on the torch, and handed it to a nurse, suggesting that she obtain some candles from the manager's office.

Finally, in the darkness, he entered his father's room. What he saw before him remained etched into his memory for the rest of his life. Illuminated by candlelight, his father lay there with his mother kneeling beside him. In silence, he got down beside her and, taking hold of his father's hand, began to say a prayer.

George Edward Stanhope Molyneux Herbert, the fifth Earl of Carnarvon, lay at peace, his colourful career over at the age of 57. Yet with his release from this troubled world went certain closely guarded secrets regarding what really had occurred when he, Carter, Lady Evelyn and the engineer Arthur 'Pecky' Callender had entered the tomb under the cover of darkness at the end of November the previous year. They were secrets that had bound together these individuals for over four months. Secrets, that if revealed would not only have ruined Lord Carnarvon's reputation as a straightforward English aristocrat with immense respect throughout the world, but also Howard Carter's role as the most famous Egyptologist the world had ever known. Secrets that might well have contributed to the untimely death of Lord Carnarvon. Secrets that, if they had become common knowledge at a time when the international media were focused daily on the discoveries surrounding the tomb, would have caused not only a political and religious scandal, but might also have changed the world for ever.

PART ONE
TUTANKHAMUN

1. THE KING IS DEAD

THE VALLEY OF THE KINGS, EGYPT, c. 1339 BC[1]

It was a time of great mourning and sorrow across the whole of Egypt. Tutankhamun, the boy-king, who had reigned over the empire for just nine years, was dead. Amid scenes of unimaginable grief in the southern capital Thebes, a funerary procession snaked its way through the hot desert valleys. Underneath a colourful canopy, the mummified body of the king was being transported across the rough terrain on a wooden sledge pulled by twelve trusted individuals, including Pentu and Usermont, the ministers of Upper and Lower Egypt, both adorned in their distinctive robes of office. All wore white linen bands of mourning around their heads.

Behind the funeral hearse women cried, wailed and tugged desperately at their hair in an attempt to express the great sense of loss that the whole of Egypt felt at this time. Then came the king's grieving widow, Ankhesenamun; as well as priests of the Temple of Amun, personal friends, courtiers, officials and Aye, the future king. He would attend the funeral both as a *sem*-priest, able to perform magical rituals on behalf of the king, and as the living embodiment of the sun god Horus. In this role he was to conduct the rites of passage that would enable the pharaoh to enter the next world, who in death had become at one with Horus' father, Osiris, Lord of the Underworld.

Trailing up the rear of the funeral procession were dozens of bare-chested men, each carrying items that the king would require in the afterlife. There were couches, thrones, chariots, weapons, toys, divine statues, and box after box of personal belongings, linen garments, cooked food and hundreds of *ushabtis*, servants in the form of small mummified figurines, to take care of any work the king would be called upon to do in the next world. All would be taken down into the four chambers that made up the king's tomb, cut out of the solid limestone cliff face in a dried-up riverbed, or wadi, beneath Meretseger, the omnipresent pyramid-like peak that would come to mark the site of some thirty royal burials.

THE EMBALMING PROCESS

Seventy days had elapsed since the expiry of the young king, who was no more than eighteen years old when he died so tragically following a blow to the head, most probably after a fall from a chariot (see Appendix I – 'The Death of Tutankhamun'). During this time of national mourning his body had been washed and purified by the royal embalmers at Per-Wabet, the Place of Purification, located most probably in the Temple of Karnak, north of the city. Very quickly, they had removed the soft tissue and viscera, or sacred organs, which were extracted via the left side of the central abdomen. Afterwards, the carcass had been drained of fluids, which ran off into a basin. Only the brain, worked out of the cranium through the use of a wire hook inserted up the nostril, was thrown away. The other organs extracted – the stomach, kidneys, liver and intestines – were preserved in order that they might be wrapped before being placed in four mummiform gold coffinettes, which were in turn contained in a calcite canopic chest placed in a special room alongside the pharaoh. Only the heart was left in place, so that the king's soul might be able to read the magic spells as he made his exit from the tomb.

Once this delicate process had been completed, the body had been enveloped for 35 days in a bed of natron, a natural soda and salt, which would absorb any remaining fluids. It was then transferred to Per-Nefret, the Place of Beautification, where it was embalmed with rich oils, resins and spices. Afterwards, it was sewn up, and priests wearing canine masks representing Anubis, the jackal-headed judge of the underworld and god of embalming, wrapped the body in layer after layer of bandages. Between the layers were placed a multitude of protective amulets and talismans, brought to life by a series of magical utterances spoken by the officiating priests.

With the embalming and mummification process completed, the body of Tutankhamun was prepared for its final journey to the Valley of the Kings. A gold diadem was placed on the king's brow, on which were the vulture and cobra goddesses, Nekhbet and Wadjet, protectors of the Two Lands, Upper and Lower Egypt. A solid-gold death mask, fashioned in the likeness of the pharaoh, was placed over the mummy's head, while on his chest were placed a pair of crossed golden hands, which held the king's crook and flail.

LIVE AGAIN, FOR EVER!

Once the funeral procession had come to a halt in front of the intended tomb, a long line of court officials and their servants started to fill up each of the chambers with grave goods. At the same time preparations were being made to conduct one last ritual to enable the dead king's soul to transcend from its earthly form to that of an *akh*, or 'glorious spirit'. This would take place only after it had made a treacherous journey through the strange world known as the *am-duat*, or underworld, in which it would encounter frightening monsters and serpents and undergo a series of trials and tribulations. If successful, the deceased pharaoh would be able to leave the underworld at a gate on the eastern horizon, and in the dawn twilight be born anew amid the circumpolar stars that surround the northern star, the pivot of the celestial universe.

The ritual, known as the Opening of the Mouth, required the participation of twelve priests and officials, and was led, traditionally, by the king's successor, in this case Aye. When all was ready, priests placed four censers of incense in the four quarters to mark out an area of sacred space around the gilded shrine containing the royal coffin. Others took water from four vases, which was sprinkled towards the four corners of the earth. Then came an invocation of the gods, and the sacrifice of various animals in celebration of Horus' triumph over the god Set, slayer of his father Osiris. They included two bulls, one each for the north and the south, as well as ducks and gazelles. A leg and heart were taken from one of the bulls and offered up to the mummy, while the rest of the offerings were to serve as food for the pharaoh in the afterlife.[2]

Aye then picked up a ritual instrument known as an adze, made either of wood or of meteoric iron, and touched its crooked tip on the king's nose, eyes, ears, mouth, hands, genitals and feet in order to imbue each one with a magical reality. When this was done he uttered words and incantations from 'The Book of the Opening of the Mouth' in the name of Anubis and Horus, ending with the words 'live again, forever'.[3]

At last the burial could take place.

Carefully, the king's mummy was taken from the sledge and carried by pallbearers down the sunken staircase that led into the tomb's Entrance Corridor. Beyond this was the Antechamber and on its right-hand side was the Burial Chamber and Treasury, where the calcite canopic chest containing the viscera had been installed inside a gilded shrine. Around this had been placed life-sized golden statues of the four tutelary goddesses of death – Neith, Selkit, Isis and Nephthys. Between the shrine and the entrance into this chamber two other protective devices were placed in position, one a wooden head of a cow representing the goddess Hathor and the other a black wooden statue of Anubis, in his form as the jackal.

Within the Burial Chamber, the walls had been painted with scenes meant to aid the king's soul to enter the afterlife, while in the centre of the room was a huge sarcophagus in rose-coloured quartzite. Inside this were a series of three gilded anthropoid coffin bases, one inside the other, like some kind of giant Russian doll. Their mummiform lids bore the likeness of the pharaoh in his guise as Osiris, and one by one these were lowered on to their respective coffin bases. As this was taking place those present, including perhaps the king's widow, placed garlands of flowers on the brow and chest of each living image of the pharaoh as oils and resins were poured over the coffins. Once the lids had been fastened down using either gold or silver nails, a fine linen shroud was placed over the outermost coffin.

An enormous red granite lid was then manoeuvred slowly into position, so that the king's resting place might be sealed for ever. Yet, as this was taking place, disaster struck. Coming down a little too fast, the lid cracked in two, an ill omen if ever there was one. With no one able to do anything about this terrible mishap, the two pieces were simply pushed together and the crack was filled with a gypsum mortar. Hastily, carpenters then went to work assembling a series of four prefabricated 'houses', or gilded shrines, each a little larger than the one before, which were then positioned around the sarcophagus. On the floor between them, and around the outermost shrine, were placed a series of magical items required by the pharaoh on his treacherous journey through the underworld. The door handles of each shrine were then bound with hemp rope and their knots stamped with the seal of the royal necropolis – the god Anubis as the jackal, seated above nine bound enemy captives.

Having completed their work in the Burial Chamber, priests erected and activated two life-size sentinel figures in black and gold, which held in one hand a mace and in the other a pole-like staff. As representations of the king's *ka*, or 'ghost', they were placed one each side of the entrance into the Burial Chamber as guardians of the king's final resting place.

Gradually, those who had witnessed the burial of the king withdrew, leaving only the king's widow and friends to enjoy a funerary banquet in which they ate a small portion of the sacrificial offerings from the Opening of the Mouth ceremony. Afterwards, the tableware was ritually broken and the floor swept clean before everything used, including the white mourning bands and embalming equipment, was placed inside twelve large storage jars located in the Entrance Corridor, away from the sterile environment of the tomb.

When everything was done in the four chambers, the doorways into all rooms, with the exception of the Treasury, were sealed using loose stones. Each entrance was then rendered flush with mortar and stamped with the seals of Tutankhamun and the royal necropolis. Finally, the dead king could be left in peace, with only soldiers of the royal necropolis guarding his final resting place.

The years rolled by, and despite two attempts by tomb robbers to steal the gold and precious items contained in the tomb, during the reign of Aye or his successor Horemheb, the mortal remains of Tutankhamun were never violated. Despite the ill omen presented by the cracking in two of the sarcophagus lid, the gods looked favourably on the fate of the boy-king. Very quickly the whereabouts of his earthly remains were forgotten, and some two hundred years after they were interred a much larger tomb for the pharaoh Rameses VI was hewn out of the rock directly above that belonging to Tutankhamun. Workers involved in its construction built their huts directly over the concealed entrance to the smaller tomb, confusing any attempts by treasure hunters to uncover it in more modern times. Thus the boy-king remained undisturbed for over a million passings of the sun, forever forging his immortality, until one day an Englishman named Howard Carter began digging in the Valley of the Kings.

2. MYSTERY IN THE VALLEY

For more than three thousand years the boy-king evaded discovery as every other tomb in the Valley of the Kings was plundered and looted. Not even the concerted efforts of the Italian strongman, explorer and adventurer Giovanni Belzoni (1778–1823), who discovered five tombs in the Valley, including that of Seti I in 1817, brought the world anywhere nearer to finding the resting place of Tutankhamun. In 1820, despite his earlier success, Belzoni gave up, declaring that there were 'no more tombs' to be found in Bibân el Molûk, the Arab name for the Valley. On his departure others took up the mantle, and more tombs were found: Champollion, Rossellini and Lepsius are names connected with explorations in the Valley, the last mentioned having opened the tomb of Rameses the Great and explored the greater part of King Merneptah's mausoleum.

Then came Theodore M Davis (1837–1915), a lawyer and millionaire from Boston, USA, with a passion for archaeological discovery. In 1902 he was granted an excavating concession – a kind of digging permit issued by the Service des Antiquités, then headed by the distinguished French Egyptologist Gaston Maspero – to begin exploration in the Valley of the Kings. Over a period of twelve years he somehow managed to achieve immense success, finding and excavating the tombs of key figures from Egypt's celebrated past, including those of the female king Hatshepsut, Thutmose IV, both from the Eighteenth Dynasty (see the time chart on page 12 for the chronology of different periods of ancient Egyptian history), and Siptah, who reigned during the Nineteenth Dynasty. All had been extensively plundered in antiquity.

In addition to these, Davis came across the royal tomb of the military genius Horemheb, c. 1335–1308 BC, who succeeded Aye as king. In the nearby Valley of the Nobles he unearthed the tomb of Yuya and his wife Tuya, the parents of Tiye, the Great Royal Wife of the pharaoh Amenhotep III, who was the father not only of the 'heretic' king Akhenaten, c. 1367–1350 BC, but also, very probably, of Tutankhamun. In addition to the intact mummies of the couple, who were both of non-royal descent, the tomb contained well-preserved funerary furniture and a dismantled chariot, the best examples found prior to the discovery of Tutankhamun.

THE MYSTERY OF TOMB 55

Then, in January 1907, Davis discovered what is arguably the most enigmatic tomb in the whole of the Theban necropolis, and identifying its incumbent will become crucial to our understanding of the chaotic times in which Tutankhamun lived. Designated KV 55 by the Antiquities Service, it was found

EGYPTIAN PERIOD	DYNASTIES	RELEVANT KINGS	HIGHEST DATED YEAR	DATES BC	SUGGESTED DATES BC OF CORRESPONDING BIBLICAL EVENTS
PREDYNASTIC (GERZEAN/ NAQADA II)				3500–3200	
PROTODYNASTIC	0			3200–3100	
ARCHAIC	I–II			3100–2700	
OLD KINGDOM	III–VII			2700–2137	
FIRST INTERMEDIATE	VIII–X			2137?	
MIDDLE KINGDOM	XI–XII			2134–1786	1996–1821' – AGE OF ABRAHAM
		XII SENWOSRET III	33	1878–1843	
		SOBEKNOFRU	3	1789–1786	
SECOND INTERMEDIATE (INCL. HYKSOS)	XIII–XVIII (XV–XVI)			(1730/1650–1575)	
		XVII KAMOSE	3?	1578–1575	
NEW KINGDOM	XVIII–XX			1575–1308	
		XVIII AHMOSE	22	1575–1550	
		AMENHOTEP I	21	1550–1528	
		THUTMOSE I	9/4	1528–1510	
		THUTMOSE II	18	1510–1490	
		HATSHEPSUT	22/20	1490–1468	
		THUTMOSE III	54	1490–1436	
		AMENHOTEP II	23	1436–1413	
		THUTMOSE IV	8	1413–1405	
		AMENHOTEP III	39/38	1405–1367	1370–1250?* – LIFE OF MOSES
		AMENHOTEP IV (AKHENATEN)	17	1367–1350	
		SMENKHKARE	3?	1352–1350	
		TUTANKHAMUN	9	1347–1339	
		AYE	4	1339–1335	
		HOREMHEB	28/27	1335–1308	
		XIX RAMESES I	2	1308–1307	
		SETI I	14/11	1308–1291?	
LATE DYNASTIC	XXI–XXXI	RAMESES II	67	1290–1224	1250–1150?* – CONQUEST OF CANAAN
		MERNEPTAH	10	1224–1214	
		SETI II	6	1214–1208	
		SIPTAH	6	1208–1202	
		XX RAMESES III	32	1182–1151	
		RAMESES VI	7	1141–1134	
		RAMESES IX	17	1134–1117	
				1087–332	1091' – SAUL, KING OF ISRAEL
					1065' – DAVID, KING OF ISRAEL
					1015' – SOLOMON, KING OF ISRAEL
					1004' – DEDICATION OF TEMPLE
					976' – DEATH OF SOLOMON
					976' – REHOBOAM, KING OF JUDAH
					JEROBOAM, KING OF ISRAEL
					897' – JEHORAM, KING OF ISRAEL
		XXII OSORKON II	29	881–852?	
					838' – AMAZIAH, KING OF JUDAH
					640' – JOSIAH, KING OF JUDAH

NOTE: All Egyptian dates are based on the chronology of 'The Kings from Manetho, the King-Lists, and the Monuments', included as an appendix to Gardiner, *Egypt of the Pharaohs*. Suggested dates for biblical events are based on the findings of this current work* and MG Easton, *The Illustrated Bible Dictionary*, after James Ussher (1580–1656), Archbishop of Armagh.'

Fig. 1. Chronology of ancient Egypt, listing kings featured in the text and corresponding biblical events.

to contain a damaged gilded coffin, inlaid with coloured glass. It had fallen to the ground when the wooden bier supporting it had collapsed under the weight, partially displacing the coffin lid and revealing the mummy within. Everything in the tomb was in disarray, causing utter confusion when attempts were made to identify the body. Left in the entrance corridor were panels from a dismantled gilded shrine on which was an inscription proclaiming that it had been made for Tiye, Great Royal Wife of Amenhotep III, by her son Akhenaten. Other smaller items strewn around in the sepulchre also bore her name.

Four 'magic bricks', placed in the four directions in order to protect the person's *ka*, or 'ghost', from malevolent influences, were located, and these had at one time borne Akhenaten's prenomen Neferkheprure-wa'enre.[1] On the coffin itself were inscriptions honouring Akhenaten. Although originally the words of a female, a royal wife, her name had been removed from the coffin and the feminine emphasis of her utterances altered to that of a royal male. Yet then later both the new name and that of Akhenaten had been removed following the collapse of the latter's religious regime (see Chapter Three), presumably at the point when the burial took place. Careful research in more recent times has shown that the missing name is probably that of Kiya, a lesser wife of Akhenaten.[2] Four canopic jars in alabaster, containing the viscera of the deceased, were found in a recess in one wall. Their stoppers had each been fashioned into the head of a royal female wearing a Nubian-style wig, thought now to represent Kiya. Unfortunately, the inscriptions on the jars had been ground away, and thus the identification of their original owner can never be certain. So whose body lay in KV 55?

At the time of its discovery, Davis employed the services of two medical men, one a doctor and the other a surgeon, to examine the body *in situ*.[3] Having removed some of the bandages, the doctor posited that, from the width of the pelvis, and the burial position of the body, it could only be that of a royal wife. Without attempting to confirm these findings, Davis concluded that he had discovered the body of Queen Tiye.[4] Yet to everyone's surprise, when the remains were examined a few months later by George Elliot Smith, the professor of anatomy at the Cairo School of Medicine, it was found that the bones belonged to a young man aged no more than 25 or 26.[5]

New theories had to be devised and Edward Ayrton, the British archaeologist working in the Valley on behalf of Davis, concluded that the mysterious occupant was none other than Tutankhamun, a theory that obviously proved to be incorrect. On the other hand, Ayrton's colleague Arthur Weigall decided that the magic bricks identified the body as that of Akhenaten, a view shared by Smith. It was considered that the heretic king's remains had been transferred hastily to the Theban necropolis from the royal tomb constructed into the cliffs of the so-called Royal Wadi beyond Akhetaten, the city in Middle Egypt he built and occupied during the last twelve to thirteen years of his seventeen-year reign. So, had KV 55 been prepared as the resting place of the heretic king?

Fig. 2. Queen Tiye, the Great Royal Wife of King Amenhotep III.

PROFESSOR HARRISON'S FINDINGS

In December 1963 a team of scientists, led by Professor Ronald G Harrison of Liverpool University, examined the body found in KV 55, first in the Egyptian Museum and later at the Qasr el-Aini Hospital.[6] In his subsequent report on the subject, he concluded that the 'remains are undoubtedly from a man, less than 25 years of age, and about 5 ft. 7 ins. [1.70 metres] in height at the time of death'.[7] He revealed also that if 'certain valuable anatomical criteria (for instance, the state of wear of the teeth, state of the symphyseal surface of the pubis, degree of union of clavicular, humeral, and other epiphyses) are to be utilized, it is possible to be more definite that the age at death occurred in the 20th year'.[8] These findings tended to confirm earlier examinations of the body by anatomical experts working in the Egyptological field of study. Elliot Smith had concluded that it was of a male around 25 or 26, while Dr Douglas E Derry, then professor of anatomy at the Egyptian University, examined the body in 1931 and determined that the bones were those of a young man not more than 23 years of age.[9] These findings were finally confirmed in 2000, when Joyce Filer, the special assistant for human and animal remains in the Department of Egyptian Antiquities at the British Museum, was given the opportunity to examine the skeleton in the Egyptian Museum. For a number of reasons, she was able to set an upper limit on the age of death of the person at 25, and possibly younger still.[10]

So to whom did the body really belong?

Akhenaten was married to one of the most famous, and most beautiful, women in Egyptian history. We speak, of course, of Nefertiti, whose extraordinary life-size painted limestone bust was found in the ruins of a sculptor's workshop at the site of Akhenaten's city by the German archaeologist Ludwig Borchardt in 1912. Before her elevation to the role of co-regent around Year 14 of her husband's seventeen-year reign (see Chapter Three), the couple produced six daughters, who in paintings and reliefs of the period are shown in the company of their parents. After this time, the eldest child, Meritaten, took over her role as chief wife, even though she retained the title 'king's daughter', and within just a year or so she gave birth to a daughter, possibly sired by her father. In this knowledge, she must have been at least thirteen or fourteen when she became a royal wife. Surmising that Akhenaten was in his mid- to late teens when he ascended the throne, it would imply that he was at least in his mid-thirties at the time of death. If so, then the body in KV 55 could not have been his; it had to belong to someone else.[11]

Interestingly enough, Dr Douglas Derry determined that, anatomically speaking, there was a close correspondence between the measurements of the skull from KV 55 and that of Tutankhamun, suggesting very strongly that they were brothers.[12] These same findings were deduced by Harrison, who also examined Tutankhamun's remains (and once again confirmed by Joyce Filer in 2000[13]). As a consequence, he commissioned a reconstruction of the head of the incumbent of KV 55 based on the skull, carried out by Mr DJ Kidd, a medical artist to the Faculty of Medicine at Liverpool University. The final reconstruction displayed, according to Professor Harrison, 'a striking resemblance' to the face of Tutankhamun as depicted on the mummiform coffins, but no resemblance whatsoever to Akhenaten.[14] Much later blood serum tests carried out on both bodies indicated that they had the same blood group, which, although of a common type, was yet more evidence of their close kinship.[15]

Since the burial in KV 55 took place during the years of turmoil and strife referred to by Egyptologists as the Amarna heresy, it could only be one of the four kings who ruled during this time. Yet it was not Akhenaten, because the mummy did not fit the evidence of the person's age at death. Neither was it Aye, an elderly member of the family, who ruled for four years after the death of Tutankhamun, and whose tomb had already been found in the Western Valley. Obviously, it was not Tutankhamun, since his tomb was found eventually in 1922. This left just one possible candidate whose body was unaccounted for – Smenkhkare. The British draughtsman Norman de Garis Davies first proposed his name as the internee of KV 55 soon after its discovery. Yet his contemporaries chose to ignore his suggestion in favour of perpetuating the idea that the body was that of

Akhenaten. The matter was not picked up again until 1931, when the British Egyptologist Reginald 'Rex' Engelbach, a former pupil of Derry, concluded that the defaced inscriptions from KV 55 indicated very strongly that the body in the golden coffin was that of Smenkhkare.[16] So exactly who was this obscure Amarna king?

SMENKHKARE

Shortly before Akhenaten's death in c. 1350 BC, Smenkhkare (pronounced *smen-car-ray*) is known to have ruled Egypt from both Tell el-Amarna and Memphis, Egypt's administrative centre in Lower Egypt, for anything up to three years. For his royal wife he took Meritaten, who had already produced a child by her father. In addition to the name Smenkhkare, he used the prenomen Ankhkheperure, and there exist inscriptions that speak of a co-regent who ruled with Akhenaten named Ankhkheperure Nefernefruaten, who was assumed to be Smenkhkare. Confounding the matter somewhat is the fact that Nefertiti also used the name Nefernefruaten. What then can we make of this strange puzzle?

It is now generally accepted by scholars of the Amarna period that Nefertiti adopted the title Ankhkheperure Nefernefruaten on becoming a co-regent with her husband Akhenaten during the final years of his life. However, on her departure from the scene, Smenkhkare ascended to the throne and confused the issue still further by adopting the name Nefernefruaten himself, perhaps to emphasise that he was Nefertiti's chosen successor. This whole debate on Nefertiti's co-regency has led some Amarna experts to assume that Nefertiti and Smenkhkare were one and the same person, a conclusion that the authors regard as untenable (see Notes and References for a longer discussion on this subject[17]).

A large number of funerary items found in the tomb of Tutankhamun had originally borne the name of either Ankhkheperure or Nefernefruaten (both occasionally coupled with the name Meritaten), which had been erased and replaced with that of Tutankhamun. Among the objects usurped for this purpose included the canopic coffins, the lid of one box, a large number of golden sequins once stitched into linen palls, two faience bracelets, a pectoral and a composite bow.[18] It has even been proposed that Tutankhamun's great sarcophagus was designed originally for Smenkhkare, before being sequestered for use by the latter's successor.[19] If these items did not come from a storehouse somewhere in Thebes, then the likelihood is that they were removed from his tomb, and if this was KV 55, just across the Valley, then it makes perfect sense.

Strangely enough, Smenkhkare is not mentioned in any textual inscriptions, nor is he depicted in any form, until he is elevated suddenly to the position of King of Upper and Lower Egypt towards the end of Akhenaten's reign. Yet from this fact alone it would appear that he must have been closely related to Akhenaten, even though he is unlikely to have been a son. It is plausible that he was a son of Amenhotep III, although his mother remains a mystery. It is conceivable also that Tutankhamun, who was himself never depicted in art before his ascension to the throne, was likewise a brother or half-brother of Akhenaten and perhaps a full brother of Smenkhkare. This solution would make sense of the anatomical resemblance between the skull from KV 55 and that of Tutankhamun.

The only textual evidence that sheds any light on Tutankhamun's parentage is a granite lion statue found at Soleb in northern Sudan, ancient Nubia. It bears an inscription in which the boy-king makes reference to his 'father Nebmaatre Amenhotep',[20] i.e. Amenhotep III, who is known to have constructed twin temples at Soleb, one for himself and the other for the Great Royal Wife, Tiye. They were both completed by Tutankhamun as an expression of his descent from Amenhotep III, as opposed to the heretic Akhenaten. Whether or not this can be seen as evidence of Tutankhamun's actual father, or simply his ancestral 'father', has never been determined. Whatever the solution, it demonstrates Tutankhamun's descent from Amenhotep III.

Whoever Smenkhkare might have been, he becomes the best candidate by far for the identity of the body in KV 55,[21] despite concerted efforts in more recent times to revive the theory that it is Akhenaten.[22] Indeed, the body was tentatively identified as Smenkhkare again in 1960 by the British Egyptologist HW Fairman,[23] and confirmed in 1966 by no less a person than Professor Harrison. Having assessed the pathological evidence offered by the remains, he was of the opinion that:

> From considerations of physique, age at death, and facial appearance … it is impossible to concede a resemblance between the present remains and Akhenaten. The striking similarity in facial appearance with Tutankhamûn, and the age at death point much more forcibly to the conclusion that these remains belong to Smenkhkarē.[24]

So, if Smenkhkare's tomb was discovered in 1907, where was his brother, or half-brother, Tutankhamun to be found?

THREE CLUES TO TUTANKHAMUN

Theodore Davis chanced upon various telltale signs that suggested the presence somewhere in the Valley of Tutankhamun's missing tomb. For instance, during the 1905–6 season Ayrton unearthed from under a rock a beautiful blue faience cup that bore Tutankhamun's throne name Nebkheperure.[25] Then, during the first week of the 1907–8 season, Ayrton came across what he first took to be a tomb at a depth of 7 metres. It was in fact a room filled with dry mud, demonstrating that it had been flooded at some point (a perennial problem in the Valley, which is, of course, a dried-up wadi or riverbed). At its base he found an unnamed alabaster statuette, the arms crossed upon the breast, possibly of the pharaoh Aye, as well as 'a broken box containing several pieces of gold leaf stamped with the names of Touatânkhamanou and his wife Ankhousanamanou'.[26] One piece of gold leaf bore a design that showed Tutankhamun hunting in a chariot,[27] another depicted the king slaying a prisoner as his queen, Ankhesenamun, stands behind him and Aye, shown as a royal fan bearer and 'divine father', stands before him.[28] Others also bore the name of Tutankhamun, while a few carried the names of Aye and his wife Tey.

A few days after this discovery Ayrton uncovered a roughly hewn pit (later designated Pit 54) some 1.9 by 1.25 metres in size, and a metre and a half deep. It was located on a hill above the tomb of King Seti II and some 120 metres from the tomb of Rameses VI, c. 1141–1134 BC (under which Tutankhamun's tomb would eventually be found). Inside the pit were a dozen large storage jars with sealed mouths and inscriptions on their shoulders. Davis had them removed to his home in the West Valley, and there they were opened ceremoniously in the presence of the British Consul-General to Egypt, Sir Eldon Gorst. Within them were broken drinking cups and wine jars; fragments of painted pottery vases; linen bags containing natron salts and chaff; rolled-up bandages; broad collars of flowers and leaves, sewn on a papyrus base; two hand brooms; and the bones of animals and birds, as well as a gilded funerary mask.[29] That these jars originated from the tomb of Tutankhamun seemed clear, for their clay seals bore either the king's throne name Nebkheperure or the seal impression of the royal necropolis – the god Anubis in the form of a seated jackal above nine bound enemy prisoners.

Since they possessed very little monetary value, the American millionaire eventually released the contents of Pit 54 to the Metropolitan Museum of Art in New York, who were always eager to purchase antiquities from archaeologists working in Egypt. On their arrival, they were stored away, and it was not until several years later that their true significance was realised by the museum's assistant curator, Herbert E Winlock (1884–1950). He recognised immediately that the bags of natron and bundles of linen were leftovers from the actual embalming process and mummification of the pharaoh. The rest of the items constituted the remains of the funerary banquet held inside the tomb, most probably after the sarcophagus had been sealed. It appeared to have involved eight individuals, each wearing a floral and leaf wreath and a linen headband, one of which was inscribed Year 8 of Tutankhamun's reign.[30]

The funeral meal had consisted of five ducks, two plovers and a haunch of mutton, all washed down with wine and beer. The tableware had then been broken in a ritual manner and placed inside the storage jars, while the brooms were used to sweep the floor of any remains. When the tomb itself was discovered, Carter and Winlock concluded that the jars had originally been left in the entrance corridor, but when, after the first break in, it had become necessary to fill its interior with rubble they were deposited in a nearby pit.

It was these three clues that led Davis finally, and rather presumptuously, to assume that this room was the tomb of the boy-king, declaring afterwards that 'I fear that the Valley of the Tombs is now exhausted'.[31] To Theodore Davis, it was not going to yield up any more treasures, and so in 1914 he decided not to renew his concession to dig. Yet one enthusiastic young draftsman cum archaeologist from England, who had been quietly waiting in the wings, did not share this same view. His name was Howard Carter.

3. CARTER'S QUEST

Born at 10 Rich Terrace, Kensington, London, on 9 May 1874, Howard Carter was the son of a watercolour painter of animals and an illustrator for the *London Illustrated News* named Samuel John Carter. He grew up with two unmarried aunts in the Suffolk village of Swaffham, where he received only a limited education. Yet, like his father, he was able to paint, and these skills were soon recognised by Lord William Amhurst Tyssen-Amherst (later first Baron Amherst of Hackney) a great collector of Egyptian antiquities as well as a founding light and chief benefactor of the Egypt Exploration Fund (EEF), later the Egypt Exploration Society (EES). After Carter had completed a number of successful commissions at his request, his artistic talents were recommended to Professor Percy Newberry (1869–1949). A member of the EEF, he was at the time excavating the rock tombs at Beni Hasan, on the east bank of the Nile in Middle Egypt. After three months in employment at the British Museum inking in pencil drawings, the seventeen-year old Howard Carter was invited to Egypt in order to help capture in watercolour the likeness of the exquisite reliefs to be found at both Beni Hasan and El-Bersha, a few miles up river. The date was September 1891, and it was to be the beginning of a forty-year relationship with Egypt, which would eventually lead him to become one of the most famous Egyptologists of all time.

Carter was a stern, thoughtful-looking individual with a long face and neatly trimmed moustache. He found it difficult communicating with others, and possessed an acute stubbornness that would eventually lead him into trouble on numerous occasions during his long career. Yet he was a proficient draftsman and painter, and very quickly impressed his peers. It is even said that he learned to read hieroglyphs on his own.

Carter worked sufficiently well for Newberry, and was asked eventually by Baron Amherst to join excavations being undertaken by the EEF at the site of Akhenaten's ill-fated city in Middle Egypt, under the supervision of one of the great pioneers of scholarly Egyptology, William Matthew Flinders Petrie (1853–1942). He needed help in uncovering the lost past of the heretic pharaoh, who constructed his city of Akhetaten, 'the horizon of the Aten', on the east bank of the Nile at a virgin site that later became known as Tell el-Amarna.

THE AMARNA HERESY
Having reigned from the New Kingdom capital of Thebes for four years, in a manner no different from any other pharaoh of his time, Akhenaten broke away from the traditional polytheism that had been practised in Egypt for nearly two thousand years. In its place, he adopted a form of monotheism, central to which

was the *Aten*. According to the inscriptions left to us this was an omnipotent, bisexual force symbolised by the light and heat of the sun's rays. In art it was depicted as a sun-disc – encircled by the *uraeus*-snake, a symbol of sovereignty – from which emanated rays of light that ended in hands, some of which offered *ankhs*, the Egyptian cross of life.

At the same time, Akhenaten forbade the worship of any other god or goddess. He deposed their priesthoods, allowed their temples to fall into ruin, diverted their incomes to the Temple of Aten at Akhetaten, outlawed all forms of idolatry and chiselled out the names of the old gods. The most powerful religion in Egypt before this period was that of the Theban god Amun, or Amun-re, whose main temple was at Karnak, located a few kilometres north of Thebes (modern Luxor). Its priesthood presided over all rites of kingship in Upper Egypt and held immense sway over the royal family. To see their power, influence and revenues stripped away virtually overnight could not have pleased them, and it would have been a similar story at temples all over the empire. The only ones to remain functional were those that served the cult of the sun god Re (sometimes spelt 'Ra'), who, in his guise as Re-harakhty (*harakhty*, 'Horus on the Horizon'), was adopted as a form of the Aten.

Fig. 3. Akhenaten and Nefertiti venerating the Aten sun-disc from a boundary stela at Tell el-Amarna (after Cyril Aldred).

As we shall see, Akhenaten initiated not only a religious revolution, but also a cultural and artistic revolution using motifs and styles that were totally alien to the existing Egyptian society. More than this, he established a form of worship that his subjects were encouraged to embrace, something that went against the exclusivity of the former state religions. On special occasions Akhenaten would appear with his wife and their daughters in what was called a 'window of appearance', a kind of viewing balcony that overlooked his 'dream' city, and from this they could address the assembled crowd, bringing to mind the Pope's weekly address in St Peter's Square.

THE RISE OF TUTANKHAMUN

Akhenaten's reign ended suddenly. No one knows why, although the fact that a number of key members of the royal family were to die in the final years of his reign cannot be unconnected. His dream lasted for just twelve to thirteen years, and, after the brief reign of his successor Smenkhkare, the restoration of the old religions began in earnest under the next king, Tutankhamun, who at this time bore the name Tutankhaten. He married the king's second eldest surviving daughter, Ankhesenpaaten (later Ankhesenamun), whom Akhenaten had already taken as his chief royal wife following Meritaten's marriage to Smenkhkare.

Initially, Tutankhaten reigned from Akhenaten's city at Tell el-Amarna, but very quickly the boy-king moved out of Akhetaten and established his royal court at Memphis. At the same time Thebes resumed its role as the chief religious centre of Upper Egypt – where a royal palace was also re-established, especially for use at times of great festivals. Moreover, both the king and queen revised their names to honour Amun instead of the Aten.

Tutankhamun cannot have been any more than nine years old at this time, and so the day-to-day running of the country was placed in the hands of others more capable. General Horemheb became the king's Deputy and Regent, taking charge of military and political affairs from Memphis, while Aye, Akhenaten's old vizier, became the boy-king's personal adviser and the administrator of all matters relating to religion. Yet even though Tutankhamun and his wife Ankhesenamun would appear to have abandoned the Aten faith focused on the city of Akhetaten, the young pharaoh did little, if anything, to quell the Amarna heresy. Indeed, it is quite clear from several key objects found in his tomb that both he and Ankhesenamun continued to venerate the Aten throughout their lifetimes.

THE RESTORATION

Some idea of the situation in Egypt at the end of Akhenaten's reign can be gleaned from a crucial piece of historical evidence dating from Year 1 of Tutankhamun's reign. Known as the Restoration Stela, this commemorative stone slab, found in 1907 amid the sprawling religious centre at Karnak by the French archaeologist Georges Legrain, reads:

> His Majesty was crowned King, the temples of the deities from Elephantine down
> to the marshes in the Delta had fallen into decay, their sanctuaries were deserted

and had become ruins, overgrown with weeds. Their chapels were as if they had never been while their processional routes served as footpaths. The land was turned upside down and the gods had turned their backs on the entire land ... If one prostrated oneself before a god to ask a favour, god did not respond ... But after many days My Majesty arose upon the throne of his father and ruled over the territory of Horus, both the Black Land and the Red Land being under his control.[1]

A relief on the wall of the colonnade in Luxor's great temple depicts the boy-king reintroducing the so-called *Opet* ceremony, in which statues of the god Amun (in his form as the ithyphallic god Min) and his consort Mut were carried in great ceremony to the Temple of Luxor. Here they were united to commemorate the divine conception of their son Khonsu. This archaic festival was accompanied by several days of celebration, during which time free food and drink would be distributed to the local population. None of this had occurred during the reign of Akhenaten, who forbade traditional religious celebrations and instead created new ones in the name of the Aten, which absorbed attributes of the old gods, including those of Amun and Mut.

THE TIME OF THE REBEL

The price Akhenaten paid for abandoning the old gods was terrible. Under the orders of the military general Horemheb, who took the throne after Aye's brief four-year reign, the city of Akhetaten was dismantled right down to its foundations. All reference to the dreaded Aten was expunged from inscriptions, and statues of Akhenaten were buried or destroyed. Moreover, Horemheb had the names of the four Amarna kings – Akhenaten, Smenkhkare, Tutankhamun and Aye – struck from official records, and extended back his own reign to begin in the year that Akhenaten's father, Amenhotep III, initiated a co-regency with his son. Thereafter Akhenaten's memory, and, indeed, that of his successors, was banished entirely from Egypt; he was never to be mentioned again by name. In legal documents dating from Horemheb's reign there is reference only to the time of 'the rebel' or the 'criminal of Akhetaten'.[2]

As an example of the manner in which Horemheb saw fit to banish even Tutankhamun from the official records, his name was chiselled out of the Restoration Stela and replaced by his own. Since he himself had directed the restoration of the old religions during the boy-king's reign, he obviously believed that he had every right to put claim to this great achievement.

LIFE AT AMARNA

The Amarna heresy, or revolution, is one of the most fascinating and compelling periods in Egyptian history, and it was certainly one that drew the interest of Howard Carter as Petrie put him to work at Tell el-Amarna. In his first year there, he was asked to make sketches of objects recovered from Akhenaten's great temple and palace, and he even drew the first surveyed map of the city.[3] Once it was completed, Petrie suggested that it be dispatched to the Antiquities Service in Cairo in order to create a good impression. So Carter promptly went down to

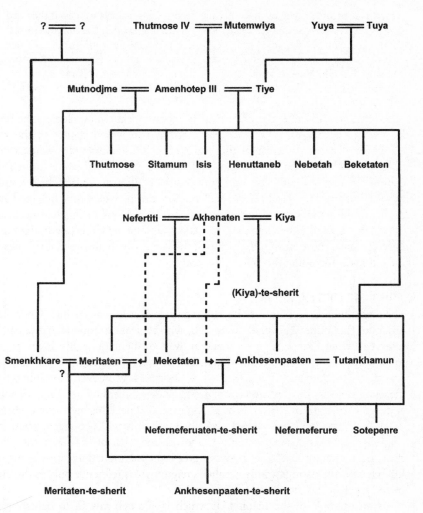

Fig. 4. Amarna royal family (after Graham Phillips).

the nearby town of el-Minya and dropped it in the post. Unfortunately, it must have been lost, or stolen, in transit, as the Antiquities Service denied later that it had ever been deposited with them.[4] This was perhaps Carter's first taste of the perceived imbecility of the French-run bureau, which as the years went by he grew to despise with intensity.

It was not long before Carter tried his own hand at excavation, the first time he had done so. He made various useful finds almost immediately and by the end of the 1891–2 winter season had catalogued a list of seventeen fragments of statues found by himself – twelve said to represent Akhenaten and five of his wife Nefertiti.[5]

Petrie had been moved enough by the huge assortment of finds being made at Amarna to write an early work on the life and times of Akhenaten entitled *Tell el-Amarna*, published in 1894. It dispelled the myth that the heretic king had in fact been a woman, or a eunuch, theories inspired by the often bizarre representations of him found both on the site of his city of Akhetaten and among the ruins of an Aten temple built at Karnak.[6] These often colossal statues showed the pharaoh with an elongated head, serpentine face and neck, slit eyes, pouting lips, full breasts and rounded thighs and abdomen, as well as chicken-like legs and no genitalia! The king adopted this new style of representation from Year 5 of his reign, when he moved the royal court to Amarna and changed his name from Amenhotep (the Greek Amenophis) IV, which honoured Amun, to Akhenaten, which means 'the glorified spirit (*akh*) of the Aten'.[7]

Fig. 5. Akhenaten from a fresco found at Tell el-Amarna. Note the elongated features of the face.

Petrie realised that the manner in which Akhenaten had portrayed both himself and, to a lesser degree, his family marked a significant shift in artistic style.[8] This was heightened further by the fact that for the first time carved reliefs and wall paintings to be found in temples, tombs and residences showed the king and his royal wife engaged in purely aesthetic pleasures. In one instance Akhenaten is seen openly kissing his wife as they ride along on a chariot, while in another she sits on his knee as their baby daughters play in their midst, like some family snapshot of the modern era. Gone almost entirely are more militaristic scenes of battle and victory. In Petrie's opinion,

> His domestic life was his ideal of the truth of life, and as part of his living in truth he proclaims it as the true life to his subjects. Thus in every line Akhenaten stands out as perhaps the most original thinker that ever lived in Egypt, and one of the great idealists of the world.[9]

STRANGE ART

Exactly why Akhenaten should have wanted to portray himself as a hermaphrodite with a long, serpentine face is not properly understood. It has been speculated that, along with other members of his immediate family, he suffered from some kind of pituitary disorder, such as Froehlich's syndrome. This was first proposed by G Elliot Smith following his examination of the remains of KV 55, which he took to be those of the heretic king. In his opinion, the skull showed signs of hydrocephalus, abnormal growth caused by fluid on the brain, which he believed, could have caused a delay in the ossification of the bones (thus leading him to assert a higher age for the person at the age of death). Yet this diagnosis was proved to be incorrect when Dr Derry carefully reconstructed the skull and found that Smith had been incorrect in his assumption that it belonged to a person suffering from hydrocephalus. In his opinion,

> The skull is undoubtedly of an unusual shape, but the type was not uncommon in the Old Empire particularly in members of the royal families, Meres-'Ankh, the granddaughter of Cheops, having had a skull of very similar form, and the type with its peculiar flatness of the vault is regularly portrayed in the reliefs of the period … It belongs to a type known to anthropologists as Platycephalic, in which the skull is flattened from above downwards and correspondingly widened.[10]

Despite this discrepancy, the idea that Akhenaten may have suffered from some kind of endocrine deficiency such as Froehlich's syndrome has remained.[11] The disease itself develops mainly in males through damage caused to the pituitary gland, a tiny gland at the base of the brain which secretes hormones that help control other glands in the body. For instance, the effect of the hormones on the thyroid gland, which controls growth and metabolism, can result in 'lantern jaw' and an extended neck. In addition to this, the effect on the hypothalamus, which regulates water distribution, results generally in a build-up of fluid in the cranium that enlarges the skull, as Elliot Smith concluded in the case of the remains found in KV 55. This may also explain why a number of carved busts and reliefs of Akhenaten's daughters show them with bizarre elongated heads. Lastly, the effect of the hormones on the adrenal cortex, which regulates steroid distribution, can produce feminine features in male victims such as the enlargement of breasts, thighs, abdomen and buttocks, explaining perhaps Akhenaten's bisexual physiognomy in Amarna art.

It is easy to see why some scholars have considered that Akhenaten and his family may have suffered from a disorder of this sort. However, Alwyn L Burridge of the University of Toronto, who has made a special study of the physical abnormalities in Akhenaten's family, observed in this respect:

> Reduced hormonal levels, particularly adrenalin, render Froehlich's sufferers lethargic. However, in contrast to his apparent habit of lounging about with family members, Akhenaten inspired a flurry of activity during his reign. To his credit, he initiated massive building projects and engendered a new expressiveness in art and poetry, in his dedication to the worship of the Aten. These accomplishments far exceed the capabilities of a severely mentally and physically challenged individual.[12]

In addition to this, he pointed out that:

> Men suffering from Froehlich's Syndrome are almost always impotent – the chemical imbalances prevent the maturation and function of the gonads. The male sexual organs are present, but remain infantile.[13]

Quite clearly if Akhenaten was impotent, then he would have been unable to sire at least six daughters. Furthermore, as the historical writer Graham Phillips points out, since any cranial enlargement would have occurred early in life, when the skull was still malleable, it makes nonsense of a whole number of busts and reliefs that show the king with a perfectly normal physiognomy before Year 5 of his reign.[14] Lastly, as Burridge has also noted, Froehlich's syndrome is not an inherited disorder: 'it is the result of trauma or congenital defect',[15] meaning that it cannot explain the long face, protruding chin, elongated head shape and paunch seen in the art depicting other members of his family, particularly the daughters.

Burridge's own theory on the cause of Akhenaten's strange physique is that he was suffering not from Froehlich's syndrome, but a genetic disorder called Marfan's syndrome.[16] This produces deformities in its victims, including a long face, elongated extremities, slender fingers, abnormally elongated skull, slit eyes, tall stature, wide pelvic girdle and abnormal prominence of the sternum. It can be inherited by offspring, thus explaining the abnormalities of his daughters, and can lead to early death, accounting perhaps for the large number of fatalities in Akhenaten's immediate family during the final years of his life. Even though Marfan's syndrome can distort the head and body, it leaves the victim neither cognitively nor emotionally impaired, allowing the king to continue his royal duties.

Burridge's proposals with respect to the strange physiognomy of Akhenaten and his family in Amarna art are far more convincing than the suggestion that the king suffered from Froehlich's syndrome. However, examinations made of the remains from KV 55, thought by some scholars even today to be the heretic king, have found no signs that might indicate that the person suffered from Marfan's syndrome. All Derry determined was that the skull revealed a peculiar 'flatness of the vault', which closely resembled the skulls of royal individuals from the era when the Great Pyramid was constructed at Giza, c. 2550–2500 BC. Similar findings were echoed again by Joyce Filer of the British Museum, following her own examination of the skull in 2000, the most recent to date. In her opinion there were no pathological features of note regarding the skull, described as brachycephalic in shape, although she did note that it is 'reminiscent of some Predynastic and Old Kingdom skulls'.[17] In other words, Akhenaten's family might well have been linked genetically with the very earliest dynastic Egyptians, who appeared on the scene around 3100 BC.

If nothing else, Burridge has convincingly shown that Akhenaten wanted to portray both himself and his family in a manner that can be said to resemble an extreme form of Marfan's syndrome. If this is correct, then what on earth can have inspired him to do such a thing? The answer seems to lie not in medical disorders within the family but in the religious and spiritual ideals adopted by him during the early years of his reign. At the same time that he proclaims the Aten to be the one and only divine principle, he changes his name to honour this omnipotent force, creates a new capital city and revolutionises the art style in Egypt. The whole thing coincides exactly, and must therefore be linked in some way. Although we do not have the full answers, it is possible that, by expressing himself as a hermaphrodite, Akhenaten was attempting to convey the idea that as the first prophet of the Aten he embodied the bisexual qualities of the Aten. In addition to this, Akhenaten's desire to represent himself with an elongated head, slit eyes and a long, serpent-like face and neck might be related in some way to his strong interest in the concepts of *Sep Tepi*, the First Occasion or the Place of the First Occasion. This was the term used to express the moment of first creation in the universe, which Akhenaten associated with the concept of divine rule and kingship in ancient Egypt.[18] Indeed, it was his fascination with this subject that would seem to have led him to construct his city of Akhetaten exactly midway between the ancient religious centre of Heliopolis in the north and Thebes in the south.[19]

Whether or not these same religious principles were behind the fashioning of busts and reliefs that show his daughters with strange elongated heads is more difficult to decide. There must exist a possibility that the children's skulls were deformed deliberately by being wrapped tightly in bandages during infancy. This practice was common among the prehistoric peoples of northern Syria and eastern Turkey, whose direct descendants were the Mitanni, a kingdom that thrived in this same region during the Amarna age.[20]

CARTER – THE EARLY YEARS
After failing to impress Flinders Petrie, Carter went on to work with other key archaeologists in Egypt, one of whom was the Swiss Egyptologist Edouard

Naville (1844–1926). Under his guidance he was set to work copying in watercolour the beautiful imagery to be found on the walls of the splendid funerary temple at Deir al-Bahri, built into a cliff just beyond the Valley of the Kings. It had been erected for Hatshepsut, one of Egypt's few female rulers, who controlled Upper and Lower Egypt for a twenty-year period, sometime between c. 1490–1468 BC.

The merits of Carter's artistic endeavours in Egypt during this period, many examples of which adorn the walls of New York's Metropolitan Museum of Art, have been said to display 'punctiliousness, verisimilitude and no life at all'.[21] Yet this is difficult to accept, since they also exude a simple perfection and exactness that is easy on the eye. There is no question that Carter, like his father before him, was a fine artist. He conducted his duties with the greatest precision and competence, and this eventually brought him to the attention of others who could further his career in Egyptology.

In 1899, the head of the Antiquities Service, Gaston Maspero (1846–1916), decided to offer Carter the post of inspector-general of monuments of Upper Egypt and the Sudan. He readily accepted, taking up the position in January 1900. It left him in charge of the administration and upkeep of all ancient monuments in the south of the country, and also brought him into contact with the Valley of the Kings for the first time.

Here he was requested to excavate the tomb of Amenhotep II, in which had been found several royal mummies moved here for their own safety during troubled times in ancient Egypt. The Frenchman Victor Loret, then director of the Cairo Museum, had first become aware of the cache when in the early 1890s a number of prize items, quite clearly from a royal tomb, started to surface on the black market. It transpired that a family living in nearby Qurna had known about the tomb for several years, and had been gradually stripping its mummies of their fineries in order to lead a comfortable lifestyle. Working on behalf of Davis, Carter also excavated a number of other tombs that, although ransacked in antiquity, were previously unknown to the archaeological community. They included the resting place of Akhenaten's grandfather, Thutmose IV, opened in 1903.

INTO THE VALLEY OF THE KINGS

In 1904 Carter became the inspector-general of monuments in the north of the country, but, following an unsavoury incident in which blows were exchanged with some drunken Frenchmen who attempted to enter the Serapeum at Saqqara without paying admission, he resigned his post. This allowed him to return to his by now first love – the Theban necropolis on the west bank of the Nile. He eked out a living taking commissions and painting watercolours of Egyptian life, both ancient and modern. In addition to this, he conducted guided tours of the various sites of interest, and here and there he worked for Theodore Davis (for instance, working alongside Ayrton and Weigall, he helped record the objects discovered in the tomb of Yuya and Tuya, Akhenaten's grandparents). He also became a dealer in *antika*. This was the Arab word for ancient artefacts bought and sold on the black market, and for which there was a huge demand both in Europe and in the United States. With the right contacts, a good transaction could be secured on objects that at an auction in London, Paris or New York would fetch ten times as much. Quite obviously the greater majority of these antiquities had been pilfered from tombs or disturbed cemeteries by local families, generally from nearby Qurna, who spent their entire life in this pursuit.

It was around this time that Carter started to survey the entire Valley and produced a detailed map, which showed all the tombs discovered and every find made. He noted too where professional and amateur explorers had carried out successful and even unsuccessful excavations over the past two hundred years or so. Carter began also to imagine that there was still one more royal tomb to be found, and very soon he was to decide that it belonged to Tutankhamun.

Carter knew that the boy-king was buried somewhere in the Valley, and the clues unearthed by Davis and Ayrton in 1905 and 1907 indicated that his tomb was within reach. The blue faience cup found under a rock, as well as the gold leaf found with other items bearing the name of Tutankhamun, pointed to its having been plundered in antiquity. Yet the fact that the raiders had not returned to pick up their booty suggested that they were apprehended and the tomb resealed. Then there were the contents of the earthenware jars found in Pit 54 – the embalming equipment, floral wreaths, linen headbands and gilded funerary mask were more difficult to explain. Yet they hinted once again at the proximity of the tomb, and this is why Carter now became so eager to dig in the Valley. His dream became a reality when in 1914 Theodore Davis finally gave up all hope of finding any further royal tombs and left Egypt for good.

In the autumn of that first year, Carter began some exploratory work in the Valley of the Kings on behalf of Lord Carnarvon. Yet it would not be until 18 April 1915 that an official permit[22] was given to his patron, bestowing on him the exclusive rights to excavate in the Valley.[23] It was the tomb of Tutankhamun that Carter was after, and, with the precious digging concession now under his belt, he was going to remove every ounce of sand and waste from that desolate place until he found it.

4. THE SEARCH COMMENCES

Whenever it had been stated that the Valley of the Kings had yielded up its final secrets, another tomb was always found, leaving Carter optimistic that his endeavours would be rewarded in the coming seasons. Never before had any explorer conducted such a systematic survey as he intended: all they had done before was to dig wherever they felt inclined to do so. As a consequence, vast piles of debris excavated from the mouths of earlier tombs filled the Valley, rising and falling like sand dunes, which would all have to be removed with the assistance of literally hundreds of local men and boys. Each would be paid a fee, using money from the pocket of Carter's patron, the fifth Earl of Carnarvon, relative to the number of baskets full of rubble they were able to carry on any particular day.

A FATEFUL JOURNEY

Lord Carnarvon was introduced to the pastime of Egyptology through a very unusual set of circumstances. Born in 1866, he developed a passion in early life for horseracing (he created a stud farm at his country estate of Highclere Castle in Hampshire), sailing (he almost completed a yacht cruise around the world at the age of 21), gambling (he sponsored Howard Carter) and motorcars. In fact, he had been driving cars in Europe even before they became legal in Britain. Indeed, on several occasions he was hauled before the magistrates for speeding, and, according to the magazine *The Autocar*, he was said to have passed cyclists and pedestrians at a near dangerous speed of 20 miles per hour![1]

Some believed Carnarvon had an unhealthy thirst for fast cars, and they were to be proved right when around 1901 he had a serious motoring accident in southern Germany. Accompanied by his chauffeur, Edward Trotman, who on more than one occasion sat in the passenger seat, Carnarvon hurtled his car down an almost dead-straight road, through a forest, towards the town of Schwalbach, where he was to rendezvous with his wife, Almina. Suddenly, Carnarvon crested a blind summit and there in the dip below them were two bullock carts drawn up right across the road. Swiftly, he applied the brakes and swerved to avoid them, but the wheels hit some boulders and the car turned over, trapping the earl, and throwing his chauffeur clear. It was only through Trotman's quick thinking and the services of a local doctor that the British aristocrat managed to get out alive. As it was, Carnarvon suffered severe concussion, a swollen face, burns to his legs, a broken wrist, temporary blindness and injuries to the palate of his mouth and jaw.[2] Indeed, he was barely alive when he was pulled free of the wreckage; had he died, then the world might still be waiting for Tutankhamun's tomb to be discovered.

Back in England he was given the best possible medical treatment and made a good recovery. Yet his injuries left him with a weak chest and difficulty in breathing, particularly during the cold and damp English winter months. Egypt, with its warm dry climate, had in those days become something of a health resort for recuperating European convalescents and so, on the advice of his physician, Dr Marcus Johnson, Carnarvon travelled to Cairo for the first time in 1903. Returning each season, he soon became bored with the expatriate way of life and the endless round of parties attended by the myriads of gossiping socialites. The earl knew that his period of convalescence would be lengthy, and that it was necessary for him to keep coming to Egypt for its health benefits, but he desperately needed something meaningful to occupy his mind. Surrounded by the monuments of a long dead civilisation, Carnarvon's interests eventually turned towards digging up the past and furthering his growing collection of Egyptian antiquities. Thus in the autumn of 1907, with the help and advice of the British Controller-General in Egypt, Lord Cromer, he received his first-ever concession and began digging at a site called Sheikh Abd el-Qurna on the west bank of the Nile.

Each morning Lord Carnarvon – a tall, slim, warm-mannered aristocrat with a long face, a moustache and a love of sports jackets – would leave his room at the Winter Palace Hotel in Luxor, a reasonably high-class residence for foreigners visiting Upper Egypt. From here he would journey out to the dig site, where he would enter a specially prepared wire cage that helped protect him from flies and dust. Safely inside, he could observe and direct the workforce of local men removing tonne after tonne of rubble, sand and dirt. After six weeks of digging all Lord Carnarvon had to show for his efforts was a mummified cat! Yet despite the scarcity of finds he was overjoyed that he had found something missed by previous excavators, which in turn bolstered his enthusiasm for his newfound hobby of archaeology. Yet, realising his limitations and lack of experience in the field of excavation, he knew he desperately needed some expert advice and a guiding hand – someone experienced, someone who could bring him greater success for the time, effort and money he was prepared to devote to the cause. And so, having voiced his misgivings to the director-general of the Egyptian Antiquities Service, Gaston Maspero, Lord Carnarvon was eventually introduced to the brilliant, yet virtually destitute and unemployed, Howard Carter.

THE KAMOSE PAPYRUS

Having decided on a strategy and with a renewed enthusiasm, Carnarvon and Carter set to work exploring the Theban necropolis on the west bank of the Nile. It was now 1909, and in a very short time two tombs would be found – one belonging to an Eighteenth Dynasty mayor of Thebes named Tetiky, and the other (listed as Tomb No. 9) producing two inscribed wooden tablets. One of these contained the beginning of an account of how the pharaoh Kamose (c. 1570 BC) had launched a counterattack against the seminomadic warlords of Asiatic origin known as the Hyksos, or 'shepherd kings'.[3] They entered Egypt from Syria-Canaan during the so-called Second Intermediate Period, sometime between 1730 and 1650 BC, and took control of the country for a period of between 75 and 155 years. The Hyksos waged war against the pharaohs of the ruling dynasties and won easily, due in the main to their vastly superior military capability. To begin with they used compact bows, which were more powerful and had a much better range than those employed by the Egyptian army. Yet more importantly, the Hyksos had war chariots, against which foot soldiers were no match.

Having subjected Lower Egypt to their rule they established a capital at Avaris, modern Tell ed-Dab'a in the Eastern Delta, and settled into an Egyptian lifestyle. Although they adopted as a divine patron Set, or Sutekh, the Egyptian god of the burning wastes (see Appendix II – 'Pork Abstinence and the Worship of Set'), they also established close links with the ancient cult centre of the sun god Re at Heliopolis. Its priests had been responsible for the coronation of kings of Lower Egypt for more than 1,500 years, and the Hyksos felt it essential that, in order to legitimise their right to the throne of Egypt, they should adhere to the religious rites and customs of the native Egyptian pharaohs.

Meanwhile, in the south of the country, a feeble royal dynasty emerged in Thebes, centred on the cult of Amun, the hidden one, which plotted to overthrow the Hyksos. The kings of the Seventeenth Dynasty, as it was known, were buried in tombs located at a cemetery near Qurna in the Theban west bank. Very carefully its generals learned how to utilise the military techniques introduced by the Hyksos. Compact bows and chariots were issued to the Egyptian army, making the two sides more equal in battle. Under the command of Kamose, and later his brother Ahmose, the Theban dynasty was finally able to drive the Hyksos out of Egypt and back to their original homeland sometime around 1575 BC. Thus began a new phase in Egyptian history, marked by the commencement of not only the Eighteenth Dynasty, beginning with the reign of Ahmose, but also the New Kingdom c. 1575–1087 BC. During this period Egypt would grow to become an empire that stretched westwards to Libya, eastwards to the borders of the Assyrian Empire, northwards to the borders of the Hittite Empire in northern Syria, and southwards to the land of Kush, present-day Ethiopia.

Carter's finds, made under the patronage of Lord Carnarvon, were encouraging, and afterwards he continued his exploration of the Theban West Bank, making several more discoveries of note, including various minor tombs belonging to private individuals. He also cleared away rubble from beneath the temple of Hatshepsut at Deir el-Bahri, finding more minor tombs here. Many of these discoveries were written up in a book written jointly by Carnarvon and Carter entitled *Five Years' Explorations at Thebes: A record of work done 1907–1911*, published in 1912.[4] It received warm reviews from the Egyptological community, and cemented a firm bond between the two individuals, which showed that they were now a force to be reckoned with. Two years later Theodore M Davis relinquished his concession to dig in the Valley of the Kings, which was duly handed over to the Earl of Carnarvon by Gaston Maspero. Yet Carter's dream to uncover the tomb of Tutankhamun now had to be put on hold, as unexpected developments in the world began to cast their ominous shadow over Egypt.

CARTER AND THE WAR EFFORT

With the declaration of war in Europe in August 1914, an air of uncertainty and dread filled the air. Egypt was ruled by Abbas Hilmi, a khedive under the direct control of the Sultan of Turkey. When in November that year he pledged his allegiance to the Central Powers, headed by Germany, fears rose that Egypt's Arab population would revolt against its British administration, which was regulated by the Foreign Office through the Egyptian High Commission in Cairo. Acting quickly, the British authorities persuaded Abbas Hilmi to abdicate and go into exile in order that his uncle, the pro-British Hussein Kamil, should replace him.[5] With no one in Egypt quite sure when the Turks would advance through the Sinai peninsula or coastal lowlands of Palestine and attack the Suez Canal, everything was held in abeyance.

Carter offered his services to the Foreign Office, but had to continue digging in the Valley until March 1915 before he was given a job. He was employed eventually by the office of the High Commissioner, Sir Henry McMahon, and acted as a message carrier and translator between members of the intelligence service and Arab contacts working on behalf of Hussein ibn Ali, the Sharif of the Hejaz region of Arabia (see Chapter 24). Yet his contribution to the war effort was, surprisingly, short lived. Somehow, he fell foul of the Egyptian High Commission and was quietly dropped from any further duties. There is no official record of what happened. Carter returned to the Valley of the Kings in October 1915, and was soon involved in an incident that amply demonstrated his tactile nature and quick-thinking response to what could have been a very dangerous situation.

TROUBLE AT QURNA

One afternoon, while at his residence in the village of Qurna on the Theban west bank, he was approached by the village elders, who informed him that a cave containing a tomb had been found on the western side of the mountain, above the Valley of the Kings. One group of workmen were busy rifling its contents, when a second group had appeared on the scene. A fracas broke out, and the original group were ousted, and now, having licked their wounds, they planned to return in order to take their revenge. Carter was asked to intervene in order to avoid any unnecessary bloodshed. So, without any hesitation, or thought for his own personal safety, he gathered together a band of villagers from among those who had not been seconded into the Egyptian army and set off for the disputed cave, which was reached around midnight. A rope hung over the sheer face, and listening quietly he could hear the distinct sound of voices drifting out into the moonlit sky. Thinking quickly, Carter cut their ropes in order to block their escape, and replaced them with his own. He was then lowered into the darkness until he came upon a gaping hole in which were a 'nestful of industrious tomb robbers', eight in number.[6] Apparently, there was a moment or two of uneasy silence, before he delivered an ultimatum: either they make their exit using his rope or stay where they were without any means of escape. Eventually, the villagers saw reason and departed without resistance. Climbing back up the rope himself, Carter waited till dawn and then went back down to explore the rock-cut tomb.

For the next 28 days Carter attempted to clear the debris from the deep cavern, which was so well concealed from either the cliff top, 40 metres above, or the valley bottom, 67 metres below, that no one would ever have suspected its presence. The tomb itself contained a corridor some 16 metres in length, which turned sharply downwards into a chamber 5.5 metres square. Expecting that an elaborate treasure remained concealed in a second chamber, the tomb robbers had dug a further tunnel 27 metres long. Despite the obvious assumption that such a well-concealed tomb must hold, as Carter put it, 'a wonderful treasure',[7] he was to be disappointed by the results of his excavation. The sepulchre had never been finished, or occupied, although it did contain a crystalline sandstone sarcophagus. This also was unfinished, although it did bear an inscription indicating that it had been intended for the female ruler Hatshepsut.[8] For reasons that will never be known, she abandoned any plans to use the tomb, and instead chose one alongside the other kings in the Valley. This was probably a bad move on her part, for, as Carter observed in this respect, 'She would have been better advised to hold to her original plan. In this secret spot her mummy would have had a reasonable chance of avoiding disturbance: in The Valley it had none. A king she would be, and a king's fate she shared'.[9]

SYSTEMATIC SEARCH

As Howard Carter himself recorded, 'In the autumn of 1917 our real campaign in The Valley opened'.[10] At last he was able to initiate his plan to 'systematically dig right down to the bedrock'. Indeed, according to his colleague, the eminent American Egyptologist James Henry Breasted (1865–1935),

> To make absolutely certain that not a square inch of its [the Valley's] floor and slopes should escape his examination, he [Carter] made a large-scale map of it upon which he subdivided the terrain into convenient sections; and as his excavations of an actual area progressed and he had completely satisfied himself that it contained nothing of value, he checked off the corresponding sections of the map.[11]

A triangular area that stretched between the tombs of Rameses II, Merneptah and Rameses VI defined the area in which he would search for the tomb of Tutankhamun.[12] Each individual square would be cleared of sand, rubble and debris in the hope of uncovering some evidence for the presence here of an undisturbed entrance passageway. Despite this methodical approach nothing was to be found in the first season, other than a series of workmen's huts set on a thick base of flints in the proximity of the tomb of Rameses VI. Carter, however, decided against investigating further, since extended excavations might mean cutting off the path to the entrance of this tomb, which was a favourite with tourists visiting the Valley. Had he done so, he would have saved himself a lot of fruitless digging elsewhere, not to mention a good deal of Lord Carnarvon's money.

Carter returned to the Valley for the 1918–19 season, but still he was denied the breakthrough he wanted so much. Yet never did his spirit wane: he just kept on unabated. The next season, 1919–20, work resumed in the area of the tomb of Rameses VI, and once again a considerable amount of debris was removed down to the bedrock. Yet still the area that enclosed the workmen's huts was left, since they were themselves considered to be of primary archaeological interest. The only items of any importance that did come to light were a small cache of thirteen alabaster jars, bearing cartouches of either Rameses II or his son Merneptah, which Carter concluded were most probably from the tomb of the latter. He did record, however, that Lady Carnarvon, who was present with her husband, 'insisted on digging out these jars – beautiful specimens they were – with her own hands'.[13]

Giving up in this area, Carter transferred his efforts to the far end of the Valley, beneath the tomb of Thutmose III. Here the workforce excavated extensively, but found nothing, other than the abandoned tomb of one Meryt-re-hatshepsut, the wife of Thutmose, which had later been sequestered for use by a Theban official named Sen-nefer.

Having dug in the Valley for three seasons and found nothing, Carter now came under increased pressure from his patron, the Earl of Carnarvon, to make the breakthrough that everyone desired so dearly. Should they begin excavations outside of the Valley, where the returns for their money and hard labour might be more profitable? Carter's reply to this question was clear: 'so long as a single area of untouched ground remained the risk was worth taking'.[14]

Carnarvon was not so convinced, and at the end of the 1921–2 season the British aristocrat decided to pull the plug on the whole affair. Yet, in an attempt to convince his patron that the matter was worth pursuing further, Carter visited Highclere in the hope of convincing him that he should sponsor one more season of excavation in the Valley. Lord Carnarvon listened to what Carter had to say, and expressed his appreciation of the years of effort put into the project, but stated that 'in view of post-war economic stringency he would find it impossible to support further this obviously barren undertaking'.[15]

Carter insisted 'that their consistent failure to find anything had not in the slightest weakened the conviction he had held for years, that The Valley contained at least one more royal tomb, probably that of Tutenkhamen [sic], the existence of which was strongly indicated by circumstantial evidence'.[16] Furthermore, he told him that the plan for the 1922–3 winter season was finally to investigate the ground beneath the area occupied by the workmen's huts at the right-hand side of the tomb belonging to Rameses VI. It was the only place in the whole of the designated triangle not yet explored fully down to the bedrock. Carter's fixation with this area of the Valley is never properly explained, although he himself added that he 'always had a kind of superstitious feeling that in that particular corner of the Valley one of the missing kings, possibly Tut-ankh-Amen, might be found. Certainly the stratification of the debris there should indicate a tomb'.[17]

Pre-empting Carnarvon's reservations about continuing to back the project, Carter then offered to fund the operation himself, and his proposal was in no way a bluff. He did indeed have sufficient funds to finance his own excavations, a fact confirmed by the author Thomas Hoving in his book *Tutankhamun – The Untold Story*.[18] He argues that during this period Carter had built up considerable wealth through the sale of antiquities to museums and private collectors, which he had bought from Egyptian dealers. Moreover, papers in the Metropolitan Museum reveal that he discussed ongoing operations with the museum's officials, suggesting that they pick up the concession should it lapse, an offer that had met with a favourable response.[19]

Realising that Carter's dogged persistence might just pay off, and being a gambling man by nature, the fifth earl decided to take a chance by agreeing to fund one more season of excavations in the Valley. Carter was jubilant, and so, with smiles all round, the two men shook hands, sealing the future of what was to become one of the most extraordinary years ever in the history of archaeology.

5. DEATH OF THE GOLDEN BIRD

> At last have made wonderful discovery in Valley; a magnificent tomb with seals
> intact; re-covered same for your arrival; congratulations.[1]

With these words a jubilant Howard Carter cabled Lord Carnarvon to announce
the discovery of the tomb of Tutankhamun. The message was received at
Highclere on Monday 6 November 1922 by the British aristocrat, who that same
day called his close personal friend, the philologist Sir Alan H Gardiner, in order
to inform him of the wonderful discovery made in the Valley of the Kings.[2]

Carter had returned to Luxor only nine days beforehand, and so what on
earth could have happened in this short space of time? Having spent four days
organising the season's operations and enrolling workmen from the local villages,
he had been back at work in the Valley by Wednesday, 1 November. Almost
immediately, his labourers began clearing away debris from the site occupied by
the workmen's huts, close to the entrance of Rameses VI's tomb. By the evening
of Friday 3 November, the foundations had been exposed and recorded, and
were now ready to be removed. There was about one metre of unexplored soil
beneath them that would need to be cleared away as quickly as possible the
following day. As dusk fell, Carter bade goodnight to the gaffirs, or headmen, and
made his way back to his house, known locally as Castle Carter, which stood at
the head of the road leading into the Valley.

THE FIRST STEP

Carter rose early the next morning and made his way to the excavation site,
unaware that this was the day that would dramatically change his life for ever.
On his arrival he was perplexed by the strange silence that greeted him, for it
meant that the workforce had downed tools and were awaiting his presence.
On approaching his now idle gang of workers, he was informed by the chief
gaffir that below the foundations of the first stone hut they had uncovered a
step cut into the bedrock. He felt it almost too good to be true, but, sure
enough, with a little extra removal of surface debris it became clear that a step
had indeed been found just four metres beneath the entrance to the tomb of
Rameses VI. In his words: '... I almost dared to hope that we had found our
tomb at last'.[3]

The strangest thing is that twice before Carter had come within a few metres
of that step: 'The first time was years ago when I was digging for Davis, and he
suggested we shift our work to some "more promising spot". The second was
only a few seasons ago when Lord Carnarvon and I decided to reserve clearance
of this area for a time when we wouldn't interfere with visitors to the tomb of
Rameses VI'.[4]

THE DOORWAY UNCOVERED

Work continued feverishly throughout the rest of the day, and as first twilight and then darkness fell the excitement among the workforce rose steadily. That evening the upper edges of what was quite obviously an opening had been revealed. Carter went home as the full moon rose high in the eastern heavens, casting an eerie glow on the face of Meretseger, the pyramid-shaped mountain peak that dominated the skyline. What he might have felt that night and what dreams haunted his nocturnal slumber are not recorded, but whatever the case he must have known, instinctively, that this was the breakthrough that he had been waiting for. Yet, not knowing what really lay under the sand and rock beneath his feet, Carter probably experienced not only self-doubt but also a myriad other fears that would have come creeping into his mind, spoiling those fleeting moments of exhilaration. Had he found the tomb of Tutankhamun? Was it intact? Had it been ransacked in antiquity like all the others? Or perhaps it was

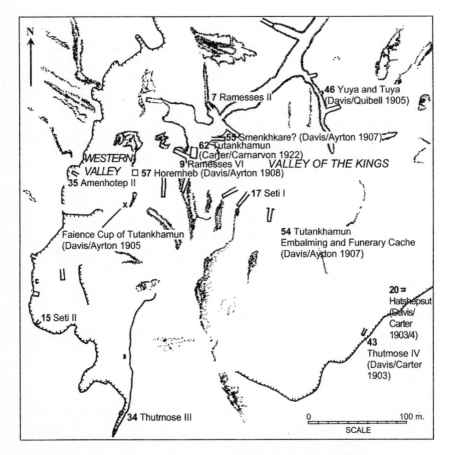

Fig. 6. Valley of the Kings showing relevant tombs and positions of finds.

unfinished, like the one he had found in the upper end of the Valley, which was meant to contain the mortal remains of Thutmose III. Over the next few weeks Carter's fears of failure would evaporate like the morning mist in the heat of the Egyptian sun.

On Sunday 5 November Carter watched in utter joy as, one by one, no fewer than twelve steps of a sunken staircase (about 4 metres by 1.60 metres in size) came into view, and then, finally, towards sunset, the upper part of a blocked doorway, plastered and sealed, was exposed. Recording his delight, Carter wrote, 'A sealed doorway – it was actually true, then! Our years of patient labour were to be rewarded after all, and I think my first feeling was one of congratulation that my faith in The Valley had not been unjustified.'[5]

At the top of the doorway a wooden lintel had become exposed, while beneath this, stamped into the remaining mortar, were distinctive seal impressions showing the god Anubis in his form as the seated jackal above nine bound enemy captives. Carter recognised it as the seal of the Theban royal necropolis, convincing him that the tomb had not been entered since the construction of the workmen's huts, built directly above it during the reign of Rameses VI.

Unable to hold back his curiosity any longer, Carter made a small peephole in the mortar, large enough for him to gaze inside. Using an electric torch, he became disappointed when he realised that the passageway beyond was filled with rubble. 'Anything, literally anything, might lie beyond that passage, and it needed all my self-control to keep from breaking down the doorway, and investigating then and there'.[6]

What did lie beyond the sealed doorway? It was a severely frustrating moment for Carter, and he must be commended for his restraint – a restraint that he was unable to match later on in the discovery.

WONDERFUL DISCOVERY

With some reluctance, Carter decided that he could go no further before informing Carnarvon of the good news. So he refilled the stairwell with debris and, as we saw at the start of this chapter, dispatched the famous cable to his friend and patron. The next day, the workmen continued to fill in the excavation, covering the sunken entrance with debris, which included many of the flint boulders used in Pharaonic times to construct the now demolished workmen's huts. So, just 48 hours or so after the discovery of the tomb, it had vanished from sight, making it difficult to persuade himself that the whole episode had not been a dream.

Yet news of the discovery travelled fast, and on Tuesday 7 November Carter began receiving notes of congratulation, offers of help and other enquiries of a type that would flood in thick and fast as the weeks and months passed by. He also realised that the job ahead would require expert assistance. So on Thursday 9 November he requested the help of his old friend Arthur J 'Pecky' Callender, who came within a day or so. Callender was a British-born engineer and former employee of the Egyptian State Railways. After his retirement he had settled in

Upper Egypt and now managed a small farm in Ermant, just a few miles south of Luxor. Carter and Callender's working relationship extended back in time to a period some years before the discovery of Tutankhamun's tomb when Carter had reason to call upon him for his engineering expertise and 'companionship'.[7] Callender, described 'as a low-keyed, placid man of saturnine expression',[8] would, in the coming months and the succeeding years prove himself to be a vital component of the excavation team and an ideal 'second man'.

Already, Carnarvon had cabled Carter to say that he would arrive at Alexandria on the 20th in the company of his daughter, Lady Evelyn Herbert. Conspicuously absent was Carnarvon's wife, Almina, who had become increasingly disenchanted with her husband's obsession for digging up the dead. Although she was perhaps not aware of it at the time, she too had developed her own obsession by becoming infatuated with a new man in her life. An infatuation that, as we shall see, was destined to lead her to remarry within eight months of her first husband's death.

HARBINGER OF ILL LUCK

Carter travelled to Cairo on Saturday 18 November in order to purchase a number of items, including wood, nails, cable and lamps, to illuminate the interior of the tomb using the available electrical sockets already present inside the tomb of Rameses VI. Everything went according to plan, although on his return to Luxor Carter learned that something rather portentous had occurred in his absence. Apparently, the house was left in the care of Pecky Callender, who had been assigned to look after a canary bought at the start of the season by Carter in order to brighten up the place and keep him company. One afternoon Callender suddenly heard a fluttering and squeaking, and so instantly made his way towards the portico where the bird cage could be found. On arrival, he had been aghast to see a cobra inside the canary's cage apparently in the process of swallowing the poor creature.[9] This was indeed unfortunate, for when Carter first introduced the bird to the foremen and guards they had all said, 'The bird will bring good fortune!'[10]

According to a letter written by Herbert Winlock, assistant curator of Egyptology at New York's Metropolitan Museum of Art, to its director Edward Robinson, the gaffirs had told Carter: 'Mabrook ["congratulations" in Arabic] – it's a bird of gold that will bring luck. This year we will find inshallah (God willing) a tomb full of gold'.[11] This was confirmed when, just a few days later, the first step of the flight of stairs leading down into the tomb was uncovered, which was promptly named the 'tomb of the Golden Bird'[12], or the 'Tomb of the Bird'.[13] As Winlock whimsically pointed out, 'The canary almost had a halo around its cage'.[14]

So news that the canary had been gobbled down, 'halo and all',[15] by a cobra, which was not only a rare sight in the Valley but also an ancient Egyptian symbol of sovereignty, worn on the pharaoh's headdress, was not greeted very well. In the minds of the highly superstitious Arab-Egyptians employed in Carter's service, the 'golden bird' had gone from being a good omen, comparable with the hawk that in Pharaonic times was a symbol of divine sovereignty, to a harbinger of ill luck. As Winlock ominously concluded, 'And the sequel was equally obvious – at least to them, though I admit to have lost some links in the chain of argument – that before the winter was out someone would die'.[16]

Herbert Winlock was a very well respected Egyptologist who played a major role in the events surrounding the discovery of the tomb of Tutankhamun. He was also a good friend to Carter and, indeed, Carter once admitted that Winlock was his only true friend.[17] Thus Winlock's comments with respect to this matter cannot be dismissed simply as flights of fancy.

Charles Breasted, quoting the words of his father, James Henry Breasted, the American Egyptologist and orientalist, who joined Carter's team in mid-December 1922, records a slightly different version of the story. He tells of how

> One day soon after the discovery Carter sent an assistant to fetch something from his house which happened to be empty, the servants having gone to the weekly market at Luxor [thus probably Tuesday 21 November]. As the man approached the house he heard a faint, almost human cry. Then all was silent again – even the bird had stopped singing.
>
> Upon entering, he looked almost instinctively at the cage and saw coiled within it a cobra holding in its mouth the dead canary.
>
> News of this spread quickly and all the natives now said: 'Alas, that was the King's cobra, revenging itself upon the bird for having betrayed the place of the tomb – and now something terrible will happen!'[18]

Whichever version of the story comes closest to the truth, that the incident occurred need not be doubted, even though some historians writing on the subject of Tutankhamun have questioned its authenticity.[19] Even though Carter's diary makes no mention of the incident (which is scant in detail, anyway), his entry for Friday 24 November is very revealing for it records that 'Lady E[velyn] arrived and brought bird',[20] which is very probably the replacement canary Carter is known to have given to Minnie Burton, wife of the photographer Harry Burton, when he returned to England at the end of the 1923–4 season.[21]

What is truly intriguing, if not downright ominous, about Winlock's letter is that it was written on 28 March 1923, just eight days before Carnarvon met his fate and joined Tutankhamun in the netherworld. Perhaps not unnaturally, Carnarvon's demise was seen by some as the fulfilment of the strange portent presented by the ill-timed death of the 'golden bird', a matter taken up in Chapter 10.

LORD CARNARVON ARRIVES

After rendezvousing in Cairo with Lord Carnarvon and Lady Evelyn on Monday 20 November Carter left for Luxor the following morning. Two days later, Carnarvon arrived in Luxor, eager to inspect the tomb. After settling in at Castle Carter, he and Carter went out to the dig site, where Callender had begun uncovering the rubbish that filled the sunken staircase.

According to Carter, the following day, Friday 24 November saw the arrival of

Lady Evelyn[22] (even though elsewhere she is said to have arrived with her father the day before[23]). After she, her father and Carter had shared a late lunch they travelled out to the Valley to see the final debris being removed from around the entrance doorway. Another four steps came into view, making sixteen in all, and on the lower section of the sealed doorway Carter now noticed seal impressions bearing the cartouche of Tutankhamun's throne name Nebkheperure, confirmation at last of the tomb's true age. More disquieting, however, was the fact that he could see that there were two places in the upper part of the doorway that had been breached and then resealed. It clearly implied that the tomb had been entered at least twice in antiquity. He realised also that the part of the doorway bearing the seal impressions of the royal necropolis denoted the replastered area, while the bottom section displaying the royal seal of Tutankhamun was original.[24]

There was no question that the tomb was, as Carter stated, 'not absolutely intact, as we had hoped'.[25] It had been entered and resealed on two occasions and, as the workmen's huts were directly over the entrance, this could only have occurred prior to the construction of Rameses VI's tomb. Indeed, Carter was later to decide that the resealing could not have occurred any later than the reign of Horemheb, thus within thirty years of Tutankhamun's death.[26] More frustration was to follow. Within the debris at the very base of the steps he found masses of

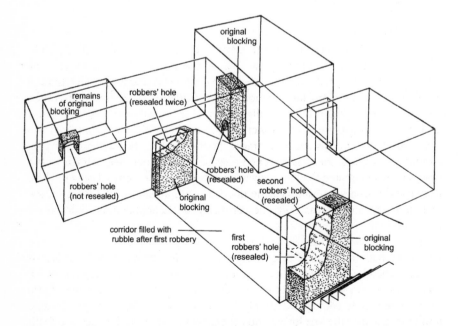

original
blocking

remains
of original
blocking

robbers' hole
(resealed twice)

robbers' hole
(resealed)

second
robbers' hole
(resealed)

robbers' hole
(not resealed)

original
blocking

corridor filled with
rubble after first robbery

first
robbers' hole
(resealed)

original
blocking

Fig. 7. Three-dimensional plan of Tutankhamun's tomb (after Nicholas Reeves).

potsherds and fragments of boxes bearing the names of Akhenaten, Smenkhkare and Tutankhamun. Even more worrying was the fact that, in addition to these items, Carter found among the debris a scarab from the reign of Thutmose III and a fragment on which was the name of Akhenaten's father, Amenhotep III. Did the tomb contain some kind of cache, like that found in the tomb of Amenhotep II, further up the Valley?

That evening Carter slept the night at the tomb. The next day, Saturday 25 November, plans were made for the removal of the sealed doorway. Already, Callender was busy co-ordinating the manufacture of a heavy wooden grille that would replace it, since it was essential that the utmost security be applied to the tomb from the outset. Once the seal impressions had been recorded, the doorway, which consisted of rough stones stacked from the threshold to the lintel plastered over with mortar, was dismantled. Beyond it was a long descending passage the same width and height as the entrance and around 2 metres high. As previously noted, it had been filled with local stone and rubble, some of it produced during the excavation of the tomb, and this would have to be cleared before going any further. As it was removed, another fact emerged. Corresponding to the resealed section in the upper left-hand corner of the doorway, was a robbers' tunnel filled in with dark flint and chert stones.

At the end of Saturday, a large amount of the rubble blocking the passageway had been removed, but the job would have to be completed the following day, Sunday 26 November. This Carter was afterwards to describe as 'the day of days, the most wonderful that I have ever lived through, and certainly one whose like I can never hope to see again'.[27]

THE DAY OF DAYS

The night must have been tense with expectancy. But, by breakfast on the 26th, the final clearance of the passageway was under way, yet here and there work came abruptly to a halt in order that the team could catalogue and draw a number of delicate items found among the rock debris. They included broken pottery, jar sealings and other smaller items, such as alabaster jars, whole and broken, coloured pottery, and water skins, which would have contained the water needed to replaster the entrance doorway after the first break-in. By around two o'clock they had reached a second sealed doorway, similar to the first, having penetrated the passageway for a distance of 9 metres. Using torches, Carter and Carnarvon examined the door's seal impressions. Like those on the first doorway, some areas bore the cartouche of Tutankhamun, while others belonged to the royal necropolis.

It was becoming clearer what had happened at the tomb soon after the interment had taken place. Originally the corridor between the two sealed doorways had been left empty, a fact confirmed in the knowledge that one of the two breaches on either door did *not* relate to the tunnel dug through the debris. This robbers' hole corresponded only to the second breach on each doorway, implying that after the first forced entry the necropolis officials had decided to fill the passageway with rubble in order to deter further violation of the tomb. Before this was done, embalming equipment and other leftovers of the funerary meal deposited in the corridor had been transferred to the pit (Pit 54) found in 1907 by Edward Ayrton and Theodore M Davis.

Carter realised something else as well. The staircase, passageway and entrance passageways resembled very closely the design of Tomb 55, which was positioned directly opposite the entrance to the new tomb. At the time he shared the opinion, held by some of his contemporaries, that it was originally a cache that contained the bodies of Queen Tiye and Akhenaten. Its doorways had likewise borne the royal seal of Tutankhamun. Carter thus became convinced that *his* tomb might be an Amarna cache, containing the bodies of other key members of Akhenaten's family, buried hastily during the reign of Tutankhamun. Whatever the answer, it showed that the two royal tombs belonged to exactly the same period of history.

EVERYWHERE THE GLINT OF GOLD

Carter, Callender, Carnarvon and Lady Evelyn watched as the very last debris was removed from the base of the door, exposing it completely. The sense of anticipation must have been unimaginable, and then came the decisive moment they had all been waiting for. His hands trembling, Carter made a small breach in the upper left-hand corner of the doorway. With the use of a testing rod, he probed the hole and was heartened to find that it was not obstructed by anything solid. As a precaution, he next conducted a candle test in order to check for any foul gases lurking in the dark interior. Finding none, he passed the candle through the spyhole until his hand was lost from view. Carter then peered inside to see what lay beyond the door, as Carnarvon, Callender, Lady Evelyn and the *reises*, or gaffirs, looked on. It took a few moments for his eyes to adjust to the eerie reflections of the candlelight, but then, gradually, he began to make out features, shapes, and objects, which seemed to fill the room:

> At first I could see nothing, the hot air escaping from the chamber causing the candle flame to flicker, but presently, as my eyes grew accustomed to the light, details of the room within emerged slowly from the mist, strange animals, statues, and gold – everywhere the glint of gold.[28]

Momentarily, Carter was struck dumb with amazement, as the others stood by waiting patiently for the verdict. Finally, Carnarvon, unable to hold back any longer, enquired anxiously, 'Can you see anything?'

'Yes,' Carter replied. 'Wonderful things.'[29] ('Yes, it is wonderful' is the response recorded in Carter's notebook.[30]) Enlarging the hole still further, he inserted an electric torch to gain a clearer picture of what lay inside the room, which would become known as the Antechamber. Piled one upon another were objects that seemed familiar, while others were entirely new to him. Never had he imagined making such a marvellous discovery, and so his total bewilderment at the spectacle seems understandable.

The other adventurers – Carnarvon, Lady Evelyn and Callender – peered through one after the other and became transfixed by what they saw. So much lay just out of reach beyond the doorway that it seemed utterly breathtaking. Directly in front of them were three gilded couches, almost unbelievable in appearance, carved into the form of wondrous animals, their golden heads gleaming in the torchlight. To the right were two life-size standing figures, facing each other like sentinel guardians, their bodies painted black. Each wore a gilded kilt and their heads were crowned with the *uraeus*-serpent, which rested on their foreheads. In their left hand they held a long pole-like staff while in their right hand was a mace with a gilded pear-shaped head. Later investigation revealed that they bore inscriptions identifying them as representations of the king's *ka*, or 'ghost'.

These were the objects that first attracted their attention, but as their eyes became increasingly more accustomed to the darkness they beheld much more – much more indeed – for, as Carter records in his notebook for that fateful day,

Our sensations and astonishment are difficult to describe as the better light revealed to us the marvellous collection of treasures: … ornamental caskets; flowers; alabaster vases, some beautifully executed of lotus and papyrus device; strange black shrines with a gilded monster snake appearing from within; quite ordinary looking white chests; finely carved chairs; a golden inlaid throne; a heap of large curious white oviform boxes; beneath our very eyes, on the threshold, a lovely lotiform wishing-cup in translucent alabaster; stools of all shapes and design, of both common and rare materials; and, lastly a confusion of overturned parts of chariots glinting with gold, peering from amongst which was a mannikin. The first impression of which suggested the property-room of an opera of a vanished civilization. Our sensations were bewildering and full of strange emotion. We questioned one another as to the meaning of it all. Was it a tomb or merely a cache? A sealed doorway between the two sentinel statues proved there was more beyond, and with the numerous cartouches bearing the name of Tut.ankh.Amen on most of the objects before us, there was little doubt that there behind was the grave of that Pharaoh.[31]

According to Carter's published account of the incredible discovery, after gazing for too long at the amazing sight before them they resealed the hole and exited the passageway, locking the wooden grille behind them. Then, leaving a trusted man on guard, they finally departed the Valley on donkeys towards Castle Carter, 'strangely silent and subdued'.[32]

They are said to have spent the evening discussing excitedly what each had seen, with one recalling this and another that: 'Each of us had noted something that the others had not, and it amazed us next day to discover how many and how obvious were the things that we had missed. Naturally, it was the sealed door between the statues that intrigued us most, and we debated far into the night the possibilities of what might lie behind it.'[33] Finally, after all the speculation had died down, they retired to bed: 'I think we slept but little, all of us, that night'.[34]

Indeed, they did not sleep at all well, for, despite Carter's official version of the story recorded in the first volume of his book *The Tomb of Tut.ankh.Amen*, co-written with Arthur C Mace, associate curator at New York's Metropolitan Museum, it has now been established that Carter, and seemingly his three co-conspirators (see Chapter 6), physically went ahead and entered the tomb's Antechamber and its adjoining Annexe that same afternoon. Moreover, there is overwhelming evidence to show that the same four individuals returned to the tomb within the next few days and, quite illegally, breached the sealed doorway between the two sentinel statues and came face to face with the dead king's final resting place. It is these transgressions that we must evaluate next in order to place them in the context of the much greater story to be told in the second half of this book.

6. UNOFFICIAL OPENING

Let him [the reader] imagine how they appeared to us as we looked down upon them from our spy-hole in the blocked doorway, casting the beam of light from our torch – the first light that had pierced the darkness of the chamber for three thousand years – from one group of objects to another, in a vain attempt to interpret the treasure that lay before us.[1]

These are Howard Carter's thoughts after he first set eyes on Tutankhamun's final resting place, sometime around two o'clock on Sunday 26 November 1922.[2] Yet what the British Egyptologist fails to disclose in his written testimony is that he went on to enlarge the spyhole and climb inside, without waiting for official permission to do so. This fact is recorded in a draft article on the events leading up to the great discovery by Lord Carnarvon dated Sunday 10 December 1922,[3] which was in fact a variation of an article that appeared in *The Times* of London on Monday, 11 December.[4] It provides a more realistic spin on what transpired that all-important day in the Valley of the Kings when he, Carter, Pecky Callender and Lady Evelyn Herbert reached the sealed doorway between the entrance passageway and the Antechamber:

I asked Mr Carter to take out a few stones and have a look in. After a few minutes this was done and he pushed his head partly into the aperture. With the help of a candle he could dimly discern what was inside. A long silence followed until I said, I fear in somewhat trembling tones, 'well, what is it?' 'There are some marvellous objects here' was the welcome reply![5]

Gone is Carter's famous reply of 'Yes, wonderful things', as published in Carter and Mace's *The Tomb of Tut.ankh.Amen*, and repeated often in books and TV documentaries on the subject. Carnarvon goes on to describe how, after Carter had given up his place, he and Lady Evelyn moved forward to peer through the hole:

At first sight with the very inadequate light all one could see was what appeared to be gold bars. On getting a little more accustomed to the light it became apparent that these were colossal gilt couches with extraordinary heads, boxes here and boxes there.[6]

So far there is no real difference between Lord Carnarvon's account of events of that day, and the published account by Carter and Mace. Yet it is what Carnarvon records next that is of greater interest, for, instead of simply peering through the hole, his lordship recalls how:

We enlarged the hole and Mr Carter managed to scramble in – the chamber is sunk 2 feet [0.7 metres] below the bottom of the passage – and then, as he moved around with the candle, we knew that we had found something absolutely unique and unprecedented.[7]

There seems no reason to doubt Lord Carnarvon's rendition of what took place that afternoon, even though Carter and Mace wrote that the four of them entered the tomb for the first time on the following day, Monday 27 November:

By noon [on the 27th] everything was ready and Lord Carnarvon, Lady Evelyn, Callender and I entered the tomb and made a careful inspection of the first chamber (afterwards called the Antechamber).[8]

So why the apparent deception? Why did Carter claim to have entered the Antechamber for the first time a day later than he actually did? The answer would appear to be petty politics. Article 3 of the digging concession officially issued to Lord Carnarvon in 1915 (and renewed annually) made it clear that the 'Permittee', i.e. Howard Carter on behalf of Carnarvon, should 'give notice at once' to the chief inspector of the Antiquities Service for Upper Egypt at Luxor of the discovery of any tomb or monument.[9] At the time the position of chief inspector was held by the British Egyptologist Reginald 'Rex' Engelbach, who had been kept informed of all developments at the tomb, and only two days beforehand, on Friday, the 24th, had 'witnessed part of the final clearing of rubbish from the [first] doorway'.[10]

Yet on this day Engelbach had been the bringer of bad tidings, for he informed Carter and Carnarvon that Pierre Lacau, the director-general of the Antiquities Service, wished them to know that he, Engelbach, or one of his colleagues should be present at the opening of any chamber found.[11] This was despite the fact that Article 4 of the digging concession asserted that 'the Permittee himself shall be reserved the privilege of opening the tomb or monument discovered, and of being the first to enter therein'.[12]

Realising the implications of what he was saying, Carter and Carnarvon protested most strongly to Engelbach, whom they loathed and alluded to rather derogatorily as 'Trout'.[13] In their opinion Lacau's proposal was not only unworkable, but also an affront to the terms and conditions of the concession. More than this, Carter would have seen the Frenchman's interference as a prime example of the way in which the Antiquities Service was attempting to undermine his work. Lastly, Lacau's insistence that Engelbach be present when the tomb was opened suggested that he wanted to keep a watchful eye on the proceedings to make sure that nothing untoward took place during the opening of the tomb, if not to gain a little fame by association.

So, when the inner doorway at the end of the Entrance Corridor had come into view for the first time, Carter and Carnarvon were faced with a dilemma. Did they down tools, notify Engelbach, and then wait for him to arrive before proceeding any further, or did they press ahead and enter the tomb? If their discovery was made known, then they could wait days before being allowed to continue their work, and, worse still, Lacau might insist that he himself travel to Luxor to oversee the opening of the tomb. However, they realised only too well that, if they did proceed without an official being present, then they risked invalidating Article 3 of the concession, which implied that they must 'give notice at once' of any discoveries made.

In the end, Carter, and, as we shall see, Carnarvon, Lady Evelyn and Callender, pressed ahead and entered the tomb. Yet, since their actions would have been seen as a breach of Article 3 of the digging concession, there was no way that they could admit to entering the tomb without having first notified Engelbach. So, in order to circumnavigate this problem, Carter and Carnarvon had first to ensure everyone's word that they would never mention anything about entering the Antechamber that day. Afterwards, Carter notified Engelbach, in order that he could 'make an official inspection' as soon as possible.[14] As long as the four of them, and, of course, Carter's trusted guards, who were also in on the secret (see below), kept their mouths shut, there would not be a problem.

HOVING'S REVELATIONS

Aside from Lord Carnarvon's typewritten draft article on the events leading to the discovery of the tomb, as well as an earlier handwritten version of the same article (see below) and a few careless whispers by the British aristocrat, the group's unofficial entry into the Antechamber managed to escape public notice for more than seventy years. It was finally brought to the attention of the world with the publication in 1978 of a sensational book entitled *Tutankhamun – The Untold Story*, written by Thomas Hoving, a former head of New York's Metropolitan Museum of Art. In 1975 he co-ordinated the American leg of the Tutankhamun exhibition, which went under the title of 'The Treasures of Tutankhamun'. Hoving's privileged position at the museum enabled him to root out dozens of previously unpublished documents that lay forgotten in its dusty archives. Many of these items either directly or indirectly related to the events surrounding the discovery of Tutankhamun, in particular the museum's relationship with Carnarvon and Carter, and among them were allusions to the pair's clandestine forays into the tomb.

Using the material he found in the Metropolitan Museum, along with Carnarvon's draft article of the events of that night and two brief papers by the British chemist Alfred Lucas, who worked with Carter on the tomb for nine seasons, Hoving attempted to reconstruct the events of 26 November 1922 (see Chapter 7).[15] According to him, it was Lady Evelyn, and not Carter, who was first to enter the Antechamber, simply because she was the smallest in the party.[16] It makes sense, although there is no confirmation that this was indeed the case. After she had wriggled through successfully, Hoving has the intrepid crew enlarging the hole as Lady Evelyn peered in awe at the treasures piled up before her. Gradually, the remaining three members of the team made their way through into the Antechamber.

THE ANTECHAMBER

Inside the north–south-oriented chamber, 8.08 metres by 1.68 metres in size, were hundreds of unimaginable objects stacked from floor to ceiling, but it was the little things that Carter recalled most during those first brief moments inside the tomb of Tutankhamun. There was the half-filled bowl of mortar, used to replaster the door into the Burial Chamber, and the blackened oil lamp, as well as the fingermark on a freshly painted surface and a well-preserved garland of flowers, discarded at the threshold. The waft of unguents, oils and perfumes pervaded the air, adding to the hypnotic setting that must have tugged at the group's sanity as they moved around, gazing mesmerically at everything they came across. As Carter was to write, 'Time is annihilated by little intimate details such as these, and *you* feel the intruder [authors' italics]'.[17]

THE ANNEXE

Once inside the Antechamber, the party of four would presumably have gone on to discover the small north–south-oriented chamber, measuring 4.35 by 2.6 metres in size and 2.55 metres high, which became known as 'the Annexe'. Its sealed doorway remained hidden behind and beneath one of the three beautiful gilded couches stacked against the west wall. Tomb robbers had forced their entry into this room through a hole made below the legs of this exquisite piece of Pharaonic furniture. Carter and Carnarvon crept underneath the ancient treasure and peered in through the opening. Everywhere inside the Annexe were objects piled high, many in a state of disarray, for as Carter records:

> One [intruder] – there would probably not have been room for more than one – had crept into the chamber, and had then hastily but systematically ransacked its entire contents, emptying boxes, throwing things aside, piling them one upon another, and occasionally passing objects through the hole to his companions for closer examination in the outer chamber. He had done his work just about as thoroughly as an earthquake. Not a single inch of floor space remains vacant, and it will be a matter of considerable difficulty, when the time for clearing comes, to know how to begin.[17]

One can understand, without much difficulty, why Carter made the decision to enter the Antechamber that afternoon. We can imagine him becoming drunk on the flow of adrenaline – the sheer buzz – that must have accompanied his first sight of the marvellous treasures within. There would have been an overwhelming compulsion to probe deeper and find out exactly what it was that glistened gold in the flickering light of the candle. We can forgive Carter and his colleagues for their understandable enthusiasm. Yet the group's indiscretions went far beyond simply entering the Antechamber without official permission, for there is now indisputable evidence to show that sometime between Tuesday 28 November and Thursday 30 November 1922, the four of them breached the sealed doorway in the north wall of the Antechamber and explored the king's inner sanctum. This, it must be stressed, was almost three months before the official opening of the Burial Chamber when Carter and Callender broke down the doorway in front of a distinguished group of invited guests on Friday 16 February 1923 (not Friday 17 February, as is recorded incorrectly by Carter and Mace in their book[18] – an error repeated again and again in modern accounts of the discovery of the tomb).

'HERE IS THE SECRET'

The first inklings of this greater transgression on the parts of Carter and Carnarvon came to light with the publication in 1972 of a book entitled *Behind the Mask of Tutankhamen*, penned by the historical writer Barry Wynne.[20] Having gained the trust and respect of the sixth Earl of Carnarvon (1898–1987), who wrote a testimonial for the book, Wynne was able to draw from the slowly fading memories of the ageing aristocrat for a more personal account of his father's life and times. In addition to this, Wynne examined the diaries of the fifth earl's half-brother, the Hon. Mervyn Herbert (1882–1929), who was present at the official opening of the Burial Chamber. These items are currently housed in the Private Papers Collection at the Middle East Centre, St Antony's College, Oxford, where they were viewed during the preparation of this book.[21]

Mervyn, at the time a diplomat with a position at the British Embassy in Madrid, had decided to take a well-earned break in Egypt with his wife Elizabeth. Having gone sightseeing in Cairo, the couple moved on to Luxor, taking up residence at the Winter Palace Hotel, where Mervyn's half-brother, the fifth earl, or 'Porch' as he called him, also had a suite. The two men were very close, and on the morning of Friday 16 February 1923, the day of the official opening, Mervyn went to Porch's room to say good morning, as he did every day. Yet, on receiving him, the fifth earl asked Mervyn if he was free, since he wanted him at the opening of the tomb. The British aristocrat admitted that he needed a little moral support, but added, 'I am afraid I shall not be able to show you anything'.[22]

Mervyn was delighted to receive the invitation, but so tight was the schedule that he had time only to return to his room and inform Elizabeth of his plans, before he was whisked off towards a waiting motorcar. Had she been dressed there and then, she might well have been able to accompany him, a matter that Mervyn felt some regret about afterwards. Yet, had she done so, the chances are that his diary entry for that day would have been a whole lot different, for what he records as happening next is of paramount importance to our understanding of the sequence of events following the initial discovery of the tomb:

> Porch and Evelyn and I started in his ford and after we had been going a few minutes he said that it would really be alright and he could quite well get me in while the tomb was being opened. Then he whispered something to Evelyn and told her to tell me. This she did under the strictest promise of secrecy – it is a thing I would never give away in any case and it is one which I think ought not to be known at any rate not at present. Here is the secret. They had both already been into the second Chamber! After the discovery they had not been able to resist it.

They had made a small hole in the wall (which they afterwards filled up again) and climbed through. She described to me very shortly some of the extraordinary wonders I was soon to see. It was a most exciting drive I cannot remember anything like it. The only others who knew anything about it are the workers, none of whom would ever breathe a word to a soul about it [authors' italics].[23]

The vehicle arrived in the Valley, and, as Lord Carnarvon, Lady Evelyn and Mervyn Herbert stepped out, they were greeted with a warm round of applause from the waiting spectators. Carter was already present as the group made its way through the crowds that had gathered in expectation around the entrance to the tomb. While members of the press and dozens of tourists looked on, Carter and Carnarvon greeted their guests as they arrived by motorcar. Very slowly the assembled group, which included Abd el Halim Pasha Suleman, the Minister of Public Works; Pierre Lacau, Rex Engelbach and three inspectors from the Antiquities Service; Sir William Garstin, the Inspector General of Irrigation for the Egyptian Ministry of Public Works; the king's equerry, Sir Charles Cust, who was a friend of Lord Carnarvon; the Hon. Richard Bethell, Lord Carnarvon's personal secretary; members of Carter's team, including Professor Henry James Breasted and Dr Alan H Gardiner; Albert Lythgoe and Herbert Winlock of the Metropolitan Museum of Art; as well as Carter, Carnarvon, Lady Evelyn and Mervyn Herbert – some twenty people in all – descended the sixteen steps into the Entrance Corridor.

Once inside the Antechamber, which was stiflingly hot and sweaty, the party sat down on rows of chairs that faced towards the north wall, where a wooden boxlike platform had been set up between the two black and gold guardian statues. These were the only items left *in situ* within the room, and even they had been encased in wooden frames for their own protection. The assembled crowd waited patiently for the entertainment to begin. Not one of them, save for Carter, Carnarvon, Lady Evelyn and Callender, could have anticipated the extraordinary nature of this great moment in archaeological history. Yet, as Mervyn Herbert implied in his diary entry for that day, all was *not* as it seemed. Each and every one of the invited guests was being duped into thinking that the Burial Chamber was being opened for the first time, something that we now know to be completely untrue. Mervyn's account of the events of that long afternoon is worth quoting in detail:

Rows of chairs had been arranged in the first chamber of the tomb which had been entirely cleared except for the 2 statues of the King at one end. Between them was the sealed entrance and at the bottom of this sealed door was *a little wooden platform which concealed the hole made in the wall when they had got in before.* Porch, poor old fellow was nervous, like a naughty schoolboy, *fearing that they would discover that a hole had already been made.* He was also and most naturally very excited. Although he knew a good deal about what was there he cannot have helped feeling that this was one of the very great moments that happen to few people. He began by making a very nice little speech to all of us – short and to the point – one of the main things being thanks to all the workers but principally to the Americans who had very generously given their services free. Then Carter made a little speech, not very good – he was nervous – almost inarticulate & talked mainly about science & the immensity of the discovery.

Then they began to work. Carter beat away the mortar and took out great stones starting at the top & handing out the rubble to Callender. The work went slowly for a bit but presently he had made a hole big enough to fit his head through. He looked in with a large electric torch & said that he saw a large gold & blue box – which was of course the tabernacle. After he had increased the size of the opening we were all allowed to look in and got a good but an incomplete view of the marvellous tabernacle. The work proceeded and eventually he got an opening big enough to let people through. He went in – then Porch – and then eventually all of those who were there [authors' italics].[24]

According to Mervyn Herbert, the 'little wooden platform' set up between the guardian figures 'concealed the hole' made by Carter and Carnarvon when they had first entered the Burial Chamber. In Carter's version of the events presented in *The Tomb of Tut.ankh.Amen*, he recorded that the breach had first been examined on his entry into the Antechamber:

Our first objective was naturally the sealed door between the statues, and here a disappointment awaited us. Seen from a distance it presented all the appearance of an absolutely intact blocking, but close examination revealed the fact that a small breach had been made near the bottom, just wide enough to admit a boy or a slightly built man, and that the hole made had subsequently been filled up and re-sealed. We were not then to be the first. Here, too, the thieves had forestalled us, and it only remained to be seen how much damage they had had the opportunity or the time to effect.[25]

So the position of the breach deemed to have been made in antiquity by tomb robbers was identical to the position of the 'hole made in the wall' by Carter and Carnarvon when they illegally entered the Burial Chamber a full three months beforehand. Does this imply therefore that they broke through the original breach and then resealed the opening again shortly afterwards?

The evidence of the resealing of the doorway is for ever preserved in the photographs of the Antechamber taken by Henry 'Harry' Burton (1879–1940), the accomplished British photographer lent by the Metropolitan Museum of Art to Carter in order to record the discovery of the tomb. A set of Burton's photographs, preserving the entire archaeological operation at Tutankhamun's tomb, is housed in the archives of the Griffith Institute in Oxford. One particular photograph (No. GB7 282 see Plate 11) clearly shows the resealed hole covered by a slightly darker mortar bearing the stamped seal of the royal necropolis.

From Meryvn Herbert's diaries and Alfred Lucas's revelations, reviewed shortly, we can be certain that Carter et al. did indeed make a hole in the wall and shortly afterwards resealed it. Since Burton did not join the archaeological team working on the tomb until mid-December, this photograph can only be evidence of Carter's handiwork and not a record of a resealing in remote antiquity.

Certainly, this conclusion is implied by Mervyn Herbert's diaries. They tell us that Carter and Carnarvon, and presumably Callender and Lady Evelyn as well, feared that someone among the selected party present when the Burial Chamber was opened on 16 February 1923 would realise that the mortar and seal impressions were only three months old, and not 3,300 years old, as Carter claimed. For this reason Carter and Carnarvon deliberately placed a wooden platform across the bottom quarter of the doorway in order to hide what they had done. Then, little by little, Carter, with the help of Callender, pierced a hole in its upper section and gradually enlarged the opening until a person could climb through to the chamber beyond. Even after Carter, Carnarvon and their awestruck guests were able to examine the inner sanctum containing the gilded shrine of the boy-king, the wooden platform remained in place. Burton's photographs recording the day show this fact quite clearly. Conveniently, it was not until after the guests had left the Antechamber that this was taken away and the lower part of the doorway removed.

To accept such a version of the events surrounding what is arguably the greatest archaeological discovery of all time is a little difficult. Can we really conceive of the notion that Carter, Carnarvon, Callender and Lady Evelyn secretly broke through into the Burial Chamber shortly after their initial entry into the Antechamber? Is it really possible that they went to all the trouble of making a replica stamp bearing the seal of the necropolis and impressing this into the wet mortar, before hiding the breech in the doorway in the vain belief that no one would notice? The whole thing seems incredible, if not a little farcical.

THE QUESTION OF THE ROBBERS' HOLE

That this is indeed what happened can be shown from two obscure articles written by Alfred Lucas (1867–1945), the Manchester-born chemist who worked with Carter from the winter of 1922–3 through until the 1930–1 season, conserving many of the thousands of objects brought out of the tomb. Carter said that without Lucas's help no more than 10 per cent of the treasures would have reached the Cairo Museum in a fit state for public exhibition. Lucas was with Howard Carter when, in the spring of 1926, Tutankhamun's famous gold mask was transported by train under armed escort from Luxor directly to the museum.

The articles in question appeared in the *Annales du service des Antiquités de l'Egypte*, the journal of the Egyptian Antiquities Service. The first of them, published in 1942 and entitled 'Notes on Some of the Objects from the Tomb of Tut-ankhamun', was intended to correct errors found in certain books that had appeared to date on the subject of the tomb of Tutankhamun.[26] They included the British archaeologist Arthur Weigall's *Tutankhamen and Other Essays* and the Belgian Egyptologist Jean Capart's *The Tomb of Tutankhamen*, both rushed out in 1923, as well as Carter's own work, *The Tomb of Tut.ankh.Amen*, published in three volumes respectively in 1923 (co-written with Arthur C Mace), 1927 and 1933. In Lucas's words, 'Certain statements in some of those books are wrong and need correction'.[27]

Starting his list of corrections with the first volume of Carter's trilogy, Lucas drew attention to the so-called robbers' hole in the doorway between the

Antechamber and the Burial Chamber. He pointed out that on pages 101 and 102 of this work 'it is stated that "close examination revealed the fact that a small breach had been made near the bottom ... and that the hole made had subsequently been filled up and re-sealed".'[28] Lucas says that 'a considerable amount of mystery was made about this robbers's [sic] hole'. Moreover, that on first examining it around Wednesday, 20 December 1922, he saw that the breach was hidden behind:

> ... [a] basketwork tray, or lid, and some rushes taken from the floor that Mr. Carter had placed before it ... Lord Carnarvon, his daughter and Mr. Carter certainly entered the burial chamber and also entered the store chamber [or Treasury], which latter had no door, before the formal opening. Whether Mr. Callender, who was present at the time, also entered the burial chamber, I am not sure, but he was a very big man and I once heard a remark that made me think that the hole was too small to admit him.[29]

Lucas was no fool. His detailed forensic work helped determine when exactly the tomb had been breached in antiquity, so his assertion that Carter et al. had broken into the Burial Chamber before its official opening cannot be treated lightly. His confession also backs up what Mervyn Herbert recorded in his diaries, making it now impossible to deny that the whole episode took place.

As to whether the breach into the Burial Chamber was open or closed when Carter and Carnarvon first entered the Antechamber, Lucas felt it did not matter, since he believed that their decision to reseal the hole was in the best interests of the tomb and its treasures. Otherwise Carter would have been inundated with requests to see the contents of both the Burial Chamber and Treasury before the outer chambers had been cleared, and this might have led to the damage of objects.

Lucas's second paper on the same subject was published in the 1947 volume of the *Annales du service des Antiquités de l'Egypte*.[30] Its purpose was to update the previous article published in 1942, and after introducing certain new written sources on the subject of Tutankhamun, and giving an analysis of some bread found in the tomb, he returned to his earlier statements regarding the breach in the door to the Burial Chamber:

> I stated [in the earlier paper] that 'Lord Carnarvon, his daughter and Mr. Carter certainly entered the burial chamber'... This leaves to the imagination the identity of the person who closed the door and the date when it was closed, and to that extent is ambiguous, an ambiguity that I now wish to remove. Mr. Carter states that 'close examination revealed the fact that a small breach had been made near the bottom ... and that the hole made had subsequently been filled up and re-sealed'. This is misleading, since the hole unlike that in the outermost doorway, had not been closed and re-sealed by the cemetery officials, but by Mr. Carter. Soon after I commenced work with Mr. Carter he pointed out to me the closing and re-sealing, and when I said that it did not look like old work he admitted that it was not and that he had done it'.[31]

So the cat was out of the bag: Carter did make the hole. Yet why did Lucas not mention this fact in his original article of 1942? The most likely explanation is that he was protecting the good character of Howard Carter, who had died only three years beforehand in 1939. Yet Lucas, having quite obviously been called to question regarding his revelations concerning the unofficial entry into the Burial Chamber, now felt it necessary to reveal all he knew to the Egyptological community.

How Lucas's article might have been received by his contemporaries is not recorded. Indeed, it would seem that instead of embracing the realisation that Carter's account of his discovery of the tomb was not only misleading, but a downright fabrication, Egyptologists the world over either failed to understand the significance of Lucas's revelations or simply chose to ignore them. The discovery of Tutankhamun was unquestionably the greatest archaeological achievement ever, and to have the handling of the affair tarnished by murmurs of gross indiscretions by its chief excavator would have been detrimental to the honoured profession of Egyptology. It was quite obviously better to hope that the whole matter would simply fade away.

So, according to the written account of the British chemist Alfred Lucas, a close friend and colleague of Howard Carter, there had been no resealed hole between the Antechamber and the Burial Chamber when the tomb was entered for the first time on 26 November 1922. This suggests that Carter, Carnarvon and Lady Evelyn were able merely to wriggle through the robbers' hole and enter the Burial Chamber and Treasury, something that the larger-framed Pecky Callender was unable to do because of his size. Then, after they emerged from the tomb's inner sanctum, the robbers' hole was covered over, in the style of the outer doorway to the Entrance Corridor, using stones, mortar and a newly made seal impression.

Yet this conclusion on Lucas's part is based solely on his own observation of the resealed area, either during or directly after the clearance of the Antechamber, as well as Carter's confession that he sealed the robbers' hole to avoid unnecessary interest in the chamber beyond. Since we know that Carter was inclined to be somewhat economical with the truth when he recounted events surrounding the discovery of the tomb, then it is probable that Lucas, being a man of science, saw the logic behind Carter's explanation and accepted it without question. Either that or this was never what Lucas intended to say in his articles, for it seems bizarre that he could ever have truly believed that the robbers' hole was left open by the officials of the royal necropolis, for we know it *was* sealed when Carter et al. examined it for the first time on 26 November 1922. This evidence comes from a copy of a never-before-published, handwritten account of the discovery of the tomb by Lord Carnarvon housed today in the British Library Manuscript Collection. Although undated, it would appear to have been written sometime between Sunday 26 and Thursday 30 November 1922.[32]

In similar to the typewritten draft article penned by Carnarvon on Sunday 10 December 1922, and cited elsewhere in this chapter, the handwritten account starts by outlining the history of the Valley and the various people who had excavated there since the time of Belzoni at the beginning of the nineteenth century. Having then described the initial discovery of the tomb's stone steps and Entrance Corridor, he recalls how the inner doorway became exposed and an examination was made of its seal impressions, before going on to say:

> After taking a photograph we decided to take down a small portion. This was done and by the uncertain light of a candle a wonderful sight was exposed to our excited eyes. Gilt couches boxes of all sorts & other objects in the dim light were just visible. Luckily just above us lies the large tomb of Rameses 6. This is a favourite tourist tomb, and is lit by electric light. Having tapped the wire & enlarged the opening we were able to enter & examine what proved to be the first chamber.
>
> Between the two statues of the king a walled & plastered up entrance again covered with the royal cartouche and the seal of the necropolis. In one place a robber had made a small hole and had evidently entered, *the hole had been carefully plastered up & sealed by the inspectors* [authors' italics].[33]

So there can be no dispute over what state the doorway was in when originally found. Carter et al. had breached the robbers' hole with scant regard for the delicacies of archaeology and entered inside the Burial Chamber. This is additionally confirmed by a remarkable letter written by Carnarvon to the British philologist Sir Alan H Gardiner (1879–1963) dated Tuesday 28 November 1922, just two days after his and Carter's initial entry into the Antechamber. In it Carnarvon states clearly, 'Tomorrow [the 29th is] the official opening and before I leave we peep into the walled chamber …'[34]

This last statement is crucial, for, if the robbers' hole had been left open, there would have been nothing stopping them from entering the Burial Chamber at the same time as they entered the Antechamber. This proves conclusively that the doorway *must* have been resealed in antiquity. Yet the letter from Carnarvon to Gardiner offers us more than simply this, for it also gives us a fix on when exactly he and Carter first entered the Burial Chamber. Carter's diary records that Lady Evelyn – whom we know from Mervyn Herbert's diary entered the inner sanctum before its official opening – left Luxor for Cairo on Saturday 2 December 1922. Her father left two days later on Monday 4 December, and after meeting up in Cairo the pair sailed back to England. This implies that the Burial Chamber had been entered by the latest Friday 1 December, the last day that Lady Evelyn could have visited the Valley. Yet she would have needed time to pack her cases and say her goodbyes, so it seems improbable that the group would have made the decision to enter the Burial Chamber on her last full day in Luxor.

Much more likely is that Carter et al. peeped into 'the walled chamber' sometime between Tuesday 28 November, the day that Carnarvon wrote to Gardiner, and Thursday 30 November. As extraordinary as this assessment of the facts might seem, no other scenario fits all the evidence. The cheek of the matter is that the dirty deed was done right under the noses of the Antiquities Service, who failed to notice the freshly applied mortar that was hidden from view behind a reed basket lid, placed there by Carter or Carnarvon, during their frequent inspections of the tomb at the end of November 1922. So what happened next? What happened when Carter, Carnarvon and Lady Evelyn first caught sight of the great gilded shrine containing the mortal remains of the boy-king Tutankhamun? It is this part of the discovery that we must reconstruct next.

7. THE TREASURE OF TUTANKHAMUN

Once Howard Carter, probably with the help of Pecky Callender, had breached the replastered robbers' hole at the bottom of the sealed doorway leading into the Burial Chamber, one of the assembled party of four – perhaps the smallest, Lady Evelyn Herbert – wriggled through to the other side. She would have found herself in a slender corridor at right angles to the north–south orientation of the Antechamber. Yet the handheld light, powered by electricity cabled down from the tomb of Rameses VI, would quickly have shown Lady Evelyn that the shimmering gold wall before her was in fact one side of an enormous gilded shrine.

Carter would have known that this great tabernacle contained a nest of smaller shrines, the innermost of which protected the royal sarcophagus. Within this was a series of gilded mummiform coffins, each one smaller than the one before. Inside the last of these, he knew only too well, would be found the intact mummy of Tutankhamun, since a very similar nest of shrines surrounding a sarcophagus containing the mummified body of a king appears in a papyrus showing the cross section of the tomb of Rameses IV, c. 1151–1145 BC.[1] Indeed, before this time it provided the best possible evidence of what an intact tomb might actually look like.

Not only Lady Evelyn, but also Carter and Carnarvon, entered into the Burial Chamber on that fateful night, sometime between Tuesday 28 November, and Thursday 30 November 1922. Yet Callender, it seems, was too big and too heavy to fit through the small breach in the doorway, leaving him to keep guard in the Antechamber. The other three members of the group must have examined the tall sides of the immense shrine, covered in gold and inlaid with blue faience. It was of wooden construction and filled the room almost entirely, leaving only a 46-centimetre space between it and the walls of the chamber, which measured 6.37 by 4 metres in size with a height of 3.63 metres.

Adorning three sides of the gilded shrine were hieroglyphic inscriptions and fearful symbols of protection, while occupying its final side, which faced east, was a huge double door with handles. Carter and Carnarvon must have slid back its bronze lock bolt,[2] enabling them to swing out the hinged doors to reveal another wooden shrine, over which was draped a linen funerary pall festooned with golden rosettes. Behind this was the second shrine's double door, bound by hemp rope and stamped with the seal of the royal necropolis. It was all the evidence that Carter, Carnarvon and Lady Evelyn needed to confirm that the body of the king remained intact. On the floor between the first and second shrines were many beautiful objects, including a small gold box, some staves and canes and an assortment of alabaster urns. The stopper of one of these had been fashioned into a reclining lion with a protruding red tongue.

After carefully closing and bolting shut the double door of the first shrine, the three of them moved northwards, being careful not to tread on the various items left on the floor of the chamber. They included alabaster vases, large clay jars and stoppers positioned in a seemingly random fashion, as well as a collection of no fewer than eleven sacred paddles carefully laid out in a line.

BURIAL SCENES

The electric light would additionally have revealed the simple, but nonetheless striking, murals that adorned the tomb's four walls. Looking towards the east wall, they would have seen the pharaoh in his guise as Osiris, Lord of the Underworld. His mummified body lay inside a garland-bedecked shrine being pulled on a sledge, representing the king's funerary barge, by ten high officials of the palace as well as the chief ministers of Upper and Lower Egypt.

On the north wall were two scenes. The first showed Tutankhamun, again in the form of the god Osiris, standing before his successor, Aye, as the god Horus, who wears the blue crown and the leopard skin of a *sem*-priest. Using the instrument known as an adze, Aye performs the Opening of the Mouth ceremony to ensure the correct burial of his godfather Osiris (in order to inherit the throne) and to bring forth the *ka*, or 'ghost', of the deceased. The second scene showed Tutankhamun as a living king, wearing the *nemes*-headdress, and holding a mace and stave, being greeted by the sky goddess Nuit. To their left the king could be seen embracing Osiris, as Tutankhamun's *ka* likewise embraces his living counterpart.

On the south wall, surrounding the entrance doorway, was the king, wearing the *khat*-headdress, being greeted in the afterlife by the goddess Hathor. She offers him life in the form of an *ankh*, the cross of life, which is held to his mouth. Behind them stands Anubis, the jackal-headed god of embalming and guardian of the dead, and Isis, the wife of Osiris. She was also the mother and protector of Horus, whose living form the pharaoh embodied during his lifetime.

Finally, on the west wall were scenes taken from the *am-duat*, the 'Book of that which is in the Underworld'. Here the dead king, in the form of the dung beetle, Khepera, stands before the solar barque, next to which are five lesser deities of the underworld. Below them are twelve baboons representing the twelve hours, or divisions, of the night through which the deceased must navigate before he can be reborn anew as an *akh*, or 'glorious spirit', in the afterlife. It was for this treacherous voyage that the pharaoh would require the eleven paddles carefully laid out on the floor between the south wall of the shrine and the north wall of the tomb.

THE TREASURY

After gazing in awe at the wall paintings, the three of them must have moved on to the northeast corner of the chamber, where they would have found an open doorway. It led into yet another room, the store chamber of the tomb, thereafter called the Treasury, which measured 4.75 by 3.8 metres in size and 2.33 metres in height. In here was the greatest treasure of all. For, as Carter records with respect to its official discovery on Friday 16 February 1923, 'Facing the doorway,

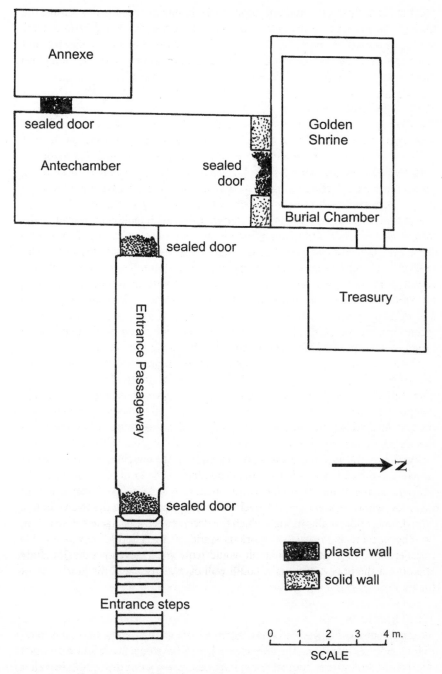

Fig. 8. Ground-plan of Tutankhamun's tomb.

on the farther side, stood the most beautiful monument that I have ever seen – so lovely that it made one gasp with wonder and admiration'.[3]

Carter was referring to a large gilded shrine of immense beauty, surmounted by tiers of *uraei*-serpents, inside which would be found a calcite canopic chest containing the four mummiform canopic jars. Within each of these were the wrapped viscera, or sacred organs, of the king. Midway along each of the four walls of the shrine was a free-standing gilded statue representing one of the four tutelary goddesses of the dead – Neith, Selkit, Isis and Nephthys. Carter described them later as 'gracious figures with outstretched protective arms, so natural and lifelike in their pose, so pitiful and compassionate the expression upon their faces, that one felt it almost sacrilege to look at them'.[4] Two of the wonderful statues, those to the left- and right-hand sides of the entrance, had their heads turned over one shoulder to gaze at anyone who dared enter this sacred place. It gave the spectacle an eerie quality previously unimagined in connection with the burial of the dead in ancient Egypt.

Guarding the way to the Treasury's gilded shrine was something even more unnerving – a life-size wooden statue of Anubis in the form of a seated jackal. Painted black and inlaid with gold, it sat resplendent on a portable box sledge equipped with carrying poles, its body and legs draped with a child's shirt, shawl and scarf. Between it and the shrine stood a gilded wooden head of a cow – a form of the goddess Hathor – with gazing eyes and long black horns, its neck draped in a linen cloth. Stacked on the south side of the chamber were a large number of black boxes and shrines in different shapes and sizes, some made of wood, others of ivory. All were closed except for one, which contained, among other things, golden statues of the pharaoh, each one standing on a black leopard.

At the far end of the Treasury were yet more boxes and chests, some of which included hundreds of tiny mummiform coffins, sealed, and later found to contain *ushabtis*, tiny mummified figures that were to carry out any work that the king was called on to do in the next world. Some of these cases were of exquisite design in gold inlaid with faience. Carter raised the lid of one and found it to contain 'a gorgeous ostrich-feather fan with ivory handle, fresh and strong to all appearance as when it left the maker's hand'.[5] Other chests and boxes contained such items as jewellery – including necklaces and gold rings – sceptres, richly decorated robes, sandals, faience cups and the king's underclothes and childhood toys. Around the walls were also heaps of other treasures, including a large number of model boats, one even with sail and rigging, as well as a dismantled chariot like those found in the Antechamber.

In addition to these wonderful items, the Treasury contained two mummified foetuses enclosed within separate nests of coffins. Undoubtedly, they were the sad result of Tutankhamun and his wife Ankhesenamun's failed attempts to perpetuate the Amarna royal line. In another nest of miniature coffins bearing Tutankhamun's name was a small uninscribed gold statuette of Amenhotep III, alongside which was a separate coffinette bearing the name of Queen Tiye and containing a lock of her hair. These items alone have given rise to the theory that if Amenhotep III and Akhenaten reigned jointly for a period of eleven to twelve years, as now looks certain (see Chapter 17), then Tiye might have borne him a son in her late forties.

HOVING'S VIEW

Exactly how long Carter, Carnarvon and Lady Evelyn studied the multitude of objects that littered both the Burial Chamber and Treasury is impossible to say. One hour? Two hours? Three, perhaps? Yet, after they could take in no more, they squeezed back through the robbers' hole in the Antechamber, where Callender awaited them.

Sometime afterwards, perhaps even that same day, Carter and Callender made good the breach by filling it with loose debris and plastering it over with carefully prepared mortar. Then, using a replica wooden seal impression, prepared most probably by Carter, the wet surface was stamped with the seal of the royal necropolis[6] before the whole thing was hidden behind the lid of a reed basket and other items, such as a variety of jars and loose reeds gathered up from the chamber floor (see Plate 10). As had been the case with the unofficial entry into the Antechamber, the small group of conspirators probably made a pact to ensure that none of them would ever reveal their indiscretions to the outside world.

Thomas Hoving, who first exposed this extraordinary story in his book *Tutankhamun – The Untold Story,* suggested that Carter et al. had entered the Burial Chamber at the same time as their unofficial opening of the Antechamber on Sunday, 26 November 1922. This he deduced from Lucas's article in the 1947 volume of *Annales du service des Antiquités de l'Egypte,* which states that Carter admitted to resealing the robbers' hole, thus supposing it was open when found. Yet Lord Carnarvon's handwritten draft article, written sometime between 26 and 30 November 1922, speaks of their coming across the doorway between the two guardian statues and noticing the robbers' hole, which had been 'carefully plastered up & sealed by the inspectors'.[7] That they did not enter the Burial Chamber there and then is confirmed in a letter from Carnarvon to Alan H Gardiner dated 28 November 1922, which speaks of his intention to 'peep into the walled chamber' before his departure for England at the beginning of December 1922.

WHY DID THEY DO IT?

Whatever motivated Carter and Carnarvon – both distinguished men who were being hailed as heroes in the international media – to risk jeopardising their precious digging concession is impossible to determine so long after the event. However, the answer probably lies not so much in their uncontrolled compulsion to explore deeper and deeper into the forbidden chambers of the boy-king but, once again, in petty politics. Pierre Lacau's insistence that a member of the Antiquities Service be present when each chamber was opened incensed Carter to such a degree that he had begun to take matters into his own hands. He saw Lacau and Rex Engelbach as being there merely to hinder, and not encourage, his work at the tomb. Having entered the Antechamber without informing the authorities, and having afterwards penetrated through into the Burial Chamber just a few days later, Carter and Carnarvon were obviously becoming a law unto themselves. This, as we shall see, may well have led to even greater indiscretions on their part that were really inexcusable. Yet before we go on to elucidate further on this matter it will be necessary to reveal a little more about the problems that dogged Carter and his colleagues as they set about clearing the tomb.

THE EXCLUSIVITY DEAL

After the discovery of Tutankhamun's tomb, Carter and Carnarvon were deluged by reporters and special correspondents, all wanting a piece of the action (in addition to the myriad high-society lackeys all waiting in line for a glimpse of the tomb). Yet neither was willing to reveal details of the discovery in the knowledge that Carnarvon at least stood to gain a substantial amount of money by selling world media rights to one of England's leading daily newspapers. Thus on his arrival back in England on 18 December 1922, Carnarvon is said to have received offers from various newspapers including the *Illustrated London News*, the *Daily Mail* and *The Times*. In the end he agreed an exclusivity deal with *The Times*, which came into effect in January 1923. Under this agreement the newspaper gained exclusive rights to publish news bulletins prepared by their correspondent in Luxor, Arthur Merton, and also reproduce Harry Burton's superb-quality photographs. A prerequisite of the contract required that Carnarvon and Carter would speak only to *The Times*. This would carry all developments concerning the discovery of new chambers and the continuing clearance of the tomb. All other newspapers would have to go through *The Times* for news of the discoveries and to use Burton's copyrighted photographs, which would be made available at a price only after first publication in *The Times*. The only exception would be the Egyptian press, which would not be charged for use of news stories or photographic illustrations.

What this exclusivity deal meant was that Merton was the only journalist allowed access not only to the tomb, but also to Carter and Carnarvon, who would give interviews to nobody else. Quite obviously, this whole situation infuriated other journalists, who felt they were being forced to stand among the crowds that gathered daily around the entrance to the tomb in order to pick up any scraps of news that might come their way. It was not an ideal state of affairs, although it was one that Carter and Carnarvon believed would allow them to continue their scientific work unhindered.

It is commonly believed that the exclusivity deal ironed out between Lord Carnarvon and *The Times* was not finalised until early 1923, two months after the discovery of the tomb. Indeed, Alan H Gardiner records that when he was lunching with Carnarvon in London, probably at the earl's residence in Seymour Place, a few days after his return from Egypt shortly before Christmas 1922, George Geoffrey Dawson (1874–1944), the paper's editor, turned up unannounced. The footman conveyed this fact to his lordship, who was rather annoyed at having his lunch interrupted. Turning to Gardiner, Carnarvon asked him to see Dawson on his behalf, which he agreed to do. The editor then proceeded to explain to Gardiner that the discovery of Tutankhamun's tomb was big news and worth a lot of money. Eventually, Carnarvon relented and agreed to see Dawson, who explained that *The Times* was eager to purchase the monopoly on the story. Dawson eventually departed, leaving Carnarvon to think the matter over as he finished his lunch.[8]

What this story implies is that the first discussions of an exclusivity deal between the two parties took place only after the fifth earl returned from Egypt. Yet the authors have discovered that this was not the case at all. Lord Carnarvon had already offered *The Times* the story within days of receiving Howard Carter's telegram informing him of the tomb's discovery. This, therefore, must have taken place *before* he left for Egypt in mid-November. This new evidence is revealed in a memorandum, marked 'Confidential', from George Geoffrey Dawson, *The Times*' editor, to Alfred Gordon Robbins (1883–1944), the associate editor, dated Tuesday 14 November 1922, housed today in the Times Newspapers Ltd (TNL) archive at the Archives and Records Office of the News International Group, which reads as follows:

> Lord Carnarvon, who is leaving to-morrow for Egypt, has just received news of the discovery on the site which he is excavating in Egypt of an untouched (apparently Royal) tomb in the Valley of the Kings. He is anxious for us to have the first and exclusive news of the discovery and of the contents of the tomb when it is opened. I have given him a letter to Merton, so that the necessary arrangements may be made. The news should arrive in about a fortnight's time.[9]

From this document it is clear that Carnarvon had no real intention of offering any other newspaper the chance to bid for the rights to an exclusivity deal; *The Times* had the whole matter sewn up even before the discovery of the Antechamber. Despite the fact that Carnarvon obviously thought he was doing the right thing, it was a situation that would cause increasing problems for Carter, especially after the untimely death of the fifth earl in April 1923 (see Chapter 8). Being a good deal more diplomatic than Carter, the British aristocrat had taken care of all business and social matters concerning the discovery of the tomb. Soon, though, he would be gone and Carter would be left to deal with them himself and his bombastic, hot-headed nature was destined to get him into a lot of trouble, not least of all with the Egyptian government.

8. SIX WEEKS TO LIVE

The events that preceded the unfortunate death of the fifth Earl of Carnarvon during the early hours of Thursday 5 April 1923, can be traced back to the days following the official opening of the Burial Chamber, a little under seven weeks beforehand. Once it became obvious for all to see that the boy-king awaited discovery within the nest of shrines inside its interior, the pressure on the 57-year-old British aristocrat increased immensely. Everywhere he and Howard Carter went they were hounded by journalists, each hoping to achieve a major scoop on any new developments surrounding the tomb of Tutankhamun.

One example of just how much Lord Carnarvon was being affected by the constant presence of the international press is seen from an entry in the unpublished memoirs of the British vice-consul to Cairo, Sir Thomas Cecil Rapp (1893–1984). He was responsible for the formalities regarding the transfer of his lordship's body to England after his death, and had this to say about him:

> To Lord Carnarvon sudden fame had proved a very mixed blessing and placed his ever robust constitution under too great a strain. His Cairo dentist told me how he would arrive early for his appointments so that he could sit quietly in his waiting room free from the importunties [sic] of journalists and others.[1]

Carnarvon began also to argue with the ever-cantankerous Carter on matters that might never have irritated him before this time. The situation only worsened, and in a letter dated Monday 12 March 1923, written to Charles Breasted by his father, the American Egyptologist James Henry Breasted (1865–1935), who had joined the Tutankhamun team in a philological capacity, this 'painful situation'

> resulted in such strained relations between Carter and Carnarvon that a complete break seemed inevitable. Alan Gardiner and I succeeded in pouring oil on the waters, but in so doing we both fell from Carter's good graces. The man is by no means wholly to blame – what he has gone through has broken him down.[2]

Charles Breasted, who had been with his father in Luxor when the Burial Chamber was officially opened, goes on to claim that Carnarvon paid a visit to Carter's house, in order to settle any problems in their working relationship. Moreover, he says that, during this meeting, 'Bitter words were exchanged, and in anger Carter requested his old friend to leave his house and never to enter it again'.[3]

There is no doubting that the relationship between Carnarvon and Carter had become severely strained during the hectic period leading up to, and shortly after, the opening of the Burial Chamber, yet there is no evidence that Carter told Carnarvon to 'leave his house and never to enter it again'. TGH James, the former curator of the Department of Egyptian Antiquities at the British Museum, examined the diaries of Minnie Burton and Lindsley Hall, an artist and draftsman on loan to Carter from the Metropolitan Museum, and also letters from Arthur Mace to his wife, and found no corroborating material to support Charles Breasted's account. Moreover, there is nothing in James Breasted's letters to his son about an argument in which Carnarvon was asked to leave Carter's house and never return.[4] Despite this enigma, a letter written by his lordship to Carter dated only 'Friday evening', although unquestionably Friday 23 February, demonstrates that a rift had indeed formed between the two friends:

> I have been feeling very unhappy today, and I did not know what to think or do, and then I saw Eve and she told me everything. I have no doubt that I have done many foolish things and I am very sorry. I suppose the fuss and worry have affected me but there is only one thing I want to say to you which I hope you will always remember – whatever your feelings are or will be for me in the future my affection for you will never change.
>
> I'm a man with few friends and whatever happens nothing will ever alter my feelings for you. There is always so much noise and lack of quiet and privacy in the Valley that I felt I should never see you alone altho' I should like to very much and have a good talk because of that I could not rest until I had written you.[5]

That Carnarvon chose to send Carter such a letter instead of personally calling upon him strongly suggests that the two men were not on very good terms at the time. The 'quiet and privacy' that the fifth earl so desired could easily have been had at either Carter's house or at Carnarvon's own dwelling, which was situated a few hundred metres away. There are elements in the letter of regret, sorrow and even remorse, although what exactly it was about, and what Evelyn might have told him to make sense of earlier feelings or actions, remains uncertain. Thomas Hoving wrote that the bust-up between the two men was over revelations concerning Lady Evelyn's affections for Howard Carter,[6] yet there is little evidence to support this contention. It is more likely that the rift between the two men came about through the pressures put upon them by the constant harassment of visitors to the tomb and the strain of the *Times* exclusivity deal, which was beginning to take its toll, with news articles almost daily condemning their perceived prostitution of Tutankhamun. Whatever the cause of the breakdown of friendship, for Carnarvon the shadow of death was looming ever nearer.

FINAL DAYS

It began, so is commonly believed, with a mosquito bite on the cheek. Yet when and where Lord Carnarvon suffered this minor inconvenience no one seems to know for sure. What we do know is that on Wednesday 28 February, just a few days after Carnarvon's letter of reconciliation to Carter, his lordship, in the company of Lady Evelyn, Arthur Mace and Sir Charles Cust, an equerry to King

George V as well as a personal close friend of the Carnarvons, embarked on a Nile cruise to Aswan. It was to be a holiday, a change in scenery, in order to recover from the traumas surrounding the opening of the Burial Chamber, and a chance for Mace to find some good health as he had been suffering considerably of late. It has been suggested, and with all likelihood, that the mosquito bite was sustained during this trip.[7]

Other sources have assumed that the fatal mosquito bite took place in the Valley of the Kings. For example, Arthur Merton's report on Lord Carnarvon's death, which appeared in *The Times* on Friday 6 April 1923, says that the British aristocrat returned from Aswan on Tuesday 6 March, and 'while he was up the Valley of the Kings' two days later was 'bitten on the right cheek – by a mosquito it is believed'.[8] But, as Professor Percy Newberry pointed out at the time, there are no mosquitoes in the Valley.[9] So, if not sustained at Aswan or on the cruise, then the bite must have occurred on the other side of the Nile, possibly at the Winter Palace Hotel in Luxor.

What happened next varies considerably, but according to Merton:

> He [Lord Carnarvon] paid no attention to the bite, and in shaving took off the scab. The minute exposed wound became infected, possibly by dust, but more probably by a fly, and a slight swelling showed itself in one of the glands. Medical aid was sought at Luxor, and when he left for Cairo on March 14 he was decidedly better.[10]

Merton's account of what happened became, quite clearly, the official version of the story. The same sequence of events is given by Charles Breasted in the biography of his father:

> When he [Carnarvon] shaved the following morning he slightly cut the small welt raised by the sting, and for several succeeding mornings his razor scraped off the little scab which had formed each day over the original cut. He neglected to apply a disinfectant; and one morning an ordinary – which is to say, unspeakably filthy – Egyptian fly settled upon the tiny wound just long enough to infect it.[11]

Others have slightly different variations of what occurred. For instance, Nicholas Reeves in his comprehensive work *The Complete Tutankhamun*, paints the picture as follows. Having suffered a mosquito bite while at Aswan, he tells us that

> Shaving with his cut-throat razor, he [Carnarvon] inadvertently opened the bite, which reddened angrily. Despite treating the wound with iodine from his well-stocked medicine chest, a fever set in and Lord Carnarvon, worn out by events and running a temperature of 38.3°C (101°F), allowed his daughter Evelyn to confine him to bed to rest and recover. This seemed to do the trick, and two days later he was up and about, eager to visit the tomb.[12]

Charles Breasted describes how Lord Carnarvon failed to apply disinfectant to the wound whereas Reeves states the opposite, explaining how he applied iodine on the wound as a disinfectant. Add to this the confusion concerning when and where the mosquito bite was sustained and it becomes obvious that a precise knowledge of what happened to Lord Carnarvon is distinctly lacking, with the recorded accounts coming purely from hearsay.

Merton states in his aforementioned report on the death of Lord Carnarvon that his lordship made the decision to leave Luxor for Cairo on Wednesday 14 March, taking with him Lady Evelyn and booking rooms in the Grand Continental Hotel. The express purpose of the visit was, it seems, to attempt to come to some sort of decision with Pierre Lacau of the Antiquities Service over the division of the tomb's contents.

Yet Merton's report is clearly inaccurate and demonstrates that no one seems really to know what was going on at the time of Carnarvon's illness. Lady Evelyn left Luxor for Cairo not with her father on 14 March, but three days earlier on Sunday, 11 March, with her maid, Marcelle, to arrange her passage back to England following an operation for appendicitis.[13] Carnarvon's travelling companion on the train from Luxor to Cairo on 14 March was in fact the Hon. Richard Bethell, son of the third Baron Westbury. He was keenly interested in Egyptology and had joined the expedition as Carnarvon's secretary.[14]

Alan H Gardiner, who at the time was working, alongside James Breasted, on translations of Middle Kingdom Coffin Texts in the Egyptian Museum, sums up what happened after Lord Carnarvon arrived in Cairo:

> He [Carnarvon] might, perhaps, have recovered from the mosquito bite which he got at Luxor if he had taken better care of himself. Disregarding the doctor's advice he came down to Cairo and invited me to dine with him at the Mohammed Ali Club. He expressed himself very tired and despondent but insisted on going to a film. There he said that his face was hurting him and I begged him to go back to his hotel, the Continental. But no, he would see the film to a finish and he was never out of doors again.[15]

By the third week of March, Carnarvon's health had deteriorated considerably. As Arthur Merton records,

> At Cairo ... Lord Carnarvon suddenly became worse and on the 17th erysipelas and streptococcic blood poisoning of the head and neck developed. As soon as the germ had been identified and the necessary culture made he was given a serum injection, which was promptly effective.[16]

In a letter written to Howard Carter on Sunday 18 March, Lady Evelyn reveals Pierre Lacau's own ill health before going on to report on her father's worsening condition:

> Pups asked me to write you to say that Lacau is laid up with influenza so is hors de combat and what is much more important is the old Man is very very seedy himself and is incapable of doing anything. You know that mosquito bite on his cheek that was worrying him at Luxor, well yesterday quite suddenly all the glands in his neck

started swelling and last night he had a high temperature and still has today. He feels just *too* rotten for words. I have got [Captain W] Fletcher Barrett [of the Royal Army Medical Corps] looking after him and I think he is competent, but oh! the worry of it all and I just can't bear seeing him really seedy. However there it is. I've made a point of making rather light of it to most people as I don't want an exaggerated account in the papers. Of course they may never get hold of it at all but since you've all become celebrities I feel there is nothing one does or thinks that they don't know! But I like *you* knowing exactly what's happening to us. We miss you and I wish Dear you were here.

I will let you know how he goes on.

with our fond love,

Eve[17]

Even before the letter would have been received by Carter in Luxor he would have opened a telegram from Lady Evelyn dispatched on Monday 19 March. It emphasised the severity of her father's ill health and advised him that Lady Carnarvon had been wired. As a result of this telegram, Carter decided to leave Luxor for Cairo in order to see if there was anything he could do for his friend and patron. His departure from the tomb of Tutankhamun was to be a long one, for he was to remain in Cairo until after Carnarvon's body left Cairo for transportation by boat back to England on Saturday 14 April.

On Tuesday 20 March, the day that Carter left for Cairo, Albert Lythgoe of the Metropolitan Museum of Art wrote to him, updating the situation:

Lady Evelyn says her father's condition is a little bit better today – for which we are all very thankful. Yesterday was a most anxious time for everyone, but his temperature has lessened today and they apparently feel the trouble is more localized or restricted.[18]

Although it was expected by all that Carnarvon would make a full recovery, sadly this was not to be the case. By the following week, his lordship had taken a turn for the worse, and those around him had begun to believe that he was terminally ill. From what Arthur Merton tells us, his 'temperature ... ran high during the next few days, and he was in great pain, as the inflammation affected the nasal passages and the eyes'.[19] Further bad news came in a letter written to Carter on the 19th by Richard Bethell from the nearby Shepheard's Hotel:

I am sorry to tell you that C. is seriously ill. Eve does not want it known how bad he is, but that poisoned bite has spread all over him and he has got blood poisoning. His temperature this morning was 104[° Fahrenheit]. Eve has telegraphed to Lady C[arnarvon]. I suppose she will get out next week ... There is hope that he may throw it off in a day or two, but otherwise I am afraid it looks pretty serious.[20]

Yet just one week later, on Monday 26 March, Merton reported that 'the poisoning had, for all practical purposes, disappeared'.[21] Unfortunately, it was to be only a temporary recovery, for the next day 'pneumonia of the right lung set in and the patient's condition again gave rise to much anxiety. Again and again he rallied and when Lord Porchester arrived on April 1 his condition was quite hopeful'.[22] Yet there could be a discrepancy here in Merton's account, for, according to the sixth earl's published memoirs, he did not arrive in Cairo until the afternoon of Wednesday 4 April![23]

In a letter dated Sunday 1 April, written by Alan Gardiner to his wife, the Egyptologist tells of his visits to the bedside of the stricken earl and of his admiration for Lady Evelyn's dedication to her father:

> I saw him on Tuesday [27 March] for five minutes, and on Wednesday came his relapse. I have just come back from seeing Evelyn; it has been a bad day and he had a terrible crisis just before six o'clock this evening, I was quite miserable about it … why am I so fond of him? And that poor little girl nearly breaks my heart with her devotion.[24]

On Monday 2 April, Lord Carnarvon's condition deteriorated still further as 'the left lung became infected, and he had to be kept going with oxygen stimulants'.[25] By the next day it did not seem as if he would live through another night, but by the morning of Wednesday 4 April, he had made another dramatic recovery. According to Merton, 'The temperature dropped and he seemed to have taken a turn for the better and called for a barber to shave him'.[26] Under the influence of intravenous injections, he had even been permitted a brief conversation with a few intimate friends.[27] There was an air of optimism among those present for the rest of the day, in contrast to the dreadful pessimism that had come over everyone just 24 hours beforehand.

Lord Carnarvon experienced a relapse again around midnight on 4 April, but once more he seemed to recover. Yet, by 1.40 in the morning,[28] he had begun coughing violently, 'which caused him much distress'.[29] Nurses rushed to his aid, but 'his heart could no longer stand the strain'.[30] His family were summoned, and very quickly Lady Carnarvon and Lady Evelyn knelt by his side as he passed away, with Lord Porchester, now the sixth Earl of Carnarvon, reaching his room only some five to ten minutes later. There ended the life of George Edward Stanhope Molyneux Herbert, the fifth Earl of Carnarvon.

THE CAUSE OF DEATH

From the varied reports of his demise, a pretty good picture of exactly what happened to him in the six to seven weeks before his death can be achieved. Having been bitten by a mosquito on the right cheek either in Aswan or Luxor, Carnarvon suffered an infection either because he failed to apply disinfectant to the wound, or because a fly landed on the scab at some point later. Whatever the cause, his neck and face became swollen and painful and he developed a high fever, which confined him to bed. Gradually, the inflammation affected his nasal passage and eyes, and he suffered extremely high temperatures, which seemed to fluctuate considerably, making it appear as if he were recovering one day, only to suffer a relapse the next. Accordingly, he was diagnosed with 'erysipelas' and 'streptococcic blood poisoning of the head and neck', which in the end brought on pneumonia, attacking both lungs until his body could take no more.

Erysipelas is an infection of the soft tissue caused by the presence in the bloodstream of streptococcal bacteria. Its symptoms can include a swelling of the head and neck glands, as was the case with Lord Carnarvon. In addition to this, it can produce an acute inflammation, whereby blood-red or copper-coloured rashes, with sharply defined edges, form on the skin. In severe cases these blotches can blister or swell out like burns. Along with chills and fevers, erysipelas can in a matter of 24 hours spread from the head and neck throughout the entire body, leaving the person susceptible to diseases such as pneumonia. Interestingly enough, erysipelas often spreads from an infected wound or scratch, very much in the manner of Lord Carnarvon's own demise. There is no question that a bacterial infection caused by a mosquito bite exacerbated Lord Carnarvon's ill health and brought on other medical conditions, which led eventually to his unexpected death. Indeed, Dr Marcus Johnson, the family physician, who arrived in Cairo shortly after his lordship's death, stated that 'Lord Carnarvon was always most susceptible to poisoning from any kind of bite'. Whenever he was bitten, Dr Johnson 'habitually inoculated him immediately'.[31]

Yet those closest to the British aristocrat at the time of his death were surprised at the suddenness and severity with which the malady had overtaken his body. As Alan Gardiner points out, 'The death was announced to me early one morning by [Algernon] Maudslay [a public servant[32]] and was a great shock. I had thought that his recovery was almost certain'.[33]

A DEEP INFECTION

Yet it is a fact that Carnarvon's deterioration in health did not begin with a mosquito bite. He had been unwell since the terrible motoring accident he suffered in Germany about 1901, which was the reason why his physician, Dr Marcus Johnson, recommended that he spend the winter months in a country with a much drier climate, the original reason behind his annual vacations to Egypt. The discovery of the tomb of Tutankhamun also took its toll on Carnarvon's health, as did the constant round of politics that followed, particularly those surrounding the exclusivity deal with The Times. Carnarvon was described as a 'weak man'[34] at this time, suffering greatly from the sweltering heat both in the Valley and inside the tomb of Seti II, which was used as a laboratory. Yet it is clear as well that, even before he was bitten, Carnarvon was suffering from some inexplicable malady, for as Thomas Hoving points out,

> Carnarvon's physical condition, which had been slowly deteriorating, now began rapidly to fail. Every few days one of his teeth chipped or just fell out. He did not realize it at the time, but this was one symptom of a deep infection exacting a terrible toll upon his body.[35]

This description of an ailing Lord Carnarvon alludes not to his final month in Cairo, but to the period immediately before he left for Aswan on a Nile cruise

– in other words, *prior* to his suffering the fatal mosquito bite. Moreover, this 'deep infection exacting a terrible toll upon his body' seemed to include his teeth daily either chipping or falling out, certainly not a symptom of erysipelas, blood poisoning, pneumonia or pleurisy. Is it possible that the whole saga surrounding Carnarvon's contraction of blood poisoning and erysipelas might well have been masking some more deep-rooted complaint that combined, with the other medical conditions, to hasten his death? What we can say is that it was not something that had been taking its toll on the man for years, slowly diminishing his health month by month. Over the Christmas and New Year period 1922–3, while he was negotiating the exclusivity deal with *The Times,* it is a fact that his lordship found time for some heavy-duty hunting expeditions on his country estate at Highclere, shooting in one day alone 'seventeen hundred head, nearly all rabbits, and five hundred [the] next day'.[36] It would have taken a fit man indeed to have bagged this number of animals in such a short space of time.

So, if Lord Carnarvon had been in relative good health during the winter of 1922–3, how was it possible that his health declined so rapidly around the time of the opening of the tomb? Was it really the consequences of an infection brought about by a mosquito bite, or could it have been something else – a malady perhaps originating from a completely different source?

Interestingly enough, on the very day that the Burial Chamber was officially opened the British Egyptologist Arthur Weigall, one of the disgruntled journalists standing with the crowds waiting avidly outside, made some very pertinent remarks about Carnarvon's health. As he watched the excavator's party climb back up the sixteen steps into daylight around 4.30 p.m., he observed:

> Lord Carnarvon, always a delicate man, looked pale and exhausted as he came up out of the depths; and on the face of all those who had been present there were marks of fatigue and over-excitement.[37]

Yet this scene of lethargy had been in stark contrast to Carnarvon's attitude when he first greeted the select group of guests around one o'clock that afternoon. After joking about how he and Carter were going to give a concert down there in the tomb, Weigall had turned to the person standing next to him and said, 'If he goes down in that spirit, I give him six weeks to live'.[38]

This prophetic utterance, why ever it was said (and Weigall could give no suitable answer when asked at a later date), was strangely true, for it was just over six weeks later that the British aristocrat did indeed die. In so doing, he somehow managed to catalyse the greatest ever supernatural drama in the history of Egyptology – the curse of Tutankhamun (see Chapter 9).

Lord Carnarvon's body was transported back to Highclere, where it was carried to its final destination on the top of Beacon Hill, an ancient British encampment, which overlooks his family's ancestral home. At 11 o'clock on the morning of Saturday 28 April 1923, the fifth Earl of Carnarvon was finally laid to rest during a private ceremony, attended only by close family and a few trusted estate employees. Yet the curse of the mummy's tomb was not about to let the memory of the fifth Earl of Carnarvon rest in peace, and nor would the hot-headed actions of his former friend and associate Howard Carter.

PART TWO
THE CURSE

9. THE CURSE OF CARNARVON

It is certain that, had he lived, the fifth Earl of Carnarvon would have believed in the curse of Tutankhamun, for it seems that the British aristocrat was deeply influenced by spiritualism and the occult. He was also an active member of the London Spiritual Alliance.[1] On numerous occasions Carnarvon organised séances in the East Anglia Room at Highclere Castle. Present would be his daughter Lady Evelyn Herbert, the politician and lawyer Sir Edward Marshall Hall KC;[2] Lady Cunliffe-Owen and, when in the country, Howard Carter.[3]

In his published memoirs the sixth Earl of Carnarvon says that his father became 'keenly interested in the occult' as he and Howard Carter waited restlessly for hostilities to cease during World War One.[4] Moreover, he recalls attending one of these séances organised by his father. It occurred during a month spent with the family following his return from military duty with the 7th Hussars in Mesopotamia in the late spring of 1919, when Carter was also present. He remembers how, in the company of his sister Lady Evelyn, he proceeded to the East Anglia Room, where his father, along with Howard Carter, Louis Steele, 'a brilliant photographer domiciled in Portsmouth',[5] and Helen Cunliffe-Owen were readying themselves for the psychic session. When everyone had settled down, Steele began to utter some form of 'incantation' that sent Lady Cunliffe-Owen into a trance in which she began speaking Coptic.[6] By 'Coptic' he presumably meant the language used by the original inhabitants of Egypt, as opposed to the Greek immigrants, in the wake of Alexander the Great's celebrated entry in 332 BC. It was adopted as the language of the Coptic Christians, who trace their lineage back to St Mark the Evangelist. The sixth earl records that only Howard Carter understood Lady Cunliffe's strange utterances, and afterwards she had no recall whatsoever of what had been said.[7]

The sixth earl goes on to say that Lady Evelyn was then placed in a similar trance, 'but she was so overcome by the experience that she had to go into a nursing home in London for a fortnight's rest'.[8] What supposedly happened next stretches the imagination to the extreme:

> To round off that session, my father said, 'If we sit round the table holding hands, I believe we shall achieve a levitation.'
>
> 'What does he mean?' I whispered to my sister.
>
> 'I think he hopes the flowers on the table will rise several feet into the air,' she replied and they did.[9]

These are the words of the sixth Earl of Carnarvon, a greatly respected British aristocrat who moved in high society circles before his death in 1987. That he believed these events took place does not seem to be in doubt, as they are recorded in his published memoirs. However, exactly what transpired at

Highclere Castle that night in 1919 is probably lost for ever. All that the authors have been able to ascertain is that the sessions did indeed take place in the East Anglia Room, something that is looked on with some embarrassment by the tour guides, reflecting perhaps the feelings of the present-day Carnarvon family. Indeed, when the authors visited Highclere and met the future eighth Earl of Carnarvon in August 2001, special permission had to be gained to enter the East Anglia Room, which is currently out of bounds to the general public. They were finally able to enter the room, used today as a dressing room for wedding parties, in the company of Tony Leadbetter, the godson of Lady Almina Herbert, the fifth earl's wife. He insisted that she loathed the séances and would have nothing to do with them, since they frightened her greatly.[10] As we shall see, the fifth earl's powerful belief in all things supernatural might not have helped dampen rumours that his untimely death was connected in some way with the opening of the tomb of Tutankhamun.

THE REBIRTH IN EGYPT

Lord Carnarvon's interest in the occult was not unique for his era. Many wealthy, well-to-do people in British society shared a belief in the omnipotent powers of ancient Egypt. To them this distant land, beneath the hot desert sun, was an exotic paradise, where the ancient gods still lived on in the invisible world. These very humanlike deities were seen not simply as the product of the superstitious fears of a bygone race, but as the power and motivation behind the great civilisation that built the Great Pyramid and flourished for nearly 3,000 years before its decline at the time of the Roman Empire.

With the spread of spiritualism from the United States to Europe in the mid-1800s, the idea of communicating with perceived celestial intelligences suddenly became more acceptable. And, if an American Indian chief or a Chinese philosopher could act as a spirit guide, then so could long-dead Egyptian spirits and even the gods and goddesses of that wonderful country. More significantly, the revival in the mystic powers of ancient Egypt was embraced by a number of occultists of the era, who felt some kind of sympathetic connection with this unseen world. More importantly, it was the influence of one such mystic that may well have convinced Lord Carnarvon that his destiny was linked inextricably not only with coming events connected with the resurrection of the Amarna age in popular consciousness, but also with the opening of the tomb of Tutankhamun.

We speak of 'Cheiro' (pronounced *ki-ro*), alias Count Louis le Warner Hamon (1866–1936), the world-renowned fortune-teller and palmist of Irish birth, who during the late Victorian period read palms, cast horoscopes and made psychic predictions for the rich and famous. His first client is said to have been Arthur James Balfour, the future Conservative Prime Minister and the signatory on the so-called Balfour Declaration of 1917 (see Chapter 23).[11] From the 1890s onwards, Hamon attracted an elite clientele both at his Indian-style salon in London's trendy Bond Street, and while on his travels abroad. The list is mind-boggling, and apparently included, among others, Mark Twain, Sarah Bernhardt, the British statesman Sir Austin Chamberlain, the writer Oscar Wilde and the

Dutch dancer and spy Mata Hari, with whom he became a close acquaintance.[12] Sir Ernest Shackleton, the explorer of the Antarctic, went in disguise to his Bond Street address in order to test him, but was told, correctly, that he would not return from a second expedition.[13] When Field Marshal Horatio, Lord Kitchener, the hero of the Sudan, turned up to see Hamon he was informed that his death would come at sea.[14] He was to die when his cruiser, HMS *Hampshire*, struck a mine and sank in the North Sea, off the Orkney Isles, in June 1916.

As Hamon's reputation as a fortune-teller grew, he was introduced to more and more clients of distinction. Among them was the King of Italy, Humbert I, whom he met in Rome in 1900 and predicted correctly that he would be dead within three months.[15] Another was the Shah of Persia, whom he met in Paris that same year. Hamon informed him that his life was in grave peril, prompting the shah's police guard to foil an assassination attempt by an anarchist.[16]

Most famous of all Hamon's clients was Edward VII, for whom he predicted the exact date of his coronation in August 1902 and subsequent death in 1909.[17] Through the British king he was introduced to other members of the royal family, for whom he cast horoscopes and made predictions. It was also through Edward VII that Hamon came to meet Tsar Nicholas II of Russia, about whom he predicted that around '1917 he will lose all he loves most by sword or strife in one form or another, and he himself will meet a violent death'.[18] So intrigued was the Tsar by this prediction that in late 1904, on a visit to St Petersburg, Hamon was invited to dine with him at the Summer Palace. During his stay Gregori Rasputin came to meet Hamon one afternoon in January 1905.[19] As with the Tsar, he predicted that Rasputin would suffer 'a violent end within a palace. You will be menaced by poison, by knife, and by bullet. Finally I see the icy waters of the Neva closing above you'.[20] It goes without saying that both Rasputin and the Tsar were to lose their lives in the manner prescribed.

MARSHALL HALL QC

It is certainly not the place here to extol any further the apparent predictions of Count Louis Hamon, alias 'Cheiro', whatever their basis in truth. Yet what is significant to the story behind the discovery of Tutankhamun's tomb is that the author Barry Wynne in his 1972 book *Behind the Mask of Tutankhamen* claimed that Lord Carnarvon was one of Hamon's clients.[21] Indeed, it is recorded that in 1899 Hamon had cause to ask the Earl of Carnarvon's close friend and lawyer, Sir Edward Marshall Hall QC, to defend him, after he was named as a co-respondent in a case brought against him by the husband of a woman client who had become infatuated by the celebrated palmist.[22] In the end the petitioner withdrew his claim, and paid the damages and costs, but only after Hamon was able to prove his innocence. At the time, the fortune-teller revealed to Marshall Hall psychic imagery that would foreshadow, and even predict, his election win at Southport some sixteen months later in October 1901.[23]

Since Marshall Hall was one of the participants in the séances that took place at Highclere Castle, it seems reasonable to assume that by this time Hamon had become a personal acquaintance of the Earl of Carnarvon. This should be borne in mind as we review the strange psychic warning that Hamon sent to Lord Carnarvon shortly after the discovery of the tomb of Tutankhamun.[24]

CHEIRO'S WARNING

Later he would claim that it had been delivered to him in the form of automatic writing by Meketaten, one of Akhenaten's daughters, whose mummified hand he believed he had been given by an elderly Egyptian guide at the Temple of Karnak in the mid-1880s.[25] Yet, regardless of its original source, the unnerving nature of the message must have sent a chill down the British aristocrat's spine, for, according to Hamon,

> It was to the effect that on his arrival at the tomb of Tut-Ankh-Amen he was not to allow any of the relics found in it to be removed or taken away. The ending of the message was 'that if he disobeyed the warning he would suffer an injury while in the tomb – a sickness from which he would never recover, and that death would claim him in Egypt'.[26]

Rightly or wrongly, Hamon sent the warning message to Lord Carnarvon at Highclere, which was received by him shortly after his return from Egypt in mid-December 1922. He was said to have 'read it over to one of his companions, the Hon. Richard Bethell, and to a close friend of Admiral Smith Dorrien, whose letter relating these facts I have still in my possession'.[27] Apparently, Carnarvon was 'deeply impressed by the warning', yet responded with the words, 'If at this moment of my life all the mummies in Egypt were to warn me I would go on with my project just the same'.[28]

Yet Hamon goes on to reveal that it was 'common knowledge what happened' next, for, according to him, 'Lord Carnarvon took numerous relics out of the tomb and sent them on to England. He would probably have taken still more if the Egyptian Government had not interfered'.[29]

This outrageous claim made in Hamon's autobiographical work *Real Life Stories*, published in 1934, must have infuriated not only the fifth earl's friends and family, but also the entire Egyptological community, including Howard Carter, who had completed his clearance of the tomb just two years beforehand. Yet, whatever Hamon's source was for this information, it proved to be staggeringly accurate, for as we shall see in Chapter 13, there is overwhelming evidence to show that Carnarvon and Carter did indeed illegally remove art treasures from the tomb.

RIDICULOUS STORIES

That a warning of the sort described by Hamon was received by his lordship around the time of the discovery of the tomb is confirmed by the sixth earl's memoirs, which tell us:

Upon the news of the discovery of the tomb he [Hamon] had written to my father warning him not to become involved. This matter preyed on my father's mind and he decided to consult his own clairvoyant, Velma.[30]

With the fifth earl's deep interest in the occult, there is no doubt that such a warning would indeed have 'preyed' on his mind. The fact that it had come from the world-renowned fortune-teller Count Louis Hamon, to whom both he and Marshall Hall seem to have been admirers, must have increased his anxiety still further.

Nowhere is it recorded what Carnarvon's feelings might have been after the discovery of the tomb – whether he felt he was destined to find it or that some kind of karmic retribution would result from its discovery. Yet according to Arthur C Mace, one of Carter's team on loan from the Metropolitan Museum of Art, Carnarvon 'was one of the most superstitious men he had ever met'.[31]

Carter, on the other hand, openly dismissed the idea of a curse connected with the death of Lord Carnarvon in the second volume of *The Tomb of Tut.ankh.Amen*. Towards the end of the Preface he states that he does not intend to 'repeat the ridiculous stories which have been invented about the dangers lurking in ambush ... in this tomb, to destroy the intruder'.[32] Moreover, he says, 'So far as the living are concerned curses of this nature have no place in the Egyptian ritual'.[33] Yet these words do not reflect what he truly believed, for, according to an article that appeared in the *Daily Express* the day after Carnarvon's death, Carter had told 'a friend' only days beforehand that 'This tomb has brought us bad luck'.[34] More significantly, an entry in the unpublished memoirs of the then British vice-consul to Cairo, Sir Thomas Cecil Rapp (1893–1984), tells us:

> He [Carter] was suffering too from a superstitious feeling that Lord Carnarvon's death was possible nemesis for disturbing the sleep of the dead, a nemesis that might also extend to him. But he was to survive for seventeen years.[35]

This is an important revelation, never before made public, which shows a more vulnerable side of Carter's character. That he also participated in the séances held at Highclere Castle, and even identified the language spoken in trance by Lady Cunliffe-Owen as Coptic, hints strongly that, like his friend and patron, he was motivated by spiritual beliefs linked intrinsically with the legacy of ancient Egypt.

HIS SOUL SHALL BE DESTROYED FOR EVER

It seems certain that the fifth Earl of Carnarvon will have felt a little uneasy after reading Hamon's letter so soon after clandestinely entering the tomb's Burial Chamber and removing a number of choice pieces for his own purposes. Yet would there be a price to pay? Hamon obviously thought so, and Carnarvon would have had every reason to believe so, too, for, contrary to what Carter wrote in his book, magical formulas *were* sometimes left behind in tombs in order to deter intruders. For example, Arthur Weigall in his book *Tutankhamen And Other Essays*, rushed out in 1923 during the wave of massive public interest in all things Egyptian, records a curse that was inscribed on a mortuary statue of a person named 'Ursu', a mining engineer who lived less than a hundred years before Tutankhamun:

> He who trespasses upon my property or who shall injure my tomb or drag out my mummy, the Sun-god shall punish him. He shall not bequeath his goods to his children; his heart shall not have pleasure in life; he shall not receive water (for his spirit to drink) in the tomb, and his soul shall be destroyed for ever.[36]

Similar curses have been found in other tombs as well. For instance, Weigall cites another example inscribed on the wall of the tomb of Harkhuf at Aswan, which dates from the Sixth Dynasty, c. 2340 BC:

> As for any man who shall enter into this tomb ... I will pounce upon him as on a bird; he shall be judged for it by the great god.[37]

It is inconceivable to think that Carnarvon would *not* have been aware of such curses, and would therefore have been concerned that in violating an Egyptian tomb he was playing into the hands of occult forces. Publicly he would have shrugged off such thoughts, but quietly, when he was on his own, such convictions may well have haunted him. Perhaps this is why Lord Carnarvon went in search of answers, or at least some form of solace, from his personal seer and palmist known only as 'Velma'.

Like Hamon, Velma was famed for his predictions, which included the assassination of the Tsar of Russia and his son, Alexis Nicoleavitch, as well as the death of Francisco Pancho-Villa, the bandit turned Mexican President, whose palm he had read when in Mexico City.[38] One of his most celebrated prophecies concerned the then Duchess of York, who went on to become the Queen Mother (she died in March 2002). Velma had met her during an Elizabethan pageant at the seat of the Cecil family at Hatfield in Hertfordshire. During this meeting he predicted that her marriage would be enhanced greatly

> by the arrival of a child who will be worshipped from one end of the [British] Empire to the other. You are, at the present time, in a mansion that stood in Elizabethan times and this is an Elizabethan Fête. It may well be that all the great characteristics of the queen of that name will be found in the princess of your house ...[39]

He was referring, of course, to the birth of the future Queen Elizabeth II, Britain's reigning monarch for over fifty years.

Yet Velma's advice to Lord Carnarvon was not of such a positive tone. Having explained the contents of the communication from Hamon, the palmist took hold of his hands and pointed out a fairly long lifeline, which was thin at the centre with ominous spots that might indicate death at this point in his life.[40]

Similar combinations in other areas of the hand led Velma to advise: 'I do see great peril for you ... Most probably – as the indications of occult interest are so strong in your hand – it will arise from such a source'.[41] According to the writer Barry Wynne, in his 1972 book *Behind the Mask of Tutankhamen*, Carnarvon's reply to this second warning was somewhat jocular: 'Whatever happens I will see to it that my interest in things occult never gets so strong as to affect either my reason or my health'.[42]

A SECOND MEETING WITH VELMA

We cannot be certain exactly what transpired between the fifth Earl of Carnarvon and the seer and palmist named Velma during this meeting, but the work of Barry Wynne leads us to believe that his lordship put on a 'brave face' and left 'in a sombre mood'.[43] Whatever his final thoughts, Carnarvon is known to have returned to Velma for a second meeting before his departure for Egypt in January 1923. We are told that on this occasion, when Velma took his hands, the ominous spots noted before had, if anything, enlarged. As Wynne penned with a sense of drama, 'In particular, the spot on the Life Line seemed perilously close to the earl's present age'.[44]

Apparently, Velma then consulted his crystal ball and on staring into its depths saw an Egyptian temple, thick with people divided into three separate parties. The features of the individuals became clearer and Velma described those that could be seen. Yet from the ethereal mist that prevented better clarity came the words, 'To Aton ... only God ... Universal Father ...'[45] There then appeared the image of a golden mask being placed over the head of a young pharaoh: 'Nothing says so, but I believe that this is the burial of your King Tutankhamen'.[46]

Next, Velma saw what he took to be a tomb, presumably that of Tutankhamun, from which emerged flashes of light, evidence, it seemed, of supernatural influences at work. Lord Carnarvon and his associates were there too, carrying out their work, but then came images of a multitude of spirit forms that 'demanded vengeance against the disturbers of the tomb'.[47] Finally, he saw an image of Lord Carnarvon set amid this spectacle of great turmoil.

Carnarvon apparently recognised the danger implied by the vision, but played down its importance, saying that he was well aware of the possible dangers of entering the tomb and would continue the work until it was done.

According to Wynne, Velma responded with the words, 'If I were you ... I should make some public excuse and finish. I can only see disaster to you, without any adequate gain to humanity to justify the sacrifice'.[48] The sixth Earl of Carnarvon, in his memoirs, also provides details of his father's visits to see Velma, and confirms that on the second occasion the seer and palmist warned him against returning to Egypt lest disaster strike.[49]

Lord Carnarvon departed for Egypt in the company of Lady Evelyn in mid January, and was back in the Valley by Wednesday, the 31st. He examined the treasures removed from the Antechamber inside the nearby tomb of Seti II, which was being used as a laboratory, and in the days that followed hung around

Tutankhamun's tomb receiving invited guests and visitors, and generally acting as if the royal sepulchre was his own private estate.

VOICES OF DISDAIN

With the removal of various treasures from the Antechamber during the early months of 1923, the international press were provided with interim news stories that kept Tutankhamun in the forefront of people's minds. Almost daily, newspaper reports would appear written by a 'special correspondent' in Luxor, making sure that no one could get away from the splendours of ancient Egypt. It was perhaps inevitable therefore that certain individuals in the public eye would begin to draw their own conclusions about what they saw as a violation of a royal tomb. One such person was the gothic novelist Mary Mackay, better known by her nom de plume Marie Corelli (1855–1924), whose occult novels were loved by, among others, Queen Victoria. Like Hamon, Corelli was known to the rich and famous, among them the late Edward VII, whose coronation she attended, Mark Twain and the Empress Frederick of Germany.[50]

A few weeks after the official opening of the tomb of Tutankhamun, Corelli wrote a letter to the *New York Times*. In it she asserted that an old Egyptian book in her possession contained a reference to the fact that 'the most dire punishment follows any rash intruder into a sealed tomb'.[51] What led Corelli to make such an eccentric statement in the *New York Times* is unclear, and the title of the old Egyptian book in her possession was never disclosed.

It has been proposed recently that Marie Corelli was simply propounding the idea of a curse attached to Egyptian tombs and mummies featured in nineteenth-century tales of the supernatural.[52] For instance, Dr Dominic Montserrat of the University of Warwick has traced the origins of the mummy's curse to an obscure children's book written in the 1820s by a 25-year-old English author named Jane Loudon Webb. After watching a public mummy unwrapping in Piccadilly Circus by the Italian adventurer and strongman Giovanni Belzoni, she penned a story entitled 'The Mummy', about a vengeful Egyptian spirit that came back to life and threatened to strangle the hero. Then in a novel entitled *The Fruits of Enterprise*, written by an anonymous English writer in 1828, an adventure inside an Egyptian pyramid leads its characters to use mummy parts as torches to illuminate the way.[53]

Inspired very probably by these earlier works, in 1869 the American novelist Louisa May Alcott (1832–88) composed a short story called 'Lost in a Pyramid'.[54] In it an explorer again uses mummy parts, this time of an Egyptian priestess, to light the passages inside a pyramid. From here he steals a gold box containing three strange seeds. These he takes back to the United States and presents to his fiancée, who plants them in the garden. They develop into grotesque flowers, which she wears on her wedding day. Unfortunately, their peculiar scent sends her into a coma and she herself becomes a living mummy!

The same theme was used again and again by various British and American writers of the late Victorian era, culminating eventually in Bram Stoker's classic, *The Jewel of Seven Stars* in 1903, which has spawned some classic horror movies over the years.[55] Very similar influences it would seem led Marie Corelli to conclude that a swift punishment would befall anyone who dared violate the tomb of an Egyptian pharaoh.

A BIRD IS SCRATCHING MY FACE …

Whether or not Lord Carnarvon was made aware of Corelli's ramblings in the *New York Times* is not recorded. However, the earlier warnings delivered to him both by Count Hamon and Velma must have made him at least slightly uneasy about the whole situation as the Burial Chamber was officially opened on Friday, 16 February 1923. Not helping the matter one little bit was the incident regarding the strange death of Carter's canary the previous November, and the strange omens that went with it, especially the prediction that 'before the winter was out someone would die'.[56]

As we know, it was around the time of the official opening of the Burial Chamber that Lord Carnarvon became ill and, exactly as Arthur Weigall had flippantly remarked, he was to be dead just over six weeks later. Yet strange stories are told about his final night on earth. Amid the feverish delirium that accompanied the final stages of his illness, he is reported to have said over and over again, 'A bird is scratching my face. A bird is scratching my face'.[57]

By this time he was more or less in a coma, and so anything he said at this time should perhaps be taken as the ravings of a dying man. Yet the matter has intrigued certain Egyptologists, including Dr Ali Hassan, a former head of Egypt's Supreme Council of Antiquities. According to the author Philipp Vandenberg, Hassan is on record as saying, 'This sentence is of particular interest because something similar appears in a curse-text from the First Intermediate Period c.2140–2100 BC, which says that the Nekhebet [vulture] bird shall scratch the face of anyone who does anything to a tomb'.[58] We should also perhaps recall the inscription found on the wall of the tomb of Harkhuf at Aswan:

> As for any man who shall enter into this tomb … I will pounce upon him as on a bird; he shall be judged for it by the great god.[59]

It would be easy to conclude that Lord Carnarvon was himself judged by the ancient gods for entering the tomb of Tutankhamun. Yet we live in a rational world where curses are dismissed as the feeble beliefs of the weak and simple-minded. They cannot affect us, because we have no place for them in our lives. But anyone who carries around this attitude is a fool who does not understand the delicate nature of the human brain and its gross need for personal security on a psychological level.

To a greater or lesser degree, a large percentage of the human race still relies upon ritual in the belief that their individual or group rites having been upheld, nothing bad will affect their day-to-day life – whether it be twice checking that the gas and electrical appliances are off, avoiding walking under a ladder, crossing oneself to gain God's protection or adopting certain routines to avoid potential bad luck. The vast majority of us do this instinctively and are not strong-willed enough to ignore these primeval compulsions. Indeed, the human mind works in completely the opposite way, believing that, if we don't do it, then something bad *will* happen! Curses and superstitions tap into those very same neurotic insecurities.

If we violate the dead, then we naturally expect that something bad will happen, and, if the owner of a tomb *tells us* that something bad is going to happen, then in all probability it will. The more superstitious we are, the more likely it is that warnings of ill omen can and will affect our lives, and this would seem to have been a weakness of the fifth Earl of Carnarvon. He believed in the supernatural powers of ancient Egypt and paid for it with his life. Moreover, it would seem that this was a failing also of the sixth earl, who during his own lifetime made it clear that he could not be persuaded to return to the tomb of Tutankhamun, even for a million pounds![60] Why? If curses do not exist then what did he have to fear from the tomb?

The death of the fifth earl on 5 April 1923 should have brought to a close any thoughts relating to the judgment of the gods on those who desecrate tombs of pharaohs, but this was not to be the case. For, even as his lordship's body was still warm, strange occurrences began to take place that would only help compound the idea that the curse of Tutankhamun was not going to go away.

10. A SENTENCE OF DEATH

In the early hours of Thursday 5 April 1923, the now sixth Earl of Carnarvon was awoken in his hotel room by a nurse banging at his door with news of his father's sad demise. As he records in his memoirs, 'I glanced at my watch which read five to two and called, "Come in" '.[1] After she had imparted her tragic news, he put on his dressing gown, combed his hair and picked up a torch (an odd thing to do, you might say) before moving out into the hallway. As he began to make quick pace towards his father's room he records that the lights mysteriously failed in the hotel, plunging everywhere into darkness.[2] Switching on his torch, he found a nurse and handed it to her, suggesting that she find some candles as quickly as possible. Inside the room, where his father's body lay at peace, he found his mother Lady Carnarvon and his sister Evelyn kneeling beside the body. Tragically, the fifth Earl of Carnarvon had died after succumbing to septicaemia and then finally pneumonia, and there was nothing more they could do now other than to pray for his soul.

THE LIGHTS GO OUT

It was quite clear from the lack of light coming in through the windows of the Continental Hotel that a power cut had taken place across the whole of Cairo. According to the sixth earl, it was 'some five minutes' before the lights came back on again.[3] The *Daily Express* for the following day reported the sudden light failure, saying that after 'the lapse of a few minutes the lights came on again, but only to go out abruptly'.[4] Eventually, the sixth earl returned to bed and attempted as well as he could to get some sleep. At breakfast he found Howard Carter sitting alone. He looked as if he had not slept and was reading the morning papers, which, in sympathy with the death of Lord Carnarvon, who was well respected in Egypt, carried a black mourning band. More curiously, the papers contained stories suggesting that both the death of the fifth earl and the blackout, which affected the whole of Cairo, could be attributed to the curse of Tutankhamun, whose tomb had been disturbed by the British aristocrat. Indeed, it was being claimed that the electricity had mysteriously failed at the *exact moment* Carnarvon had died, before mysteriously coming back on several minutes later, all without any kind of obvious technical problem. Even General Sir Edmund Allenby, the British High Commissioner, fuelled the paranoia by announcing that he had asked the engineer on duty that night to explain why four districts had been plunged into darkness, although the man was unable to offer any kind of explanation.[5] Thus it was assumed that this curious occurrence was connected in some way with the demise of Lord Carnarvon and could be 'interpreted by those anxiously awaiting news as an omen of evil', or so wrote the *Daily Express*.[6]

The enigma of the failure of the lights of Cairo just as Lord Carnarvon's body expired has fascinated the world ever since that time. Unfortunately, the facts of the matter are not so impressive. In several books on the subject of Tutankhamun it is claimed that the electricity failed at 01.50 hours,[7] while others, including the memoirs of the sixth Earl of Carnarvon, have suggested that the failure took place about 02.00.[8] In contrast, the *Daily Express* reported that it happened shortly *before* Carnarvon's death, which it records as having occurred at 01.40.[9]

Whatever the true time of the light failure, the memoirs of the sixth Earl of Carnarvon clearly imply that the incident happened some minutes after his father's demise, which was at precisely 01.45, as his death certificate shows.[10] It *is* possible that the sixth earl was mistaken, and that the lights had already failed when he was awoken by a nurse to inform him of the bad news, especially as he says he picked up a torch before leaving the room, a strange thing to do unless the hotel was itself in darkness. Yet to claim that the lights of Cairo mysteriously went out at the exact time that Lord Carnarvon's body expired is simply incorrect. Even if this strange incident might be seen as significant, it is worth noting that Christine el Mahdy, in her definitive work *Tutankhamun: The Life and Death of a Boy King*, states that power cuts were common in Cairo even in more recent times,[11] suggesting that the light failure was nothing special.

DEATH OF A DOG

Adding still further to the strange circumstances surrounding Lord Carnarvon's death was the story, which began circulating soon afterwards, regarding his 'favourite dog, which accompanied him on journeys to Egypt, until it lost its left front leg in an accident in 1919'.[12] According to Mrs McLean, Highclere's Scottish housekeeper, when Lord Carnarvon died the animal howled, keeled over 'as if struck by lightning' and died on the spot.[13] Since the guardian keeper of the dead in ancient Egyptian religion was the jackal-headed god Anubis, this unfortunate death was construed as further confirmation of the divine wrath of the gods in the wake of the discovery of the tomb.

First the electrical failure and now the strange death of the fifth earl's favourite dog – the two incidents are regularly cited together in the same paragraph as if the existence of one were enough to give credibility to the other. Yet, as with the power failure, the reality of the story surrounding the death of the dog is much less appealing when the facts are known. The dog in question, a fox terrier bitch named Susie, actually belonged to the sixth earl and not his father, who had merely agreed to take care of the animal in Lord Porchester's absence, initially during World War One and then afterwards, when his son was posted to India. Secondly, there is the matter of the dog's untimely death.

According to the sixth earl, when his father was abroad Mrs McLean would look after the dog, which would sleep in a basket at her bedside. Apparently, 'at five minutes to four on 5 April 1923, Susie sat up in her basket, howled like a wolf and fell back dead.'[14] Note the fact that the time given here is 03.55. Yet of course there are time differences to be taken into account, and in this respect the sixth earl had this to say: 'There is, of course, two hours' difference between Cairo time and London time.'[15] The trouble is that instead of Greenwich Mean Time being two hours *behind* Egypt in 1923, as implied by the sixth earl, it was in fact two hours *ahead of* Cairo time. Since there was no adjustment for British Summer Time until 22 April that year and Egypt did not apply summer time until 1940, it means that, if Susie died at 03.55 British time, it would have been 05.55 in Cairo. Since this is a full four hours after the death of Lord Carnarvon, it rather deflates the incident's potential significance when attempting to justify the reality of Tutankhamun's curse.

TUTANKHAMUN PANIC

Once the Egyptian news media had proposed that the spirit of Tutankhamun was responsible for Carnarvon's death, it became the cue for newspapers worldwide to speak openly about the mummy's curse. Some picked up on the gothic novelist Marie Corelli's warning about the dire consequences of violating the tomb of a pharaoh and used it to corroborate the idea that by opening the tomb the British aristocrat had fallen victim to some ancient curse.

Suddenly, museums began receiving package after package of unwanted Egyptian antiquities, a situation highlighted by the *Daily Express* just two days after Lord Carnarvon's death with their front-page headline 'Egyptian collectors in a panic: sudden rush to hand over their treasures to museums: groundless fears'.[16] It reported:

> The death of Lord Carnarvon has been followed by a panic among collectors of Egyptian antiquities. All over the country people are sending their treasures to the British Museum anxious to get rid of them because of the superstition that Lord Carnarvon was killed by the 'ka,' or double of the soul of Tutankhamen. These fears are, it is hardly necessary to state, absolutely groundless.[17]

Among the multitude of artefacts received by post by the British Museum were the shrivelled hands and feet of mummies, 'porcelain' and wooden statues and other assorted relics from tombs. The newspaper remarked that the institution had become a 'godsend to the superstitious'.[17]

Tutankhamun panic was not simply a British or American phenomenon, either. In Paris, one of the capital's best-known 'seers', Monsieur Lancellin, had declared, 'Tutankhamen has taken his revenge!' One of his rivals, a Madame Fraya, added that the science of the ancient Egyptians was very advanced and that in her opinion Carnarvon had definitely been the victim of the pharaoh's *ka*, or 'ghost', 'or what is known in Egyptian and Oriental occult science as the "doctrine of the double" '.[18] Furthermore, a columnist for *The World* named Clare Sheridan wrote in all seriousness:

> Lord Carnarvon had to pay the price each one pays who dares to touch the Oriental dead. Other men have paid the penalty before. There is hardly a mummy in any museum in Europe that has not its sinister record for those who crossed its path. In my own family there is the same tale of disaster attached to the relic that a great uncle brought from Luxor.[20]

Such views only heightened people's imagination in the supernatural power of ancient Egypt, and did little to quell the growing curse mania. Even so, there were plenty of authoritative voices only too happy to dispel the myth. The well-known British Egyptologist Sir Edgar Wallis Budge simply dismissed the idea as 'bunkum', while Dr HR Hall, Assistant Keeper of the Department of Egyptian and Assyrian Antiquities at the British Museum, summed up the argument rather whimsically with the words, 'If there had been such a curse there would not be any archaeologists left today!'[21]

'DEATH SHALL COME ON SWIFT WINGS …'

Yet by now the press reaction to the escalating belief in the curse was getting out of hand. Newspapers began to publish reports that inscriptions backing up the curse theory had been found in the tomb of Tutankhamun. One written on a carved stone found at the tomb entrance supposedly read, 'Let the hand raised against my form be withered! Let them be destroyed who attack my name, my foundation, my effigies, the images like unto me!'[22]

It never existed, of course.

A second example was an exaggerated form of an inscription said by one newspaper to have been written on the mud base of a candle found by the Anubis statue that guarded the entrance into the Treasury, which read, 'It is I who hinder the sand from choking the secret chamber. I am for the protection of the deceased …'[23] But the journalist responsible for the news story, having quoted this inscription, falsely added the words '… and I will kill all those who cross this threshold into the sacred precincts of the Royal King who lives forever.'[24]

Yet by far the most enduring of the false-curse inscriptions alleged to have been found in the tomb was said to have been written on the door to the second gilded shrine found in the Burial Chamber: 'Death shall come on swift wings to him who disturbs the sleep of the Pharaoh.'[25] These words have been immortalised in books, documentaries and articles on the subject of Tutankhamun ever since the tomb was discovered. Yet, quite simply, this inscription was never found anywhere inside the tomb, and it is in fact a corruption of the warning against tampering with royal tombs made by Marie Corelli in a letter to the *New York Times* a few weeks before the death of Lord Carnarvon.

More strange still is the knowledge that a belief in the reality of the 'swift wings' curse has persisted through to modern times, with some authors even citing its existence as historical fact. For example, Philipp Vandenberg in his book *The Curse of the Pharaohs*, first published in 1973, states, with apparent full belief, that Carter found a clay tablet in the tomb's Antechamber on which the 'swift wings' curse was inscribed.[26] He goes on to say that the item was catalogued properly and the hieroglyphs 'decoded' by the philologist Dr Alan H Gardiner. Furthermore:

> Neither Carter nor Gardiner nor any of the other scholars present feared the curse then or took it seriously. But they worried that the Egyptian labourers would, and since they were dependent on native helpers, mention of the clay tablet was wiped

from the written record of the tomb's discovery. Even the tablet itself disappeared from the artifact collection – but not from the memory of those who read it.[27]

Nowhere else prior to this time is the alleged existence of the 'swift wings' inscription – here transposed mysteriously from the door of the second shrine to a 'clay tablet' – given so much credibility. Why Vandenberg, whose popular books on the Amarna period are generally well researched and informative, should have believed in this press creation is totally inexplicable.

CARTER AND THE CURSE

The one point that Vandenberg did have right was Carter's fear of what effect the sudden panic concerning the curse would have on his Egyptian workforce, who were deeply superstitious people. Already Carter must have seen how they had interpreted as an ill omen the strange death of his canary the previous November and felt it foretold that 'before the winter was out someone would die'.[28] Faced with such an extreme reaction to strange events of this sort, Carter kept private his own fears concerning the consequences of opening the tomb and issued a public statement regarding the whole curse business. As we saw in Chapter 9, in the second volume of *The Tomb of Tut.ankh.Amen* he dismissed 'the ridiculous stories which have been invented about the dangers lurking in ambush' in the tomb. Carter went on to rubbish the whole matter with the following words:

> It has been stated in various quarters that there are actual physical dangers hidden in Tut.ankh.Amen's tomb – mysterious forces, called into being by some malefic power, to take vengeance on whomsoever should dare to pass its portals. There was perhaps no place in the world freer from risks than the tomb. When it was opened, scientific research proved it to be sterile. Whatever foreign germs there may be within it to-day have been introduced from without, yet mischievous people have attributed many deaths, illnesses, and disasters to alleged mysterious and noxious influences.[29]

Whether this did the trick as he continued to work towards clearing the tomb of its treasures is unclear, although it is worth lingering for a while on his assertion that when it was first opened 'scientific research proved it to be sterile'. He was responding here to rumours suggesting that the untimely death of Lord Carnarvon could have been the result not of a strange curse but of an infection brought about by bacteria or viral agents introduced to the tomb, either by accident or design, before its final closure.

In Carter's opinion, this likelihood was impossible, for on the morning after the official opening of the Burial Chamber the British chemist Alfred Lucas began scientific work to ascertain whether any kind of life, even of the lowest form, existed in the tomb. Sterile swabs were placed in the extreme corners of the room, beyond the limits of the great gilded shrine.[30] Here they 'were wiped on the walls, on the bottom of the outer shrine and under some reeds on the floor'.[31] Afterwards, they were dispatched to the bacteriological laboratory of the Royal Naval Cordite Factory, near Wareham in Dorset, where they were examined by a

Mr HJ Bunker. In an appendix to the second volume of Howard Carter's *The Tomb of Tut.ankh.Amen*, the results are given as follows:

> … out of five swabs from which cultures were taken, four were sterile and the fifth contained a few organisms that were undoubtedly air-infections unavoidably introduced during the opening of the doorway and the subsequent inspection of the chamber, and not belonging to the tomb, and it may be accepted that no bacterial life whatsoever was present. The danger, therefore, to those working in the tomb from disease germs, against which they have been so frequently warned, is non-existent.[32]

However, what he did find present in the tomb were fungus growths, for as Lucas records:

> Fungus growths occur on the walls of the Burial Chamber, where they are so plentiful as to cause great disfigurement, and they occur also, though only to a slight extent, on the walls of the Antechamber and on the outside of the sarcophagus, but in every instance the fungus is dry and apparently dead.[33]

Could fungal growth have been in any way responsible for the creation of the curse that, aside from Lord Carnarvon, was linked with a whole number of strange deaths during this period, many of them individuals who had never even visited the tomb?

VICTIMS OF MORBIFIC AGENTS

On 3 November 1962, a physician and biologist attached to the University of Cairo named Dr Ezzeddin Taha held a press conference claiming that he had finally solved the mystery of the curse of the pharaohs. He explained how over a prolonged period of time he and his colleagues had conducted medical examinations on archaeologists and museum staff who worked regularly either inside tombs or in environments where they came into contact with mummies, or objects removed from tombs. The tests showed that many of them suffered from an unknown fungal infection, which caused feverish inflammations of the respiratory system. He concluded also that this infection was one and the same as a malady experienced particularly by those who worked with ancient Egyptian papyri known as the 'Coptic itch', the symptoms of which are skin rashes and respiratory problems.[34]

Studies revealed that these infections were caused by fungal agents, usually *Aspergillus niger*, and in Dr Taha's opinion they were resilient enough to survive in undisturbed tombs for up to several thousand years, although modern-day antibiotics were strong enough to neutralise their effects.[35] According to him,

> This discovery has once and for all destroyed the superstition that explorers who worked in ancient tombs died as a result of some kind of curse. They were victims of morbific agents encountered at work. Some people may still believe that the curse of the pharaohs can be attributed to some supernatural powers, but that belongs to the realm of fairy tales.[36]

The idea was taken up again during the 1990s by the German biochemist Christian Hradecky. Using magnified computer imagery, he noted the presence of high concentrations of the fungus *Aspergillus flavas* on the surface of various mummies examined. In addition to this, he identified deposits of the fungal agent in rotted food from earthen pots found at various Egyptian grave sites. Professor Kent Weeks of the American University in Cairo added support to this theory by pointing out that the rotted food in the containers caused the fungus to grow and accepted that there is every reason to believe that these agents can remain dormant for thousands of years before reactivating themselves.[37]

That these scientists might have identified a possible source of fungal infection among the tombs and graves of the dead cannot be denied. It is a bold discovery, and further exploration in this area of biological research should be encouraged. Furthermore, it cannot be ruled out that the fungal agents present in both the Antechamber and Burial Chamber of the tomb of Tutankhamun were not dormant forms of either *Aspergillus niger* or *Aspergillus flavas*. Yet whether it has any connection with the death of Lord Carnarvon, or any of the other untimely deaths linked with the curse, is quite another matter.

THE VICTIMS

Much could be said about the so-called victims of the curse of Tutankhamun. The fifth earl's half-brother Aubrey Herbert died unexpectedly after having his teeth extracted in September 1923. The railroad magnate Jay Gould died of pneumonia after catching a cold following a visit to the tomb of Tutankhamun, while the French Egyptologist Georges Bénédite died from a fall after he too entered the royal sepulchre. Carter's colleague Arthur C Mace, suffered from continued ill health after the discovery of the tomb and died eventually in 1928. The fifth Earl of Carnarvon's private secretary, Richard Bethell, died under unusual circumstances in 1929 at the Bath Club in London. That same year his elderly father, the third Lord Westbury, committed suicide by jumping from his seventh-storey home at St James' Court, Westminster. On the way to the funeral, an eight-year-old child accidentally fell beneath the wheels of Lord Westbury's horse-drawn hearse. The list goes on: Egyptian Ali Kemel Fahmy Bey was shot by his wife in London's Savoy Hotel not long after inspecting Tutankhamun's treasures, while the Hon. Mervyn Herbert, Lord Carnarvon's other half-brother, who was present when the Burial Chamber was officially opened in 1923, died in Rome seven years later.

All of these deaths, and many more besides, have been linked again and again with the curse of Tutankhamun. Yet to accept that these individuals died because of some kind of 3,000-year-old curse we will have to assume, quite naïvely, that the gods of ancient Egypt have awesome supernatural powers that afflict even those in distant lands who never even came into contact with the tomb of Tutankhamun. The 78-year-old Lord Westbury, for example, was deeply depressed after the premature death of his son and felt he could not live any more, while the child who fell beneath the wheels of his hearse was really only the victim of a tragic accident (although there is another side to the death of Lord

Westbury explored in Chapter 13). Even those who died after visiting the tomb, or coming face to face with Tutankhamun's treasures, are simply victims not of the curse of the pharaohs but of a curse brought about by the material world in which they lived. Other than the death of Arthur C Mace, which we shall deal with in the next chapter, none of these people's demises can be linked with the very public departure from this world of Lord Carnarvon. He alone can be seen as a genuine victim of the curse of Tutankhamun – yet it was a curse that had more to do with his own inner fears than the paranormal capabilities of ancient Egyptian gods.

As we have seen, there is some evidence to suggest that Lord Carnarvon's powerful belief in the occult may have made him fear the warnings of doom offered by fortune-tellers such as Count Louis Hamon and Velma. As with someone who has a killing bone pointed at him, his superstitious nature may have led him to believe that he really *was* under a sentence of death for violating an Egyptian royal tomb. If so, then on a purely psychosomatic level, this could have affected his will to live, leaving his body in a vulnerable state of health.

The overriding symptoms experienced by his lordship in the weeks following the fatal mosquito bite conform very well to those expected of someone suffering from erysipelas, or blood poisoning, which in due course weakened Carnarvon's immune system to such a degree that he succumbed finally to pneumonia. Yet, as was stated in Chapter 8, there are clear indications that he was suffering from some kind of inexplicable malady even before he embarked on a cruise to Aswan at the end of February 1923, where the fatal mosquito bite is thought to have occurred. As we saw in that chapter, Thomas Hoving has spoken of how one of Carnarvon's teeth fell out or became chipped every few days, indicating symptoms of a deep infection.[38]

Why exactly were Carnarvon's teeth either chipping or falling out on what seems to have been a regular basis? Was it quite simply the result of brittle teeth, caused through poor dental care, or was it a symptom of something else altogether? Teeth crumbling and falling out is most commonly associated with the introduction into the body of harmful toxins over a prolonged period of time. Is it remotely possible that Lord Carnarvon's death might have been exacerbated still further by the introduction into his body of poison?

11. THE PRESENCE OF POISON

The idea that Lord Carnarvon might have been affected by some kind of poison present in the tomb of Tutankhamun goes back to the height of the curse mania that prevailed in the wake of his untimely death in April 1923. For example, Ralph Shirley, editor of a publication called the *Occult Review*, asserted at the time: 'I should not like to say one way or another, with regard to Lord Carnarvon, since there is no evidence [of a curse]. It may have been that some native Egyptian, indignant at the Luxor operation, put poison in the tomb.'[1]

HV Morton, a correspondent writing for the *Daily Express* on the subject of Tutankhamun, fuelled the debate when writing Lord Carnarvon's obituary by noting:

> The queer atmosphere which clings to all things Egyptian is responsible for the wide-spread story that in opening the tomb of Tutankhamen Lord Carnarvon exposed himself to the fury of some malignant influence, or that he was poisoned by materials left in the tomb thousands of years ago.[2]

Having dismissed the idea that supernatural agencies, bacteria or viral agents might have been responsible for Carnarvon's death, some astute observers such as those cited above considered it possible that his illness was the result of poison having been introduced to the tomb, either in modern times or during antiquity. In the latter case, the placing of potentially lethal toxins in the tomb, perhaps in the form of scattered powder on the dusty floor, would have acted as a deterrent to intruders. Although this would not have prevented a tomb robbery, if the person afterwards became ill or died, then his family, unaware of the effects of poison, would surely have considered it divine retribution. If nothing else, it will have deterred further tomb robbery by those who came to hear of the intruder's misfortune.

And there are precedents for the presence of poisons or toxic substances in Egyptian tombs as well. Dr Zahi Hawass, Undersecretary of State for the Giza monuments, discovered one such tomb, thought to have been protected in this manner, at the Bahariya Oasis in Egypt's Western Desert. The tomb belonged to a man called Zed-Khonsu-ef-ankh, who was a vizier under the Pharaoh Apris (c. 589–570 BC) during the 26th Dynasty. Hawass described his experience of entering the tomb for the first time as follows:

> At that moment of discovery, I felt as though arrows of fire were attacking me. My eyes were closed, and I could not breath [sic] because of bad smell. I looked into the room and discovered a very thick yellow powder around the anthropoid sarcophagus. I cold [sic] not walk and did not read the name of the owner. I ran

back out because of this smell. We brought masks for the workers who began to remove the material. I found out that it was hematite, quarried nearby in Baharia.[3]

Hawass speculated that the powder might have been placed there 'to protect his tomb from unwelcome visitors'.[4] Given that Zed-Khonsu-ef-ankh's sarcophagus remained undisturbed this ploy seems to have deterred even the most determined of tomb robbers.

Other examples of noxious substances being placed in tombs to protect its occupant can be found in other parts of the world. For example, in the Mayan territories of Central America, burials were very often coated with a layer of highly toxic cinnabar, the red sulphide of mercury (HgS) and the chief mercury ore, which was also used as a pigment under the name 'vermilion'. Cinnabar's distinctive colour linked it with the underworld, the realm of the dead, which the deceased entered after leaving this world. It may also have acted as a deterrent to intruders, and, quite obviously, its presence today is a major hazard to archaeologists who have to wear protective gear in order to examine the tomb and its contents.

In addition to the cinnabar found in the royal tombs of the Maya, mercury has been reportedly found in several sepulchral monuments in China. For example, the vast, elaborate and currently unexcavated tomb of Qin Emperor Huangdi, c. 200 BC, in the X'ian Province, is said to contain a map of his empire, which includes rivers delineated with liquid mercury that surround his sarcophagus.[5] There are also thought to be self-firing crossbows that are activated by trip wires. As is the case with the Mayan tombs of Central America, the possibility of a plethora of poisons contained in the royal tomb of Huangdi has led to fears that it might be too dangerous for archaeologists to work in such an environment.[6]

Can we find evidence that any metallic or organic toxins could have been introduced to the tomb of Tutankhamun before its final closure? More importantly, could this offer an explanation for Lord Carnarvon's deterioration of health during late February 1923?

Between the date of the discovery of the tomb in late November 1922 and the onset of Carnarvon's illness some fifteen weeks later, there were approximately fifty days when his lordship could have entered the tomb. On the other hand, Carter's team, who continued working to clear the tomb when Carnarvon journeyed back to England for the Christmas and New Year period, could have spent up to eighty days inside the cramped sepulchre during the same period. Thus, those who worked on the clearance of the Antechamber, when Lord Carnarvon contracted his illness, would have had a 24 per cent higher chance of coming into contact with the same toxic substance, and yet none of them, with one possible exception, experienced similar symptoms of illness.

We must also consider the likelihood that any toxin was present only in the Burial Chamber and/or Treasury, which, as we know, was entered by Carnarvon, Carter and Lady Evelyn three months before its official opening in February

1923. However, if a toxin had indeed been present in the Burial Chamber or Treasury, then surely we should find evidence of chronic illness among those members of Carter's team who worked on clearing these rooms. But is this the case? In short, the answer is no, although there is *one* case that does require special attention – that of Arthur Cruttenden Mace.

THE CASE OF ARTHUR CRUTTENDEN MACE

Born in Glenorchy, Hobart, Tasmania, in 1874, Mace travelled to Egypt in 1897 to join the great British Egyptologist William M Flinders Petrie, a distant cousin. Mace excavated for him at Abydos, Dendera and Hiw, before going on to work with California University's George A Reisner at Giza and Naga ed-Dar until 1906, when he joined New York's Metropolitan Museum of Art. Here he helped organise its Department of Egyptian Art and went on to become its assistant curator. For a while this took him away from Egypt, but he was digging out there again between 1912 and 1914, this time working at Lisht in the Fayyûm. Then in 1915 he was enlisted into the 29th London Territorial Rifles and later the Army Service Corps. Afterwards, Mace returned to Lisht, where he remained through to the 1921–2 winter season. He was about to start a fresh season both here and at Thebes when in November 1922 he was asked by the Metropolitan to assist Howard Carter in the mammoth job of clearing the tomb of Tutankhamun.

Throughout the winter months Mace used his common sense and practical skills to assist the team, and also began to co-author the first volume of Carter's *The Tomb of Tut.ankh.Amen*, which must have been an enormous task. Yet by early 1923 Mace was clearly suffering from ill health, one of the reasons why he accepted Carnarvon's offer to join him, Lady Evelyn and Sir Charles Cust on the trip to Aswan at the end of February. Here they spent their time visiting the tombs at Qubbet el-Hawa, inspecting the unfinished obelisk at Aswan, marvelling at the dam and lazing around in the bazaars. In addition to this, the party also joined a day trip to the Island of Philae. It was following his return from Aswan that Mace famously wrote to his wife Winifred describing Lord Carnarvon and Lady Evelyn in the following terms:

> Carnarvon's a queer fish, but in spite of his oddities very lovable. He and Lady Evelyn are devoted to each other, she is somewhat spoilt and a bit slangy, but there's a lot of good stuff in her. They treat me like one of the family and say I must go to Highclere.[7]

The trip did Mace some good, for he also informed his wife that 'they all say I look ever so much better for my holiday, and I certainly feel so.'[8] It proved to be only a temporary recovery, for by 1924 his health had deteriorated to such a degree that he was forced to abandon any further Egyptological work. The last four years of his life were spent in England, and for the final few months he was confined to a nursing home at Westgate-on-Sea in Kent. He died at Haywards Heath, Sussex, on 6 April 1928, five years almost to the day after Carnarvon's own death.

ARSENIC POISONING

Occasionally, Arthur Mace's name has appeared in that long list of victims who supposedly succumbed to the curse of Tutankhamun. Yet no author of this dreaded subject seems to have picked up on the fact that strange circumstances do surround the nature of Mace's long-term illness, which began around the *same time* as Carnarvon's health also began to diminish. One biography of Mace exists, and this is the curiously titled … *the grand piano came by camel: Arthur C Mace, the neglected Egyptologist*, written by Christopher C Lee and published in 1992.

The book is a cornucopia of unknown facts about Mace's life and times, and contains much material on his gradually diminishing health. After retiring to live in England, Mace wrote regularly to his old friend Albert Lythgoe of the Metropolitan Museum of Art. In one letter dated 14 January 1927 he alludes to his illness, revealing that he is 'still breathless and suffering from indigestion'.[9] He speaks also of consulting a heart specialist, but crucially he tells Lythgoe that his present condition is 'a heritage of the arsenic poisoning'.[10]

Mace's biographer was as perplexed as anyone to read these words and was led to comment in this respect:

> It is not clear how he got arsenic poisoning. In the days before antibiotics it was sometimes used in small doses as a medicine, and it was used in museums, but principally by taxidermists. The effects of arsenic poisoning are very unpleasant and can prove fatal.[11]

Certainly, they can, although not in Mace's case. The heart specialist diagnosed that a thickening of the arteries was the root of his problems – the result most probably of his long years of digging in Egypt.[12] Indeed, Mace was later to describe his condition to Lythgoe as 'similar to that suffered by miners and caused by swallowing too much sand and dust…'.[13] He went on to add:

> That last winter I had at Lisht [1921–2] I spent weeks underground making my lungs black by blowing decayed coffin dust into them and on the tomb work I spent most of my time breathing cloth dust.[14]

The doctor failed Arthur Mace, for his condition only worsened. He grew weak and thin, until finally his body could take no more. Yet by his own admission the illness did not occur until *after* his final season at Lisht during 1921–2. Moreover, there is every reason to believe that it did not take hold of his body until the early months of 1923, for the first mention of his diminishing health occurs in the letter written to his wife after his return from Aswan. If this is correct, then he could well have contracted his illness when working on the tomb of Tutankhamun. Yet how might arsenic poisoning figure in this story? The answer remains a mystery, with Mace's biographer being unable to shed any extra light on the perplexing subject.[15]

If we choose to accept that arsenic poisoning really was contributory to Mace's poor condition as early as February 1923, then we must look at how he may have come into contact with enough arsenic to poison his system? Was it, as he himself suggests, when he worked in the dark confines of the tombs at Lisht? Did the decayed 'coffin dust' contain tiny particles of arsenic that were inhaled into his lungs? It seems unlikely, as there would surely exist many more cases of Egyptologists, both past and present, contracting arsenic poisoning while working in death-infested tombs and catacombs, and this simply isn't the case.

The only acknowledged illness that an Egyptologist might expect to contract from rummaging around in the tombs and graves of ancient Egypt is a form of bronchopulmonary aspergillosis. This, as we saw in the last chapter, is caused by fungal agents such as *Aspergillus flavas* or *Aspergillus niger*, which can return to life after being dormant for thousands of years. While it is true that in the days before antibiotics such infections might have led to feverish inflammations of the respiratory system, or worse, there is no reason to believe that this is what triggered Mace's ill health in 1923. If contagious fungal spores were present in Egyptian tombs, then once again we should be able to find many more cases of Egyptologists in the nineteenth and early twentieth centuries suffering from serious respiratory problems. Although it is possible that Mace's long years working in Egypt cannot have helped his health, there is no obvious reason why he might have suffered from arsenic poisoning which, as we shall see, produces a number of quite specific symptoms in addition to problems relating to the respiratory system.

So how else might Mace have come into contact with arsenic in the years preceding 1923? Was it, as his biographer Christopher Lee intimates, during his time at a museum, such as the Metropolitan in New York? The authors contacted the Metropolitan Museum and asked them whether the Department of Egyptian Art ever used arsenic. Dorothy Arnold, the current curator of the department, admitted that although it was possible that coffin dust might prove hazardous to Egyptologists, there was nothing to suggest that Arthur Mace's presence at the museum might have exacerbated his ill-health.[16] So if he did not succumb to arsenic poisoning when working in the museum, how was it contracted? Could he have inadvertently consumed arsenic when taking a medicine for some existing malady?

FOWLER'S SOLUTION

Although arsenic is classified as a poison, it is medically accepted that, if consumed in minute quantities, it can have beneficial effects on the body. This was noted as early as 1786 by the British physician Thomas Fowler (1736–1801), who in that year published a series of medical reports in which he proposed the effectiveness of arsenic in curing agues, fevers and headaches. This led to the formulation of something called Fowler's solution, which contains 1 per cent potassium arsenate dissolved in water. In Victorian times it was popular as a cure-all remedy, and was even taken by Charles Dickens. However, only through prolonged usage over many years would there have been any serious health risks. Yet there is no suggestion that Mace ever used Fowler's solution.

POISONOUS GROUNDWATER

One final possibility is that Mace could have drunk water contaminated by arsenic. One of the most lethal sources of arsenic is groundwater extracted from underground aquifers using tube wells. For instance, widespread arsenic poisoning has resulted from drinking infected water in various countries of the world, including the United States, Mexico, Chile, China, Argentina, Taiwan, India, Ghana, Hungary, the United Kingdom, the Philippines, New Zealand and Inner Mongolia. In 1998 a natural catastrophe on an unparalleled level concerning arsenic poisoning was brought to the attention of the outside world.

During the 1970s a shortage of clean surface water in Bangladesh and the Indian province of West Bengal led the United Nations Children's Fund (UNICEF) and the World Bank to initiate a project to sink 900,000 tube wells in the area. It was considered that these would enable unlimited drinking water to be accessed by the greater part of the population of both countries. Hundreds of thousands more tube wells have been bored since that time. Yet the high arsenic content of the subsurface water has led to an estimated 10 million people suffering from an assortment of skin diseases, cancers, keratoses and melanomas brought about by chronic poisoning. More disturbing is the fact that some 70 million people in Bangladesh and West Bengal are still relying on wells that are almost certainly contaminated. According to the World Health Organisation, the crisis is the biggest outbreak of mass poisoning in history and there is no sure way of dealing with it effectively.[17]

Although this awful tragedy in Bangladesh and West Bengal highlights the highly dangerous properties of arsenic, there is no evidence whatsoever to suggest that the groundwaters of Egypt contain dissolved arsenic, or that anyone there has suffered from arsenic poisoning by consuming its drinking water.

So what is the answer? Where did Mace contract arsenic poisoning? If it was in a tomb, then aside from the example quoted above where haematite powder was found sprinkled on the floor of a tomb in the Bahariya Oasis, what evidence is there that the ancient Egyptians were aware of either toxic or organic poisons?

POISONS IN ANCIENT EGYPT

In 'an extremely ancient papyrus in the Louvre' it says, 'Speak not the name of IAO [the Gnostic name of God] under the penalty of the peach-tree.'[18] Those responsible for compiling this text must have known that the peach tree produces a powerful toxin called prussic acid, which, if ingested, can kill a person. Pliny the Elder (AD 23–79), the celebrated Roman naturalist, countered claims to this effect by noting:

> It is not true that the peach grown in Persia is poisonous and causes torturing pain, and that, when it had been transplanted into Egypt by the kings to use as a punishment, the nature of the soil caused it to lose its dangerous properties …[19]

But he was wrong in this respect for we now know that the peach tree, which was indeed introduced to Egypt from Persia, produces prussic acid, which does induce 'torturing pain' in its victims.[20]

Papyri texts and stone inscriptions from Egypt's New Kingdom period onwards provide details of various spells to combat the effects of poison. Although most commonly associated with the venom of snakes and scorpions, other spells are more vague and could well relate to prepared potions involving toxins. However, no mention is made of what these might have been. All we know is that, aside from the peach tree, which was cultivated in special gardens, several plants grown in Egypt produce poisons. Among them is the opium poppy (*Papaver somniferum*), from which is obtained opium alkaloids, including morphine. It is mentioned in the famous Graeco-Egyptian medical pharmaceutica known as the Oxyrhynchus papyrus.[21] Other plants that contain powerful toxins are the 'thorn apple' *Datura stramonium*, used as a powerful psychotropic drug; henbane and various types of Hyoscyamus, including 'Egyptian henbane'. Both henbane and black hellebore (*Rhizoma hellebori nigri*), another potent toxin, are also listed in the Oxyrhynchus papyrus.[22]

In addition to these seemingly organic toxins, Michael Carmichael, who has made an extensive study of the archaeology of early chemistry, has identified the puffer fish among the aquatic life in a wall relief dating to the Old Kingdom period.[23] Certainly, it is known to have been a fish native to the Nile Delta in Pharaonic times. With this in mind, groundbreaking ethnobiological research by the Harvard botanist Dr Wade Davis has shown that a deadly tetrotoxin, a massively powerful poison, can be made from pulverising the puffer fish into powder.[24] He established that it had been used for hundreds of years by magicians, witches and voodoo priests of the Caribbean island of Haiti to cause death by sprinkling it on the floors of potential victims. It is feasible, therefore, that the puffer fish could have been utilised in a similar way in ancient Egypt.

RARE METALS

Carmichael thinks it reasonable to assume that, as the inventors of alchemy, the Pharaonic Egyptians isolated and used deadly toxins, especially those produced by rare metals. Alchemy was a strange mixture of magic and science in which the ultimate aim was the transformation of base matter, usually metals, into a pure state – a process reflected in the transformation of the alchemist's own spirit and soul. The word alchemy comes from the Arabic *al-kimia*, with 'kimia' coming, most probably, from the Egyptian word *kemi*, which alludes to the original matter of transmutation, i.e. the art of treating 'black metal' to produce precious metals. It also relates to the black mud that brought life to the fertile regions of the Nile after the act of First Creation and the yearly inundation of the Nile overspilling its banks. If not from the Egyptian *kemi*, the Arabic *al-kimia* might stem from the Greek *khymeia*, 'fusion', in other words, the art of producing gold and silver. It is from 'alchemy' that we derive words such as 'chemical', 'chemist' and 'chemistry'.

The Arabs embraced the concept of alchemy and through them it passed into medieval Europe, leading to the discovery of rare metals such as arsenic, first isolated in the thirteenth century by the alchemist Albertus Magnus (1193–1280). The name comes from the Greek *arsenikon*, a pale-yellow pigment that contains arsenic sulphate and is known to have been used by the ancient Egyptians.[25]

Arsenic is a highly toxic substance, found naturally in certain foods, including seafood, bone meal, and even in apple seeds. More importantly, it forms as a by-product in the smelting of copper, which the ancient Egyptians obtained from opencast mines in the Sinai. It is likely that their knowledge of copper extraction led them to discover the properties of arsenic sulphate.

That the tomb of Tutankhamun could have contained arsenic, or some other kind of poison, is a thought-provoking idea. On the other hand, we really have no evidence at all to suggest that this was ever the case. In 1938 the British chemist Alfred Lucas, who conducted a series of experiments in order to establish whether bacteria or viral agents were present in the tomb, wrote a definitive paper on poisons in ancient Egypt.[26] It makes no mention of the fact that the ancient Egyptians possessed a knowledge of rare metals, and says nothing whatsoever about the tomb of Tutankhamun in this connection. If Lucas had believed there was even the slightest chance that some kind of toxic residue might have been present inside its chambers at the time of discovery, then surely he would have said so.

Add to this the fact that no other member of Carter's team seems to have suffered from any chronic illnesses while working on the tomb, and it becomes unlikely that Arthur Mace's 'arsenic poisoning' stemmed from this source, if indeed he did suffer arsenic poisoning in the first place. If correct, then where did it originate and was it even related to Lord Carnarvon's own worsening condition as he entered the final few weeks of his life? Perhaps it is time to look a little more closely at the effects of arsenic poisoning.

THE SYMPTOMS

It begins with headaches, and is followed by confusion and drowsiness. As the arsenic takes hold of the victim's body, he or she may experience convulsions and changes in fingernail pigmentation. Then, very gradually, diarrhoea, vomiting, muscle cramps, hair loss, blood in the urine and worsening convulsions can be expected. The organs of the body most commonly affected by arsenic poisoning are the lungs, kidneys and liver. It can also lead to respiratory problems. What is more, because it is a carcinogen, blisters appear on a victim's hands and feet, which can often turn gangrenous and cancerous. Hundreds of thousands of those suffering from arsenic poisoning in Bangladesh and West Bengal experienced these cancerous blisters on various parts of their anatomy. Ultimately, when the body can take no more, a coma sets in, and death follows.

Quite obviously, a victim does not have to suffer from all of these symptoms. They come as a result of a cumulative effect, sometimes over many years, and, if the body has not reached a point where it cannot cope with any more arsenic in its system, then there are ways of reversing the process. They include the ingestion of foods that contain a lot of sulphur, such as eggs, garlic, beans and onions. Fibre also helps, as do charcoal tablets and properly administered injections of ethylenediaminetetra acetic acid.

BAD TEETH

What seems infinitely more important to our investigation of Carnarvon's illness is that teeth coming loose, crumbling and falling out is another major symptom of arsenic poisoning. Indeed, this was one of the problems that victims of a recent outbreak of mass arsenic poisoning in Oakland County, Michigan, USA, were found to have suffered. In 1983 a series of tube wells were bored in order to supply some three thousand homes with drinking water. Unfortunately, it just happened to be laced with arsenic. A recent report highlighted the case of Renee Crouch, a mother of three from Ortonville. It apparently took sixteen doctors eight years to realise what was making her hair fall out and her teeth 'crumble'.[27] Previously, they had suggested that she might have been suffering from liver cancer or multiple sclerosis, but after performing the hair shaft test on samples of her hair they finally realised that the problem was arsenic, which was then found in the water coming from the family's 91-metre-deep well.

In the knowledge that teeth becoming loose, crumbling and falling out is a clear symptom of arsenic poisoning, is it reasonable to ask whether Lord Carnarvon suffered from this same malady? Aside from the aforementioned dental problems, his mood swings and 'violent tantrums' in late February[28] and, of course, his obvious respiratory problems, he experienced very few of the symptoms associated with arsenic poisoning. Indeed, it seems impossible to escape from the conclusion that after suffering a mosquito bite at the end of February or the beginning of March 1923 Lord Carnarvon contracted erysipelas, which weakened his body to such a degree that he succumbed to pneumonia. Yet, before dismissing the idea that Lord Carnarvon's illness was in any way connected with the effects of poisoning, we should explore the possibility that he may have succumbed to the toxic effects not of arsenic but of another rare metal. The most obvious example would be mercury, which – along with copper, silver, lead and gold – was seen as one of the classic transition metals of alchemy.

MERCURY POISONING?

Simply absorbing mercury in sufficient quantities through the skin or inhaling it into the lungs can cause severe toxic poisoning. Whichever way it is introduced into the body, once it has reached the bloodstream it causes vomiting, diarrhoea, nausea and severe kidney damage. More chronic exposure results in gums becoming soft and spongy, increased salivation, the appearance of sores and, as with arsenic, teeth either becoming loose or falling out. Interestingly enough, mood swings and other mental changes can also be expected, leading patients to become irritable, frightened and depressed for no apparent reason. Criticism may upset them, since they may lose their self-confidence or become apathetic. In addition to this, they find it difficult to concentrate, and can suffer from hallucinations and even memory loss.

Mercury poisoning also affects the nervous system, leading to hands shaking involuntarily, tremors in the tongue and eyelids, and an inability to stand up straight. In worse-case scenarios, the respiratory system is affected, leading to coughs, tightening of the chest, breathing trouble and stomach complaints.

Eventually, as the body weakens still further, pneumonia sets in and this can prove fatal to the patient.

If we now apply these symptoms to Lord Carnarvon's own illness we can see that there are some uncanny parallels. The mood swings, apparent depression, dental troubles, respiratory problems and even the pneumonia are all classic signs of mercury poisoning, making it a very realistic diagnosis of his worsening condition. The only thing holding us back from making this connection is the apparent absence of mercury in the tomb of Tutankhamun, and the so-called 'arsenic poisoning' that led to Arthur Mace's deterioration of health and eventual death in 1928. Did he really suffer from arsenic poisoning, or it is possible that his physician got it wrong and he was in fact suffering from the effects of mercury poisoning? If so, then how on earth might these two men have come into contact with mercury? Could cinnabar have been present either in the tomb of Tutankhamun or in one or more of the many tombs that both men entered over the years, perhaps in a powdered form? Although Alfred Lucas's paper on poisons, published in 1938, makes no mention of organic or metallic poisons being found in the tomb, Michael Carmichael's assertion that the ancient Egyptians would have been aware of rare metals, such as arsenic and mercury, is compelling to say the least. Indeed, having read this chapter he was of the opinion that the authors 'are on the right track'. Yet he added:

> Whether or not either Carnarvon or Mace were exposed to metallic poisons through the process of excavation is, of course, impossible to determine – due to a lack of forensic evidence from their corpses. That said, if corpses exist, it still might be possible to arrange for forensic examination of samples of the hair, liver, stomach or intestines – to investigate for the presence of metallic residues or other toxins. The presence of mercury or arsenic or other toxins in these tissues would clinch the case for toxicity in these two instances.[29]

The authors will consider some of Michael Carmichael's suggestions in the final chapter of this book. Yet still there is the mystery of how Carnarvon and Mace might have been exposed to metallic toxins. It could have been from a tomb, but then again there is another possibility. As we saw at the beginning of this chapter, Ralph Shirley, editor of the *Occult Review*, put forward the view that not ancient Egyptians but 'some native Egyptian, indignant at the Luxor operation, [may have] put poison in the tomb', thus causing the eventual death of Lord Carnarvon. It is an intriguing thought, but before we can go on to explore this subject further we must return once more to Carter's indiscretions inside the tomb of Tutankhamun and the petty politics that now plagued his world.

12. LOCKOUT!

Soon after the 1923–4 digging season got under way, Howard Carter began suffering increasing interference from members of the Egyptian government in charge of archaeological exploration in their native land. Following complaints from one AH Bradstreet, the Luxor correspondent with the *New York Times*, Egypt's Minister of Public Works, Abdel Hamid Suleman Pasha, urged Carter to issue a brief bulletin to all newspapers by nine o'clock each night in order that they might carry the story in their morning edition. This was not a request, but a statement, since the minister informed Carter that he intended building it into the terms of the digging concession (to clear the tomb of Tutankhamun, not to explore the Valley further) issued since the death of Lord Carnarvon in favour of his widow Lady Almina, Countess of Carnarvon.[1] In addition to this, he would ensure that, henceforth, surveillants were posted to the tomb in order that they might observe all work being carried out by Carter and his team.

Quite obviously, Carter was having none of this, and so he travelled to Cairo in order to sort out the matter with both the minister and Pierre Lacau, the director-general of the Antiquities Service. After two days of heated debate, no agreement had been reached and Carter now threatened to inform the world of their incompetence unless he retained control over the international press and the admission of visitors to the tomb. He waited in Cairo for a week before finally returning to Luxor, and in due course he received a document agreeing to his terms, but there were conditions that made it a hollow victory.

In an unprecedented move that drew immediate suspicion, the Ministry of Public Works pressed Carter to supply a complete list of all his staff, at the same time insisting that this must include only bona fide experts in their respective fields of study. Only these persons were to be allowed access to the tomb; all others would have to apply for permission to do so from the Antiquities Service. Carter knew this was a dig at him, since he had allowed the *Times* correspondent Arthur Merton to become a member of the team at the beginning of the season, something that had upset other journalists who were left outside the tomb to fry in the heat of the Valley.

As the relations between Carter, the Minister of Public Works and the Antiquities Service deteriorated still further, Pierre Lacau came to Luxor on Wednesday 12 December 1923, in the hope of finding a solution, but Carter was ill that day and remained at his house. Owing to Carter's absence, the tomb was locked, so Lacau made a visit to the 'laboratory', where he met Arthur Merton. Lacau proceeded to tell Merton that he was the cause of all the past troubles and more of the same would follow. Suddenly, poor Arthur Merton became the focus of a major political rumpus, with the Minister of Public Works pointing out to Carter that reporters were not scientists and that Merton should be allowed in the tomb only on days when other journalists were permitted entry. Although Carter would not budge an inch concerning Merton's position, he did finally accept that in order to keep other newspapers happy he would not object to the occasional press call when representatives from major newspapers would be allowed access to the tomb. In effect, this signalled the end of the exclusivity deal with *The Times*, renewed at the beginning of the season.

UNVEILING THE SARCOPHAGUS
Around the time that these irritating problems were causing Carter extreme consternation, the removal of the nest of gilded shrines surrounding the sarcophagus got under way. On Thursday 3 January 1924, the entwined and sealed hemp rope binding together the double door into the second shrine was cut using a surgical scalpel. The doors swung back to reveal a third gilded shrine, and this also had a rope-bound double door. When this was opened, Carter found a further double door into a fourth shrine on which were reliefs of the outstretched wings of a hawk protecting the king. Beyond the doors of the fourth shrine was the highly polished, red quartzite sarcophagus of the mummified king.

One by one the shrines were dismantled and removed carefully from the Burial Chamber. Strangely, it was found that, although each one was beautifully executed, the carpenters who pieced them together had been somewhat sloppy in their handiwork. Each of the panels bore hieroglyphs marking where exactly it should go, but some sections were wrongly placed and there were instances where some of them had been banged into position by a hammer in order to make them fit into the space provided. In contrast, Carter found a number of objects of remarkable workmanship between the shrines, including a golden fan with ostrich feathers that fell to dust on being handled. On one side of its semicircular handle was an image of the king hunting ostriches, while on the other was a hunting scene showing prancing horses as well as bearers carrying away these great birds. The king was shown as well, mounted on a chariot, with the ostrich feathers used to make the fan underneath his right arm.

PARTITION OF OBJECTS
At this same time Carter received notification that the Minister of Public Works intended to suspend work temporarily at the tomb in order that thousands of visitors be allowed entry. In addition to this, the minister wanted to take charge of all undertakings made in connection with the tomb, and pointed out the department's 'right over objects discovered which are as such in the Public Domain.'[2] To Carter, this signalled a fundamental shift in the Egyptian government's attitude over the partition of objects found in the tomb, as agreed with the former director-general of the Antiquities Service, Gaston Maspero, and outlined in the digging concession, first issued in 1915 and renewed annually thereafter. Article 9 of the concession stated that tombs 'which are discovered intact, together with all objects they may contain, shall be handed over to the Museum whole and without division'.[3] Article 10, on the other hand, stated:

In the case of tombs which have already been searched, the Antiquities Service shall, over and above the mummies and sarcophagi intended in Article 8, reserve for themselves all objects of capital importance from the point of view of history and archaeology, and shall share the remainder with the Permittee.[4]

Since the tomb of Tutankhamun had been violated quite clearly in antiquity, Lady Almina expected to receive a generous portion of its treasures. Thus the Egyptian government were now going back on their assurances that this would indeed be the case. As a consequence of this change of attitude towards the division of objects, Carter informed Sir John Maxwell, the executor of Lord Carnarvon's estate, who began preparing a legal case against the Ministry of Public Works. The grave situation also infuriated the Metropolitan Museum of Art, whose staff had been on loan to Carter free of charge since the time of discovery. The museum expected to receive at least some choice objects via Lady Almina when the clearance was complete. As we shall see in Chapter 13, they were eventually to be compensated for their concerted efforts in this area, but in a manner they could never have expected.

It was time to take action, and this took the form of an open letter that praised the scientific work being carried out by Howard Carter and accused the Antiquities Service of jeopardising further work at the tomb with its pettiness, ridiculous demands and inconsequential restrictions. Directed at Pierre Lacau, it was signed by four of the world's most eminent Egyptologists: Percy E Newberry, with the staff of the Egyptian Museum; James Henry Breasted, with the Oriental Institute of Chicago; the renowned philologist Alan H Gardiner; and Albert M Lythgoe, curator of the Egyptian department of the Metropolitan Museum. The probable purpose of this letter was to intimidate Lacau – but it only served to infuriate him still further.

THE KING'S RESTING PLACE

Once the nest of shrines had been removed, Carter was able to see for the first time the entirety of the great sarcophagus. On each of its corners in carved relief were one each of four tutelary goddesses whose outstretched wings offered protection to the king's mortal remains, even in death. Yet some surprises were in store when Carter and his team came to examine the coffer's great lid. First, it was made not of red quartzite, like the sarcophagus, but of rose granite, a very strange combination. Yet Carter recalled, quite correctly, that there had been a similar anomaly when the sarcophagus of the heretic king Akhenaten was discovered in the royal tomb located in a wadi beyond the site of his city at Tell el-Amarna. That too was made of red quartzite with a lid of rose granite.

The second surprise that greeted Carter when he examined the upper surface of the sarcophagus lid was that it had been broken in two and had afterwards been repaired using a gypsum mortar. At first his heart sank as he contemplated the thought that it had been smashed by grave robbers in order to gain access to the nest of mummiform coffins within. Yet this surmise was quickly dashed when he realised that the fracture must have occurred when the lid was lowered into place. One can imagine the consternation of the necropolis officials and priests when suddenly they heard a huge crash and found that the lid had cracked clean in half!

POLITICAL CHANGES

At the time that Carter was busy examining Tutankhamun's sarcophagus, major changes were going on in the outside world. Since the 1880s Egypt had effectively been under a British administration, which meant that, although it was still a province of the Turkish Empire, with its own hereditary khedive, or ruler, it remained under the jurisdiction of Britain. The British had relinquished control of Egypt only in 1922, but the handover was delayed, owing to continued opposition from the pro-nationalist Wafdist party, which ousted the pro-British government in 1923. Not only was the new government anti-British, but it was also against foreign intervention in Egypt's cultural affairs. Indeed, it cared little for Egyptology, and even less for Howard Carter, who had become an international hero by claiming full responsibility for a tomb that was part of Egypt's national heritage. Thus it despised him, and was amenable to any plan of action, however petty, that might make life difficult for the discoverer of Tutankhamun.

On Wednesday 6 February 1924, Carter travelled to Cairo for a meeting with Morcos Bey Hanna, the new Minister of Public Works, scheduled for five o' clock the following afternoon. On entering the offices of the ministry he was informed that the appointment would be delayed for about twenty minutes and was asked to meet with Percy Marmaduke Tottenham (1873–1975) the Undersecretary of State at the Department of Public Works. During their encounter Tottenham dug out a temporary digging concession issued to Howard Carter in 1918, when he had applied to excavate a remote tomb site in a wadi north of the Valley of the Kings. Contrary to the digging concession signed by Carter on behalf of Lord Carnarvon in 1915, this permit contained a modification to Article 9, which effectively cut out the discoverer from sharing in the contents of a royal burial and also redefined the meaning of an 'intact tomb'. It read:

> Tombs of Kings, Princes, Queens, High Priests found intact and all the objects which they contain will be allocated to our Museum. But if it relates to an intact tomb of a private person, it is agreed that the Antiquities Service will give Lord Carnarvon an important object from this tomb.
>
> By the words 'intact tomb' used in the previous authorization and also here, it is agreed that it should not mean a tomb absolutely unviolated, but rather a tomb still containing its furniture in good condition and forming a whole, even if robbers have already entered the tomb to take jewels as in the tomb of the father and mother of Queen Ta'ia [i.e. that of Yuya and Tuya found in 1905].[5]

In bringing this document to Carter's attention, Tottenham seems to have been scraping the bottom of a very deep barrel to find everything and anything that would bring the discoverer of Tutankhamun's tomb to heel. Carter himself saw this as a 'disingenuous attempt on the part of the Department to prejudice the terms of Lord Carnarvon's original concession'.[6] Indeed, he questioned how a temporary permit, issued for an area outside the Valley concession, and one that had become null and void at its termination, could have any impact on the terms of the current licence concerning his work in the Valley of the Kings. Moreover, Carter rightly defended himself by noting that despite the rewriting of Article 9 in the temporary permit issued in 1918, no 'modification or addition was inserted in the Valley Concession, either in the year in which the temporary authorization was issued, or in the subsequent yearly renewals'.[7]

Concerning this issue, Carter certainly appears to have held the moral high ground, but the winds of change were fast coming his way and they were not destined to blow in his favour. In fact, the days of foreigners digging in the Egyptian sands for choice pieces to enrich private or public collections were decidedly numbered.

THE FACE OF TUTANKHAMUN

When the day came finally to raise the sarcophagus lid inside the illuminated Burial Chamber, a party of 24 individuals gathered for the ceremony. The date was Tuesday 12 February 1924, and the time three o'clock in the afternoon. Among those present were the Undersecretary of State at the Ministry of Public Works, Mohamed Pasha Zaghlul; members of the Antiquities Service; the chairman of the Metropolitan Museum, Edward Harkness; and all of Carter's team, including Arthur Merton of *The Times*.

After the giant slab, which weighed a ton and a quarter (approximately 1,270 kilograms), had been lifted just a few centimetres, angle irons were inserted along and underneath its base, thus enabling differential pulleys to raise it without fear that it might fracture once more. Very slowly rope tackle was wrapped around the lid and at the appointed time it began to lift away from the great sarcophagus. As Carter was to record later, although this may have been an insignificant event in the history of the Valley of the Kings, for him and his team it was the culminating point of their careers:

> ... a moment looked forward to ever since it became evident that the chambers discovered, in November, 1922, must be the tomb of Tut.ankh.Amen, and not a cache of his furniture as had been claimed. None of us but felt the solemnity of the occasion, none of us but was affected by the prospect of what we were about to see – the burial custom of a king of ancient Egypt of thirty-three centuries ago.[8]

Slowly the sarcophagus lid rose into the air, and when Carter shone an electric light into the depths of the great stone coffer, what greeted him must have seemed at first disappointing, for all he could see was a covering of fine linen shrouds. After Harry Burton had finished taking photographs, Carter at last began to peel away the linen to find out what lay beneath. The sight he beheld must have sent a shiver down his spine, for there before him was the face of Tutankhamun sculpted in gold upon a gilded mummiform coffin over two metres long, inlaid with faience and coloured glass and decorated with semiprecious stones. It rested upon a bier in the form of a lion, and enveloping either end of this form were the protective goddesses Isis and Neith, while the king's hands were crossed over his breasts holding the crook and flail, his symbols of divinity. Inserted into the forehead were representations of the vulture and cobra goddesses, Nekhbet and Wadjet, protectors of divine sovereignty in the Two Lands, Upper and Lower Egypt respectively. Around these symbols was a simple though touching gesture – a tiny wreath of flowers 'as it pleased us to think, the last farewell offering of the widowed girl queen to her husband, the youthful representative of the "Two Kingdoms" '.[9]

ON STRIKE!

There were handshakes and words of congratulation all round as Howard Carter climbed the sixteen steps back out into the bright afternoon sun. They were a trifle muted, however, as it had been a long tiring day, and before Mohamed Pasha Zaghlul left for Cairo Carter took him aside to discuss a few points regarding the press opening arranged for the following day. Casually, he mentioned that before it commenced he intended showing the wives of his staff the golden coffin, and hoped that this would be acceptable. Zaghlul said that he could not envisage any problems, but would inform the minister just to make sure.

All went well, and after a pleasant night's sleep Carter prepared for a leisurely breakfast in order that he might arrive at the tomb by nine, the time fixed for the excavators' wives to view the golden king. At 6.40 a.m. a messenger arrived with a note from Mohamed Pasha Zaghlul. It was to inform Carter that the Minister of Public Works could not permit the wives of his 'collaborators' to enter the tomb.[10] Utterly incensed by this slap in the face from the Egyptian authorities, Carter stormed off to the tomb clutching the communiqué. There he met up with his colleagues, who were equally outraged. Together they decided on a plan of action. The press conference would be allowed to go ahead, but thereafter they would down tools, lock up the tomb and suspend any work until a suitable agreement had been reached between themselves and the Minister of Public Works.

So this is what happened. With the one-and-a-quarter-ton sarcophagus lid still suspended rather precariously above the golden coffin, Carter and his colleagues locked up the tomb and went on strike. He even posted a notice to this effect on the bulletin board of the Winter Palace Hotel. A very grave situation had arisen, and one that could now only get worse. Later that day Carter was informed that Pierre Lacau, on behalf of the Antiquities Service, had issued a notice to the guards at the tomb not to allow entry to Carter and his collaborators.

Very quickly the whole story appeared beneath banner headlines in newspapers worldwide. *The Times* of London ran a lengthy piece giving Carter every support and severely criticising the Ministry of Public Works for hampering all efforts by Carter and his team to conduct their work in a scientific manner. In contrast, the Egyptian press severely criticised Carter, accusing him of unprofessional behaviour, which was set to endanger the future of Egypt's national treasures.

Two days into the 'strike', Carter, who possessed the only set of keys to the steel gate erected to safeguard the tomb in December 1922, was refused entry by government troops. Adding to his problems still further was the fact that when the topic came up during question time in the Houses of Parliament, the Prime Minister, Ramsay MacDonald (1866–1937), stated unequivocally that no special privileges would be afforded to Carter. Furthermore, he advocated that the matter be dealt with by the appropriate authorities in Egypt.

CONCESSION CANCELLED

Through the actions of the 'strike', the concession for the clearance of the tomb of Tutankhamun now issued in the name of Lady Almina, Countess of Carnarvon, was cancelled, leaving Carter and his colleagues out in the cold. Carter submitted two writs against the Ministry of Public Works and these were eventually heard in Cairo's Mixed Courts, the judge being an American named Pierre Crabites. On advice from the Minister of Public Works, Carter was persuaded by his lawyer FM Maxwell that if he wished for the concession to be reissued he would have to renounce any claim to the treasures of Tutankhamun.

The trial went well until Maxwell accused the government of acting like 'a pack of bandits' when they had taken possession of the tomb. This was received as an insult, since in Arabic 'bandit' means, quite literally, thief, leading the Minister of Public Works to state that he would never again negotiate with Howard Carter. Despite further attempts by individuals like Herbert Winlock of the Metropolitan and James Breasted to quell the situation and find a suitable solution to the problem, nothing was resolved and Carter persistently refused to co-operate with respect to any kind of settlement.

Carter was out of a job, and the most curious fact of all is that, when the Antiquities Service attempted to persuade other Egyptologists to take over the role of director of excavations at the tomb, all those approached refused point-blank. They included Rex Engelbach, who admitted that he was incapable of taking up the role, and Albert Lythgoe, the curator of the Metropolitan Museum, whose archaeologists already formed part of Carter's team. Yet he too refused point-blank, asserting confidently that Carter was the only man for the job.

THE CASE OF THE FORTNUM AND MASON WINE BOX

Since he could do no more at this point, Carter left Egypt on 21 March 1924 and returned to England, via Venice, in order to prepare for a major lecture tour of the United States and Canada, scheduled for the late spring of that year. Yet something then happened that was very damaging to Carter's reputation. On 29 March Pierre Lacau arrived in the Valley of the Kings with orders from the Ministry of Public Works to inspect the various tombs used by Carter and his team and make an inventory of their contents. With four aides, including Rex Engelbach, Lacau broke down the door to tomb No. 4 (formerly the final resting place of Rameses XI), which was being used as a storeroom, and went inside.

Having catalogued various items of furniture and an assortment of objects labelled and packed carefully in crates, ready for transportation to the Egyptian Museum, they moved to the rear of the dusty tomb, where they found a pile of empty cases stamped FORTNUM AND MASON, the well-known London department store. One of them marked RED WINE appeared to contain something, and on opening it Lacau found, wrapped in cotton wool and surgical gauze, a beautiful, elongated, painted wooden head. It was of a boy aged around eight or nine, emerging from a pedestal carved to represent the blue lotus flower. The item was a work of surpassing beauty, and almost certainly it represented the young king. More than this, it was fashioned in a style easily recognisable as Amarna art, intimating that it was a representation of Tutankhamun, or more correctly Tutankhaten, when he was still living with his family at Akhetaten.

Yet something was terribly wrong about the manner in which the head had been found. Not only did it bear no label, but there were no catalogue details to say where or when it had been found. What, then, was it doing, unmarked, in an old Fortnum and Mason packing case?

Lacau, not usually Carter's ally, believed there must be a logical explanation, even though his Egyptian colleagues were already in uproar and demanded that a cable be sent immediately to the Prime Minister. Lacau advised restraint, but despite this the officials went ahead and sent the message. They also made arrangements for the head to be dispatched immediately to Cairo as evidence of the dirty deed. In their opinion Carter, or one of his associates, had intended to smuggle the head out of the country.

So what was going on? Had the head been found in the tomb of Tutankhamun, or did it come from elsewhere? Had Carter been attempting to conserve it using the facilities available to him on site? Had he simply forgotten to catalogue it? Did it belong to him or to someone else, who might have asked Carter to store it on their behalf?

Questions needed answering, and fast. So, at the request of Rex Engelbach and Pierre Lacau, Herbert Winlock of the Metropolitan was asked to cable Carter, now back in England, in the hope that he might throw some light on the subject. His answers were worryingly ambiguous, for he claimed that the head had been retrieved from the debris removed from the Entrance Corridor when it was being cleared in late November 1922. On the point of why it had not been catalogued, Carter stated that all items found were first allotted group numbers before being finally indexed, and so it was awaiting final assessment and handling.

Carter's answers fell short of fully explaining his actions. Already an account of the artefacts found among the debris in the Entrance Corridor had appeared in the first volume of his and Mace's book *The Tomb of Tut.ankh.Amen*, and there was no mention here of the discovery of any head. More damning is the fact that there was no entry for the priceless artefact in Carter's own comprehensive inventory of objects found in the tomb, despite what he claimed. Furthermore, *not one* of his associates involved in the excavations admitted to having any knowledge of the priceless item before its discovery in the Fortnum and Mason packing case.

Even more difficult to justify is why Carter had not brought the head to the attention of the international press, who through *The Times* had been kept informed of any new discoveries. The fact that the object almost certainly came from Amarna and thus firmly linked Tutankhamun's boyhood with Akhenaten's capital was significant in itself, since very little evidence of his presence there had previously come to light. Furthermore, since the head emerges from the sacred blue lotus flower, like the sun god Atum emerging on the primeval mound at the point of First Creation, it intimated that Tutankhamun was destined to become king even before the death of Akhenaten, emphasising his royal lineage.

Finally, there was the simple fact that such an artefact is unlikely to have come from among the debris removed from the Entrance Corridor. The only items retrieved from here were either spoil left by tomb robbers or broken items mixed randomly into the stone debris, before it was recycled as ballast used to fill the passageway. Tomb robbers were after stealing gold, jewellery, unguents, perfumes or any prized item that could be placed into a head scarf and taken out through openings and tunnels just large enough to squeeze their bodies through. There is no way that they were going to steal a painted wooden head of a king, for it would have had no monetary value. In addition to this, as Thomas Hoving has observed regarding the matter,

> It is difficult to believe that the priests who returned twice to put the tomb in order, after the thieves departed, would have left the magical image of the King as Sun God lying on the floor of the passageway and then callously covered it with rubble.[11]

The unlikelihood of Carter's official explanation did not deter Pierre Lacau from accepting it wholesale. In many ways, perhaps he did not want to contemplate the possibility that one of the most celebrated and capable Egyptologists he had ever known was plotting to steal the lotus head. Somehow, Lacau managed to convince the Ministry of Public Works that the story was true, and the matter was dropped. Even so, it left a nasty taste in the mouths of Carter's associates, who were as shocked as anyone to find that their trusted friend and colleague could keep such a major find to himself.

It all begs the question of what the painted lotus head of the boy-king really was doing in a Fortnum and Mason packing case. Did Carter intend to ship it back to England, where it would have joined his own antiquities collection, or was it to be sold to a private collector? On the other hand, had Carter been telling the truth when he claimed that the priceless art treasure was an uncatalogued item found among the debris removed from the Entrance Corridor? For an answer to this awkward dilemma we must return to the article on the tomb and its contents written in 1942 by the British chemist Alfred Lucas, for he realised early on in the day that Carter was quietly removing objects from the tomb of Tutankhamun.

13. TOMB ROBBERS

Whether the breach into the Burial Chamber was open or closed when Howard Carter and Lord Carnarvon first entered the Antechamber was deemed irrelevant by the British chemist Alfred Lucas, since he believed their decision to reseal the hole was in the best interests of the tomb and its treasures. By itself, he concluded in the first of two articles for the *Annales du service des Antiquités*, published in 1942, that the matter seemed 'hardly worth mentioning, but ... another fact ... which *is* of archaeological significance, *depends upon it* [authors' italics].'[1]

That 'fact', so vital to Lucas's assessment of Carter and Carnarvon's activities in connection with the tomb of Tutankhamun, related to the provenance of a certain perfume box found beneath the bier that supported the outermost golden coffin placed in the rose-coloured quartzite sarcophagus.[2] The item in question is in fact a highly ornamental gold and silver receptacle for sacred unguents, some 15 centimetres in height, which Carter listed as having been removed from the tomb during the 1925–6 season.[3] Yet according to Lucas the perfume box could not have been found inside the sarcophagus because:

> I saw it at Mr Carter's house [close to the Valley of the Kings] before the official opening of the burial chamber [on Friday, 16 February 1923], and evidently it was found when Lord Carnarvon and Mr. Carter first penetrated into the burial chamber.[4]

In Lucas' opinion the perfume box was found most probably 'either outside, or inside, the outermost shrine, and I think inside.'[5] Thus it was removed at the same time that Carter et al. slid back the swing doors of the outermost gilded shrine and peered in at the sealed double door of the second shrine. The British chemist went on to add:

> This box and a few other objects, including the alabaster cup [shown as Plate XLVI in the first volume of Carter's trilogy] ... and a few pieces of broken jewellery, which latter were found on the floor of the burial chamber, just inside the hole, were taken to Mr. Carter's house for safety until the workshop had been fitted with a steel gate. They were shown to Mr. Lacau, the Director General of the Antiquities Department, and later they were taken to the workshop, where they remained until they were sent to Cairo.[6]

It is clear, therefore, that Carter and Carnarvon, in the presence of Lady Evelyn and Pecky Callender, decided to remove certain objects from the tomb during their illicit incursion into the Burial Chamber and Treasury at the end of November 1922. Since any knowledge of what awaited discovery within these rooms could not be revealed until the official opening of the Burial Chamber on

Friday 16 February 1923, it must mean that Carter stored these objects at his home until after this date. He then either replaced them carefully to enable their 'discovery', or he simply claimed at some later point that they were found wherever it was convenient for them to have been found, as was the case with the perfume box.

If nothing else, this curious behaviour on the part of Carter was a little unorthodox, if not a trifle dishonest, especially as the Egyptological community has attempted to reconstruct Egyptian funerary practices from evidence presented by this one and only intact royal tomb. Yet the fact that Carter openly admitted to individuals, such as Pierre Lacau of the Antiquities Service, that he had removed objects from the tomb for safekeeping is to his credit. There was always the chance that before a suitable security gate was put in place modern-day thieves could have raided the tomb. Yet, if this was Carter and Carnarvon's concern, why leave behind many objects of equal, or considerably more, value? Why choose only certain artefacts, and leave behind others?

The only answer is to suppose that certain items removed from the tomb by Carter held some personal fascination and were easy to carry. Whatever their motivations, the objects were returned, satisfying the concern of team members such as Alfred Lucas. There the matter might have rested were it not for even more disconcerting irregularities in connection with Carter and Carnarvon's handling of objects thought to have originated from the tomb of Tutankhamun.

THE MISSING TREASURES

It has long been known that Howard Carter and Lord Carnarvon removed certain artefacts from the tomb that never reached the Egyptian Museum, where the rest of the collection of some 3,700 items is housed today. For example, in his notes Howard Carter describes one group of objects withheld for scientific purposes. Seventeen items are listed, and many of these ended up in New York's Metropolitan Museum of Art, via the private collections of either Howard Carter or Lord Carnarvon, built up during their lifetimes (see below).[7]

There were no art treasures among this small scientific collection, simply minor items such as 'a cupful of dried-out embalming fluid; two fragments of gilded wood from the fourth shrine; a piece of crumbling linen from the majestic funerary pall; other linens from a large sack dropped between the outer and second shrines; fragments of matting that covered the floor of the Burial Chamber; and a piece of quartzite from the rose-colored sarcophagus'.[8] Most if not all of these pieces have been on display since their acquisition, even though the Metropolitan has been reluctant to admit their provenance publicly.

The American Egyptologist Thomas Hoving in his book *Tutankhamun – The Untold Story* made a careful study of these, as well as a number of other, Egyptian artefacts and art treasures that have turned up in museums and concluded that they were removed from the tomb of Tutankhamun. He lists so many that it becomes mind-boggling to say the least, but a review of at least some of them is necessary for the purposes of this book. For instance, there are the two silver nails, recorded on catalogue cards found in the archives of the Metropolitan as having come from the second coffin inside the sarcophagus. One derived originally from the Carnarvon collection, while the other came from Howard Carter.[9]

In addition to the silver nails, the Metropolitan have two gold nails from the third coffin, which also came, most probably, from Howard Carter, while a gilded bronze rosette from the pall that covered the second shrine was purchased from Carter directly in 1935.[10] In addition to this, the Metropolitan has in its collection a heavy collar of faience beads thought to have come from the Antechamber,[11] as well as a small bronze puppy of fine beauty and workmanship, its head turned delicately backwards.[12] This too is thought to have come from the floor of the Antechamber, and yet as Hoving admits, 'Considering the thousands of masterpieces from Tutankhamun's tomb that remained in the country in the Egyptian Museum, their unauthorized removal amounts to no more than a minor archaeological indiscretion.'[13]

THE CARNARVON COLLECTION

Unfortunately, the list does not end there. Some three years after the death of Lord Carnarvon in 1923 the executors of his estate, working on behalf of Almina, Countess of Carnarvon, sold off his unique collection of Egyptian antiquities, amassed over a period of around twenty years. Even though it was the staff of the Metropolitan that had formed the backbone of Carter's team, for some reason Carnarvon stipulated in his will that the British Museum be given first refusal of the collection. Nobody could understand this, since they were sure that Carnarvon would have wanted it to go to his American colleagues. So a plan was hatched whereby the solicitor representing the estate walked, unannounced, into the British Museum at ten o'clock one morning and asked them to make an offer. Yet he stipulated that, if they did want to purchase the collection, the museum had until four o'clock that afternoon to come up with the money. Quite obviously, the officials at the museum were not amused and so declined to make an offer, leaving the path open for the Metropolitan to step in and purchase the whole collection for a cool $145,000. At the time this was seen as a huge amount of money to pay (about $14 million in today's terms), although it seems quite obvious that the museum knew very well that among the carefully catalogued items were certain choice pieces that came from the tomb of Tutankhamun.

One item that springs to mind immediately is the ivory statue of a leaping horse. This has a finely painted black mane, brownish skin and raised head, its eyes inset with garnet stones, only one of which remains today. Then there is the beautiful ivory statue of an ariel, or African gazelle, standing on a decorated and painted base. Both of these objects are described in the catalogue compiled by Lord Carnarvon before his death as fine examples of late Eighteenth Dynasty art from the royal workshops of Thebes, which places them firmly in the time frame of Tutankhamun's reign.[14] Such a supposition on Carnarvon's part is supported by the sheer fact that the horse appears in the so-called 'flying leap' pose, one of the more naturalistic styles of art that emerged, briefly, during the Amarna age.

Was this record Carnarvon's cryptic way of saying that they came from the tomb of Tutankhamun? An initially misleading clue is a letter written by Carnarvon to Carter dated Sunday 24 December 1922, just days after the former's return from Egypt in the wake of their clandestine exploration of the Burial Chamber and Treasury. It speaks first of the many dignitaries and politicians who had travelled to Highclere in order to congratulate him. Yet afterwards the letter goes on to say that he had 'put the ariel and horse – *bought* in Cairo – into the wall case. They look very well. I have, after mature examination, decided that they are *early* Eighteenth Dynasty and *must* come from the Saqqareh [authors' italics].'[15]

In view of the fact that Carnarvon catalogued these art treasures as fine examples of late Eighteenth Dynasty workmanship from Thebes, which conform to known Amarna art pieces from this period, it is clear the reference in his letter to the provenance of the artefacts is an 'in' joke between him and Carter. The 'bought in Cairo' statement was simply to cover their tracks, while the allusion to the early Eighteenth Dynasty and 'Saqqareh', the Memphite necropolis south of Cairo, was pure nonsense, since Saqqara was virtually deserted at the beginning of the Eighteenth Dynasty. It is more likely that the ariel and horse were removed from one of the chambers in the tomb before Carnarvon returned to England at the beginning of December 1922.

Other objects that passed from the Carnarvon collection to the Metropolitan included a paint palette, and an ivory writing palette with a pair of reed brushes. The cover over the inset of this latter item bears the inscription, 'The King's Daughter of his Body, his beloved Meritaton, born of the Great Royal Wife Nefernefraton Nefertiti, who lives forever and ever.'[16] Meritaton was the eldest daughter of Akhenaten and Nefertiti, as well as the consort of Smenkhkare and the sister-in-law of Tutankhamun.

Albert Lythgoe of the Metropolitan Museum asked Carter where he thought the palettes had come from, to which he replied 'the tomb of Amenhotep',[17] i.e. Amenhotep III. Yet Carter simply cleared the interior of this well-known tomb, which yielded up very few artefacts, and, anyway, this was back in 1915. Since Lord Carnarvon is said to have acquired these palettes shortly before his death in 1923, they too are more likely to have come from the tomb of Tutankhamun. Other suspect items purchased by the Metropolitan as part of the Carnarvon collection in 1926 include two faience rings bearing Tutankhamun's throne name Nebkheperure, which according to Carter's own notes were found on the floor of the Antechamber.[18]

THE CARTER COLLECTION

Another influx of Tutankhamun-related art treasures came into the possession of the Metropolitan Museum after it secured a substantial part of Howard Carter's collection of Egyptian antiquities a year after his death in 1939. Among them were two ivory cosmetic boxes, carved into the likeness of ducks with their necks curled backwards over their left shoulder. Both bear a striking similarity both to Amarna art and items from the tomb of Tutankhamun, including the distinctive decoration on a pair of boxes found in the Annexe.

Then there is the alabaster perfume vase around 7.5 centimetres in height with appliqués in blue and purple glass, gold leaf, carnelian and obsidian. It shows a finely executed maiden upon a lotus flower, similar in style to post-Amarna art. The item is recorded by the museum as having come, most probably, from Tutankhamun's tomb.[19] Another item purchased by them from the Howard Carter estate in 1940 is a running hound in ivory with a movable jaw and collar. Executed no doubt as a toy, this precious object quite conceivably came from the tomb.[20]

Also in the Metropolitan's Egyptian collection is a gold ring bearing the cartouche of Tutankhamun, acquired in December 1922 by its chairman, Edward Harkness. An index card examined by Thomas Hoving suggests that before purchase this priceless item had been floating around the Cairo antiquities market since 1915.[21] Yet the sheer fact that it appears out of nowhere just days following Carter and Carnarvon's first entry into the Antechamber and Burial Chamber led Hoving to conclude: 'No doubt the ring had been given to Harkness by either Lord Carnarvon or Howard Carter as a superb token of their discovery'.[22]

Various items originally from Carter's collection, and thought to have come from the tomb of Tutankhamun, have found their way into other museums as well. For instance, there is the fabulous bronze panther with rock-crystal eyes in the Cincinnati Museum of Art and the black haematite cat in the Cleveland Museum of Art.[23]

In addition to these objects, there are the three rectangular gold sequins, each with stamped double cartouches bearing the names Ankhkheperure and Nefernefruaten, i.e. Smenkhkare, housed at the Nelson-Atkins Museum of Art at the University of Missouri, Kansas City. It has been argued academically, and is accepted by the museum, that these items came from the tomb of Tutankhamun and match almost exactly 47 other sequins found on a linen garment discovered in the Antechamber.[24] These also bear the name Nefernefruaten, although in a slightly altered form. A more or less identical gold sequin bearing the same name is to be found in the Royal Scottish Museum in Edinburgh.[25]

Then there are the various unique items in the possession of the Brooklyn Museum. They include a broad collar of faience beads, like the one purchased by the Metropolitan directly from Howard Carter in 1935; a small vase in blue glass; a carved statue of a naked girl in ivory; and an ivory spoon. A grasshopper in fine ivory on loan to the Brooklyn since 1947 is also thought to have originated from the tomb. It belongs to the Guennol Collection, which purchased it from the Howard Carter Estate.[26] All of these items conform very well with the artistic style prevalent at the end of the Amarna age, and there seems no doubt where they came from, something that was accepted by the Brooklyn's former curator of Egyptian antiquities, John Cooney.[27]

THE HANDS OF THIEVES
When Howard Carter came to compare the treasures contained in the many boxes and caskets found in the Treasury with inventory dockets written at the

time of the funeral, he concluded that some 60 per cent of the jewellery and precious-metal vessels originally interred in the room were in fact absent.[28] Yet had ancient tomb robbers taken these missing items or did Carnarvon, Carter and Lady Evelyn pocket at least some of them when they explored the Burial Chamber and Treasury at the end of November 1922? An answer to this question may lie in a comparison between the chaos found in the Antechamber and Annexe and the relative order observed in the Burial Chamber and Treasury, where it is clear that tomb robbers seem to have spent very little time.

In volume one of *The Tomb of Tut.ankh.Amen*, Carter and Mace recorded that the Antechamber and Annexe had suffered greatly from the actions of ancient plunderers. Both rooms, particularly the Annexe, were found in a state of complete chaos and disorder brought about by the frantic actions of the robbers in their hurried search by the dim light of an oil lamp for items of value. Boxes had been opened and their contents flung out in their search for gold and precious jewels. Afterwards the priests of the royal necropolis had hurriedly tidied up the Antechamber, not even bothering to place the correct items into their respective containers, while the Annexe was left in a complete jumble with overturned boxes, furniture and pots everywhere.

As anyone who has suffered a burglary will know, the chaos and disorder left behind by the hands of thieves is a hallmark of their trade. So why then should the two other rooms, the Burial Chamber and Treasury, not have suffered the fate that befell the Antechamber and Annexe? Hardly anything in either of the final two chambers had been touched or moved and nothing was broken. Despite this, Carter was adamant that tomb robbers did manage to penetrate as far as the Treasury:

> Unquestionably the thieves had entered this little room, but in their predatory quest they seem to have done little further harm than to open and rifle the treasure caskets and some boxes. Some beads and tiny fragments of jewellery scattered on the floor, the broken seals and displaced lids of caskets, folds of linen hanging from the mouths of the boxes, and here and there an overturned object, were the only evidence at first sight of their visit.[29]

In recalling the turmoil found in the Antechamber and Annexe, one has seriously to question Carter's version of events. Given that both Carter and Carnarvon are known to have removed objects from the tomb, and given also Carter's economy with the truth, it does not take a leap of faith to imagine that it was they themselves who opened the caskets and pocketed certain pieces of jewellery, leaving behind clues that they could later claim were evidence of plunderers. After all, where exactly in the tomb did those gold and faience rings come from that were inherited by Carter's niece, Phyllis Walker, upon his death (see below)?

There can be no doubt robbers in antiquity cut a hole through to the Burial Chamber from the Antechamber. Yet the careful way in which the inner chambers were treated, almost respectfully, is not the hallmark of ancient thieves, and so it seems more likely that those responsible were discovered around the time that the breach was made. Furthermore, there is ample evidence to support these bold assertions.

On the floor, in the narrow space between the outermost gilded shrine and the wall of the Burial Chamber, the ancient Egyptian priests placed a variety of funerary objects. In both corners of the east wall they had left a number of jars, as well as a pole-like Anubis standard, still positioned upright, and other ritual objects. On the floor of the north wall eleven sacred paddles had been carefully placed to assist the pharaoh in his journey to the afterlife. Against the east wall other objects were discovered, including two beautiful and delicate calcite lamps, two boxes made of reed and papyrus, a wooden goose and a wine jar (see Figure 9).

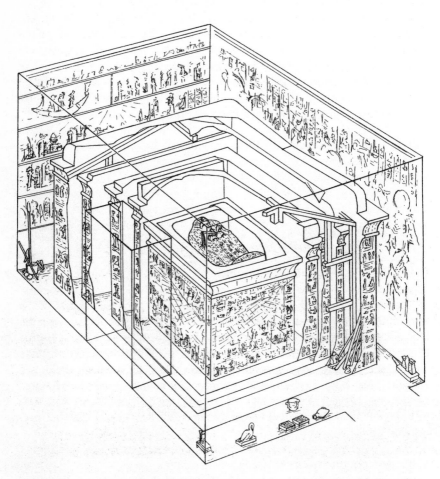

Fig. 9. Cutaway of Tutankhamun's burial chamber (after Nicholas Reeves). Note the careful positioning of objects on floor.

Any ancient tomb robbers entering the Burial Chamber would have had to navigate the narrow gap between the outer shrine and the chamber wall if they were to enter the Treasury. The shortest route would be for the robber to turn to his right, or east, upon entry, thus forcing him to move past the delicate alabaster lamps and papyrus and reed boxes. But none of these objects, when examined in February 1923, showed any sign of having been kicked over, broken or, in the case of the lamps, chipped even. The same thing can also be said of the other objects on the floor of the west and north walls.

Are we expected to believe that tomb robbers, in their haste to grab precious items, gently tiptoed around the Burial Chamber in the semidarkness, with only a tiny flame to light their way, without breaking or displacing any of the objects? Did they go on to enter the Treasury, where they carefully opened a few caskets and boxes, selecting a few choice items, before gently tiptoeing back through the Burial Chamber to make their exit? It seems highly unlikely.

If it was Carter, Carnarvon and perhaps Lady Evelyn too, and not ancient tomb robbers, who pocketed at least some part of the missing 60 per cent of jewellery and precious metal vessels removed from the Treasury, then there are undoubtedly small objects from the tomb still to be identified. Some of these are likely to be in the possession of families or individuals to whom they were bequeathed long ago. One such false inheritance came to light shortly after Howard Carter joined Tutankhamun in the afterlife.

THE CASE OF PHYLLIS WALKER

On Carter's death in 1939, it was found that among the possessions he had bequeathed to his niece Phyllis Walker were five rings in gold and faience. When she realised that they bore the royal cartouche of Tutankhamun, she was 'horrified' and arranged for them to be handed over to Egypt's King Farouk.[30] These precious items joined Farouk's personal collection, which already included a gold buckle, or epaulet, showing the young king Tutankhamun in his chariot, which had almost certainly been given by Carnarvon to Farouk's father, King Fuad. All of these treasures were presented to the Egyptian Museum shortly before Farouk's abdication in 1952.[31]

That Carter's own collection of Egyptian antiquities contained various items that came out of the tomb is echoed very well by Christopher C Lee, the biographer of Arthur C Mace, Carter's assistant and co-author on the first volume of *The Tomb of Tut.ankh.Amen*, who died in 1928. Writing in 1992, Lee recounts a visit made by Mace's widow Winifred and their daughter, Margaret Orr, to see Howard Carter at his London home. According to Lee, 'Margaret still remembers her mother leaving in a very angry mood saying "he should not have those things" '.[32] By 'those things' Lee leaves us in no doubt that she was referring to priceless antiquities which came originally from the tomb of Tutankhamun.

THE CASE OF RICHARD BETHELL

Finally, we come to the comments made by Count Louis Hamon, the fortune-teller and palmist who went under the name of 'Cheiro'. In his autobiographical work *Real Life Stories*, published in 1934, he relates how, after he had passed on a psychic message warning Lord Carnarvon not to remove any objects from the tomb, he ignored his advice and 'took numerous relics out of the tomb and sent them on to England. He would probably have taken still more if the Egyptian government had not interfered'.[33]

If Hamon was correct in this respect, then his knowledge of Carnarvon's indiscretions are the earliest on record. What seems more pertinent here, though, is that his book was published when Carter was still alive. Yet there is no doubt that the distinguished excavator of Tutankhamun's tomb would have been able simply to brush off these accusations as the ravings of a madman who fooled people into thinking he had the mummified hand of Princess Meketaten!

Yet Hamon was no lunatic; indeed, he was far from it. By all accounts he was an astute, intelligent and extremely charismatic man with a deep interest in spirituality and the occult. Furthermore, he was very well connected in society circles, and it is clear that he not only knew Lord Carnarvon, but also his private secretary, the Hon. Richard Bethell, and his father, the third Lord Westbury. Both of these men were eventually to die under somewhat unusual circumstances, yet Hamon tells us that, shortly after the official opening of the Burial Chamber in February 1923, Lord Westbury voiced his anxiety over the recent actions of his son. According to Hamon, the elderly peer revealed:

> My son Richard, has brought back with him many relics and mementoes from Tut-Ankh-Amen's Tomb. He has them in his house. Do you think these things will bring him harm?[34]

This, once again, is a quite extraordinary statement. Lord Westbury is concerned here for the wellbeing of his son, who has just returned from Egypt with 'many relics and mementoes' from the tomb. Exactly what 'relics and mementoes' does this imply? We can only assume that this meeting between Westbury and Hamon took place after the death of Lord Carnarvon in April 1923. Thus the former's concern would appear to have been born more out of superstitious fear than the pure legality of the situation. That Westbury was a firm believer in the curse of Tutankhamun is not in doubt. Following the death of his 46-year-old son, who was found dead at the fashionable Bath Club on 15 November 1929,[35] it is recorded that the 78-year-old peer was frequently heard to mutter the words, 'the curse of the Pharaohs' in connection with his son's unfortunate death.[36]

Yet, when he approached Hamon in 1923, he could never have realised the tragedies in store for the family. Despite this, the world-renowned fortune-teller offered scant comfort to Lord Westbury. He simply agreed that it was dangerous for the items to be left in a private house, and suggested that they be sent to the Department of Egyptian and Assyrian Antiquities at the British Museum.

The matter, however, does not end here, for according to Hamon years later he was invited to Bethell's home at Manchester Square in London's fashionable West End where, he claimed, 'on nearly every wall were some of the relics of

Tut-Ankh-Amen's tomb just as Lord Westbury had described'.[37] Apparently, a close friend of Hamon's had rented Bethell's house, which was deemed one of the finest of its kind in the capital's aristocratic quarter. Yet in the months that followed this man suffered a series of disasters, which Hamon obviously put down to the presence of the relics in the house. Upon Bethell and his wife's return we are told that a number of strange occurrences took place in his home, including knocks and bangs, and even strange fires. After these had persisted for a while, the arsonist was found to be a trusted servant, who was duly arrested. Bizarrely, he stated in his defence that the relics from the tomb had 'got on his nerves' and thus he felt that he should 'burn down the place so as to get rid of them'.[38] Reference is made to the mysterious fires and the fact that Bethell's house 'was stocked with treasures brought from the Valley of the Kings' in an account of his death which appeared in the *Daily Mail* on 16 November 1929.[39]

The authors ask the reader to put aside the nature of these peculiar occurrences and ponder more on the accuracy of Hamon's statements regarding the 'relics' supposedly removed from the tomb. As previously mentioned, the fortune-teller, although somewhat negligent with historical facts in his books here and there, held a fond passion for Egypt's Amarna period, and would surely have been able to recognise artefacts dating from the reign of Tutankhamun. Thus we must assume that not only Lord Carnarvon but also his personal secretary was known among the social circles of London to have spirited out art treasures from the tomb of the boy-king.

As mentioned in Chapter 10, Lord Westbury's death followed just three months after that of his son, Richard. Unable to get over his unexpected death, the elderly peer leaped from the balcony of his seventh-storey apartment in St James' Court, West London. He plummeted on to a glass veranda, severing his neck and finally dying on impact with the pavement.[40] A suicide note read, 'I cannot stand any more horrors', which the *Daily Express* at the time said alluded to the 'age-old curse of the Egyptians' which had troubled him since the death of his son the previous November.[41] There is little question that the 'horrors' he was referring to related to the continuous round of disasters that had befallen the family since the official opening of Tutankhamun's tomb. There is no question that Lord Westbury's suicide was connected with the curse of the Pharaohs, but in this instance it really was one of his own making.

FATE OF THE LOTUS HEAD

We come now to the fate of the lotus head of the boy-king discovered by Pierre Lacau in a Fortnum and Mason packing case after Carter stopped work at the tomb in early 1924. What can we say about this item in the light of the damning evidence against both Carter and Carnarvon? Carter claimed that it was found among the debris that filled the tomb's Entrance Corridor. He said it was still to be properly catalogued, even though a full account of the objects found in the passageway had been published in the first volume of his book *The Tomb of Tut.ankh.Amen*. The case of the perfume box seen by Alfred Lucas on Carter's desk before the official opening of the Burial Chamber makes it clear that Carter misled, quite deliberately, his Egyptological associates with regard to the circumstances surrounding the discovery of this and, we must presume, other items as well. Moreover, the fact that a selection of objects from the tomb ended up in both Carter and Carnarvon's private collections suggests very strongly that the lotus head was destined for the same fate.

SUITABLE REMUNERATION

Cited within these pages are examples of professional misconduct on the part of Howard Carter and Lord Carnarvon. They stand accused of removing, without permission, a substantial number of art treasures from the tomb of Tutankhamun and spiriting them out of Egypt for their own purposes. So what exactly were their motivations behind this selfish, and somewhat illegal, activity?

The answer probably lies not simply in their desire to possess that which was immensely appealing to them, and thus irresistible, but also in the archaeological climate in Egypt. Antiquities were being stolen by local people from tombs and cemeteries all over the country and then sold to wealthy European and American collectors and museums, often via Egyptologists who would act as go-betweens. It was happening all the time, and there is no question that Carter and Carnarvon became caught up in this lucrative market.[42]

In addition to the trade in antiquities, another motivation behind Carter and Carnarvon's actions is likely to have been a mixture of bitterness and resentment aimed at the Antiquities Service, and through them the Egyptian government. There had been Anglo-French rivalry for many years, and this had led Carter to despise the organisation to such a degree that he came to believe that its members were out to make life difficult for him. The Egyptian government, on the other hand, were seen by Carter in particular as selfish and corrupt, and no better than the villagers of Qurna who made their living selling stolen antiquities.

Add to this the terms and conditions of the concession, which made it uncertain whether Lord Carnarvon would ever receive his share of the treasures from the tomb (as was proved correct in 1924), and the reasons behind his and Carter's removal of objects from the tomb become a little clearer. Rightly or wrongly, it was their way of ensuring that they gained suitable, and immediate, remuneration for the many years of hard work spent in the pursuit and eventual discovery of Egypt's only intact royal burial. In other words, they felt that they could help themselves to a few choice objects from the tomb for services rendered to Egypt and the world as a whole. And who are we to judge the actions of two people who did so much for Egyptology by revealing one of the greatest archaeological treasures ever found.

WEIGALL'S WARNING

Curiously enough, it does appear as if rumours regarding Carter and Carnarvon's nefarious activities inside the tomb did leak out. Both their unauthorised entry into the Antechamber on Sunday 26 November 1922, and the fact that they were in a position to remove objects illegally, came to the notice of the British Egyptologist Arthur Weigall (1880–1934). He had worked previously alongside

Carter, but in early 1923 was employed by the *Daily Mail* as their special Egyptological correspondent in Luxor, making daily news bulletins on the progress inside the tomb. Incensed by the exclusivity deal Lord Carnarvon had struck with *The Times*, Weigall had written to Carter from the Winter Palace Hotel, Luxor, on Thursday 25 January 1923, in an attempt to persuade him to defuse the mounting resentment being hurled against him and Lord Carnarvon in the international press. At one point in the lengthy letter – sent with genuine concern from one Egyptologist to another – Weigall stated, quite bluntly:

> The situation is this. You and Lord Carnarvon made the initial error when you discovered the tomb of thinking that the old British prestige in this country is still maintained and that you could do more or less what you liked, just as we all used to do in the old days. You have found this tomb, however, at a moment when the least spark may send the whole magazine sky-high, when the utmost diplomacy is needed, when Egyptians have to be considered in a way to which you and I are not accustomed, and when the slightest false step may do the utmost disservice to our own country. You opened the tomb before you notified the Government representative, and the natives all say that you may therefore have had the opportunity of stealing some of the millions of pounds' worth of gold of which you talked. (I give this as an instance of native gossip about you.)[43]

Pulling no punches, Weigall had hit the nail on the head. Carter and Carnarvon could not simply go around doing exactly what they pleased any more. The situation had changed in Egypt, and they needed to respect that fact as much as any other visitor to the country. Since Weigall had himself dealt in antiquities for some years, he realised easily what was going on. His letter to Carter was necessarily diplomatic. Yet reading between the lines it is clear that Carter and Carnarvon's exploits inside the tomb were spreading among the local Egyptian population, who will have heard stories from the guards working alongside Carter at the tomb. It is likely that Weigall got to hear of these rumours and wanted to alert Carter and Carnarvon to this fact in the knowledge that if the matter became more widely known it would lead to an unprecedented uproar that could only result in the closure of the tomb. All the letter achieved, however, was to alienate Weigall still further from Carter and Carnarvon's camp.[44]

It has been with some regret that the authors have felt it necessary to highlight the more shadowy elements behind the discovery of the tomb of Tutankhamun. Digging up such disquieting material will merely serve to tarnish still further the already fragile reputations of Howard Carter and the fifth Earl of Carnarvon. Yet it was felt that an investigation into the two men's more covert activities in connection with the tomb and its treasures was essential if the reader is to understand their connection with what Perry Mason would call 'the case of the missing papyri'.

14. A SCANDALOUS ACCOUNT

It was the spring of 1924, and all was lost to Carter. He had ordered his colleagues to down tools in protest at the way they were being treated by the Ministry of Public Works and the Antiquities Service, and the fact that his colleagues' wives had been denied entry into the tomb of Tutankhamun. The concession issued to Almina, Countess of Carnarvon, had been revoked and a fierce court battle to reverse this decision had ended in mayhem. At Luxor, hordes of invited dignitaries, as well as their families, friends and indeed anyone who knew someone in a position of power, were being allowed admittance into the tomb without even the slightest care for the hundreds of objects still *in situ*. Antiquities already removed to the 'laboratory' were simply left where they stood, unattended and without any process of preservation being carried out on them. As far as Carter was concerned no one seemed to give a damn about the whole sordid business.

Carter came to believe that there was only one recourse left open to him: to seek the assistance of the British Consulate at the Residency in Cairo. He considered that the High Consul and the other British diplomats posted there were in a position to apply pressure on the Zaghlul regime in order to get the Antiquities Service to issue a new concession to Lady Carnarvon. Previously, Egypt's High Commissioner, General Allenby, had offered his support for Carter's cause and had even given the impression that he backed in full his struggle against governmental interference.

Yet now Allenby was conveniently unobtainable, and so, before his departure for England via Venice on 21 March, Carter decided that he would pay the British Consulate a visit in order to determine exactly what the position was with regard to his claims of unfair dismissal. With his temper frayed, Carter was in no mood for quiet discussions: he wanted the consulate's full support forthwith and nothing less would do.

Inside the Residency, Carter was led into the office of an official,[1] where he began sounding off his grievances, fully expecting him to sympathise with his predicament and offer some means of resolving the problem. Although the British official did indeed sympathise with Mr Carter, he also made it clear that the consulate could do nothing to influence the decisions of the Egyptian government and the Antiquities Service. It was simply beyond British jurisdiction.

Carter, never the best tempered of men, was incensed by this attitude and flew into a rage. Heated words were exchanged. Carter spoke of the total inadequacy of the department and the imbecility of its staff before exclaiming that:

... unless he received complete satisfaction and justice, he would publish for the whole world to read the documents that he found in the tomb giving the true account according to the Egyptian Government[2] of the exodus of the Jews from Egypt.[3]

Realising the potential damage that such revelations might have on the delicate situation existing between Britain and Egypt, and being aware also of the growing Arab hostility towards the establishment of a Jewish homeland in Palestine, the British official lost his temper. Without thinking, he forsook his code of diplomacy and let fly at Carter a half-full inkwell that stood on his desk. Carter ducked just in the nick of time to avoid injury, leaving the projectile to bounce wildly off the wall – the resulting mess making it necessary for the whole room to be redecorated. Eventually, both men calmed down 'and an adjustment was made so that Carter was silenced and the threat never materialised'.[4]

KEEDICK LECTURE BUREAU
We know that the explosive exchange between Carter and a British official in Cairo actually took place because it is recorded in the memoirs of Lee Keedick, president of the Keedick Lecture Bureau. It was his company that organised Carter's immensely successful lecture tour of the United States and Canada, which commenced at New York's prestigious Carnegie Hall on 23 April 1924. Carter's presentations, supported by a total of 358 black-and-white glass slides taken by Harry Burton, was an instant success both with the audience and the critics.

Off stage, Carter struck up a friendly acquaintance with Lee Keedick and it was probably during one of their long conversations as the pair travelled by train from one city to another that details of the incident in Cairo were revealed. Exactly why Carter decided to make known his actions to Keedick, a man of business with probably little interest in the fields of politics and Egyptology, will doubtless remain a mystery. Yet for Carter these events were still fresh in his mind, having happened only a few weeks earlier[5] and, it would seem, were something he needed to talk about, at least in private. What is more peculiar, however, is the threat he made to 'publish for the whole world to read the documents that he found in the tomb giving the true account according to the Egyptian Government of the exodus of the Jews from Egypt'. What exactly did this mean, and why should Carter have felt that threatening the British official in the manner described would persuade him to support his cause for a fair deal?

The most likely explanation, if one simply wishes to dismiss the whole affair, is that it was merely an idle threat or a bluff meant to shock British diplomats in Cairo to support his cause. This certainly seems to be the conclusion drawn by Thomas Hoving in his book *Tutankhamun – The Untold Story* who wrote:

Carter had, of course, found no papyri or ancient documents of any sort in the tomb, much less documents of a sensitive political nature. The only explanation for his bizarre threat is that, angered beyond toleration by all that had happened to him, he wanted, perversely, to outrage the British vice-consul.[6]

Hoving's conclusions regarding Carter's outburst are certainly reasonable, yet they are not the only ones that can be reached. The existence of the papyri can be neither proved or disproved, yet it is clear that both Carnarvon and Carter did state that they had found papyrus documents in the tomb.

MISSING PAPYRI

Ever since the opening of the tomb in November 1922, Tutankhamun's 'missing' papyri have been the subject of both rumour and speculation by newspapermen and historical writers. As we saw in Chapters 6 and 7, on Tuesday 28 November 1922, Lord Carnarvon dispatched a letter to his friend and colleague the philologist Alan H Gardiner describing the contents of the tomb. If we look again at what it said, we can see that it refers quite specifically to the discovery of papyri:

> The find is extraordinary. It is a cache and has been plundered to a certain extent but even the ancients could not completely destroy it. After some slight plundering the inspectors shut it again. So far it is Tutankhamon – beds, boxes and every conceivable thing. There is *a box with a few papyri in* – the throne of the King the most marvellous inlaid chair you ever saw... [authors' italics][7]

The discovery of papyri is alluded to in another letter written by Carnarvon in connection with the opening of the tomb, this time to Sir Edgar A Wallis Budge, the Keeper of Egyptian and Assyrian Antiquities at the British Museum. On Friday 1 December 1922, he wrote:

> One line just to tell you that we have found the most remarkable 'find' that has ever been made, I expect, in Egypt or elsewhere. I have only so far got into two chambers [perhaps a little short of the truth here], but there is enough in them to fill most of your rooms at the B.M. (upstairs); and there is a sealed door where goodness knows what there is. I have not opened the [innumerable] boxes, and don't know what is in them; *but there are some papyrus letters*, faïence, jewellery, bouquets, candles on ankh candlesticks. All this is in [the] front chamber, besides lots of stuff you can't see [authors' italics].[8]

The letter is quoted in full in Budge's 1923 book *Tutânkhamen: Amenism, Atenism and Egyptian Monotheism*, although there is no mention in the text of the nature of these so-called 'papyrus letters'.

NEWSPAPER ACCOUNTS

Yet it was not only in private correspondence that the existence of the papyri was revealed. Arthur Merton's bulletins were dispatched each day from Luxor and in one of these he brought to the public's attention the discovery of the papyri. His initial announcement of the discovery of the tomb was published on Wednesday 29 November 1922, and this was followed a day later with a more detailed account of the contents of the Antechamber. Various items are noted, including exquisite alabaster vases, some blue faience pieces, provisions for the dead and 'some remarkable wreaths, still looking evergreen'. Yet then, directly after this entry, he states that 'one of the boxes contained rolls of papyri which are expected to render a mass of information.'[9]

First-hand knowledge of this kind could have come only from Carnarvon, whose responsibility it was to deal with the release of press information. It could be argued that perhaps Carnarvon was mistaken in his assessment of the treasures initially noted in the tomb. Yet Carter, an experienced Egyptologist who had seen many papyri during his time in Egypt, seems not to have corrected him on this supposed error. Indeed, even as late as Sunday 17 December 1922, Carnarvon was still claiming that they had discovered papyri in the tomb. On his way back to England the fifth earl was interviewed by a *Times* special correspondent at the French port of Marseilles where he is quoted as saying:

> One of the boxes contains rolls of *papyri* which may be expected to shed much light on the history of the period, and other *papyri* may be discovered in other of the boxes which have yet to be examined.[10]

Clearly, he was convinced that he and Carter had found papyri in the tomb and would, no doubt, have discussed this matter with Alan Gardiner on his return to England. Indeed, there is some evidence that Gardiner was cabled by Carter in the hope that he would agree to undertake 'the philological work in connection with the papyrus find in the antechamber to the tomb'.[11] Thus, initially at least, Carter would seem to have shared his patron's belief in the existence of the papyri, for it was not until after the fifth earl's death and the publication of the first volume of *The Tomb of Tut.ankh.Amen* that he claimed that there had been a misidentification (see below).

ALAN GARDINER

Gardiner would probably have responded favourably to Carter's request for help on the papyri, as he had already been tipped off regarding the contents of the tomb in a letter written to him by Carnarvon on Tuesday 28 November. He would also have read the report on the discovery of the papyri in *The Times* on Friday 1 December, and so would not have been in any doubt as to their existence. Such was the speculation surrounding the contents of the tomb that Gardiner was asked by the newspaper to comment on the significance of the find, including, of course, the alleged papyri. His views, published in *The Times* on Monday 4 December, are very revealing indeed:

> My own predilections lead me to be particularly interested in the box of papyri which has been found. It is possible – it is even probable – that this papyri will turn out to be no more than 'Books of the Dead,' as they are called, such as were buried with practically every king and person of note, and which consisted of incantations ensuring the dead king's welfare in the other world. On the other hand, these documents may throw some light on the change from the religion of the heretics [i.e. the Amarna kings] back to the old traditional religion, and that would be exceedingly interesting. We have one lengthy document, the longest known, which

was found in the tomb of Rameses III., and is known as Papyrus Harris. This document is in the British Museum, and relates to the benefits which Rameses III. had conferred upon the different gods of Egypt. It is possible that we may find in this tomb something of the same kind, with sidelights on the troubled times that had gone just before.[12]

After such a huge build-up concerning the likely significance, or not, of these papyri, nothing more was said on the matter. Although Gardiner did join the team to undertake philological duties, we are told that these only included making translations of inscriptions found on the walls of the Burial Chamber and on individual items, such as the great gilded shrines and mummiform coffins.

BOX NO. 101

Obviously, rumours began to circulate regarding the missing papyri, for it would seem that Carter was compelled finally to say something about the matter. In the preface to the first volume of The Tomb of Tut.ankh.Amen, co-written with Arthur C Mace and published in late 1923, he refers to the initial entry into the Antechamber and the alleged discovery of papyri in the following manner:

When, by the dim light of a candle, we made the first cursory examination of the Antechamber, we thought that one of the caskets (No. 101) contained rolls of papyri. But, later, under the rays of a powerful electric light, these proved to be rolls of linen [seemingly loincloths], which had even then some resemblance to rolls of papyri.[13]

Thus the mystery was solved. He goes on to outline the team's frustration in this respect:

This was naturally disappointing, and gave rise to the suggestion that the historical harvest, compared with the artistic value of our discovery, will be unimportant because of the lack of literary evidence concerning King Tut.ankh.Amen and the political confusion of his time.[14]

It would be easy to accept that Carter and Carnarvon made a genuine mistake when they explored the contents of the Antechamber for the first time. We can imagine them holding up a flickering candle and attempting to identify whatever they could without actually touching a thing. We can understand too their disappointment when during the clearing of the room of its treasures between December 1922 and January 1923, the presumed 'papyri' turned out to be nothing more than King Tut's underpants! There would have been such a great embarrassment among Carter's team, especially in the wake of Gardiner's speculation in The Times as to the probable contents of the papyri.

Yet can we believe Carter's word on the matter? The answer to this question is yes: we should be able to believe his word. Yet we know that he deliberately misled the world regarding his and Carnarvon's first entry into the tomb. We know too that both Carter and Carnarvon were illegally removing valuable art treasures from the tomb.

In addition to this, Carter's explanation for mistaking rolls of linen for papyri is inadequate. He tells us that the contents of Box No. 101 were illuminated only by flickering candlelight. Yet we know that, from the very first occasion he, Carnarvon, Lady Evelyn and Callender entered the tomb on Sunday, 26 November 1922, an electricity cable was channelled through from the nearby tomb of Rameses VI in order to illuminate the room fully. This is confirmed in Carnarvon's unpublished account of the party's first entry into the tomb preserved in the British Library:

> Luckily just above us lies the large tomb of Ramesses 6. This is a favourite tourist tomb, & is lit by electric light. Having tapped the wire & enlarged the opening we were able to enter & examine what proved to be the first chamber.[15]

So there was no excuse from the outset of investigations inside the tomb for simple mistakes such as confusing rolls of papyri with linen garments, apparently triangular loincloths. Furthermore, it would seem that other authors, writing on the subject of Tutankhamun, have had reason to doubt the absence of papyrus documents in Tutankhamun's tomb. For instance, the British Egyptologist Nicholas Reeves has been fascinated by the idea of papyri being found in the tomb of Tutankhamun and actually wrote a paper on the subject.[16] He pointed out that at the time of the tomb's discovery there was 'the prospect of a rich harvest of papyri' and that they were likely to be found in still sealed coffers or, indeed, inside the sarcophagus. Yet as he himself admitted, 'Apart from a single, badly decayed "ritual" recovered from the mummy itself, however, no papyri were found: in the tomb of Tutankhamûn, this particular class of inscriptional material was notable only by its absence.'[17] The reason for this absence which, he said, was quite remarkable in itself, considering the number of inscriptions in other places, could be because 'Carter and his contemporaries had simply misdirected their search'.[18]

Reeves drew attention to the fact that rolled papyri had been secreted inside wooden funerary statues, like the ones recorded as having been found in the tomb of Seti I by the Italian adventurer Giovanni Belzoni in 1817. These examples were described as 'standing erect, four feet [1.22 metres] high, with a circular hollow inside, as if to contain a roll of papyrus, which I have no doubt they did'.[19] Yet Reeves notes also that a statue found by the traveller and archaeologist Henry Salt (c.1797–1873) 'in the King's Tomb, on the Hill to the left, on going up the Valley', possibly that of Rameses IX, has been noted as having a similar function. This representation of an underworld deity, who grasps its beard with both hands and has 'its upper torso turned at ninety degrees to its legs'[20], has a hole 'hollowed out to hold papyrus'.[21] In addition to these examples, a full-sized 'guardian' statue in the British Museum has a recess beneath its triangular kilt almost certainly to hold a rolled document.[22]

Suspicions regarding the purpose of these hollow cavities was confirmed when in 1898 the tomb of Amenhotep II yielded up a small wooden statuette in which was a rolled-up funerary papyrus containing a version of the Book of Caverns, one of the so-called Books of the Dead.[23] The idea would seem to have pre-empted the use of actual containers in which papyri could be concealed.[24]

THE AMHERST PAPYRUS

Perhaps the most important example of a concealed papyrus being found inside a statue is the so-called Amherst Papyrus, which dates to Year 16 of the reign of Rameses IX, c. 1134–1117 BC. It details the trial of ancient tomb robbers who plundered the tomb of a king who reigned during the Seventeenth Dynasty of Egyptian history, c. 1600 BC. One half of this document belonged to the extensive collection of Egyptian antiquities owned by the Amherst family of Didlington Hall in Norfolk, and it was only in 1935 that the other half popped out of a wooden funerary statuette in the Musées Royaux d'Art et d'Histoire in Brussels.[25]

It does not take much imagination to see where Nicholas Reeves was going with his research into this subject. As we have noted, on either side of the sealed doorway into Tutankhamun's Burial Chamber stood a life-sized guardian figure in black and gilt holding a mace in one hand and a pole-like wand in the other. At Carter's insistence they remained in situ until long after the clearance of the Antechamber, although exactly why is unclear. Yet it could be suggested that Carter left them in place so that other members of his team did not examine the underside of their kilts too closely, for, if Carter had tampered with the statues in search of papyri, then perhaps he had been forced to make them good again prior to their removal.

Reeves concluded his article, which was published in 1985, by admitting that

> at least a proportion of a king's funerary papyri could, on occasion, be deposited within one or more of the royal or divine representations buried with him – all indications of their presence being concealed beneath a coating of resin or a layer of gilded gesso. It is a reasonable deduction, therefore, that Tutankhamûn's 'missing' religious texts were concealed in a like manner – and, if this is so, that these texts still await discovery.[26]

So did the guardian statues of Tutankhamun's ka, or 'ghost', really contain papyri? Sadly, the answer seems to be no, for X-ray examinations of both statues have shown that they are both solid.[27] This was, of course, a great disappointment for those who have speculated on the whereabouts of Tutankhamun's 'missing' papyri. Despite this fact, rumours implying that documents were removed from the tomb and that Carter and Carnarvon failed to make them public have led key writers on Tutankhamun to make pertinent statements about this subject.

BUDGE AND BRACKMAN

Take, for example, Sir Edgar A Wallis Budge in his book *Tutânkhamen: Amenism, Atenism and Egyptian Monotheism,* published in 1923. In its preface he comments on claims made by 'some' writers that Lord Carnarvon's 'find' has made it necessary to rewrite and recast the history of Egypt's Eighteenth Dynasty. He sweeps away such far-fetched views in a veiled reference to the alleged papyri found in the tomb mentioned in the letter from Carnarvon dated 1 December 1922:

> Lord Carnarvon may have obtained from the tomb information that would amplify our knowledge of the reign of Tutânkhamen, but if he did so he did not publish it. As matters stand we know no more now about the reign of this king than we did before Lord Carnarvon made his phenomenal discovery.[28]

Carnarvon's letter and Budge's own response to it were picked up by the US writer Arnold C Brackman in his 1976 book, *The Search for the Gold of Tutankhamen*:

> Did Carter and Carnarvon find papyri in the tomb? If so, did they suppress them? This hardly seems likely, given Carter's obsession with integrity. For Carter to suppress a discovery would have been wholly, inexplicably out of character. For that matter, the same may be said of Carnarvon. One must assume, therefore, that in the general excitement of discovery, articles that appeared to be rolls of papyri were simply something else …
>
> But if, just for the sake of discussion, something were suppressed, what could it conceivably have been? The only plausible material of a highly combustible nature would be evidence about the relationship between the two great monotheists of that millennium, Akhenaten – Tutankhamen's father and/or father-in-law – and Moses.[29]

Brackman raises some important points here and ones that we shall explore fully in subsequent chapters. It is interesting, however, to note that Brackman's book appeared two years *before* the publication of Thomas Hoving's *Tutankhamun – the Untold Story*, which presented, for the first time, Lee Keedick's account of Carter's explosive argument with a British official in Cairo during the spring of 1924. Never before had this material been seen by the outside world, meaning that at the time of writing his book Brackman cannot have been aware that Carter threatened to reveal what Hoving referred to as

> documents contained in unrevealed papyri he had found in the tomb, documents presenting the true *and scandalous* account of the exodus of the Jews from Egypt [authors' italics].[30]

It is certain that Mr Brackman would have been stunned by the revelations contained in Hoving's book concerning the supposed missing papyri. He would also have been quite shattered to read that Carter's 'obsession with integrity', as he puts it, was seriously eroded in the light of the knowledge that Carter and Carnarvon failed to record their clandestine forays into the tomb and illegally removed various items for their own purposes. Had Brackman been aware of this information when researching his own book, it seems probable that his statements on the 'missing' papyri would have been a whole lot different.

Brackman would appear to have got it right when he predicted, for the sake of discussion at least, that any papyri found in the tomb and suppressed by Carter and Carnarvon must have contained 'material of a highly combustible nature'. In his opinion only one subject would have caused gross consternation at the time of the discovery and this was the possible relationship between Akhenaten, Tutankhamun's monotheistic father-in-law and half-brother, and Moses, the Israelite lawgiver who, according to Old Testament tradition, led the Exodus.

In this knowledge we can better understand why Carter stated that the papyrus documents said to have been found in the tomb concerned 'the exodus of the Jews from Egypt'. As we have seen, this fact was conveyed only during a heated argument between the Egyptologist and an official at the Residency in Cairo in spring 1924. Thus there is always the possibility that the outburst, as Hoving has proposed, was merely an idle threat meant to spur the embassy officials into action in the belief that Carter could heighten tensions between the Arabs and Jews in the Middle East.

So had Carter been bluffing? Was he simply trying to wind up a British official already agitated by the escalating Palestinian problem? If this was the case, then why did Keedick record that, after things had calmed down between the two men, 'an adjustment was made so that Carter was silenced and the threat never materialised'.[31]

Keedick could have said words to the effect that eventually Carter admitted that his claims were untrue and agreed not to spread malicious rumours of this kind. But the American businessman said nothing of the sort. His words, which we must remember are based on conversations with Carter, make it clear that the British official took the threat seriously and, later, persuaded him to keep silent about the matter. Of course, Carter could have been bluffing as he had nothing to lose at the time but much to gain. However, if we examine the nature of his threat in more detail, facts emerge that suggest very strongly that he was privy to knowledge regarding the relationship between the tumultuous Amarna period of Egyptian history and the events surrounding the life and times of Moses. This knowledge, at the time of the discovery of the tomb, had little place either among biblical archaeology or conventional Egyptology.

So crucial is this matter to the story being told that in the remaining half of the book it will be necessary to challenge not only the orthodox views on the timeframe and route of the biblical Exodus, but also the origins of the Israelite race and the foundations of the worship of Yahweh, the Hebrew name for God. We must look too at the evidence for the true site of the Mountain of God, or Mount Sinai, and Israel's conquest of Canaan – all of which will seriously bring into doubt traditionally held beliefs concerning the origins of Jewish religion and Israel's divine right to inherit Palestine, the land of its deliverance. In so doing, the authors will attempt to demonstrate that Carter and Carnarvon really did suppress documents found in the tomb of Tutankhamun which, if allowed to reach the public domain, might well have changed the face of the Middle East for ever.

PART THREE
MOSES

15. AGE OF THE EXODUS

According to Old Testament tradition, the Hebrews came to Egypt at a time of great famine that raged in the land of Canaan. Chief among them was Joseph, the son of Jacob, who was sold into bondage by his brothers but rose to fame in the royal court because of his ability to interpret the dreams of Pharaoh (the name given in the Bible to the ruler of Egypt). Joseph's wise words enabled the king to avert a major economic and humanitarian disaster, and as a reward his father Jacob, along with the rest of his family, was allowed to settle in Egypt. Later, Jacob took the name Israel, and his descendants – the children of Israel, or Israelites – multiplied greatly, making Pharaoh despise them, and thus began the time of their 'affliction'.

Afterwards, there ruled a king of Egypt 'who knew not Joseph'.[1] He saw how much the Hebrews had multiplied, and how they grew ever mightier. He noted too how when Egypt was at war, the Hebrews would join with their enemies. So he appointed 'taskmasters to afflict them with their burdens', and thereafter they were forced to build for Pharaoh the 'store cities, Pi-thom and Raamses'.[2] Yet the more the Egyptians afflicted them, 'the more they multiplied and the more they spread abroad'.[3] So even harsher labour was forced upon them in order to make them 'serve with rigour'.[4]

Thereafter Pharaoh attempted, with the aid of the midwives, to kill every male child born of Hebrew parents. Yet these women feared the Hebrew god, and so refused to carry out the king's demands. When Pharaoh learned that his orders had been disobeyed, he issued a public proclamation that all Hebrew male babies were to be thrown into the river, yet once again his commands were not carried out to the full.

AFLOAT AMONG THE REEDS

Among the Hebrew families ordered to cast out their newborn son was that of Amram, a Kohathite of the house of Levi, one of the twelve sons of Jacob.[5] He lived with his wife Jochebed and their two other children – Aaron, aged three, and Miriam, aged around fifteen. They concealed their child for three months. Yet, when this became increasingly more difficult, Amram and his wife placed the baby in an 'ark of bulrushes',[6] which was set afloat among the reeds. Very quickly the ark was drawn to the attention of the king's daughter, who had come to bathe at the water's edge. Marvelling at the sight of the child, which she recognised was of Hebrew parentage, the princess turned and saw Miriam, who had followed the passage of the baby. She asked whether it would be wise to bring a nurse from among the Hebrews, in order that they might nurse the child. The princess agreed, and so Miriam brought the mother of the boy, who was given the name 'Moses', because the king's daughter 'drew him out of the water',[7] and so by this means the boy was restored to her.

Moses was brought up as the child of Pharaoh's daughter, and thus he was 'instructed in all the wisdom of the Egyptians'.[8] According to the writings of Flavius Josephus, a Jewish historian of the first century AD, Moses led the Egyptians in a war against the Ethiopians, who had advanced forward from the south and taken many cities,[9] and thus he became a mighty general of the Egyptian army.

Afterwards, Moses settled into an Egyptian lifestyle, but soon he became disenchanted by their ways. He went out among his brethren, and saw for himself their affliction. Then one day Moses, who was now forty years of age, saw a Hebrew being smitten by an Egyptian. So disgusted was he by this injustice that he struck out and killed the man, and then hid the body in the sand. Yet by the next day his deed was well known, and very soon it reached the ears of Pharaoh, who sought to slay Moses. Knowing that he could remain no longer in Egypt, Moses fled to Midian, the land of the Midianites.

For forty years Moses remained in Midian as a shepherd, watching over the flock of Jethro, whose daughter Zipporah he had married. Then one day he found himself at 'the back of the wilderness, and came to the mountain of God, unto Horeb'.[10] Here the Lord appeared to him in the form of a fire that was about a bush, but did not consume it.[11] He told Moses to take off his shoes as this place was holy and, afterwards, the lawgiver was charged with freeing the bonds of his people and delivering them out of Egypt so that they might go 'unto a good land … flowing with milk and honey'.[12] Through various signs Moses became convinced of the power of the Lord, prompting him to enquire as to his name. In response, the Almighty said simply, 'I AM THAT I AM',[13] and that Moses was to tell the children of Israel that 'I AM', or 'Yahweh', 'hath sent me unto you'.[14]

THE EXODUS

On his return from Midian, Moses met his brother Aaron, and together they sought out the elders of the children of Israel before beseeching Pharaoh to release his people. But, even after Moses had offered signs which demonstrated that the power of Yahweh was stronger than that of the Egyptian gods, Pharaoh refused to allow the Hebrews their freedom, and thus the Lord unleashed ten great plagues on Egypt. One by one they weakened Pharaoh, until finally he relented and allowed the Israelites, their wives, their children and their cattle to leave his country. Yet after Moses had led his people out of Egypt, Pharaoh changed his mind and ordered that his horsemen, chariots and army go and bring them back. He even took charge of the expedition himself to ensure their return.

Very soon the Israelites, numbering 600,000 able men and their families, came upon 'the Red Sea' (Hebrew *yam-sûp*, the Suph Sea, literally 'the Reed Sea'), and, with the Egyptian army in sight, Moses called upon Yahweh to intervene in order to save his people. Thus 'the Lord caused the sea to go back by a strong east wind all the night, and made the sea dry land, and the waters were divided'.[15] This enabled the children of Israel a safe passage across to the opposite side. The waters then returned and drowned the horsemen, chariots and army of the Egyptians, which had followed in pursuit of the enemy.

Thereafter, the children of Israel entered the 'wilderness of Sin',[16] where Moses climbed 'mount Sinai',[17] or 'mount Horeb',[18] and Yahweh delivered unto him the holy laws – the Ten Commandments. Yet in his absence the Israelites turned to Aaron and asked him to make for them 'gods'. They had used the golden rings belonging to their wives in order to fashion them into a 'molten', or golden, calf.[19] Before this Aaron constructed an altar on which offerings were burned, and the next day the people rose early to eat, drink and play. So angered was Moses by what he saw on his return that he smashed the two tablets of the law, and made new copies only after the sons of Levi had rooted out and killed no fewer than 3,000 individuals who had strayed from the faith of the Lord.

Following many adventures, the Israelites came upon the plains of Moab, modern Jordan, in readiness to cross the River Jordan into the Promised Land. It was then that Moses delivered his final counsels to the elders of the twelve tribes, before ascending 'mount Nebo, to the top of Pisgah, that is over against Jericho'.[20] From here he gazed down on Canaan, the land of their inheritance. Afterwards Moses died, being now 120 years of age. He was buried 'in the valley in the land of Moab, over against Beth-peor; but no man knoweth of his sepulchre unto this day',[21] and the children of Israel wept for thirty days.

Such is the story of Moses the lawgiver and prophet of the children, or descendants, of Israel, whose story is told in the Torah, or Pentateuch, the names given to the first five books of the Old Testament: Genesis, Exodus, Leviticus, Numbers and Deuteronomy. Yet what about the historical reality of Moses and the Exodus? What do we really know about the world in which he lived over three thousand years ago?

During the spring of 1924 Carter marched into the offices of a British official in Cairo and threatened to 'publish for the whole world to read the documents that he found in the tomb giving the true account according to the Egyptian Government of the exodus of the Jews from Egypt'.[22]

Provided this incident was faithfully reported by Lee Keedick of the Keedick Lecture Bureau, then we must ask ourselves why Carter considered that he could persuade the British administration in Cairo to fly into action simply by admitting he had in his possession papyrus documents that gave 'the true account' of the Exodus. We can only assume that the material must have been of a politically sensitive nature that was better suppressed than placed in the public domain. So what exactly did Carter have up his sleeve? How did he expect to pull off this little stunt? The most likely explanation is that the documents contained a form of the Exodus story contradictory to the one accepted by biblical scholars in Carter's day. If this is true, then it becomes necessary to understand exactly what was known, or at least accepted, about the historical background to the Exodus in 1924. Only then can we go on to decide what exactly the papyri might have said, and why Carter believed he could use them as bargaining power.

MIGHTY RAMESES – PHARAOH OF EGYPT

Only isolated quotations found here and there in different books of the Old Testament offer any clues regarding the historical validity of Moses and the events surrounding the Exodus. All too often this meagre information is used either to support or condemn different theories regarding both his identity and the age in which he lived. In Carter's day, notions regarding Moses's historical background were centred upon one particular pharaoh – Rameses II (c. 1290–1224 BC), styled Rameses the Great. He was seen as the Pharaoh of the Oppression, 'who knew not Joseph'. For example, MG Easton's *Illustrated Bible Dictionary*, first published in 1894, tells us:

> Rameses II., the son of Seti I., is probably the Pharaoh of the oppression. During his forty years' residence at the court of Egypt, Moses must have known this ruler well. During his sojourn in Midian, however, Rameses died, after a reign of sixty-seven years, and his body was embalmed and laid in the royal sepulchre in the Valley of the Tombs of Kings beside that of his father.[23]

Bible scholars noted that during his long reign the mighty Rameses embarked on a series of building programmes of incredible proportions, the remnants of which can still be seen today. For instance, he commissioned the construction of the colossal seated stone figures that flank the entrance to the mighty temple, carved from solid rock, at Abu Simbel, close to the border with Sudan, in order to warn Nubian invaders to advance no further. It was also a 1,000-tonne, 20-metre-high statue of Rameses II found at the Ramesseum, situated on the Theban West Bank, that inspired Shelley's famous poem 'Ozymandias', about the fall of even the greatest of civilisations. Was it Rameses who forced the enslaved Israelites to build the 'store cities of Raamses and Pi-thom'?

The book of Genesis speaks of Joseph, his father Jacob, and his eleven brothers settling at Pharaoh's command in 'the land of Goshen',[24] known also as 'the land of Rameses'.[25] In order to help pin down its whereabouts, biblical scholars have attempted to identify the store city of Raamses, which was presumably in 'the land of Rameses'. Its obvious name association suggested that it had been built during the reign of Rameses the Great. Moreover, Egyptian inscriptions made reference to a lost city named Pi-Ramesse, 'the House of Rameses', known to have been located in Egypt's Eastern Delta, close to the border town of Sile. Not unnaturally, it was concluded that Pi-Ramesse was one and the same as the biblical city of Raamses.

In Carter's day Pi-Ramesse was identified with the ruined city of Tanis, situated on the Tanitic branch of the Nile. This was itself identified with the biblical city of Zoan, said to have been built seven years before the Canaanite city of Hebron.[26] Zoan is named in the book of Psalms as the place where Jacob and his descendants lived.[27] Tanis' association with Pi-Ramesse came about because of its location in the Eastern Delta and the fact that in Carter's day all that remained of this lost city was a vast area of scattered building blocks, stelae (carved upright stone slabs with rounded tops), obelisks and statues, many bearing Rameses II's name. Thus it was assumed that Tanis was Rameses' northern capital, constructed by the enslaved Israelites during the age of Moses. According to Easton in *The Illustrated Bible Dictionary*, Zoan, or Tanis, 'was the frontier town of Goshen. Here Pharaoh was holding his court at the time of his various interviews with Moses and Aaron'.[28]

In addition to being identified with Pi-Ramesse and the biblical Zoan, Tanis was also considered to be Avaris, the capital of the Hyksos, the Asiatic kings who overran Egypt and ruled from the Eastern Delta for a period of between 75 and 155 years during the so-called Second Intermediate Period, c. 1786–1575 BC. It was during their time in Egypt that some Bible scholars came to believe that Joseph and Jacob, who, like the Hyksos, were of Semitic origin, came to settle in the same region.

A PLACE CALLED TELL ED-DAB'A

Over the last hundred years or so, opinions have changed regarding the whereabouts of Pi-Ramesse and Avaris, throwing new light on this intriguing subject. In the summer of 1882 the Swiss philologist Edouard Naville began excavations at the site of a tel (occupational mound) named Tell ed-Dab'a in the Eastern Delta province at Sharqiya. At over 500 metres in diameter, it seemed to represent an urban development of immense proportions. Moreover, it was found to stretch westwards for a distance of 1 kilometre to the nearby villages of Khata'na and Ezbet Helmy, situated on the old Pelusiac branch of the Nile.

Very soon the excavation site, which also extended northwards for a distance of 2 kilometres to the village of Qantir, started to produce evidence of Asiatic occupation coincident to the presence in Egypt of the Hyksos. It had then been abandoned for a period of around 250 years before being occupied again during the reign of Horemheb, and thereafter continued to be an extensive town through until the time of Rameses the Great.[29] For instance, at Qantir an extensive palace begun during the reign of his father Seti I was uncovered by an Austrian expedition, including a beautiful doorway, now in the Louvre. In addition to this, the remains of a well and the houses of several princes and high officials dating from the reign of Rameses II were also found. Moreover, the hard limestone base of a colossal statue of the king, which would once have stood 10 metres high, was unearthed in 1953 by the Egyptian archaeologist Shehata Adam at Qantir,[30] who decided that Rameses II must have 'built a temple of great importance here'.[31]

From this evidence alone it became clear that this massive site had been a major Ramesside city, very possibly Rameses' northern capital, rebuilt over the ruins of an earlier foundation that stretched back to the Old Kingdom.[32] More importantly, it had been occupied during the Second Intermediate Period by Asiatic peoples coming in from Syria-Palestine, all strongly suggesting that this was the site of Pi-Ramesse, and thus the biblical store city Raamses. Or so believed the Egyptian archaeologist Mahmud Hamsa, who first proposed this theory in the mid-1950s.[33] The view was seconded by Labib Habachi, who additionally proposed that the Tell ed-Dab'a site was none other than Avaris,[34] the

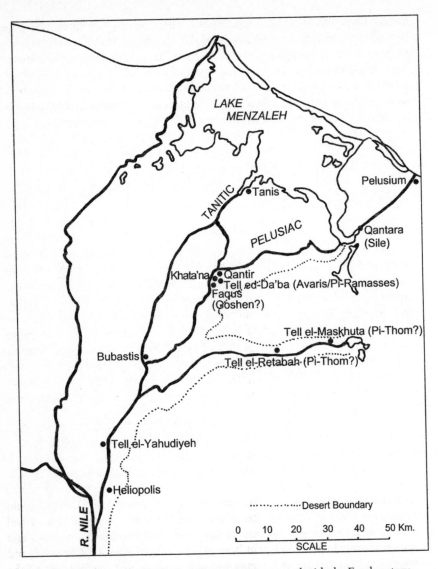

Fig. 10. The eastern delta showing relevant sites connected with the Exodus story.

capital of the Hyksos, a theory developed by the Canadian Egyptologist John van Seters.[35]

In addition to this, Edouard Naville pointed out something important recorded in the Septuagint, the Greek Bible used by Greek-speaking Jews in the Graeco-Roman world and thought to have been translated using Hebrew scriptures in Alexandria around the third or second century BC. In this it identifies Goshen, the land of the Hebrews, with an Arabian *nome*, or area, of the

Eastern Delta, the chief city of which was Phacusa. Its original name in Egyptian could be read as *gsm*, or *gsmt*, within which Naville, perhaps correctly, saw the name Goshen. Today Pharcusa is the town of Faqus, which is just 6 kilometres from Tell ed-Dab'a.[36]

There is confirmation of Naville's identification of Goshen with Faqus in the writings of a certain Abbess Aetheria, who travelled the Holy Land as a pilgrim between AD 533 and 540. In her words,

> But from the town of Arabia [Faqus] it is four miles [6.4 kilometres] to Ramesses. We, in order to arrive at Arabia, our stopping place, had to pass through the midst of Ramesses, which town of Ramesses is now fields, so much so that it does not possess a single habitation. It is true that it is visible, since it both was huge in circuit and had many buildings; for its ruins, however tumbled-down they may be, appear endless even to this day.[37]

Such was the situation when in July 1966 Dr Manfred Bietak of the Institute of Egyptology at the University of Vienna began excavating at Tell ed-Dab'a. Since that time he has conducted an exhaustive survey of the area, and unearthed an extensive town site of Asiatic origin, beginning during the Middle Kingdom and extending through to the end of the Second Intermediate Period, when the Hyksos were finally run out of Egypt by the army of the pharaoh Ahmose. Among the discoveries made at Tell ed-Dab'a are two large Asiatic temples, strikingly similar to others found at Megiddo and Hazor in Palestine.[38]

Bietak found that the city of Tell ed-Dab'a covered an area of around 4–5 square kilometres.[39] His research, which continues to this day, has led him to confirm that, in his opinion,

> All the evidence taken together – the cultural and the stratigraphic – would fit well the identification of the site on the one hand with the capital of the Hyksos, Avaris, and on the other hand with the Delta residence of the Ramessides, Piramesse ...[40]

Bietak has even cleared up the confusion surrounding Tanis' age-old association with the biblical cities of Zoan and Raamses. For some years it had been suspected that the majority of Ramesside building blocks, obelisks and statues scattered about Tanis had been pilfered from the Tell ed-Dab'a site, and were thus in secondary use. Bietak was able to show that this was indeed the case. Moreover, he determined that this massive reconstruction project had taken place after the silting up of the Pelusiac branch of the Nile, on which the Tell ed-Dab'a site was once situated, an event that took place during the Twenty-first and Twenty-second Dynasties, c. 1087–730 BC. The city, which was up until this time the northern capital of the Ramesside kings, very quickly lost its importance and so was transferred, in some cases block by block, to the site of Tanis, situated on the still flowing Tanitic branch of the Nile. Thereafter the desert reclaimed Pi-Ramesse as the nearby city of Tanis grew in size and prominence. It was this transfer of power from one capital city to another that Bietak believes created confusion among later Jewish scholars when it came to identifying the true locations of Goshen, 'the land of Rameses' and the store city of Raamses, all wrongly equated with Tanis.[41]

Even though Manfred Bietak has brought to life the city of Pi-Ramesse, which he believes (probably rightly so) was the Old Testament site of Raamses, his findings throw little, if any, light on the identity of the Pharaoh of the Oppression, and the time frame in which Moses lived. As we have seen, Rameses II was not the founder of Pi-Ramesse: he and his father, Seti I, simply reconstructed the site and turned it into his northern capital. It was renamed Pi-Ramesse, the House of Rameses, in his honour, meaning that there is no reason to assume that he was the Pharaoh of the Oppression. Indeed, the king who would seem to have initiated the first phase of reconstruction at the Tell ed-Dab'a site, following its abandonment by the Asiatic kings, was Horemheb. So could Horemheb have been the Pharaoh of the Oppression? It is a matter we shall return to in Chapter 17.

PHARAOH OF THE EXODUS

Having assumed that Rameses II was the Pharaoh of the Oppression, biblical scholars in Carter's day considered that, when Moses returned to Egypt after forty years in the land of Midian, the king on the throne was his son and heir Merneptah, who reigned c. 1224–1214 BC.[42] If this was correct, it would have made him the Pharaoh of the Exodus, who ruled when Yahweh unleashed the ten plagues on Egypt and the Israelites were finally able to obtain their freedom.

Yet never have any hard facts emerged from archaeological exploration in either Egypt or Palestine to support this theory. Indeed, the exact opposite seems to be the case. For instance, in 1896 the British Egyptologist William M Flinders Petrie unearthed an enormous black granite stela while excavating the site of Merneptah's mortuary temple at Thebes, modern Luxor, (a fragmentary duplicate was found also in the Temple at Karnak).[43] As we shall see, its discovery has completely altered our understanding of the very foundations of ancient Israel.

THE VICTORY STELA

Known to Egyptologists as the Victory Stela (sometimes the Israel Stela) this proclamation stone housed in the Egyptian Museum (No. Cairo 34025) dates to Year 5 of Merneptah's eventful ten-year reign. It commemorates his defeat of the Libyans, the peoples of North Africa who lived in the lands to the west of Egypt. After describing this great event, it recounts how the gods held a court session and proclaimed Merneptah the victor, after which peace returned to the land. This is followed by a poetic eulogy that extols the king's triumph over not only the Libyans, but also Egypt's enemies in its northern empire. It reads,

> The princes are prostrate, saying: 'Mercy!'
> Not one raises his head among the Nine Bow:
> Desolation is for Tehenu; Hatti is pacified;
> Plundered is the Canaan with every evil;
> Carried off is Ashkelon; seized upon is Gezer;

Yanoam is made as that which does not exist
Israel is laid waste, his seed is not;
Hurru is become a widow for Egypt!
All lands together, they are pacified;
Everyone who was restless, he has been bound ... [authors' italics][44]

All of these towns and territories are seen to have been conquered or pacified by the king, 'the Nine Bow' being the term used to describe the traditional enemies of Egypt (depicted on the seal of the royal necropolis as nine bound enemy prisoners). The Tehenu are the Libyans, while Hatti is the land of the Indo-European peoples known as the Hittites, who ruled supreme in Turkey and occupied parts of northern Syria. They had fought a major battle with the Egyptian army at Kadesh in Northern Syria during the reign of Merneptah's father, Rameses II.[45] Indeed, it would seem that in writing 'Hatti is pacified', the son was simply highlighting the military glories of his father, even though the military conflict fought at Kadesh was actually a draw! Moving on, we find that Canaan was an Egyptian province of this name in ancient Palestine, even though it was also used to denote Gaza, the province's capital. Ashkelon and Gezer were southern coastal towns in the land of Canaan; Yanoam was an important town in the north of the country, while the Hurru, Khurru, or Hurrites, were the peoples of Greater Palestine.[46]

The mention of Israel on the Victory Stela is quite remarkable for two reasons. First, it is the oldest acknowledged reference by at least 300 years to what might just turn out to be the descendants of Jacob. Secondly, it provides us with clear evidence that by this time the children of Israel were seen as a force strong enough to be a threat to Egypt's northern empire. The other curious fact is that 'Israel' is written as a personal name, suggesting that it refers to a tribe or clan, plausibly one without any fixed territorial homeland.

That the Victory Stela tells us that 'Israel is laid waste, his seed is not' ('Israel is wasted, bare of seed' in one translation[47]), implies that, although defeated in battle, its leaders had posed a major threat to Egypt, which controlled large parts of Canaan from the coastal lowlands north to the borders of the Hittite Empire.

In view of the slight rewriting of history in the case of the Hittites, we cannot say whether Israel really had been 'laid waste' by Merneptah, nor whether the Israelites had managed to establish themselves in Canaan by this time. Yet the chances are that they did not pose a problem to Egypt until after they had begun to get too unruly and threatened the shaky stability established in Canaan by Merneptah's father, Rameses II. This is an important realisation, for the Bible tells us that, before the children of Israel entered the Promised Land, they wandered for forty years in the wilderness. So, even if the Hebrews had crossed over the River Jordan when the Israel Stela was inscribed in Year 5 of Merneptah's reign, it implies that in strict biblical terms the Exodus must have taken place at least forty years earlier – conceivably, many decades beforehand. This means that Merneptah could not have been the Pharaoh of the Exodus. The role would have to be assigned to his father, Rameses II, while the Pharaoh of the Oppression, who reigned a full four decades earlier, must have been another king altogether, conceivably Rameses' father Seti I, c. 1307–1291 BC. His own father, Rameses I, was an old man when he took the throne in 1308 BC, and reigned for only a year or so before his death.

With all these facts in mind, any notion suggesting that the enslaved Hebrews built the store city of Raamses, or Pi-Ramesse, in the reign of Rameses the Great, has to be abandoned. They can have been involved in its construction only much earlier, either in the reign of Rameses' father, Seti I, or earlier still, perhaps during the reign of Horemheb. Yet then, of course, the city could not have been known by the name Raamses, while the land of the Hebrews would not have been 'the land of Rameses', showing that these names are anachronisms. In other words, they were added to the Exodus account only long after the events described, plausibly several centuries later when the Pentateuch was committed to written form for the first time.

LOOKING FOR PI-THOM

What about Pi-thom, the other store city said to have been built by the enslaved Israelites? Might a search for its location offer some clue regarding the time frame of the Exodus? Unfortunately not, for identifying this location has been just as problematical as finding the city of Raamses. In Carter's day, Egyptologists and Bible scholars agreed that, like Raamses, Pi-thom was situated somewhere on the edge of the Eastern Delta. Most probably it was the fortress of Per-Atum (*Pr-Itm*), the House of the god Atum, alluded to in a number of ancient texts. For example, it features in a dispatch made by an Egyptian official of this region during the reign of Merneptah:

> ... This is a dispatch for [my master's] information ... to wit, we have finished admitting the Shasu-tribes of Edom (through) the fortress of Merneptah-hotpe-hi-ma'at which is (in) Tjekku to the water holes of [Pr-Itm] the House of Atum-of-Merneptah-hotpe-hi-ma'at which (are in) Tjekku, for their own subsistence and that of their flocks.[48]

Here in the so-called Merneptah Stela we gain a glimpse of the manner in which 'Shasu-tribes' – the name given to pastoral nomads, or ancient Bedouin – were able in times of hardship to enter Egyptian territory in order to graze their herds on its more fertile pastures. For this privilege they would come all the way from Edom, a mountainous region north of the Gulf of Aqaba and east of the Dead Sea in the Transjordan, part of the modern-day Republic of Jordan (see Chapter 18).

In 1883 Edouard Naville felt he had found Per-Atum, and thus Pi-thom, when he began investigating an occupational mound named Tell el-Maskhuta, located at the eastern end of the Wâdî Tumilât, close to Lake Timsah at the southern end of what is today the Suez Canal.[49] Inscriptions found among the scattered ruins included one, apparently from the reign of Rameses II, that mentioned the place name *Thuku*, the 'Tjekku' of the Merneptah Stela,[50] which formed part of

Per-Atum. In addition to this, a red granite statue of a squatting man from the reign of Osorkon II, c. 881–852 BC, was found to be inscribed 'Ankh sher nefer, the good Recorder of Pithom [i.e. Per-Atum]'.[51] Other inscriptions also mentioned Per-Atum, leading Naville to conclude that he had discovered Pi-thom, which he felt was also synonymous with Succoth, the first place of encampment of the Israelites after they left the land of 'Rameses' at the time of the Exodus.[52]

Among the ruins of Tell el-Maskhuta Naville found a series of rectangular brick structures, which he described as 'store-chambers'.[53] These he saw as the granaries said to have been built by the enslaved Israelites.[54] He noted too that in some places the chamber walls were constructed of bricks made without straw, in his opinion a unique feature, recalling the popular, although entirely false, notion that the Hebrews were forced to produce bricks without straw for the construction of the biblical store cities.[55]

Subsequent work at Tell el-Maskhuta by John S Holladay of the American Research Center of Egypt (ARCE) completely contradicted the earlier work of Naville, and without sufficient explanation. He determined that the site had supported an Asiatic Bronze Age settlement around 1600 BC, but was then abandoned and had not been occupied again until the Saite and early Persian periods, c. 610–486 BC.[56] Curiously, he would seem to have found no evidence whatsoever of a city built here during Ramesside times.

Holladay's findings make it difficult for Egyptologists and Bible scholars to accept that Tell el-Maskhuta is the site of Pi-thom. Despite this setback, the fact that archaeology has thrown up no other evidence of its whereabouts, Tell el-Maskhuta remains the only obvious candidate for the title. Recently, however, there has been an attempt to show that Pi-thom was in fact Tell el-Retabeh, a dynastic site at the west end of the Wâdî Tumilât, as building blocks bearing the cartouche of Rameses II have been found there.[57] Whatever the location of the second store city built by the Israelites, it does little to help us pin down the age of the Exodus.

BIBLICAL CHRONOLOGY

Another system used very much in the past to define the historical time frame of key events of the Old Testament is biblical chronology. It is a subject that cannot be mentioned without reference to James Ussher (1580–1656), the Archbishop of Armagh and a professor of theology, whose own rigid chronology, published posthumously in 1660 within his treatise *Chronologia Sacra*, still features in creationist research today. By using a complicated system involving the coincidence of solar and lunar cycles he determined that Creation occurred in 4004 BC. With this date as a starting point in biblical history, he was able to calculate to his satisfaction the chronology of all major events contained in the Bible.

In this knowledge, certain isolated quotations taken from the Old Testament have been cited in order to calculate the date of the Exodus. For example, in 1 Kings 6: 1, it tells us that Solomon's Temple was built 'in the fourth year of

Solomon's reign over Israel', which is 'the four hundred and eightieth year after the children of Israel' gained their freedom. Since biblical chronology implies that Solomon's Temple was founded in c. 1012 BC,[58] this provides a date of c. 1492 BC for the Exodus, nearly 300 years before the age of Rameses II and his son Merneptah.

Another similar quotation, this time from the book of Exodus, tells us that before their departure from Egypt, the 'sojourning of the children of Israel' was 'four hundred and thirty years'.[59] Bible scholars have proposed that the earliest Hebrew settlers in Egypt were nomadic peoples forced by famine to leave Syria and Canaan during the reign of the Middle Kingdom pharaoh Senwosret III, c. 1878–1843 BC.[60] Since this unsubstantiated view parallels the manner in which Jacob and his sons found their way into Egypt, it has been assumed that Senwosret's reign marks the beginning of Israel's sojourn in Egypt.[61] If so, then it suggests that the Exodus took place 430 years later, thus somewhere between 1448 and 1413 BC, around 200 years before the age of Rameses the Great. So are we at least in the right time frame now?

SYMBOLISM IN NUMBERS

Figures representing periods of time found in both the Old and New Testament clearly have a symbolic meaning, and do not seem to relate directly to real time. For example, at the age of forty Moses is said to have departed Egypt after killing an Egyptian he found maltreating a Hebrew slave. He then spent forty years in the land of Midian, before returning to Egypt to persuade Pharaoh to release his people from bondage. Only after a further forty years of wandering in the wilderness with the children of Israel did Moses ascend Mount Nebo and gaze out over the Promised Land before promptly expiring on the spot. Moreover, on the occasion that Moses was given the Tablets of the Law on Mount Sinai, he remained there for forty days and forty nights. Clearly, to the writers of the Old Testament the number forty held some special significance, reflected in the life and times of their chief prophet. The same symbolic value is most probably behind the fact that, in the Gospels, Jesus, prior to embarking on his ministry, is said to have spent forty days and forty nights in the wilderness.

The Bible historian Ian Wilson has proposed that the number 120, cited for the age of Moses when he died, reflects a state of perfection, since it is a multiple both of 12 and 40.[62] With this in mind, we should look again at the reference in 1 Kings 6: 1 to the fact that Solomon's Temple was built in 'the four hundred and eightieth year after the children of Israel' departed Egypt at the time of the Exodus. As Wilson goes on to point out, 480 is 12 × 40, revealing the number's obvious symbolic value and showing us that it would be disastrous to assume that this figure referred to actual years.[63] Even more damning is the fact that the Septuagint, the Greek Bible, records that Solomon's Temple was built 440 years after the Exodus and not 480 years, as is stated in the Bible. This fact alone makes the whole idea of utilising biblical chronology to define age-old biblical events that much less appealing. So how then can we determine the exact time frame of the Exodus? Was there anything at all that could define with some kind of precision the era in which it occurred?

Howard Carter obviously thought so when he marched confidently into the offices of the British authorities in Cairo in 1924 and threatened to release the contents of the supposed Exodus papyri. Yet it was his old rival Arthur Weigall who only months beforehand had proposed a solution to the age of the Exodus that might just throw some considerable light on what Carter had at his disposal.

16. MOSES THE EGYPTIAN

When Tutankhamun's Burial Chamber was opened officially in February 1923, the British Egyptologist Arthur Weigall stood patiently in the blazing sun above its busy entrance. Alongside him were crowds of excited tourists and newspaper reporters, held back by a line of Egyptian guards. Everyone was eager to learn what was occurring inside the tiny subterranean sepulchre, out of sight of prying eyes. Weigall, who was there in his official capacity as Egyptological correspondent for the *Daily Mail*, had not been chosen to witness this historic event at first hand.

Yet Weigall had his own agenda when it came to the discoveries relating to Tutankhamun, for even at this early stage in the proceedings he was preparing an account of the events surrounding the finding of the tomb for an upcoming book, commissioned by his publisher, Thornton Butterworth of London. It appeared that autumn under the title *Tutankhamen And Other Essays*. Around the same time, Howard Carter's 'official' version of the events (co-written with Arthur C Mace) also hit the bookshelves, a situation that must have infuriated him, since he saw Weigall as a despicable rival, whom he would have nothing to do with in any capacity. The main reason for the animosity between the two men was Weigall's objection to the exclusivity deal Carter and Carnarvon had agreed with *The Times* of London. In his opinion it deprived the Egyptian people of first-hand news of the greatest archaeological discovery ever in their country, something that was made clear in letters written to Carter during the spring of that year (see Chapter 13).

As might be expected, it was Carter's breathtaking description of his and Carnarvon's first peek inside the Antechamber, and their grand entry into the Burial Chamber, that captivated the imaginations of the general public and ensured that *his* book became an instant classic. On the other hand, Weigall's own book must have sold reasonably well, before fading eventually into obscurity. Yet, despite its obvious intent to cash in on the discovery of Tutankhamun's tomb, both in Britain and abroad, *Tutankhamen And Other Essays* was more than simply a second-hand account of the discovery of a long-dead Egyptian pharaoh.

Already Weigall had written a highly successful book entitled *The Life and Times of Akhenaten*, first published in 1910.[1] It proved to be such a popular work that in just twelve years it was revised three times, with four printings alone appearing in the wake of the discovery of Tutankhamun's tomb. Weigall was an outstanding scholar on the Amarna period, having spent time in the company of the pioneering British archaeologist William M Flinders Petrie during his early years in Egypt. In addition to this, as the Chief Inspector of Antiquities for Upper Egypt in 1905, he had worked on the clearance of the virtually intact tomb of

Yuya and his wife Tuya, the grandparents of Akhenaten. With him on the excavation had been his fellow countryman James Quibell, the American millionaire and sponsor Theodore Davis and a young Howard Carter. Having recently resigned his post as Inspector of Antiquities in Northern Egypt, he was on hand to make drawings of the many wonderful finds that emerged from the tomb. It was an experience that would serve Carter well when seventeen years later he was to discover the final resting place of Tutankhamun.

Weigall's *Tutankhamen And Other Essays* dealt with a fascinating array of subjects in a thought-provoking and very readable manner. In addition to containing a detailed account of the tomb's discovery, drawn from first-hand accounts supplied by Carnarvon and other members of the team, the book also contained parts devoted to more unorthodox material. For instance, in the wake of the untimely death of the British aristocrat in April 1923, one chapter featured cases exemplifying the supernatural consequences of disturbing the ancient dead; it also cited various curse inscriptions found in Egyptian tombs.

In addition to this, Weigall's book carried a reasonable account of the life and times of Tutankhamun, placing the boy-king in the context of the turbulent events surrounding the Amarna heresy. Yet he went further, for after describing Akhenaten's rise to power, he began extolling the virtues of the intangible, formless Aten, seeing it in terms of an archaic representation of 'the worship of the true God, almost as we understand Him now'.[2] He drew attention to the uncanny similarities between Psalm 104 and the so-called 'Hymn to the Aten', an ode to the omnipotent powers of the sun-disc, often said to have been composed by Akhenaten himself. For Weigall it was the 'undoubted original of our 104th Psalm, many of the verses of which in the hieroglyphic script are almost word for word those of the Hebrew version'.[3]

WEIGALL ON MANETHO

In addition to this, *Tutankhamen And Other Essays* contained Weigall's views on the life of Moses and the age of the Exodus. To this end he drew extensively from the writings of Manetho the Sebennyte, an Egyptian scribe and priest from the temple of Heliopolis in Lower Egypt, who is accredited with having written in his native Greek language no fewer than eight books, between c. 280 and 250 BC.[4] Among them was a history of his country, complete with the chronicles of the kings, commissioned by Ptolemy II Philadelphus, the founder of the famous library of Alexandria. Entitled *Aegyptiaca*, or *The Egyptian History*, it is no longer extant. However, fragments of Manetho's *History* are to be found in a work entitled *Flavius Josephus Against Apion*, or *Contra Apionem*, written by Flavius Josephus (c. AD 37–97), the Jewish writer who witnessed, and then chronicled, some of the most important events in Jewish history. In this respect, he was the author of two definitive works *History of the Jewish Wars*, c. AD 75, and *Antiquities of the Jews*, c. AD 93.

Contra Apionem was written as a form of literary attack on those Graeco-Egyptian and Graeco-Roman writers who had compiled works that presented what Josephus saw as derogatory, if not blatantly false, renditions of events in the history of the Jewish race. As suggested by the title, among those at the receiving end of his sharp criticisms was Apion, a Greek grammarian who lived in the Egyptian city of Alexandria around AD 38. Yet by far the most significant writer to have come under attack from Josephus in *Contra Apionem* was Manetho, who, as we shall see shortly, wrote that the Jews were descended from lepers. These fragments, Weigall claimed, had been constantly ignored 'as legendary and fanciful' by his Egyptological colleagues, yet in his scholarly opinion they were 'a fairly accurate account of the Tell-el-Amârna episode as viewed by those who were opposed to it.'[5] So what exactly did Manetho have to say about the life of Moses that was not found in the Bible?

MANETHO'S ACCOUNT

Manetho's account begins with the introduction of a pharaoh named 'Amenophis' who, desiring to see the gods ('as had Orus, one of his predecessors in that kingdom, desired the same before him'[6]), sought out the advice of his namesake 'Amenophis, the son of Papis', a wise man with 'the knowledge of futures'.[7] Having listened to the king's request, Amenophis insisted that the only way this could be achieved was to rid the kingdom of all 'the lepers' and 'impure people'.[8] Thus it came about that 80,000 unclean individuals were rounded up and dispatched to the stone quarries, 'which are on the east side of the Nile', where they worked segregated from the rest of the Egyptian population.[9] Among their number were 'some of the learned priests that were polluted with the leprosy'.[10]

Despite his formula for fulfilling the pharaoh's desire, Amenophis, son of Papis, felt uneasy about what he had set in motion, for as Manetho records:

> Amenophis, the wise man and the prophet, was afraid that the gods would be angry at him and at the king, if there should appear to have been violence offered them [i.e. 'the wise priests'].[11]

Knowing full well the consequences of his words, he predicted that 'certain people would come to the assistance of these polluted wretches', who would rise up, depose the king and remain in charge of the kingdom for thirteen years.[12] Unable to face the consequences of bringing this matter to the attention of the king, Amenophis recorded his prophecy before taking his own life.

Having learned of the death of his namesake, and the predictions he had made, Amenophis the king decided that he would try to rectify the improprieties he had forced on 'the lepers' and 'impure people'. They had begged him to assign them as a dwelling place the deserted city of Avaris, the former home of the Hyksos, and the place of worship since earliest times of Typhôn (i.e. Set),[13] and this the king now consented to do. As we may recall, this was also the site of Pi-Ramesse and the biblical store city of Raamses, identified by Manfred Bietak et al. as Tell ed-Dab'a, in the Eastern Delta.

Having occupied the city, 'the lepers' and 'impure people' used Avaris as a base for revolt and elected themselves a leader 'out of the priests of Heliopolis'.[14] His name was Osarsiph, or Osarsêph,[15] and to him the people swore an oath of obedience, and in return he made new laws that were 'mainly opposite to the customs of Egypt'. He told them not to 'worship the Egyptian gods' or 'abstain from any one of those sacred animals which they have in the highest esteem, but kill and destroy them all'. Moreover, Osarsiph ordered that they should 'join themselves to nobody but to those that were of this confederacy'.[16]

Afterwards, this Osarsiph, the priest of Heliopolis, spoke to 'the impure people' telling them that they should work no longer in the quarries. Instead, they were to build walls around the city and prepare themselves for a war against King Amenophis. Osarsiph then secured the 'friendship' of the 'other priests and those that were polluted with them' and dispatched ambassadors to 'Jerusalem' in the hope that they might persuade the 'shepherds', i.e. the Hyksos, to rally to their cause. Earlier in *Contra Apionem*,[17] Josephus had recounted Manetho's story of the expulsion of the Hyksos under King 'Thummosis', or 'Amosis', unquestionably Ahmose, who ruled c. 1575–1550 BC, saying that on their return to Syria, i.e. Canaan, they had built the city of Jerusalem. This is despite the fact that in the Old Testament Jerusalem did not become important in Israelite tradition until the time of the united monarchies under David and Solomon, hundreds of years after the time of Moses. In acknowledgment of their support, Osarsiph promised the shepherds the city of Avaris, which they had been forced to abandon after their departure from Egypt several generations beforehand.

After accepting the offer, some 200,000 Hyksos came to Osarsiph's aid and together they seized control of Egypt. Amenophis, who had gathered into the city of Memphis all the sacred animals, where already could be found the Apis bull,[18] then fled with his five-year-old son Sethos and 300,000 of his most 'war-like' men to Ethiopia, where the king was 'under an obligation to him'.[19] As had been promised, Avaris was returned to the shepherds. Yet 'the people of Jerusalem', having united with 'the polluted Egyptians', began to treat the Egyptians in 'a barbarous manner':

> … those who saw how they subdued the forementioned country [i.e. Egypt], and the horrid wickedness they were guilty of, thought it a most dreadful thing; for they did not only set the cities and villages on fire, but were not satisfied till they had been guilty of sacrilege, and destroyed the images of the gods, and used them in roasting those sacred animals that used to be worshipped, and forced the priests and prophets to be the executioners and murderers of those animals, and they ejected them naked out of the country. It was also reported that the priest who ordained their policy and their laws, was by birth of Heliopolis; and his name Osarsiph from Osiris, who was the god of Heliopolis; but that when he was gone over to these people, his name was changed, and he was called Moses.[20]

After thirteen years in exile Amenophis reassembled his army, and with the assistance of a second army raised by his son, 'Rhampses' (earlier 'Sethos, who was also named Ramesses from his father Rhampses'[21]), they returned to Egypt and joined in 'battle with the shepherds and the polluted people, and beat them and slew a great many of them, and pursued them to the bounds of Syria'.[22]

Such is the story presented by Manetho in his *Aegyptiaca*, and noted by

Weigall in his own book. In his opinion, there seemed little question that the thirteen-year rule of Osarsiph-Moses constituted 'the thirteen years of the Aton "heresy" at Tell-el-Amârna'.[23] In his opinion,

> The 80,000 unclean people I take to be the heretic Aton-worshippers, and their removal to the quarries on the east bank of the Nile corresponds very strikingly to the historic transference of the whole capital to Akhnaton [sic] from Thebes to Tell-el-Amârna.'[24]

Weigall correctly surmised that, because Horemheb backdated his reign to the death of Amenhotep III, it explained why Manetho saw all of these events as having occurred during the reign of a single king, Amenophis, who is loosely based on Akhenaten's father, Amenhotep III. In other words, at least some of the events Manetho describes actually occurred over an extended period beginning with the final years of Amenhotep and culminating during the reign of Horemheb, whom Weigall saw as responsible for having finally ejected the 'lepers', 'impure people' and 'shepherds' from Egypt.[25]

In the knowledge that the leader of the 'impure people' and Asiatics was an Egyptian priest of Heliopolis named Moses, Weigall proposed that he had been 'born in the reign of Amenhotep III; [and] that', as the Moses of biblical tradition, 'he fled to the land of Midian in the reign of Akhnaton'.[26] Thus he suspected 'that Tutankhamen was the Pharaoh under whom Moses returned to Egypt and organised the exodus of his enslaved countrymen.'[27]

Although this conclusion flies in the face of biblical tradition, which seems to paint an entirely different picture of Moses' life and times, Weigall's words must be seen in the context in which they were written. As he himself admits, in 1923 Egyptologists and Bible scholars alike were of the opinion that the Pharaoh of the Oppression was Rameses II and the Pharaoh of the Exodus was Merneptah. Yet, in order to overturn this long-held belief, Weigall showed the implausibility of this view by highlighting the weaknesses of biblical chronology. For example, he pointed out the fact that the 480 years said to have elapsed between the Exodus and the building of the temple of Jerusalem in 1 Kings 6: 1 proves this wrong.[28] Weigall cited also the number of generations that 1 Chronicles 6 suggests had elapsed from the time of the Exodus down to the age of King David (actually eleven or twelve) to pin down the date of the former in the region of c. 1360–1330 BC, well within the range of Tutankhamun's reign.[29]

TACKLING THE CONQUEST

According to Weigall, the Amarna letters (the body of documents found on cuneiform clay tablets unearthed by local villagers digging on the site of Tell el-Amarna in 1887) demonstrated how at the end of Akhenaten's reign there were uprisings against Egypt's vassal kings in Syria and Canaan, especially by the Habiru (the 'Apiru of Egyptian inscriptions). They were a class of Near Eastern society, mostly of Western Semitic origin, who would leave their homes, where the prospects were poor, and offer their services to wealthy benefactors in neighbouring city-states. Sometimes they would travel for thousands of kilometres to carry out domestic duties for little more than the price of food, lodgings and a few state benefits. However, another class of Habiru/'Apiru derived from Semitic warrior stock. As fierce mercenaries they would offer their services as ready-made armies to whichever petty prince paid the highest prices. They had no fixed allegiances, and are known to have switched sides in the middle of battles.

Weigall pointed out that, during the reign of Akhenaten and later Amarna kings, large groups of Habiru/'Apiru mercenaries had fought alongside Canaanite princes such as Abdi-ashirta and Labaya, under whom they sacked and burned various fortresses, and generally laid waste to the countryside. Moreover, there was every reason to assume that the Habiru/'Apiru were synonymous with the term Hebrew, the name given to the children of Israel by the Egyptians and Philistines in the Old Testament, an expression that might well have had a derogatory usage.

Today we know that theories linking the Habiru/'Apiru with the conquest of Canaan, and the origin of the Hebrews, cannot be viewed as valid, since the question of the ethnic and cultural background of these peoples is far more complex than anyone could have imagined back in 1923.[30] Yet, for the time, it was a bold attempt at trying to define the age of the conquest in historical terms, and Weigall knew full well that his radical reappraisal of the Exodus story had profound implications for our understanding of the Bible. As he observed in this respect,

> I need not point out how wide an area of thought is opened up by this supposition that Moses lived through the Aton heresy; for the question as to what connection there was between the Hebrew monotheism and this earliest known monotheism of the Egyptians will at once present itself to the reader. It is a subject which deserves the fullest study.[31]

No one else before Weigall had come close to making the connections between the age of Akhenaten and the biblical story so familiar to us.[32] Yet he was not the only one to deal with the matter that year, for 1923 also saw the publication of Sir Ernest A Wallis Budge's *Tutānkhamen, Amenism, Atenism and Egyptian Monotheism*.

BUDGE'S REBUTTAL

As Keeper of Egyptian and Assyrian Antiquities at the British Museum, Budge had been encouraged by Lord Carnarvon, in the wake of the discovery of the tomb, to draw together everything that was known about Tutankhamun and his era for a book on the subject. It was to include his own opinions on the possible relationship between the Amarna age, the story of Moses and the Exodus from Egypt. Yet, unlike Weigall, Budge was not in favour of this assumed connection, and, in words that seemed to have been directed at Weigall himself, the matter was dismissed in the following terms:

Other writers [he does not state which ones] again have tried to show that Tutankhamen was the 'Pharaoh of the Exodus,' and also that it was his wife Ankh-s-en-pa-Aten (or Amen) who took Moses out of his ark of bulrushes and brought him up. But there was more than one Exodus, and Tutankhamen was not King of Egypt when any of them took place.[33]

Budge did not elaborate on these sweeping statements, and instead attempted to dispel any notion that there was a relationship between Atenism and the worship of God as exemplified in the Bible. Since Budge was infinitely more influential than Weigall, his views were taken more seriously, dampening any future attempts to make the link between Moses and Akhenaten until the psychoanalyst Sigmund Freud was to express the same basic hypothesis in the 1930s. In two major articles for the German magazine *Imago*, which subsequently appeared in a more expanded form in the book *Moses and Monotheism*, published for the first time in 1940, the by then elderly inventor of modern psychology proposed that Moses had been an Egyptian in the court of Akhenaten.[34] He put forward some stimulating evidence to back up his thesis, including the fact that the Hebrew word for 'Lord', *Adonai*, or *Adon*, becomes *aten*, the name of the sun-disc, when written in Egyptian.[35] This observation makes considerable sense of Exodus 12: 12, which speaks of the slaughtering of the firstborn among the Egyptians on the night of the Passover: '... against all the gods of Egypt I will execute judgements: [for] I am the Lord'.[36] If 'the Lord', i.e. Adonai, is replaced with the word Aten, the passage reads: '... against all the gods of Egypt I will execute judgements: [for] I am the Aten'.

CARTER'S SOURCE MATERIAL

We have already seen in Chapter 14 Carter's threat to reveal the contents of papyrus documents found in the tomb of Tutankhamun, which contained the 'true account ... of the exodus of the Jews from Egypt'. The date of the encounter with the British official is revealing, for it was time enough for Carter to have read and digested Weigall's book *Tutankhamen And Other Essays*, published the previous autumn. Whether historically accurate or not, the book contained compelling new evidence to link the life of Moses with the Amarna age, and, as we have seen, it proposed 'that Tutankhamen was the Pharaoh under whom Moses returned to Egypt and organised the exodus of his enslaved countrymen.'[37]

Can this conclusion implicating King Tutankhamun in the Exodus story have gone unnoticed by Carter? The answer is almost certainly no, for, even though the mere existence of Weigall's book must have infuriated him, he would at least have examined a copy, either before his departure for Egypt in November 1923 or on being handed one sometime during the 1923–4 digging season. If nothing else, he would have needed to check that it did not contain any material or photographs under his copyright jurisdiction.

WEIGALL'S INFLUENCE

Are we to imagine Carter flicking through the pages of Weigall's popular tome and stopping to read the section on the relationship between Manetho's story of

Osarsiph-Moses and the Amarna age? Did he mull over the proposed link between the events of the Exodus and the reign of Tutankhamun and conceive of some kind of foolhardy plot to use this new vision of the biblical story to scare the British authorities in Cairo into making them jump to his aid? If so, could the Exodus papyri have never existed, the whole idea being an almighty bluff conceived after Carter had read the relevant pages in Weigall's book? The answer could be yes, but the weight of evidence argues against it.

Why should Carter have taken seriously anything that Weigall might have said? Carter disliked the man intensely, and it is unlikely that he would have accepted his theory that Manetho's account of Osarsiph-Moses somehow preserved an ancient Egyptian rendition of the biblical Exodus. Indeed, Carter is more likely to have sided with the opinions of Budge, whose book on the life and times of Tutankhamun, along with its relationship to the Aten religion and Egyptian monotheism, was encouraged originally by Lord Carnarvon. As we have seen, Budge dismissed outright any notion that Tutankhamun might have been the Pharaoh of the Exodus. In theory, Carter would have taken the same view, which was shared by the entire Egyptological community. In spite of his role as special Egyptological correspondent for the *Daily Mail*, by 1923 Weigall was seen as a maverick, a loose cannon, and his book on Tutankhamun must have been treated more with mild amusement than scholarly acknowledgment. We must not forget that it contained a serious chapter on curses in ancient Egypt, something that would not have been greeted too warmly at the time.

Yet Carter obviously did become convinced that the Exodus occurred before the final closure of the tomb of Tutankhamun. Otherwise how could he claim that papyrus documents found inside the sepulchre revealed a 'true account' of this monumental event in Jewish religious tradition? Any documentary evidence unearthed in the tomb had to date either to the reign of Tutankhamun or to one of his predecessors, most plausibly Smenkhkare or Akhenaten. If so, then somehow Carter's scandalous revelations concerning the Exodus story would seem to parallel, almost exactly, Weigall's own theories on the subject. We must ask ourselves 'why?'

As the authors will demonstrate shortly, there is undeniable evidence to link Manetho's account of Osarsiph-Moses with the Amarna age. However, can it be shown to preserve a clearer picture of the biblical Exodus? The answer is yes, for we find that other early writers also recount these self-same events concerning the expulsion from Egypt of 'impure' Egyptian priests in the company of a multitude of Asiatic peoples. Moreover, they are linked implicitly with the Exodus story preserved in the Jewish holy books.

HECATAEUS OF ABDERA

In all likelihood the source material behind Manetho's Moses account came from the library rooms at Heliopolis. Yet one possible influence on his writings is a work composed a generation or two beforehand by the Greek historian Hecataeus of Abdera. In 320 BC, just twelve years after Alexander the Great's celebrated entry into Egypt, Hecataeus stayed at the court of the first Hellenic king, Ptolemy I, and afterwards wrote his own *Aegyptiaca*, or *History of Egypt*. Although it is no longer extant, fragments from it are quoted by Diodorus Siculus, or Diodorus of Sicily (c. 8 BC), in his work *Bibliotheca Historica*, the 'Library of History'.[38]

Even though Manetho makes no mention of Hecataeus' work, it is certain that both authors must have drawn on similar material for their narratives. According to Diodorus, this is how Hecataeus introduces the story of the Exodus:

> When in ancient times a pestilence arose in Egypt, the common people ascribed their troubles to the workings of a divine agency; for indeed with many strangers of all sorts dwelling in their midst and practising different rites of religion and sacrifice, their own traditional observances in honour of the gods had fallen into disuse.[39]

Thus on being expelled from the country, the foreigners are forced to find a new homeland. Some of them, under the leadership of Danaüs and Cadmus, end up colonising Greece while another group, led by Moses, settle in Judaea, i.e. Palestine, which at the time was said to have been 'uninhabited'. Afterwards, they go on to found the city of Jerusalem.[40]

Even though Hecataeus' account would seem to have been influenced by the biblical narrative (perhaps with Diodorus' help), it contains elements of the biblical story of the Exodus and yet constitutes the oldest gentile recollection of these events. Furthermore, in Chapter 17 we shall meet again with the theory that a plague might have been responsible for the Exodus.

APION'S MOSES

Although no earlier forms of the Osarsiph-Moses narrative survive, several versions that postdate Manetho do exist and some of them display interesting variations on the life of Moses. Among them is the account provided by the first-century Greek grammarian Apion of Alexandria. He has left behind some quite remarkable statements concerning Moses the Egyptian in his own now lost *Aegyptiaca*, which were preserved, quite fortunately, by Josephus in his *Contra Apionem*. According to Apion:

> I have heard of the ancient men of Egypt, that Moses was of Heliopolis, and that he thought himself obliged to follow the customs of his forefathers, and offered his prayers in the open air, towards the city walls; but that he reduced them all to be directed towards the sun-rising, which was agreeable to the situation of Heliopolis; that he also set up pillars instead of gnomons [obelisks] …[41]

Like Manetho before him, Apion goes on to state that this wise man united 'the lepers' and 'impure people' against the might of the ruling pharaoh of Egypt and for which they were driven out of the country. Once again we read that Moses was not an Israelite but a priest of obviously high rank from Heliopolis. Furthermore, we learn that he adopted a new form of sun worship 'agreeable' to

Heliopolis, the place of the cult of the sun god Re, whereby he lowered the city walls enough for the morning sun to be greeted each day.

THE CULT OF HELIOPOLIS

There seems little doubt that, when speaking about Moses, Apion is in fact recalling the religious revolution that occurred during the reign of Akhenaten. On ascending to the throne as Amenhotep IV, he proclaimed himself to be the First Prophet of the Aten. Despite this, the omnipotent Aten was not known exclusively by this name until Year 9 of his reign. Before this time it additionally bore the title Re-Harakhty, Horus on the Horizon. This was a falcon-headed form of the sun god Re, which embodied the dual aspects of the double horizon – the sun-disc in the west at sunset and in the east at sunrise.

The ancient religious centre of the cult of Re was Heliopolis, Greek for 'city of the sun'. In the Bible it is referred to as On, a variation of its original Egyptian name *Aunu*, *'Ounû* or *Iwnw*, the 'pillared city', and in Arabic it became known as *Ain Shams*, literally the 'sun-eye' or 'spring of the sun'. Today its sprawling splendour has gone, and *Ain Shams* is no more than a busy suburb of northeast Cairo, close to the international airport.

Akhenaten championed the Heliopolitan cult of Re, adopting at the beginning of his reign its religious principles, priestly titles and methods of worship, which included, as Apion stated, the construction of open-air temples in which the sun would be greeted each morning. Inscriptions from Akhenaten's reign speak of Re as the hidden light of the Aten, while in the Aten temple at Karnak Re-harakhty was shown in his form as a male god with the head of a falcon surmounted by the sun-disc. In addition to this, one of the chief priestly titles at Heliopolis was 'Greatest of Seers', a position held by Mery-re II, Akhenaten's personal vizier, as high priest of the Aten at Amarna.[42]

In similarity with Manetho's Osarsiph-Moses, Akhenaten forbade the worship of idols and dispensed with the veneration of sacred animals. For instance, in his reign there were no Apis bulls buried at the Serapeum in the Memphite necropolis at Saqqara, a firm indication that he abandoned this age-old tradition. It was not reintroduced until the reign of Tutankhamun, when one of these sacred creatures is known to have been interred in the Serapeum with full honours.[43] On the other hand, it is certain that Akhenaten revered the sacred Mnevis bull of Heliopolis, which was seen as an incarnation of Ur-mer, described in inscriptions as the 'life of Re'.[44] Each bull would be allowed to live out its life in luxury, and after death its carcass was embalmed and interred in a specially prepared grave at Heliopolis. After his move to Amarna, Akhenaten had a large tomb dug in the Royal Wadi – where his own family's tomb was constructed – to be used when the current Mnevis bull died.[45] It is not known whether or not any bull was actually interred in the bovine sepulchre, although its existence alone demonstrates Akhenaten's devotion to the religious practices of Heliopolis.

Lastly, there is Akhenaten's fascination with the *benben*-stone, perhaps the most important cult object in Heliopolitan tradition. This was a sacred stone shaped like a cone, a pyramidion or stepped object, originally mounted on a perch in an open court at Heliopolis known as the Mansion of the Benben, or the Mansion of the Phoenix. In Year 4 of his reign, Akhenaten began the construction of a temple at Karnak known also as the Mansion of the Benben; this would unquestionably have contained its own *benben*-stone. Then in Year 6, following his move to Amarna, work began on an open-air temple called the Great House of the Aten. At its eastern end was a Mansion of the Benben, within which was placed yet another *benben*-stone. This is known to have taken the form of a round-topped stela of quartzite, mounted on a stone dais.[46] Akhenaten is even known to have erected a stone stela resembling a *benben*-stone at Heliopolis, where his father had built a temple to the Aten during his own lifetime.[47]

Akhenaten's unique fascination with the *benben*-stone, which in ancient Egyptian cosmology symbolised the Point of First Creation or *sep tepi*, the age or place of the First Occasion, would seem to explain why Apion stated that Moses 'set up pillars instead of gnomons'. By gnomons he was referring to the towering granite obelisks that dominated the precincts of Heliopolis, as well as other great religious centres such as Karnak and Tanis.[48] It would seem that many hundreds of years after the collapse of the Amarna heresy, some memory of the activities attributed to its now anonymous First Prophet lingered at places such as Heliopolis, which was a key centre for the cult of the Aten. Akhenaten was still seen as a religious reformer of great renown, but now his deeds were linked integrally with that of Osarsiph-Moses, and probably others as well.

If one period more than any other can be said to reflect the events surrounding the biblical Exodus, it is the Amarna age – not the reign of Rameses II or that of his son Merneptah. Such a conclusion makes perfect sense of the facts at hand, even if other time periods in Egyptian history might have *contributed* to the narrative presented in the book of Exodus.[49]

This, we must assume, was the knowledge available to Carter when he marched into the offices of the British administration in Cairo during the spring of 1924 and made his outrageous demands. Yet did it come from papyrus documents discovered inside the tomb? Did they reveal how Moses was an Egyptian belonging to Akhenaten's monotheistic faith of the Aten? If so, then what part did the Amarna royal family play in this fascinating story? Taking Arthur Weigall's lead, we must examine more closely the writings of Manetho, as well as other ancient writers, in order to assess the true relationship between the age of Akhenaten and the biblical Exodus.

17. DIVINE RETRIBUTION

That Manetho, priest of Heliopolis and historian to Ptolemy II, preserved some echo of the tumultuous events that occupied Egypt during and directly after the Amarna age now seems certain. According to the surviving fragments of his *Aegyptiaca*, Osarsiph-Moses, the elected leader of 'the lepers' and 'impure people', was said to have established new laws and customs contrary to those of Egypt. His brethren were not to 'worship the Egyptian gods' or 'abstain from any one of those sacred animals which they have in the highest esteem, but kill and destroy them all'.[1]

CULT OF THE SUN-DISC

There is no question that these commands mimic the manner in which Akhenaten forbade the worship of any god or goddess other than the deity symbolised by the Aten sun-disc, and, as Manetho states, actively 'destroyed the images of the gods'.[2] Whether or not his followers abstained from venerating 'those sacred animals that used to be worshipped, and forced the priests and prophets to be the executioners and murderers of those animals' and then 'ejected them naked out of the country'[3] is another matter. However, it is quite likely that the transition from polytheism to monotheism was not a pretty thing in many instances.

Manetho records also that Osarsiph-Moses ordered his followers to 'join themselves to nobody but to those that were of this confederacy'. Does this reflect the manner in which Akhenaten advocated the veneration of a single god, and transferred the seat of power from Thebes to the newly constructed city of Akhetaten ('horizon of Aten'), being built on the east bank of the Nile, some 277 kilometres down river?

Akhenaten would have attracted to his dream city tens of thousands of loyal subjects, including administrators, architects, artisans, artists, builders, sculptors and painters from every part of the kingdom. The priesthood itself consisted of many hundreds of individuals, who would have taken up their posts in earnest to venerate daily the reappearance of the solar orb upon the eastern horizon. Akhenaten's subjects were encouraged to take part in religious festivals in which the king, in the company of Nefertiti, would have ridden through the cheering crowds on a horse-drawn chariot. Thousands of people will have also attended the regular addresses the royal couple made from the balcony, the so-called 'window of appearance', which overlooked the city's central square.

To what degree Akhenaten's subjects discarded their belief in the old religions and truly embraced Atenism is unclear, especially as a large number of small statuettes of Egyptian gods and goddesses have been unearthed on the site of the city. However, it is likely that a great many people, especially those linked to the priesthood, would have viewed the Aten as some kind of new divine saviour that would ensure peace and prosperity in Egypt for all eternity; they were, of course, to be proved quite wrong in this respect.

THE FALL OF AKHETATEN

All of this was swept away quite suddenly at the end of Akhenaten's reign, when first Smenkhkare and then Tutankhamun transferred the royal court to Memphis and re-established Thebes as the great religious centre of Upper Egypt. Those who had relocated to Akhenaten's city for practical reasons alone, would simply have packed their bags and gone back to wherever they had come from in the first place. Yet the many converts to the new religion are unlikely simply to have walked away from Akhetaten, leaving behind everything they had believed in so passionately for the past thirteen years or so. Thus diehard followers of Akhenaten and his Aten faith quite probably remained in the city, attempting to continue the daily offerings, ceremonies and celebrations to the sun-disc, before the eventual collapse of its social infrastructure would have forced them to abandon the place for good. Thereafter Akhetaten quickly became little more than a ghost town, occupied only by nomadic tribesmen who would have taken

Fig. 11. Akhenaten and Queen Nefertiti bestowing collars upon favoured courtiers. Three young daughters help with the proceedings.

e from the Burial Chamber of
nkhamun showing the dead king as Osiris
ding before his successor Aye, who
orms the Opening of the Mouth ritual.

The Restoration Stela of Tutankhamun, found
at Karnak in 1907, which relates how the gods
turned their back on Egypt after the temples
had been abandoned.

ve The perplexing sight that awaited the
erican archaeologist Theodore M. Davis
n he first entered Tomb 55 (KV55) in the
ey of the Kings in 1907.

t Bust of Queen Tiye, the Great Royal
e of Amenhotep III and mother of
enaten.

The head of Akhenaten showing the strange elongated, viper-like features and slanted eyes he adopted in Year Five of his reign.

Bust of Queen Nefertiti found at the site o Akhenaten's city at Tell el-Amarna by Ger archaeologist Ludwig Borchardt in 1912.

Above (left to right) Arthur Weigall, Theodore M. Davis and Edward Ayrton in picture taken in 1907, when Davis held the digging concession for the Valley of the Kings.

Left Why were Akhenaten's daughters depicted with elongated heads like this example?

Right Castle Carter, Carter's home at the head of the Valley of the Kings, where, strangely, his canary was killed by a cobra soon after the tomb's discovery.

Right After Carter resealed the doorway to the Burial Chamber the lid to a reed basket, as well as other inconsequential items, was used to hide his handiwork.

Above Harry Burton's photograph (No. GB7 2) shows the hole resealed by Carter between the tomb's Antechamber and Burial Chamber.

Above A wooden platform hides Carter's handiwork, as he (left) and Carnarvon break down the doorway into the Burial Chamber during its official opening on 16 February 1923.

Left (left to right) Lady Evelyn Herbert, her father the 5th Earl of Carnarvon, Howard Carter and A. R. 'Pecky' Callender stand at the entrance to Tutankhamun's tomb.

Right Highclere Castle, the seat of the Carnarvon family in the English county of Hampshire, where seances regularly took place in the East Anglia Room.

The leading lawyer and Member of Parliament Sir Edward Marshall Hall, KC, who took part in the seances organised by Lord Carnarvon at Highclere Castle.

Count Louis Hamon, alias 'Cheiro', the famous palmist and fortune teller (pictured), warned Lord Carnarvon to remove objects from the tomb at his own peril.

ght The wooden Anubis statue that guarded e entrance to the tomb's Treasury. It became e focus of the curse story after the reported ath of Lord Porchester's dog.

low Members of the excavation team *(left right)*: Arthur Mace, Carnarvon's secretary hard Bethell, A. R. Callender, Lady elyn, Carter, Lord Carnarvon, the chemist red Lucas and photographer Harry Burton.

tus head of Tutankhamun found in a m and Mason's packing case in the sed to store objects removed from hamun's tomb.

This image of Tutankhamun and Ankhesenamun beneath the rays of the sun-disk, from the throne chair found in the tomb, reveals their continued interest in the Aten faith.

Above The story of Pharaoh's daughter Scota's journey
Egypt to Spain by boat, as depicted in this fifteenth-cent
Scotichronicon, provides crucial information about the Ex

Left The Victory, or Israel, Stela, dating to Year Five of
Merneptah's reign, c.1220 BC, contains the earliest refere
to 'Israel' in its penultimate line.

Above Hittite king making a libation to invoke the storm-
god. Mursilis II believed that the plague which ravaged Hatti
was divine retribution for failing to supplicate the storm-god
properly.

Right Egyptian relief showing one of the semi-nomadic
peoples from the Transjordan known as Shasu, who seem
synonymous with the earliest Israelites.

Below Miriam, the sister of Moses, whom the Book of Numbers tells us died and was buried at Kadesh, identified with the rock city of Petra in Jordan.

Above The six-metre tall obelisks of Zibb Attûf (Merciful Phallus), which act as a gateway to Petra's elevated sanctuary known as al-Madhbah, the High Place.

bove Ain Mûsa, the spring of Moses, in the own of Wadi Mûsa, east of Petra. Was it here nat Moses struck the rock and brought forth ne waters of Meribah?

ight The end of the breathtaking narrow avine at Petra known as the Siq, or Cleft of Aoses, through which the waters of Ain Mûsa nce flowed.

Above Petra's al-Madhbah, the High Place, showing the sunken rectangular area on which is the raised Mensa Sacra, or offerings table.

Below The High Place's circular basin.

Below The High Place's carved stone altar.

Below Jebel al Madhbah, Petra's holiest site. Is this the true site of Mount Horeb, Mount Sinai and the Mountain of Yahweh?

Below Carved 'feet of God' among archaic rock art at the base of a mountain in Wadi Rum, between Petra and Aqaba.

Left Betyl containing a god-block with twin columns surmounted by crescent moons located beneath the summit of Petra's Jebel al-Madhbah.

Below Do these triangular carvings found at Petra also represent the god of the mountains? Note the twin gouges meant to represent eyes.

e Hemispherical god-block in a niche in Petra's Siq. Does this strange carved represent Dhushara, the Nabatean god of mountains?

t Stamp-seal from Tawilan, an Edomite ment near Petra, showing a star and ent upon a staff or pole. It is thought to sent the Edomite god Qaush.

Right The Shrine of Aaron in which is a crypt containing the alleged tomb of Aaron, Moses' brother. Note the column drums in its walls from an earlier building.

Right Summit of Jebel Harûn, the traditional site of the biblical Mount Hor, with the whitewashed Moslem shrine of Aaron in view.

Above View from the altar of Petra's High Place across to Jebel Harûn, unquestionably the most holy spot in the whole of the Seir, or Shara, mountain range.

Right Michaelangelo's Moses in the Vatican. Is his story a memory of the deeds of an Asiatic tribal alliance led by Egyptian followers of the Aten?

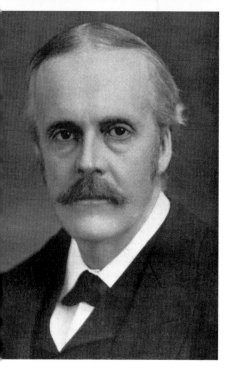

Above Chaim Weizmann (left), the leading Zionist Jew and future first president of Israel, with Feisal ibn Hussein, the Hashemite leader of the Arab Revolt, taken in June 1918.

ove Arthur James Balfour, the senior
tish statesmen who played a crucial role in
establishment of a Jewish National
meland in Palestine.

ht T. E. Lawrence, alias 'Lawrence of
bia', the British army officer who worked
ngside Feisal ibn Hussein during the Arab
olt (1916–1918).

ow President Woodrow Wilson (right),
h his close aide Colonel Mandel House.
entry of the United States into World War
was crucial in the issuing of the Balfour
claration in November 1917.

Above What was behind the threat made by Howard Carter (left) to reveal the contents of papyri found in Tutankhamun's tomb? Was Carnarvon (right) aware of their alleged contents?

Above Almina Wombwell, the future Countess of Carnarvon, was the illegitimate daughter of Alfred Rothschild, a grandson of the founder of the British branch of the House of Rothschild.

Above As part of the marriage arrangement between Almina (pictured) and Lord Carnarvon, Alfred Rothschild agreed to pay his existing debts of £150,000 and provide a dowry in the region of £500,000.

Above Before her husband's untimely death in April 1923, Almina had begun a relationship with Lt. Col. Ian Onslow 'Tiger' Dennistoun (pictured here with Almina), whom she married that same year.

shelter in its once great buildings, until finally it was dismantled right down to the foundations during the reign of Horemheb.

Those priests and individuals who did remain loyal to the outlawed faith of Akhenaten would have been seen as heretics, to be rejected by society if they did not embrace Egypt's polytheism once more. In some ways we might compare them to the earliest Christians of Jerusalem and later Rome, who were shunned and rejected by Romans and Jews alike. It is not unlikely that they would have become known as social 'lepers', or the 'impure people', terms used by Manetho to describe Osarsiph-Moses's followers, although they were neither ill nor corrupt, simply outcasts of society. Let us read again the Egyptian writer's words regarding the attitude of Amenophis, the son of Papis, towards the followers of Osarsiph-Moses:

> ... there were some of the learned priests that were polluted with the leprosy; but that still this Amenophis, the wise man and the prophet, was afraid that the gods would be angry at him and at the king, if there should appear to have been violence offered them ...[4]

Who were these 'learned priests that were polluted with the leprosy'? Is it possible that they constitute a distorted memory of renegade priests of the Aten faith, who remained loyal to the outlawed religion after Akhenaten's death? It seems a most likely explanation.

OSARSIPH-MOSES AS AKHENATEN

Let us review now the thirteen years that Osarsiph-Moses and his followers, with help from the 'shepherds' from Jerusalem, are alleged to have seized control of Egypt. As the British Egyptologist Arthur Weigall obviously recognised, it was in Year 5 of Akhenaten's seventeen-year reign that he abandoned the name Amenhotep IV and, just one month later, arrived at the site of his future city. Here the heretic pharaoh made offerings at an open-air altar in order to proclaim its foundation, before taking up residence in a great tent until the royal palace was ready for occupation in Year 6. This must be seen as the starting point of the heresy, which continued for twelve to thirteen years until Akhenaten's assumed death in Year 17, corresponding to the thirteen years of Osarsiph-Moses's own rebellion. Weigall realised this was no coincidence, and so have Egyptologists in more recent years. For example, the Canadian Amarna expert Donald Redford, although advocating a connection between the expulsion of the Hyksos from Egypt and the biblical Exodus, sees Manetho's story of Osarsiph-Moses as a straight reflection of the religious reforms instituted by Akhenaten. In his opinion:

> The occupation of a deserted area, set apart (though in the modified form of the story replaced by Avaris), sounds like the hejira to Amarna; and the 13 years of woe wrought by lepers and shepherds can only be the term of Akhenaten's stay in his new city. *The figure of Osarsiph-Moses is clearly modelled on the historic memory of Akhenaten* [authors' italics].[5]

We should read this final line again: 'The figure of Osarsiph-Moses is clearly modelled on the historic memory of Akhenaten.' Donald Redford is no lightweight. He is professor of Egyptology at the University of Toronto, and is the author of several books and key articles on the Amarna period and ancient Egypt's association with Western Asia. His findings must be taken seriously. Similar ideas have been echoed again recently by Jan Assmann, professor of Egyptology at the University of Heidelberg, who sums up Manetho's Osarsiph-Moses narrative in the following terms:

> The story of the lepers can thus be explained as a conspicuous case of distorted and dislodged memory. In this tradition Egyptian recollections of Akhenaten's monotheistic revolution survived. But because of the banishment of Akhenaten's name and monuments from cultural memory, these recollections became dislocated and subject to many kinds of transformations and proliferations.[6]

In spite of such admissions from the Egyptological field, there is a growing movement within its ranks that sees the biblical character of Moses as in some way attached to the memory of the expulsion of the Hyksos during the reign of King Ahmose, c. 1575–1550 BC.[7] Yet if this crucial event in Egyptian history did have an influence on the formulation of the Exodus story, then it was a minor one, the bulk of the story having emerged out of the chaos of the Amarna age.

THE CO-REGENCY

Manetho tells us that the pharaoh who opposed the 'lepers' and 'impure people', and was forced out of Egypt, before returning to expel both them and their Asiatic allies, was Amenophis. In the first instance we can identify him as Akhenaten's father Amenhotep III, in whose reign lived a celebrated minister named Amenophis-son-of-Hapu, unquestionably the historical character behind Manetho's 'Amenophis, son of Papis' (see below).

It seems pretty certain that during the final years of his life Amenhotep III shared a co-regency with his son, Akhenaten, perhaps for as long as eleven or twelve years. Evidence for this has come from a number of key discoveries, mostly from the site of Akhenaten's city at Tell el-Amarna. For instance, while excavating here John Pendlebury and his epigrapher Herbert Fairman found and examined two pottery fragments from wine containers on which were dockets inscribed, respectively, Year 28 and Year 30.[8] Since Akhenaten's own reign reached only Year 17, the wine dockets had to refer to that of his father Amenhotep III, who lived to see Year 38 of his reign. They argued that, because wine does not keep well in containers of permeable pottery in hot climates, they must have been bottled and delivered after Akhenaten transferred his permanent residence to Amarna in Year 5 of his reign, hinting strongly at a co-regency between the two kings.

Other evidence of co-regency includes a wall mural found in the ruins of a house at Amarna belonging to an official named Pinehesy. This depicts Amenhotep III and his royal wife Tiye adoring the Aten disc, with its name written in a style adopted only in Year 9 of Akhenaten's reign, suggesting that the old king was still alive at this time.[9] In addition to this, carved reliefs on the entrance façade from the tomb of Huya at Amarna show on one side Amenhotep III and Tiye, and on the other side Akhenaten and Nefertiti, once more in conjunction with the latter form of the Aten name.[10] In contrast, within the tomb itself is a carved representation of Tiye alone in Year 12 of her son's reign. To Pendlebury this implied

> … the death of Amenhotep III between the carving of the façade and of the interior, and suggests that Teye's visit was in the nature of a state 'progress' to her son on the occasion of his father's death.[11]

This evidence, along with other royal scenes and inscriptions found in the ruins of the city,[12] indicates that the elderly Amenhotep may well have lived at Amarna during his later life and probably had permanent residences there.[13] More than this, it provides the perfect basis to propose that the father of Tutankhamun was not Akhenaten, as many scholars have proposed, but in fact Amenhotep III, a point made by Pendlebury as early as 1936. To him this conclusion was implied not only by the suggestion of a long co-regency but also by 'his looks, by his own statement … and by the presence in his tomb of a statuette of Amenhotep III in the same "coffinette" as a lock of Teye's hair'.[14]

The matter of a co-regency having existed between Amenhotep III and Akhenaten was most famously discussed by the Amarna expert Cyril Aldred in his classic work *Akhenaten: King of Egypt*. Although it is not the place here to cite all the evidence he presents in this respect, his conclusions are clear:

> The co-regency of Amenophis III with his son, according to our view of the evidence, thus lasted for over twelve years … disturbing as this conclusion may be, we shall have no option but to accept it.[15]

The idea of a 'long' co-regency between Akhenaten and Amenhotep III of perhaps eleven to twelve years has been forcibly argued in more recent years, based primarily on artistic synchronisms between the two reigns. Despite this fact, some scholars of the Amarna period, such as Donald Redford, have attempted to dispel any idea of a co-regency, while still others have argued for a 'short' co-regency of just two years.[16] Yet the physical evidence weighs against both of these views.

If a long co-regency between the two kings can be accepted, then it is clear that Amenhotep III was still alive when Akhenaten was establishing his monotheistic religion and attempting to abolish all rival priesthoods, including that of Amun, the most powerful in the whole of Egypt. Akhenaten's actions must have caused so much consternation among the priesthoods that we can imagine them pleading for help from the elderly Amenhotep III, lest the country fall into a state of chaos and abandonment. Indeed, in the Theban tomb of Pairi constructed during the reign of Smenkhkare, we gain some idea of the desperation of the people over the loss of the old gods. A graffito left there by the scribe Pawah laments the absent god Amun, beginning with the words, 'My heart longs to see you!'[17] We can thus make better sense of why Manetho tells us that Amenophis desired so much to see the gods, almost as if they were already abandoning him. It was a request he entrusted to his sage 'Amenophis, son of Papis', who can only be based on Amenophis-son-of-Hapu, Amenhotep III's personal adviser.

AMENOPHIS-SON-OF-HAPU

From textual evidence available to us, we can be sure that Amenophis-son-of-Hapu was a favourite of the elderly monarch. Early on in his career he was appointed Scribe of the Elite Troops, a position that placed him in charge of army recruitment. Later, as Superintendent of All the Works of the King, he is accredited with the fashioning and transportation of the colossal quartzite statues of Amenhotep, each 21 metres high, which flanked the entrance to the king's mortuary chapel on the Theban west bank. It was the northernmost of these statues that in classical times was identified with Memnon, the celebrated Trojan hero.[18] Each morning the colossus of Memnon was said to have greeted his mother Eos (Aurora), the goddess of the dawn, by emitting a strange murmuring sound at the moment the sun's rays fell upon its stone surface. That was until one day, in the reign of the Roman emperor Septimius Severus (AD 146–211), an earthquake silenced the statue for ever.

We know too that Amenophis-son-of-Hapu was behind the organisation of the ageing king's first sed-festival, or 'jubilee', conducted every few years towards the end of a pharaoh's life in order to reaffirm his divine right to rule and rejuvenate his body and soul.[19] This much celebrated event – witnessed by large crowds of people, including high officials from every nome, or province, and dozens of foreign dignitaries – took place in Year 30 of Amenhotep's reign. The venue was a specially constructed temple enclosure attached to the king's palace complex at el-Malqata, near Medinet Habu, on the Theban west bank.

Amenophis-son-of-Hapu also became High Steward of the estates of Sitamun, Amenhotep's Great Royal Wife from around Year 27 of his reign.[20] In gratitude for his services to the king and his family, he was allowed to erect statues of himself at the entrance to the Tenth Pylon, or entrance archway, within the great temple complex of Karnak, where he is described as King's Scribe. Amenophis-son-of-Hapu is thought to have died shortly after the king's second sed-festival, which occurred in Year 34 of his reign (his third and final one took place in Year 37). So if there had been a long co-regency between Amenhotep III and the heir apparent, then Amenophis-son-of-Hapu would have been alive when Akhenaten founded his city at Amarna in Year 5 of his reign and must have died as late as Year 7 or 8.

The known titles of Amenophis-son-of-Hapu also make sense of Manetho's suggestion that, at the orders of the king, 'Amenophis, son of Papis' rounded up some 80,000 'lepers' and 'impure people' and dispatched them to work in quarries 'which are on the east side of the Nile'.[21] As Superintendent of All the Works of the King his duties would have included defending the Delta region from piratical attacks, and the enforcement of labour for quarrying, transport and building operations.[22] Clearly, Amenophis-son-of-Hapu would not have been alive when Akhenaten's regime collapsed, thus he cannot have been responsible for the internment of the diehard followers of the Aten who remained after the king's death. Moreover, we have no idea how he died – whether he took his own life, or even if he was a sage or prophet as was suggested by Manetho.

Yet to understand better the historical events portrayed in Manetho's account we must expand the time period to embrace the roles played by those kings who followed Smenkhkare and Tutankhamun to the throne of Upper and Lower Egypt. For instance, at the beginning of the Osarsiph-Moses account we read:

> This king [namely 'Amenophis'] was desirous to become a spectator of the gods, as had Orus, one of his predecessors in that kingdom, desired the same before him.[23]

So who exactly was 'Orus', or just 'Or',[24] as his name is sometimes written? If we turn to the *Epitome*, or dynasty-lists, originally included in Manetho's *Aegyptiaca* – and now found only in secondary use within later works written centuries later – we find him listed among the rulers of the Eighteenth Dynasty. For instance, in versions of the king-lists preserved by Josephus and certain early Christian chroniclers of history a pharaoh named Orus was said to have reigned for between 28 and 38 years, most usually 36 years 5 months.[25] Yet his entry falls not before but directly *after* the reign of a king named 'Amenophis', who is usually allotted a reign of 31 years.[26] That this Amenophis was Amenhotep III is clear from his positioning in the list of fourteen, sixteen or eighteen kings from this dynasty, depending on the source quoted.[27] This conclusion is confirmed by the fact that alongside Amenophis's entry appear the words, 'This is the king who was reputed to be Memnōn and a speaking statue'.[28] In fact, Amenhotep III reigned for 38 years, and not 30 to 31, as is stated by Manetho, although this is a minor error when compared with Manetho's entries for the remaining kings of the Eighteenth Dynasty.

We are told by Manetho in his king lists that the king named Orus reigned after Amenhotep III but before a list of kings that can only equate with the known rulers of the Amarna period. They begin with one Acenchĕrês (also spelled Acherrês, Achenchersês and Achencheres), who is undoubtedly Akhenaten, even though the twelve or sixteen years assigned to him, falls short of his actual seventeen-year reign.[29] However, it must be remembered that the confusion surrounding this list of Amarna kings stems from the fact that all memory of their reigns was obliterated from official records. This may therefore account for why in two versions of Manetho, Acenchĕrês is said to have been the daughter of Orus![30] Whether or not this had anything to do with the unusual artistic style adopted by Akhenaten, or some confusion derived from his co-regency with Nefertiti, is unclear.

Acenchĕrês is followed in two renditions of Manetho's *Epitome* by 'her brother' Rathōtis[31] (or Rathos),[32] who is allotted a reign either of six or nine years. Another version of the king-lists names the pharaoh who ruled after Acenchĕrês as Acherrês, who is allotted a reign of eight years.[33] From the names and years of rule assigned to this king, he can be none other than Tutankhamun, who reached Year 9 of his reign.

This much we can say for certain, but in the different versions of Manetho's *Epitome* there follows after Rathõtis a series of kings with conflicting entries and lengths of reign; some are simply Akhenaten again, returning under either the same or a slightly altered name. Others must be Nefertiti, Smenkhkare and Aye. Finally, the lists name a pharaoh who is recognisable – Ramessês.[34] Yet he seems to be a confused memory of both Rameses I, who reigned for just over one year after the death of Horemheb, c. 1308 BC, and his grandson Rameses II, who reigned for 67 years, c. 1290–1224 BC. Moreover, both kings belong to the Nineteenth Dynasty, and not the Eighteenth, where Manetho places them. So who exactly was Orus, the king said to have ruled between Amenhotep III and Akhenaten? The answer is Horemheb, who was responsible for all the confusion in the first place. Owing to the fact that he extended the length of his own reign of around 27 years to include that of the four kings who preceded him, he accredited himself with having reigned over Upper and Lower Egypt for a full 59 years. Not only is Horemheb the Orus of the Manetho king-lists, but he reappears under the name Harmaïs (also known as Armesis or Armaïs) for a reign of 4/5 years immediately prior to that of the above mentioned Ramessês.[35]

ACENCHĔRÊS AND THE EXODUS

One positive indication that the Exodus may be linked with this chaotic period of Egyptian history comes from a brief note written after the entry for Acenchĕrês, i.e. Akhenaten, in Manetho's *Epitome*, which reads, 'About this time Moses led the Jews in their march out of Egypt'.[36] A second form reads only slightly differently: 'In his time Moses became leader of the Hebrews in their exodus from Egypt'.[37]

Both variations are to be found in the fragments of Manetho included originally in a work entitled *Chronicon*, written in the first half of the fourth century AD by Eusebius of Caesarea (AD c. 264–340), a Greek father and chronicler. The second form of the note is found in an Armenian edition of his book, while the first comes from a work written around AD 800 by Georgius the Monk, also known as Syncellus, meaning the 'attendant', from his role as attendant to Tarasius, Patriarch of Constantinople. He copied chunks out of Eusebius's *Chronicon* for use in his own chronicle, which spanned from Adam right down to Diocletian (AD 245–313), emperor of Rome. However, after providing this curious statement to the effect that the Exodus occurred during the reign of Acenchĕrês, Syncellus tells us,

> Eusebius alone places in this reign the exodus of Israel under Moses, although no argument supports him, but all his predecessors hold a contrary view, as he testifies.[38]

What this means is that Eusebius' *Chronicon* also included fragments from other now ancient works from an earlier era, which would have given contrary views on the time frame of the Exodus. This suggested to Syncellus that Eusebius's note, to the effect that the Exodus occurred during the reign of Acenchĕrês, was not to be taken seriously. Sadly, it does not appear in any other version of Manetho's king-lists.[39] Yet his statement regarding the age of the Exodus should not be seen as merely Eusebius' creation, only that other authors are either silent on the matter, or support an alternative viewpoint.

We can never be certain whether the note from Eusebius to the effect that the Exodus occurred during the reign of Acenchĕrês-Akhenaten stemmed originally from Manetho, or whether it was information derived from a now lost source. Whatever the case, it does show that by early Christian times this tumultuous period of Egyptian history known as the Amarna age had become associated not only with the life of Moses but also the biblical Exodus.

THE POLLUTED PEOPLE

Other works from writers of the late Hellenistic period also contain variations of the Egyptian form of the life of Moses as recounted by Manetho.[40] In these the Israelite lawgiver likewise becomes the leader of diseased or polluted people who are forced out of Egypt, generally at the time of a plague that is ravaging the Two Lands. Often the account also includes a pharaoh responsible for their eviction, and when he is named it is either Amenophis, or occasionally Bocchoris.[41] In Manetho's king-list Bocchoris is the only named pharaoh of the 24th Dynasty (c. 720–715 BC). He was said to have been burned alive by Sabacôn, the third king of the 25th Dynasty, which presumably ran concurrently with the 24th. Who exactly Bocchoris might have been is unclear, since so few relics survive from this period, and how his name became associated with the story of Moses the Egyptian is even more of a mystery.

One such account is that of Lysimachos, a historian of Alexandria, who wrote during the second century BC. In his version of events, preserved by Josephus in his *Contra Apionem*, Bocchoris, i.e. Pharaoh, sends a priest to the oracle of Amun after a large number of 'leprous and scabby' 'Jews', who are also 'subject to certain other kinds of distemper', flock to the temples, where they beg for food and, through their actions, cause a scarcity throughout Egypt. The oracle pronounces that Bocchoris should cast the 'impure and impious' people from the temples into the desert, while others of a 'scabby and leprous' nature were to be drowned and the temples purged. Only afterwards would the country bring forth its fruits.

Yet those 'Jews' cast into the desert felt aggrieved, and so elected from among themselves a leader named Moses. He advised them to continue their journey until they found a place fit for habitation. Furthermore, he told them that they should have 'no kind regards for any man, nor give good counsel to any, but always to advise them for the worst; and to overturn all those temples and altars of the gods they should meet with'.[42] The people agreed that this was the right policy to adopt, and so continued on their journey until they found a land that was inhabited. Here they abused the men and plundered the temples until they reached the land of Judaea, where, using the wealth taken from the temples, they established a city named *Hierosyla*, or *Hierosolyma*, i.e. Jerusalem.[43]

Josephus condemned the work of Lysimachos, as he did that of Manetho, since he names those who were plague-ridden and cast out of Egypt as the 'people of the Jews', and, of course, the fact that their leader was named as Moses, the biblical lawgiver.[44] It must be emphasised, of course, that these 'Jews' have nothing whatsoever to do with the peoples of this name that exist today. They seem simply to have been Asiatic foreigners of uncertain ethnic origins, who had settled temporarily in areas of Egypt situated on the border with the Sinai.

Cheremon, an Egyptian from Alexandria who wrote as a priest and later became the tutor of Nero (AD 37–68), emperor of Rome, had a different spin on the traditional story. According to him, the goddess Isis reproaches King Amenophis in a dream for allowing her temple to be destroyed at times of war. In order to propitiate her, a priest suggests that the king purge Egypt of all 'polluted people', which he does, expelling no fewer than 250,000, who take as their leaders Moses and Joseph, or in Egyptian Tisithen and Peteseph. The multitude gather in the Nile Delta city of Pelusium, where they join forces with 380,000 others who have been 'left there by Amenophis', and together they invade Egypt and force the king to flee to Ethiopia. Yet Amenophis's son and successor Rameses, who was born in a cave after the death of his father, returns with an army to Egypt and defeats the 'Jews', driving the remaining 200,000 into Syria.[45] Clearly, this narrative did not go down too well with Josephus, either, as is shown by his comments on Cheremon's work in *Contra Apionem*.[46]

The Latin grammarian Pompeius Trogus in his *Historicae Philippicae* records that Moses was not an Egyptian, but the son of Joseph, even though the cult he institutes in Jerusalem is seen as 'sacra Aegyptia'. Having stolen the sacred treasures from the Egyptian temples, Moses and his followers leave Egypt, with Pharaoh's army in hot pursuit. However, the Egyptians are forced to turn back owing to terrible storms. Yet the reason for the Exodus from Egypt is once again an epidemic, which on this occasion is described in greater detail:

> But when the Egyptians had been exposed to the scab and to a skin infection, and had been warned by an oracle, they expelled [Moses] together with the sick people beyond the confines of Egypt lest the disease should spread to a greater number of people … And because he remembered that they had been expelled from Egypt due to fear of contagion, they took care not to live with outsiders lest they become hateful to the natives for the same reason. This regulation which arose from a specific cause, he transformed gradually into a fixed custom and religion.[47]

Once again we see events surrounding what amounts to a plague in Egypt causing the king to take drastic action to restore order and placate the Egyptian people, who have decided that the cause of the epidemic is the presence in their country of a large number of polluted individuals. The only way they can be purged of this misery is to rid the country of these undesirables, described as both Egyptians and 'Jews'. They come together in the Eastern Delta, the very region known in the Bible as the land of Goshen, where also the store cities of

Raamses and Pi-thom are said to have been located. They are forcibly expelled from Egypt, and so journey onwards until they come across the highlands of Palestine, ancient Canaan, where they eventually settle. Here they build the city of Jerusalem and establish their own customs and religion.

Bible scholars, from Josephus down to the modern day, have been happy to dismiss all such gentile accounts of the Exodus as fanciful interpretations of the real story found in the Pentateuch. Yet what if this is not the case, and these stories constitute a fragmentary, but obviously grossly distorted, picture of the true foundations of Israel? What if these narratives from Egyptian or Hellenistic historiographers and chroniclers really were gleaned from much older sources – indeed, older perhaps than the earliest forms of the Pentateuch, which is likely to have taken its present form in the seventh century BC (see Chapter 22)? What if these narratives contain kernels of historical information that date to the Amarna period, and also reflect very real events that actually influenced the construction of the Pentateuch, which in turn influenced the final form of these Graeco-Egyptian and Graeco-Roman narratives? These thoughts may be heretical even in this day and age, but what if they are correct? What if we are looking at the true events surrounding the rise of Moses and the Exodus from Egypt?

SCOTA, PHARAOH'S DAUGHTER

One more source must be quoted before we can leave this subject – one that may at first seem a little peculiar. It is the *Scotichronicon*, a chronicle of the peoples of Scotland, written in the mid-1440s by Walter Bower (1385–1449), an abbot of Inchcolm Abbey, located in northeast Scotland. Drawing on much older source material, including Eusebius' *Chronicon* and Nennius' *Historia Brittonum*, c. AD 800, he reconstructs the history of the Scots. Yet the story does not begin in Scotland, or even Ireland, but in one of the kingdoms of Greece, where we meet a character named Gaythelos (or Gayel). He was the son of a probably mythical king named Neolus or Eolaus, and, it seems, 'good looking but mentally unstable'.[48]

Having failed to attain a position of authority in his father's land, the young prince, provoked by anger, and with the support of many men, starts committing acts of great barbarity and cruelty and becomes the cause of many disasters across the kingdom. So outraged are the king's subjects that Gaythelos is driven out of his native land and sails to Egypt, where he teams up with Pharaoh and helps him expel an invading army of Ethiopians from his kingdom. In gratitude, he is offered the hand in marriage of Pharaoh's only daughter, Scota, which he happily accepts.[49]

It is at this time that the Exodus takes place, and Pharaoh and his army pursue the Israelites out of Egypt and drown in the Red Sea, as per the account in the book of Exodus. Since Scota was his only daughter, this now meant that Gaythelos could seize control of the country. However, the Egyptians were well aware of his cruelty, and so forced him and his wife to leave Egypt.

Realising that he can never return to his native land because of the crimes he has committed, Gaythelos decides that he will 'acquire new lands to cultivate in the remotest regions of the world'. He therefore readies a large fleet of ships and sets sail with his wife Scota and their entire household.[50] According to Robert Grosseteste (c. 1175–1253), an earlier source of material quoted verbatim by Walter Bower,

> In ancient times Scota the daughter of Pharaoh left Egypt with her husband Gayel by name and a large following. For they had heard of the disasters which were going to come upon Egypt, and so through the instructions or oracular responses of the gods they fled from certain plagues that were to come. They took to the sea entrusting themselves to the guidance of their gods. After sailing in this way for many days over the seas with troubled minds, they finally were glad to put in at a certain shore because of bad weather.[51]

That shore was in Spain, where Gaythelos and Scota built a strong town called Brigantia on the River Ebro, in the middle of which was a great tower surrounded by deep ditches.[52] Here they settled down to spend the rest of their lives. A generation or so later, two of Scota's sons, Hiber and Hymec, departed for Hibernia, i.e. Ireland.[53] The inhabitants he found here were either killed or enslaved, and afterwards they named this place Scota, in memory of their mother.[54] An Irish version of the story, preserved in the *Lebor Gabála Erenn* ('The book of the taking of Ireland'), names her husband's family as the sons of Míl, who with their father Míl, the son of Bile, sail to Egypt. Here he marries Scota, and together the party journey through the Mediterranean until they reach the Irish DílRiata where they engage the fierce inhabitants, the Túatha Dé Danaan, in battle. Although they win the day, Scota is slain and her body interred in a mound called Scota's Grave.[55] Other variations of the story have Scota herself sailing from Spain to Scotland, either directly[56] or via Ireland.[57] Once on the mainland, she journeys to Ergadia, Argyll, named after her son Erc and her husband Gaythelos.[58] Curiously enough, Scota is said to have brought with her from Egypt the '*sedile regium*', the Stone of Scone, used in royal coronations, and removed from Scotland to London by Edward I (and presented in 1996 to Edinburgh Castle, where it can be found today).[59]

Even though Walter Bower's story of Scota, the daughter of Pharaoh, did not find its final form until the fifteenth century, it is known to have been around as early as AD 800. For example, the ninth-century British monk and chronicler Nennius tells us that when the Egyptians drowned in the Red Sea in pursuit of the Israelites there was present a powerful 'nobleman of Scythia', i.e. Gaythelos. Those Egyptians who survived took counsel to expel him, lest he attack and seize control of their kingdom. As a result he took his wife, whose name was 'Scotia', and from whom 'Ireland, is said to be named', and 'wandered' for 42 years until finally they landed on the coast of Spain.[60] From references such as this, we can be certain that her story is not simply a medieval creation, but a far older legend based on some kind of distorted historical recollection of real events. But who exactly was Scota, and how can she help us fine-tune the age of the Exodus?

PHARAOH'S DAUGHTER

Scota was said to have been the daughter of Pharaoh, the Egyptian king drowned in the Red Sea in pursuit of the Israelites at the time of the Exodus. When his name is given, it is said to have been 'Chencres'. Bower, utilising an unknown version of Manetho's *Epitome*, tells us that he ruled for eighteen years, following the seven-year reign of a king called Achorisis, who succeeded to the throne after the death of a king named Acencris.[61]

Bower's Acencris is Manetho's Acenchĕrês, i.e. Akhenaten. Achorisis' seven-year rule shows him to have been Tutankhamun, while the enigmatic Chencres, the father of Scota, would seem to be simply another entry for Akhenaten. Not that he reigned twice, only that Manetho drew upon source material that spoke of the reigns of various Eighteenth Dynasty kings and, even though their names might have been curiously similar, he decided that they must have been separate individuals. Thus kings such as Akhenaten, and, as we saw earlier, Horemheb, are listed more than once by Manetho under different names. Thus Scota was conceived to have been the daughter of Akhenaten, suggesting that the plague that is alluded to not only in the story of Gaythelos and Scota, but also in various Graeco-Egyptian and Graeco-Roman accounts of the life of Moses from Hecataeus of Abdera onwards, would appear to be associated with his reign.

Does any of this make sense of what we know about the events surrounding the Amarna age? The answer is an overwhelming yes! First, the idea that one of Akhenaten's daughters ended her days in Britain is not as strange as it may at first seem.[62] Secondly, there is compelling evidence to suggest that an unprecedented plague of immense proportions swept across Egypt and the Near East towards the end of the Amarna age.

THE HAND OF NERGAL

We can trace the gradual spread of the plague and monitor its progress. For instance, one Amarna letter from the king of Alašiya (Cyprus) to Akhenaten belies the presence of the plague in his kingdom, for it speaks of 'the hand of Nergal', an underworld deity associated with pestilence and disease, 'now in my country; he has slain all the men of my country, and there is not a (single) copper-worker' to produce ingots for the king.[63] This statement, of course, implies that the epidemic was already rampant in the Near East, and had only just been carried across to the island of Cyprus, which was an important centre for maritime trade throughout the Eastern Mediterranean.

So what exactly was happening at this time on the mainland? Murmurs of the epidemic also surface during the Amarna period from Sumuru,[64] a town on the Syrian coast, and also from the Lebanese seaport of Byblos, where it struck fear into both the inhabitants of the city and its Egyptian officials.[65]

THE AGONY OF MURSILIS

In addition to this, we know that after the death of Tutankhamun the plague reached Hatti, the land of the Hittites (modern-day Turkey), after being introduced by Egyptian prisoners captured in the Lebanon. This is known from

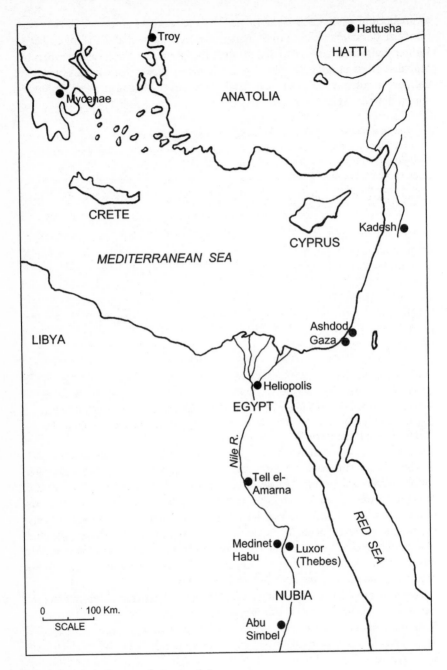

Fig. 12. Ancient Egypt and western Asia.

a cuneiform text on a clay tablet found with many others at the site of Hattusas (modern Bogazköy), the Hittite capital of Anatolia, near the city of Ankara. Written by a king named Mursilis II, the text, known as 'The Plague Prayers of Mursilis', offers a plea to the Hittite gods to restore order in 'Hatti land' by ridding its people of the plague that has raged since the time of his father Suppiluliumas.[66] The text begins,

> What is it that ye have done? A plague ye have let into the land. The Hatti land has been cruelly afflicted by plague. For twenty years now men have been dying [initially] in my father's days, [then] in my brother's days, and [now] in mine own since I have become the priest of the gods. When men are dying in the Hatti land like this, the plague is in no wise over. As for me, the agony of my heart and the anguish of my soul I cannot endure any more.[67]

Mursilis attempts to find some kind of supernatural justification behind this divine retribution brought upon his country. He asks whether it is because either he or his father had forgotten to supplicate the gods, or had caused their anger in some way. In order to establish what he could do to end the plague, he consulted an oracle, which revealed that his father failed to honour promises made on behalf of the Hittite royal dynasty to the storm-god, implying that this was the root cause of the problem. As a result of his father's indiscretions, only misery had been brought on the land of Hatti, for, as Mursilis laments,

> My father sent foot soldiers and charioteers who attacked the country of Amka, the Egyptian territory [in the Lebanon]. Again he sent troops, and again they attacked it ... But when they brought back to the Hatti land the prisoners which they had taken a plague broke out among the prisoners and they began to die ... From that day on people have been dying in the Hatti land.[68]

The toll that this epidemic took on the population of Hatti was immense. A supplementary plague text written by Mursilis speaks of the death of all the ploughmen who used to work in the fields, 'so no one works or reaps the fields of the god at all'. He laments also that 'The grinding women who used to make the sacrificial loaves for the gods are dead.' In addition to this, he says that the 'shepherds are dead', as are those who make sacrificial offerings to the gods.[69] It was a terrible natural catastrophe, and we can only imagine that it must have been the same story across the whole of the Near East.

According to the calculations of the British Egyptologist Kenneth Kitchen, the 'Second' Syrian war between Egypt and the Hittites under Mursilis II's father, Suppiluliumas, took place inside a year of Tutankhamun's death, c. 1339 BC.[70] Thus the plague was already rampant in the Near East by this time, and, since it was Egyptians who introduced it to the land of Hatti, it seems clear that it must have been present among the Egyptian garrisons of the northern empire and, we must assume, in Egypt before this time. Yet to what extent did it affect the people who lived along the Nile? Possibly we shall never know, since all the official records from this period were destroyed at the orders of Horemheb.

A CURSED NATION

Yet crucial evidence of the plague's presence in Egypt is to be found among the hundreds of Amarna letters written by vassal kings to Amenhotep III, Akhenaten and Smenkhkare during their reigns. One tablet seems to imply that Queen Tiye, Akhenaten's own mother, was herself a victim of the plague. Entitled 'Proper escort for a betrothed princess', it is addressed to Naphururea, the Akkadian name for Akhenaten, and was written by Burna-Buriyaš, the king of Babylonia. After offering cordial greetings to the king and the royal household, it begins,

> [*After the wife of*] your father had been mourned, I sent Hu'a, [my] mess[enger, and ..., an interp]reter, [*to you*]. [*I*] wrote [*as follows*], saying, 'A daughter of the king who [..., *was* (once) ta]ken [*to your father*]. Let [*them take*] another [*to you*].'
>
> [*And you yourself*] sent [Haamaš]ši, your messenger, and [... Mihuni, *the interprete*]r, [*saying*, ' ... *the wife of*] my father was mourned [...] that woman [...] she die[d] in a [pl]ague' [original italics].[71]

If the plague could have taken the life of Akhenaten's own mother, Tiye, the widow of Amenhotep III, then just how many other people did it claim? Egypt's northern empire was in the grip of an unprecedented plague, unlike any ever recorded before in the Near East. It was decimating the population, taking the lives of countless individuals, and was destined to wreak havoc for at least twenty to thirty years. What type of effect would this have had on the king of Egypt, who was seen to be the First Prophet of the Aten, the incarnation on earth of the life-giving god of light? How exactly might the spread of the plague have been seen not only by the king, but also by his subjects? Would they not have deemed it a sign that the old gods were angered by the king's choice of adopting one god above all others? The historical writer Graham Phillips, in his book *Act of God*, published in 1998, sums up the situation well:

> Such a plague may actually account for the abandonment of Amarna. Even though the ancients may not have known the true cause of disease, they knew well enough that contagious illnesses were passed from person to person. What type of epidemic this might have been is hard to tell, although it seems to have had a lengthy duration. ... For a people whose pharaoh was considered the personification of the chief god on earth, around whom the whole of society revolved, it must have seemed as if they were indeed a cursed nation.[72]

With these thoughts in mind, it is possible that the account in the book of Exodus of the smiting of Egypt's firstborn on the night of the Passover, immediately prior to the Exodus, was somehow influenced by this very real plague, which was decimating Egypt and the Near East at this time. Let us read what the Bible tells us about this event:

> And the Lord said unto Moses, Yet one plague more will I bring upon Pharaoh, and upon Egypt ...[73] And it came to pass at midnight, that the Lord smote all the firstborn in the land of Egypt, from the firstborn of Pharaoh that sat on his throne unto the firstborn of the captive that was in the dungeon; and all the firstborn of

cattle. And Pharaoh rose up in the night, he, and all his servants, and all the Egyptians; and there was a great cry in Egypt; for there was not a house where there was not one dead.[74]

Does this biblical narrative preserve a recollection of the plague that overran Egypt during the Amarna age? If the original source material behind the Graeco-Egyptian and later Graeco-Roman accounts of the life of Moses really did influence the contents of the book of Exodus, then it becomes a distinct possibility. Phillips proposed that the account of the killing of the firstborn by the Hebrew god was indeed a memory of this epidemic,[75] and the authors feel that he got it right.

Like the Hittite king Mursilis II, did the Egyptian people during the Amarna age come to believe that the plague was some kind of divine retribution, caused by the fact that the deposed gods of the old pantheon were not being appeased with suitable offerings and sacrifices? Might it have been suggested that to placate the angered gods all 'polluted' priests and followers of the Aten, as well as the Asiatic settlers, or 'foreigners', deemed to be spreading the plague, should be rounded up and either imprisoned or expelled from Egypt? Forewarned of what was about to happen, did many of these people, both Egyptian and Asiatic in origin, decide to leave Egypt of their own accord, fleeing to Syria-Palestine, where finally they integrated with native peoples? Were they afterwards joined by others who had been able to escape from Sile, modern-day Qantara, the frontier fortress situated on the border between the Eastern Delta and Sinai, where criminals and enemies of the king were enslaved during the reign of Horemheb?[76] As we have seen, he can be identified with the Orus, or Or, in Manetho's story of Osarsiph-Moses, and is likely to have been responsible for at least some of the actions attributed to Amenophis in the Exodus narrative.[77]

In other words, at least a percentage of the events Manetho describes actually took place during the reign of Horemheb, and not during that of his official predecessor Amenhotep III. This makes him the most likely choice as the true pharaoh of the Exodus (with echoes even of the pharaoh of the Oppression), which began most probably several years earlier when he became commander of the Egyptian army at the start of Tutankhamun's reign.

Are these the true roots of the Exodus, as well as the subject matter of the papyrus documents found by Howard Carter in the tomb of Tutankhamun – documents which he tried to use to his advantage during the spring of 1924? Everything points towards this extraordinary conclusion, and to explore the matter further we must venture now beyond the confines of Egypt into the wilderness of Sinai in search of the route of the Exodus and the origins of Yahweh, the god of the Israelites. Only by establishing the point of foundation of the Jewish religion can we go on to determine the historical reality of the conquest of Canaan and its implications with respect to the political situation at the time of the discovery of the tomb of Tutankhamun.

PART FOUR
YAHWEH

18. THE SEARCH FOR YAHWEH

Deep down in the Sudan, the ancient kingdom of Nubia, Amenhotep III, the father of Akhenaten and Tutankhamun, constructed twin temples at Soleb, one for himself and the other for his Great Royal Wife, Tiye. In his own temple, dedicated to the god Amun, are a series of columns on which are inscribed a register of African and Asiatic place names, or toponyms as they are known.[1] Among them are listed three places 'in the land of the Shasu',[2] one of which reads *t3 šsw yhw*, 'Yahweh in the land of the Shasu'.[3] Yahweh, of course, was the tetragrammaton, the ineffable name of the Israelite god, and yet here it was being linked directly with the nomadic peoples called Shasu and their homeland in the southern Transjordan, described textually as Seir,[4] or Edom.[5] This was the highlands region that stretched between the Gulf of Aqaba in the south and the Dead Sea in the north, and is referred to in Egyptian textual accounts as 'the land of the Shasu'.[6]

The above reference to Yahweh is the oldest on record, and so attempting to understand the relationship between the Shasu tribes and the god of the Israelites becomes essential if we are to establish the origins of the Israelite race. As we saw in Chapter 15, the Shasu (a name derived from the Egyptian *š'sw*, 'to wander'[7]) are alluded to in the Merneptah Stela, which dates to around 1220 BC. In this we read that the 'Shasu of Edom' have passed from 'the fortress of Merneptah ... to the water holes of the House of Atum' in the frontier town of Tjekku, the biblical Succoth, on the edge of the Eastern Delta, 'for their own subsistence and that of their flocks'.[8]

The annual movements of the Shasu were based on a precise knowledge of seasonal climate changes. During the winter rainy season they established their camps in the rich pastureland of the steppes and fertile plains of the Transjordan. Then in the arid summer season, when droughts were common, they drove their flocks into the coastal lowlands of Palestine and, as we have seen, even as far as the Eastern Delta, where their movements would appear to have been strictly monitored.[9] Yet the Shasu were more than simply pastoralists, moving their flocks and herds across thousands of kilometres of desert terrain each year, for somehow they grew to become a major threat to a succession of Egyptian kings of the Eighteenth and Nineteenth Dynasties.

EGYPT IN CANAAN

Even during the age of Amenhotep III and Akhenaten in the fourteenth century BC, Egyptian authorities feared that the Palestinian highlands could be used by unruly elements planning insurrection. As a consequence, they set up vassal kings in Jerusalem in the south and Shechem in the north, in order to police the regions in question. Indeed, the Amarna letters make it clear that the Egyptian authorities engineered the installation of a ruler in Jerusalem named 'Abdi-Heba, who had previously been given military training in Egypt.[10] Jerusalem thus became a strategic town with ample Egyptian influence, which included a temple once located on the site now occupied by the French Dominican Monastery of St Étienne (St Stephen). Archaeological excavations to determine its extent and origin have produced fragments of lotus columns and two alabaster vessels, as well as parts of an offering table, a statuette in serpentine and a stela dating from around the reign of Merneptah (c. 1224–1214 BC).[11]

One of the biggest thorns in the side of the Egyptian authorities was the Habiru of the Amarna letters, the 'Apiru of Egyptian inscriptions. As we saw in Chapter 16, they were displaced Semitic-speaking peoples who travelled to neighbouring city-states and countries looking to enter the service of wealthy landlords. Yet more importantly they banded together to form mercenary armies that would fight for whatever petty prince offered them the greatest return. They were a law unto themselves and, either with or without the support of local rulers, they terrorised Canaanite city-states, including those that were vassals of Egypt. The Amarna correspondence is full of accounts of attacks by Habiru/'Apiru militia, and in one letter 'Abdi-Heba of Jerusalem records his outrage over the fact that the cities of Ashkelon, Gezer and Lachish are taking in Habiru/'Apiru and offering them supplies.[12]

THE SHASU ENEMIES
Yet, in addition to the Habiru/'Apiru, who were mainly in the north country, one of Egypt's principal concerns was the build-up of the more southerly Shasu

Fig. 13. A Shasu warrior from a relief in Rameses II's rock temple at Beit el Wali in the Sudan. Note the distinctive headband and cap.

tribes, especially during the reign of Horemheb, who would seem to have launched a major offensive against Asiatic enemies in c. 1320 BC.[13] Having become a nuisance in the Transjordan, the Shasu clans began pushing westward through Arabah into the Negeb, in northern Sinai. From here they came into contact with major towns along the coastal plain, which made them a potential threat to Egypt's Eastern Delta.[14] In addition to these regions, there are references to them in the central highlands at places such as Megiddo, the Jezreel valley and Beth Shean.[15]

A view of the Shasu from this period can be gleaned from Egyptian textual records, which nearly always refer to them in a military context. Either they are fighting against the Egyptian armies in Syria-Palestine, or they appear as robber bands operating on their own. One papyrus text speaks of their infesting the mountain passes and trails of Canaan 'hidden in the brush', and 'fierce of visage with unpleasant hearts, who do not listen to persuasion'.[16] Indeed, according to Egyptian scholar William A Ward,

> The Egyptian view of the Shasu would thus seem to be of a group of free-booters, originating in Transjordan, who were encountered predominantly in their dual role of mercenaries or robber-bands serving or preying on the towns and caravan-routes of Canaan.[17]

In addition to this, we must not forget that they were also pastoralists, who used these same routes from Edom to Egypt in order to graze their flocks and herds. What is more, there exists good evidence to show that they had their own towns,[18] and may also have been involved in mining operations in the copper-mining district of Timna, some 27 kilometres north of the Gulf of Aqaba, the eastern extension of the Red Sea.[19] Yet matters would appear to have escalated, for an inscription from Year One of the reign of Seti I (c. 1309–1291 BC), speaks of an uprising among these tribal peoples:

> The Shasu enemies are plotting rebellion. Their tribal leaders are gathered in one place, standing on the foothills of Khor [or the Hurru, the inhabitants of Greater Palestine], and they are engaged in turmoil and uproar. Each of them is killing his fellow. They do not consider the laws of the palace.[20]

Exactly what was going on here remains uncertain. However, this insurrection led Seti I to mount a military campaign, which began with the capture of the city of Pa-Kanaan, modern-day Gaza. From here he pushed forward along the coastal plain, until he reached the Sea of Galilee, seemingly in pursuit of Shasu and Habiru/Apiru, who often became synonymous with each other. The cities of Yanoam (mentioned in the Victory Stela from Merneptah's reign), Beth Shean and Hammath are all said to have fallen before him, until finally he was knocking on the door of Hittite strongholds in northern Syria. It was a remarkable run of victories, celebrated with reliefs and inscriptions on the exterior walls of the Temple of Amun at Karnak.

Despite their apparent defeat at the hands of Seti I, the Shasu clans would

Fig. 14. Relief from the temple of Amun at Karnak showing Shasu warriors engaged in battle against the army of Seti I (after Raphael Giveon).

seem only to have increased in strength and number, for they began posing a major threat to the northern hill country around Shechem. They also began to infiltrate other regions of Canaan right the way across to the coast of Syria.

During the reign of Seti's son, Rameses II (c. 1290–1224 BC), a number of military campaigns were undertaken, the most famous being the battle against the Hittites at Kadesh in Syria. Yet it is also a fact that Rameses entered the southern Transjordan, the land of Edom, and here defeated unruly enemies of Egypt, including Shasu tribes. Certainly, wall reliefs at Karnak celebrate Rameses' attacks on coastal cities such as Ashkelon and depict Shasu being taken as prisoners.

Later, early in the twelfth century BC, raids against the 'tent camps' of the Shasu located in southern Canaan were made by the pharaoh Rameses III (c. 1182–1151 BC). Once again they would seem to have risen up and become troublesome and unmanageable, necessitating a military campaign to quell their actions.[21]

From records such as these it would seem that from around 1320 BC through to the end of the first quarter of the twelfth century BC, the Shasu grew to become a major headache for the Egyptian authorities. So are the Shasu to be associated with the tribal group named as 'Israel' on the Victory Stela as having been 'laid waste' by Merneptah?

YAHWEH IN THE LAND OF THE SHASU
The Shasu toponym found in the Soleb temple bearing the name 'Yahweh' implies that this tribal group were followers of the Israelite god. Moreover,

since the reference to Yahweh seems to be attached to a town, or location, it suggests that there was to be found here a shrine, or sanctuary, of this god – a theory first proposed in 1971 by Raphael Giveon, the world's leading expert on the Shasu.[22] He speculated also that 'Yahweh in the land of the Shasu' may well be the origin of the biblical term Beth Yahweh, the House of Yahweh, or Beth-el, 'House of God.[23] Furthermore, Giveon went on to propose that in this realisation the homeland of the Shasu must have been important to the development of the religion of Israel, and in particular its connection with sacred mountains.[24] Similar ideas had been voiced as early as 1947 by the Egyptologist Bernhard Grdseloff,[25] who realised that the Yahweh-Shasu toponym was perhaps the earliest attested extrabiblical reference to both the Israelite god and those who venerated this deity.[26] Indeed, as the Egyptologist Donald Redford has commented with respect to the significance of the Yahweh-Shasu toponym,

> For half a century it has been generally admitted that we have here the tetragrammaton, the name of the Israelite god, 'Yahweh'; and if this be the case, as it undoubtedly is, the passage constitutes a most precious indication of the whereabouts during the late fifteenth century B.C. of an enclave revering this god.[27]

What is more, the Soleb temple dating from the reign of Amenhotep III is not the only place where we find mention of 'Yahweh in the land of the Shasu'. It appears also among a list of some 104 African and Asiatic toponyms, many of them damaged, found at a temple dating back to the reign of Rameses II in the Nubian city of Amarah West. Among them are listed six place names 'in the land of the Shasu' including, once again, 'Yahweh in the land of the Shasu'.[28] So we can say that the Soleb entry is not simply a misreading of another name, for we find it present in two different Nubian temples built 150 years apart (although the Amarah inscriptions could have been copied from those at Soleb).

So, assuming that the Shasu did venerate Yahweh, then how might this relate to the Israel of the Bible? How can we interpret this new perspective of the origin of the Hebrew god in the knowledge that the oldest reference to 'Yahweh' dates from the reign of Amenhotep III (c. 1405–1367 BC)?

Israel, as we shall recall, was the name conferred on Jacob by God,[29] and was afterwards applied to his descendants, who became known as the 'children of Israel', or the Israelites. As outlined in Chapter 15, the mention of 'Israel' on the Victory Stela relates not to a place but a people, implying perhaps that they were a nomadic, or seminomadic, tribal group. Thus we must ask ourselves why their name appears in a list of Asiatic peoples and places during the reign of Merneptah, even though 'Israel' does not appear among the toponym register from Amarah dating from the reign of his father Rameses II. OK, so many of the place names have been damaged and are now illegible. However, the name is also missing from the earlier Soleb register dating to the time of Amenhotep III. Nowhere is there mention of 'the land of Israel'.

What do appear on both the Soleb and Amarah lists, and yet are glaringly absent from Merneptah's Victory Stela, are references to the Shasu, who we can be pretty sure Rameses II 'laid waste' during his aforementioned military campaign in Seir-Edom. Since at least some elements of the Shasu would appear to have been worshippers of Yahweh, then is it not possible that Israel denotes a particular tribe or clan? Thus Israel simply becomes one of the clans of the Shasu, and very possibly the most important of them, for it appears to have risen in notoriety enough by Merneptah's reign to have been included in the list of Asiatic enemies found on the Victory Stela. More than this, the fact that although they had been 'laid waste', and 'his seed is not', suggests that its leader, or leaders, had posed a major threat to Egypt's northern empire, which is exactly what happened in the case of the Shasu. As we have seen, following the death of Merneptah in c. 1204 BC they rose up again, prompting a military campaign against the 'tent camps' of the Shasu in the reign of Ramesses III, some thirty to fifty years later.

Attempts to link the Hebrews with other Asiatic enemies mentioned in Egyptian inscriptions have always failed. As we have seen, a relationship between the Habiru/'Apiru and the Hebrews has always been suspected, although there seems to have been no obvious ethnic, social or geographic commonality among these Semitic-speaking peoples. Moreover, it now seems certain that the term Hebrew, if it did derive from Habiru, simply became a term of abuse, used by the Egyptians and Philistines to describe a certain type of Asiatic enemy, and had little if anything to do with their ethnic background.[30] Only the Shasu appear to fit anything like the description of the children of Israel as outlined in the Bible. Thus if the Shasu were really the 'Israel' of the Victory Stela, as well as perhaps the original worshippers of the god Yahweh, then what are we to make of the biblical account of the establishment of the Israelite religion?

I AM YAHWEH

Yahweh, the tetragrammaton, or ineffable name of God, was first revealed to Moses when in Midian, the land of the Midianites, long considered to be northwest Arabia. One day, whilst tending the flock of Jethro, his father-in-law, comes 'to the back of the wilderness' and upon 'the mountain of God, unto Horeb',[31] which means 'mountain in the desert'.[32] Here he witnesses an 'angel of the Lord' in the form of a burning bush of fire, and during the encounter asks the deity for his name, to which he responds, 'I AM THAT I AM: and he said, Thus shalt thou say unto the children of Israel, I AM hath sent me unto you.'[33] Yet then God tells Moses that he is to say unto the children of Israel, 'Yahweh your fathers' deity appeared to me, the deity of Abraham, Isaac and Jacob'.[34] This passage from the book of Exodus constitutes the first disclosure of the name Yahweh,[35] linking it directly with the mountain of God.

During his encounter with Yahweh Moses is told to return to Egypt, where he is to demand from Pharaoh that he release the Israelite nation. Yet, when this simply incites the Egyptian king to inflict even more agony on the Hebrews, Yahweh delivers another message, in which he proclaims,

I am Jehovah [i.e. Yahweh], and I appeared unto Abraham, unto Isaac, and unto Jacob, as God Almighty [*El Shaddai*], *but by my name Jehovah I was not known to them* [authors' italics].[36]

This statement is important, for it confirms to us that, prior to Moses' first visit to 'the mountain of God, unto Horeb', the true name of the deity was unknown

And the angel of the Lord appeared unto Moses in a flame of fire, out of the midst of a bush: & he looked & behold, the bush burned with fire, & the bush was not consumed. Exod. III. Ch. V.

Fig. 15. Moses witnesses the Angel of the Lord in the form of a burning bush of fire on Mount Horeb, an alternative name for Mount Sinai, the mountain of Yahweh.

to him. Previously, the god of the Israelites was referred to only by epithets such as *Adon*, 'lord', or variations of El, the Canaanite name of God, such as *El shaddai*, 'God almighty', or *El-elohe-Israel*, 'mighty one, God of Israel'.[37] That the Israelites' worship of Yahweh was intimately associated with the Mountain of God is evidenced from the 'Song of the Sea', a poem from the book of Exodus, which celebrates the deliverance of Israel from Pharaoh's army. In this we read,

> Thou shalt bring them in, and plant them in the mountain of thine inheritance,
> The place, O Lord, which thou hast made for thee to dwell in,
> The sanctuary, O Lord, which thy hands have established.[38]

Yahweh was thus considered to inhabit the mountain, or at least dwell in a shrine, or sanctuary, which was deemed to have been erected by him (an inference perhaps that no one had any knowledge of its original foundation, thus implying that it was divine in origin). A more direct translation of the original Hebrew text reads:

> May you bring them and plant them in your property mountain,
> The firm seat for your sitting/throne/dwelling you devised, Yahweh,
> The sanctum, my Lordship, your hands founded.[39]

From these lines it is clear that the mountain was considered to be the seat of Yahweh, and possessed a shrine or sanctuary of some kind. We know too that it was already considered sacred because Moses was told by the voice of God, 'Draw not nigh hither; put off thy shoes from off thy feet, for the place whereon thou standest is holy ground'.[40] In addition to this, the composer of the 'Song of the Sea' tells us that it was deemed the divine right of the children of Israel, through the intercession of Moses, to approach the dwelling place of Yahweh, who appears as the *genius loci*, or spirit of the place.

MOUNT SINAI

Following the Exodus from Egypt, the book of Exodus tells us that Moses returned to the Mountain of Yahweh in the company of the 'children of Israel'. This time the location is introduced initially as 'mount Sinai',[41] although the name 'mount Horeb' is used later in the account, demonstrating that they are one and the same place.[42] Here God imparted to Moses the holy laws, which were inscribed on 'two tables of the testimony'.[43] So where might this monumental event in Jewish religious tradition have actually taken place?

The search for Mount Horeb, or Mount Sinai, is an extremely old one. Following the encampment here for a whole year at the beginning of the Israelites' forty years of wandering in the wilderness, the Bible is silent regarding the Mountain of Yahweh. Indeed, the Israelites and later Jews appear to ignore the area completely, which seems strange considering it was here that the divine laws were delivered unto Moses by the Lord himself. The only person recorded as having gone to 'Horeb the mount of God'[44] after this time was the prophet Elijah, who fled into 'the wilderness' after Jezebel, the wife of Ahab, king of Israel, who reigned c. 918–900 BC, threatened to kill him for putting to death her priests of the pagan god Baal. Here he remained in a cave for forty days and forty nights, until finally Yahweh appeared before him and asked, "What doest thou here, Elijah?"[45]

Unfortunately, the Bible gives no indication as to where Elijah might have been, other than that he passed through Beersheba immediately prior to entering 'the wilderness', beyond which was presumably the Mountain of God.[46] Thus eventually the mountain's whereabouts was lost, and not until the early Christian era did the quest begin to properly identify it.

THE CASE FOR JEBEL MÛSA

Dionysius of Alexandria, who came to live in the Sinai around AD 250, recorded that the peninsula had become a refuge for Christian refugees escaping persecution in Egypt.[47] It was even said that St Catherine of Alexandria fled initially to Sinai, but that she eventually returned to Egypt. According to the popular story, in AD 307 she was crucified on a spiked wheel and eventually beheaded. Angels carried her body through the air and placed it down on one of the Sinai's highest mountains, Jebel Mûsa (2,286 metres) or, seemingly, the more southerly placed and slightly higher Jebel Katherina (2,637 metres). Both peaks belong to the same massif and are separated only by a saddle-back indentation. The first church constructed over the spot was founded by the Empress Helena, or St Helena (c. AD 255–330), the mother of Constantine the Great, the emperor of Rome, who chose to identify Jebel Mûsa with Mount Sinai, even though there was no Jewish tradition as to its whereabouts.[48] Following her son's conversion to Christianity after the battle of Milvian Bridge in AD 312, and his election as emperor in AD 324, she had devoted much of her life to travelling the Holy Land, founding churches on the site of holy shrines and collecting religious relics. Why she regarded Jebel Mûsa as Mount Sinai will never be known. However, it is speculated that this knowledge might have been revealed through visions experienced by Constantine.

In AD 373 a monk from Canopus, Egypt, named Ammonius is recorded as having visited the holy places of Palestine. He returned via 'Mount Sinai', presumably Jebel Mûsa, in the company of a group of pilgrims.[49] Then in AD 420 some forty monks were said to have been massacred when Arabs or Saracens attacked the 'Monastery of the Burning Bush', situated on the slopes of the mountain.[50] Much later Justinianus (AD 483–565), emperor of the Eastern Roman Empire, founded a new monastery on the site of St Helena's church, which in the ninth century was dedicated to St Catherine. By this time there were as many as 6,000 to 7,000 monks and hermits living in southern Sinai under constant threat of attack from Arabs and Saracens.[51]

Only in the fourteenth century, following the Christian Crusades, were pilgrims finally able to visit Jebel Mûsa, which had by now been identified as Mount Sinai for over 1,000 years. Somewhat confusingly, nearby Jebel Serbal (2,057 metres) was seen as Mount Horeb, the Mountain of God, even though it is clear from the Bible that both sites are one and the same. Moreover, there is a long tradition linking Jebel Serbal with the site of Mount Sinai, which seems to be even older than the one attached to Jebel Mûsa. However, even this goes back only to the late Roman period.[52] Moreover, there is good reason to assume that some of the legends attached to Jebel Mûsa were originally associated with Jebel Serbal, which seems to have been the original site of pilgrimage during early Christian times.[53]

Oblivious of this knowledge, Christians and Muslims come from all over the world to visit Jebel Mûsa and pray at the spot where Moses received the Tablets of the Law and Mohammed's horse, Boraq, is supposed to have ascended to heaven. The Greek Orthodox monks of St Catherine's monastery will guide the visitor to a small oratory, lit constantly by a burning lamp, where they say the miracle of the Burning Bush took place. Elsewhere they will point out the shrine of St Catherine in which are housed the saint's bones. Also of interest is the monastery's library, which contains around 500 priceless manuscripts in Greek, Arabic, Syriac and Ethiopic, although its most precious possession is the Codex Sinaiticus, a valuable biblical manuscript dating from the fourth century AD.

All this may be so, but the original Mount Sinai is unlikely to have been situated in southern Sinai for a number of reasons. Yet if we are to discern its true location we must begin by accepting that there is some historical basis to the account of the Exodus and the wanderings of the Israelites. Even if only a small group of renegade Egyptians, and/or foreigners, were forced out of Egypt, the Bible becomes our only real guide through the wilderness.

THE FLIGHT FROM EGYPT

Thus we must assume that the starting part of the Exodus was, as the Old Testament suggests, Rameses, ancient Pi-Ramesse, modern-day Tell ed-Dab'a and its environs, the original residence of the Ramesside kings in the Eastern Delta. Here too was the land of Goshen, and indeed the city of Zoan, where the Hebrews were said to have settled at the time of Joseph and Jacob. In addition to this, we know that Tell ed-Dab'a was the Hyksos capital of Avaris, which supposedly became the home of the 'lepers' and 'impure people', under the leadership of Osarsiph-Moses and the 'shepherds', before their expulsion from Egypt.

In the book of Exodus the Israelites are said to have journeyed from Rameses to Succoth, Egyptian Tjekku, modern-day Tell el-Maskhuta, lying in front of Lake Timsah at the eastern end of the Wâdî Tumilât, an east–west-running dry river valley which they must have traversed to reach this area. Such a conclusion makes sense of the Bible account, which states that, after Pharaoh 'had let the people go',

> ... God led them not by the way of the land of the Philistines, although that was near: for God said, Lest peradventure the people repent when they see war, and they return to Egypt.[54]

The 'way of the land of the Philistines' – although an anachronism, for the Philistines did not enter Palestine until after the Exodus – was the road that passed through the Eastern Delta towns of Thel (modern Tel Abu Sêfeh) and Sile (Qantara) to El Arish, Raphia and, finally, Gaza. The coastal lowlands of Palestine did eventually become the stronghold of the Philistines, but only after 1250 BC. What would have been infinitely more of a problem for any escaping 'Israelites' (and we shall use this term since we are dealing specifically with the biblical narrative) would have been the Egyptian military garrisons. These are known to have been placed at regular intervals all along this ancient military road, referred to in ancient texts as 'the Ways of Horus'. This would explain why the Israelites were persuaded to take another route: 'Lest peradventure the people repent when they see war, and they return to Egypt'. In other words, it was feared that, the first time they came up against an Egyptian fort, the Israelites would do an about-turn and head back to Egypt. Such a route makes sense of why, after persuading the Israelites from taking the 'way of the land of the Philistines', God made them take 'the way of the wilderness by the Red Sea'.[55]

THE ROUTE OF THE EXODUS

Travelling southwards from Lake Timsah, past the so-called Bitter Lakes, they could have reached the head of the Gulf of Suez and continued along its eastern shore until they hit the Sinai peninsula. Yet here Egypt's prized copper and turquoise mines were located, and so the whole region would have been crawling with Egyptian soldiers, whom the Israelites are, once again, unlikely to have wanted to confront. Much more likely is that the path of the Exodus was from Lake Timsah south to the Bitter Lakes, the biblical Marah, meaning 'bitter', as well as the most likely candidate of the *yam-sûp*,[56] or 'reed sea', where the Israelites were able to thwart the pursuing Egyptian army led by Pharaoh himself. Once on its eastern side they would seem to have travelled eastwards 'into the wilderness of Shur',[57] still known today as the Way of Shur (which could also have been reached via the road to Beersheba and Hebron, which starts in the vicinity of Lake Timsah, a less likely route by far – see fig. 22 on page 231). South of here they could have picked up the ancient road used since time immemorial by caravan traders and nomadic pastoralists, such as the Shasu, moving between Egypt and Arabia.[58] By following this in a south easterly direction they could have journeyed unhindered, past what is today the towns of Nakhel and Et-Tamad, until the Bible tells us they came upon 'Elim, where were twelve springs of water, and threescore and ten palm trees; and they encamped there by the waters'.[59]

Although some Bible scholars place Elim on the shores of the Gulf of Suez, all the indications are that it was situated on the Gulf of Aqaba, where the Red Sea resort of Eilat is to be found today. The word Elim is a plural form of El, which can also be written Elath or Eloth,[60] a location that the Bible's first book of Kings tells us was 'besides' Ezion-Geber, where Solomon's navy was moored 'on the shore of the Red Sea, in the land of Edom'.[61] Thus Eloth and Elim are almost certainly one and the same. This is the most obvious route taken by Moses and his followers, since it must have been this same road that he followed on his way to and from the land of Midian, the land beyond the eastern shores of the Gulf of Aqaba, on the edge of which the mountain of Yahweh was situated.

Having encamped by the waters of Elim, the book of Exodus tells us the Israelites resumed their journey and on the fifteenth day of the second month after their departure from Egypt they entered 'the wilderness of Sin, which is between Elim and Sinai'.[62] Having pitched their camps at a place called Rephidim, the Israelites complained of having no water. As a consequence, Moses is said to have struck his rod on 'the rock in Horeb', where immediately water gushed forth.[63] Thus they had reached Mount Horeb, the Mountain of Yahweh, a fact confirmed when later we read that, after they depart from Rephidim, they enter the 'wilderness of Sinai', where in the third month after their departure from Egypt 'Israel camped before the mount'.[64]

So, was the 'wilderness of Sin' the same as 'the wilderness of Sinai', and why did they seem to reach Horeb, before departing again and then coming upon 'the mount' for a second time? The geographical answers will become apparent, but it is important to remember that there are many inconsistencies, anachronisms and contradictions in the Pentateuch, which indicate that it was composed by different authors from different backgrounds at different times. Thus many of the events portrayed in the book of Exodus and the book of Numbers, the two main sources for the Israelites' wanderings, are unquestionably based on oral traditions. These could have been floating around for many hundreds of years before being finally committed to written form. Thus there will be duplications of events mixed up with local folk stories from the Sinai that must be disentangled from the core source material contained within these accounts in order to provide us with a workable framework for deciding the true location of the Mountain of Yahweh.

Neither Exodus nor Numbers make it clear where the wilderness of Sin, or Sinai, was to be found. As previously mentioned, the connection between the Sinai of the Bible and what we know today as the Sinai Peninsula was determined only in Christian times. More likely is that Mount Sinai, or Horeb, was situated somewhere beyond Eilat, at the head of the Gulf of Aqaba, where the Seir mountain range, the land of the Shasu, stretches away in the direction of the Dead Sea. Yet was there any evidence to support this bold assertion?

THE CASE FOR MOUNT SEIR

We look first at a curious statement in Chapter 33 of the book of Deuteronomy, the final book of the Pentateuch, which is thought to have been composed as late as the seventh century BC.[65] This tells us that, before his death, Moses gave a blessing to the children of Israel, which began:

The Lord came from Sinai,
And rose from Seir unto them [i.e. the Israelites];[66]

These words imply that, in addition to his connection with Sinai, Yahweh emerged out of Seir. An even more interesting statement appears in the war poem known as the 'Song of Deborah' found in the book of Judges, which proclaims:

I will sing praise to the Lord, the God of Israel.
Lord, when thou wentest forth out of Seir,
When thou marchedst out of the field of Edom,
The earth trembled, the heavens also dropped,
Yea, the clouds dropped water.
The mountains flowed down at the presence of the Lord,
Even yon Sinai at the presence of the Lord, the God of Israel.[67]

If these lines do not simply relate to the final onslaught on Canaan launched by the Israelites from Seir, then it becomes the place foremost associated with the might of Yahweh. More than this, it suggests that Sinai is merely another name for Seir. So what exactly do we know about Seir, or Edom, the land of the Shasu?

Egyptian textual inscriptions link the Shasu specifically with Mount Seir,[68] the chief peak in the Seir range, and with Edom.[69] Originally, the Bible tells us Seir was the homeland of the Emim, 'a people great, and many, and tall',[70] known also as the Rephaim or Anakim,[71] a giant race said to have been descendants of the Nephilim, a fallen race that thrived before the age of the Flood.[72] Afterwards, Seir became the homeland of the Horites,[73] a troglodyte race that lived 'in their Mount Seir'.[74] They were driven out by the armies of Edom,[75] who afterwards 'dwelt in mount Seir'.[76] Seir itself took its name from the ancestor of the Horite race, named in the book of Genesis as 'Seir the Horite', whose descendants were called 'the sons of Seir'.[77] Bible scholars surmise that the Horites were synonymous with a peoples mentioned in Egyptian textual inscriptions as the Hurru, or Hurrites,[78] the inhabitants of 'Greater Palestine'.[79] This is despite the fact that the Bible places the Horites only in the vicinity of the Seir mountain range, and so it is unlikely that they were the Hurru.

A SCAPEGOAT FOR AZAZEL

In Hebrew *se'ir* means 'rough' or 'hairy', as in the coat of a mountain goat.[80] Seir was also the land of Esau, 'the father of the Edomites in mount Seir',[81] who was the elder twin brother of Jacob and son of Isaac, whose father was the patriarch Abraham. Esau, or Edom[82] – they are both one and the same – was known as the 'hairy man' (*ish se'ir*), indicating that he is merely an aspect of the god of Seir.[83] He was also identified with the 'he-goat' (*sa'ir*),[84] or more correctly the scapegoat. This sacrificial animal, the book of Leviticus tells us, was slain, or more correctly sent away to its death, by the Israelites under Moses as 'a sin offering' in order that the Israelites might atone for their sins:[85]

And Aaron shall present the goat upon which the lot fell for the Lord, and offer him for a sin offering. But the goat, on which the lot fell for Azazel, shall be set alive before the Lord, to make atonement for him, to send him away for Azazel into the wilderness ...[86]

Azazel is a fallen angel, whose name came to be associated with the word 'scapegoat' in Bible translations. Yet it in fact derives most probably from the

Fig. 16. Esau, the son of Isaac, selling his birthright to his younger brother Jacob for the price of a bowl of red lentil pottage.

Akkadian *uz*, meaning 'goat'.[87] Other sources make it clear that the scapegoat ritual was done to propitiate Samael, another chief demon and fallen angel in Jewish tradition, whose name means 'poison of God'.[88] Yet it is Azazel who is singled out in connection with Seir, for of him it was said, 'His portion among the peoples is Esau, a people who live by the sword; and his portion among the animals is the goat. The demons [*shedim*] are part of his realm and are called in the Bible *seirim*; he and his people are named Seir.'[89] The *seirim* mentioned here were not, of course, demons, but the indigenous peoples of Seir, the descendants of Esau, or Edom.

Mount Seir would seem to have been the original location of the scapegoat ritual conducted by Aaron and perpetuated each year in the Jewish feast of *Yom Kippur*, the Day of Atonement. Moreover, there is clear evidence that rabbinical scholars in medieval times attempted to disassociate this archaic practice with any kind of sacrificial offering made to the god of Seir. This seems to be confirmed in a statement issued by one Jewish rabbi who made it clear that 'The scapegoat is not (heaven for-fend!) an offering from us to him [i.e. the god of Seir], but an act of obedience to God'.[90]

So who exactly was the god of Seir? He is associated with Esau and also with Edom, whose name means simply 'red'. This colour appellation is said to derive from the familiar Bible story in which Esau is tricked out of his inheritance by his younger brother Jacob, who offers him some red lentil pottage in exchange for his birthright after he arrives home from a hunt one day ravished by hunger.[91] Yet the true purpose of this parable is perhaps to justify the animosity that existed between the two different branches of Isaac's family, which the Bible implies were bitter enemies. For example, while in the wilderness the Israelites were attacked by the Amalekites, the descendants of Amalek, the grandson of Esau and a 'duke' of Edom.[92] The Amalekites were supposed to have inhabited the territories to the west of Edom.[93] Moreover, when finally the children of Israel wished to enter Canaan, the king of Edom refused Moses and the Israelites permission to travel along the King's Highway north to Jericho, forcing them to 'compass' the land of Edom in order to reach Palestine (see Chapter 22).[94]

That Aaron, Moses' brother and the high priest of the tribe of Levi, sacrificed the scapegoat on Mount Seir in the land of Edom, where Egyptian records speak of a location called 'Yahweh in the land of the Shasu', is very interesting indeed. Here then we might expect to find the roots behind the worship of Yahweh. Yet where exactly was Mount Seir? Was any one mountain identified with this name? In order to answer these questions, we must first ask ourselves how the Mountain of Yahweh could on the one hand have been seen as the seat, throne or sanctuary of the Israelite deity, and on the other as the abode of the 'pagan' god of Seir? This awkward conundrum must be tackled before the veil can be lifted and the location of Mount Sinai revealed.

19. MOUNTAIN OF THE MOON

Following Joshua's conquest of Canaan, the lands from Mount Hermon in the north to Gaza in the south and the Jordan Valley in the east were divided among the twelve tribes of Israel. Thereafter the Israelites came under the control of a series of local magistrates or rulers, known as judges, whose influence is traditionally thought to have lasted for around 300 years. The first king of Israel was Saul, of the tribe of Benjamin, who took the throne in around 1091 BC. He was followed by David, who was anointed king of the tribe of Judah at Hebron in c. 1048 BC, and became king of all Israel seven and a half years later, choosing Jerusalem as the seat of his kingdom.

It was during the reign of David's son Solomon that the First Temple was built, making Jerusalem both the seat of royal power and the national place of worship of the Israelite god. Here, in the Holy of Holies, rested the Ark of the Covenant, the vessel in which the deity is said to have been transported from place to place. The kings of Israel were anointed, a religious act that established a special relationship with God, thus making them the 'Anointed [ones] of Yahweh'.[1] During the ceremony the spirit of Yahweh entered the candidate, enabling the anointing process to proceed in order to make the king inviolate to danger.

After Solomon's own reign of forty years internal struggles broke out among the leaders of the different tribes, and this resulted in a schism whereby the chiefs of ten tribes broke away from the next king, Rehoboam, king of Judah, who ruled from Jerusalem. This left the rest of the country in the hands of Jeroboam, the anointed king of the new Israel (which became known as Samaria), made up of the territories of the other ten tribes. Only the tribe of Benjamin, and the priestly caste known as the Levites, decided to support Judah after the division. Thereafter Judah and Israel went their own ways, each carving out its own separate history until Israel was conquered by the Assyrian empire in c. 721 BC and the ten tribes were carried off into exile, events that effectively put an end to the commonwealth of Israel. Then in c. 640 BC a man by the name of Josiah was anointed king of Judah. Unlike a number of his predecessors who had fallen into idolatry, he was a fanatical follower of Yahweh, and was said to have 'walked in all the way of David his father, and turned not aside to the right hand or to the left'.[2]

Josiah revived the worship of Yahweh as a national religion and attempted to exterminate all forms of idolatry, which had perverted the land for generations. Any religious practices or tracts from the Old Testament that intimated that the god of Israel was once attached to the land of the Edomites, Israel's hated enemies, would have been expunged. Indeed, in these actions Josiah would have had in mind the reckless deeds of his ancestor, Amaziah, king of Judah, who had come up against the 'children of Seir' some 200 years beforehand (he reigned c.

838–809 BC).[3] After slaughtering so many of them, and throwing to their deaths so many more (see Chapter 20), he is said to have brought back to Judah

> the gods of the children of Seir, and set them up to be his gods, and bowed down himself before them, and burned incense unto them.[4]

Josiah would have seen this act as an abomination against the name of Yahweh, especially as these 'gods of the children of Seir' must have been supplicated *inside* the Temple of Solomon, something that would have caused an even greater enmity towards Edom. Additionally, it is possible that Josiah instructed the copyists of the Pentateuch to dissociate the worship of Yahweh from any references to the 'pagan' god of Seir, who was henceforth denigrated into a demon or devil called Azazel or Edom. Moreover, it is plausible that Josiah severed any geographical associations between Seir and the Mountain of Yahweh, in the hope that this would resanctify the memory of the covenant made between Moses and Yahweh on Mount Sinai/Horeb. If this is true, then it may go some way to explain why in later generations the prophet Ezekiel, as 'the word of the Lord', spoke out so venomously against Mount Seir:

> I am against thee, O mount Seir, and I will stretch out mine hand against thee, and I will make thee a desolation and an astonishment. I will lay thy cities waste, and thou shalt be desolate; and thou shalt know that I am the Lord.[5]

Can all this hatred towards Edom have resulted from its king's refusal to allow Moses and the Israelites to pass through his kingdom at the time of the conquest? Clearly, the answer is no. What seems far more obvious is that later generations of Jews were somehow distancing themselves from the form of religious worship that was practised by the Edomites, the descendants of Esau. For so much hatred to have been vexed in this direction, it was quite obviously not simply a 'pagan' religion, but an inversion of the Israelites' own perception of the worship of Yahweh. In other words, the god of Seir was not a pagan deity at all. He was simply a form of Yahweh, yet one, it would seem, that the Israelites and later Jews saw as a blasphemy. So what was it that so abhorred them about this pre-Mosaic form of Hebraic worship? The answer would seem to have been Yahweh's close association with the moon.

THE SEARCH FOR SIN

In ancient times the moon was considered the oldest of the planets, preceding the sun, as day follows night. He was seen to control the cycles of nature, causing grass, trees and crops to grow. He increased the yield of flocks and herds, and was responsible for childbirth among the human race.[6] In ancient Mesopotamia, modern-day Iraq, he was worshipped under the name Sin, from the Sumerian *en-zu*, or *zu-en*, meaning 'the lord of knowledge',[7] whose chief temple was at Ur, a major city located at the mouth of the Euphrates river. His other great temple was at Harran, an ancient city on the borders of what is today northern Syria and southeastern Turkey.

Yet the most ancient worshippers of the moon god were not farmers who tilled the land, but Aramaean and proto-Aramaean nomadic pastoralists, Semitic-speaking peoples, who roamed the deserts of Syria and Arabia and were the forerunners of the Midianites and the pre-Islamic Arabs. In the Old Testament, the Aramaeans were descendants of Aram, the son of Shem and great-uncle of Abraham,[8] whose older brothers are named as Nahor and Haran.[9] Midian, the ancestor of the Midianites, was the fourth son of Abraham by Keturah, his 'concubine',[10] through whom he became the father of many nations.

Abraham is thought to have lived c. 2000–1800 BC, and is said to have been born in 'Ur of the Chaldees'[11] located in the Bible's land of Shinar,[12] ancient Sumer. As early as 1854 this city was identified by JE Taylor of the British Museum with a ziggurat hill in southern Mesopotamia named Tell al Muqayyar.[13] It was famously excavated during the 1920s by the English archaeologist Leonard Woolley, who wrote various books on the subject including *Ur of the Chaldees*, published in 1929.[14] Yet in all likelihood the biblical city of Ur is to be identified with Urfa, ancient Edessa, in southeast Turkey. This would seem to have been the location of an ancient city named in Akkadian, Sumerian and Hittite texts as Ursu.[15] Moreover, local tradition asserts that Abraham was born in Urfa within a cave situated at the foot of the citadel, which is even today a major site of pilgrimage for Muslims who descend on the city from all over the Near East.[16] More significantly, Urfa had its own temple to the moon god Sin,[17] while the term 'Chaldees', or Chaldeans, was simply another name for the star worshippers of Harran and Urfa, who were known from the eighth century onwards as Sabians (see below).[18]

From 'Ur of the Chaldees' Abraham journeyed with his wife Sarai (later Sarah), his brother's son Lot and his father Terah to Harran, a distance of around 35 kilometres. After remaining here for some time, God told him to leave his father's house (his father having died) and set out with his family and household.[19] So from Harran they went down into Canaan, and encamped first at Shechem in the northern highlands,[20] before journeying on to central Palestine, where Abraham pitched his tent near the site of Bethel, 'the house of God',[21] thought to have been located on the road between Jerusalem and Shechem.[22] Abraham then continued his journey southwards until finally a famine forced him and his family to enter Egypt. His first son, Ismael, born to an Egyptian handmaiden named Hagar, was said to have become the ancestor of the Ismaelites or Arab peoples. Abraham's second son, Isaac, born to his wife Sarah, was destined to become the father of Jacob, the ancestor of the Israelites, and Esau, the founder of the Edomite tribes.

That Abraham was brought up in 'Ur of the Chaldees', and spent his early life at Harran, both great cult centres of the moon god Sin, has constantly intrigued Bible scholars. Since he is named as the first great patriarch, the possibility of there being a connection between the god of Abraham and the moon god Sin is very tantalising indeed. Establishing this fact is especially important in view of the fact that the Mountain of Yahweh, on which Moses gained the Tablets of the Law, is named as Sinai, quite literally 'of Sin', or 'of the moon'.[23]

The ancestors of the Israelites were unquestionably nomadic and seminomadic pastoralists who, like their cousins the Aramaeans, camped temporarily in the deserts of Syria-Palestine before twice entering Egypt at times of famine, once during the age of Abraham, and then again at the time of Joseph and Jacob. Yet could they also have been worshippers of the moon, the oldest of the planets and the father of the sun, and was this religious tradition adhered to by Esau, Isaac's elder son? For an answer to these questions we have to travel back to Abraham's place of origin.

THE CITY OF SIN

As we have seen, the ancient inhabitants of Harran and nearby Urfa were worshippers of the stars and planets, and in particular the moon, Sin, whom they saw as 'God of the Gods' or 'Lord of the Gods'.[24] Indeed, Harran was actually referred to as 'the city of Sin'.[25] The myths and legends of the Harranians, known also as the Chaldeans or Sabians, are a strange amalgam of biblical stories and their own 'pagan' religious traditions. Yet some of these reveal a clear connection between the worship of the moon god and the roots of the Jewish faith. For instance, the Harranians believed that Adam, the first man, 'was a prophet, the envoy of the moon, who called people to the worship of the moon'.[26] Yet they disapprove of Seth, Adam's son, because he disagreed with his father over the worship of the moon.[27]

Quite obviously, the Harranians have much to say about their ancestor Abraham, of whom they speak in a derogatory manner. According to the Arab scholar 'Abû Muhammad 'ibn 'Ahmad 'ibn Hazm al-Qurtubi (AD 994–1063), the Harranians believed that Abraham was originally brought up among their two sects – the idol worshippers and the star worshippers – but that eventually he had turned to the *Hunafa*, i.e. those contrary to the faith.[28] However, he wrote also that there were still Sabians in his day who believed themselves to be adherents of the religion of Abraham.[29]

THE MOON-DEFICIENTS

Also of interest are the myths and legends of the Mandaeans, a people who originated in Harran, but have spread over the last 1,500 years across Lower Iran and Iraq, leading seminomadic lifestyles. Today their descendants are the Marsh Arabs, who have survived in pockets, despite genocidal persecution at the hands of Saddam Hussein, the ruler of Iraq. According to Mandaean tradition, Bahram, their name for Abraham, was originally a Mandaean from Harran. Yet then he was circumcised, which made him unclean. Bahram began worshipping Yurba, a sun spirit identified with the Hebrew Adonai, who was commanded by Ruha, queen of darkness.[30] Henceforth he destroyed all the idols in the great temple and went forth into the desert, and with him went all the unclean and 'leprous and those who were deficient – and of these *basran Sira* (moon-deficients) their descendants are unclean and deficient until the seventh generation'.[31]

Bahram's tribe grew mightier and mightier, and Yurba gave them great power in the world, as well as 'such magic power that fire was unable to burn him'.[32] He took his place on the side of darkness, and fought against the Mandaeans, whom he would catch and circumcise by force and make them unclean like himself. Yet he later decided to repent, and was told by the planet Saturn to sacrifice his son (Isaac), but being truly repentant he was allowed to let his child go free and offer up a ram instead.[33]

Such is the story told by the Mandaeans about Abraham, parts of which eerily parallel some aspects of the Exodus narrative offered by Manetho and other ancient writers. More significant is the fact that Abraham's followers were known as *basran Sira,* 'moon-deficients', with Sira, or Sera, being the Mandaean name of the moon.[34] If we ignore the claims that these people really were unclean and 'leprous', then it implies that they were renegade moon worshippers, since the moon was seen by the Mandaeans as an 'unclean' sinister influence, who is described as 'overthrower', 'striker' and the 'bringer about of deficiency'.[35] The fact that Yurba, obviously Yahweh, is identified as a sun spirit should not lessen this conclusion, as this was simply the manner in which he was perceived in the eyes of Mandaeans in much later times, and does not reflect the original religion of Abraham.

LUNAR FESTIVALS

Yet what is the evidence that the worship of Yahweh among the Israelites was ever influenced by the veneration of the moon? Although the lunar deity was important to many ancient cultures of the Middle East, it was especially revered among Semitic-speaking nomadic pastoralists. Obviously, the sun played a major role in agricultural cycles, but, to those leading a nomadic lifestyle, the moon was far more important since herds and flocks were moved by night to avoid the searing heat of the day. As already mentioned, the moon god Sin became the chief-deity of the pre-Islamic Arabs of Syria and Arabia, among whom were tribes with names such as *Banu Hilal* ('sons of the crescent moon') and *Banu Badr* ('sons of the full moon'), which honoured the lunar deity.[36] Whenever the moon would reappear after the nights of darkness, it was greeted with shouts of joy, preserved in the Arabic word *hilal,* which means both 'new moon' and 'festive shout'.[37]

From earliest times, the Arab peoples celebrated festivals at the time of the new moon. The most important of these was held in spring during the month of Ragab, the equivalent of the old Hebrew month of Abib, which corresponds with the annual appearance of the first newborn animals among the flocks and herds.[38]

FEAST OF THE PASSOVER

With the origin and nature of the Arab festivals in mind, we find that the Hebrews, who were also originally nomadic pastoralists, based their twelve-month year (thirteen months every third year) on the first appearance of the new moon, and conducted all major feasts in accordance with the lunar calendar. Like the Arabs, they would commence in the first month, Abib, modern Nisan, with a spring festival coinciding with the casting out of the young animals. We speak here of the Passover, still today one of the three most important feasts in the

Jewish calendar. It begins on the 14th day of Nisan (written 14 Nisan) with the killing of the *Pesah* animal and continues into the next night, the time of the full moon, when the victim is consumed entirely by one or more families. According to the book of Exodus, the *Pesah*, or Passover, celebrates the night that Yahweh 'passed over' the houses of the Hebrews when he sought out and killed the Egyptian firstborn. They were not affected because the Lord had told them to sprinkle the blood of the *Pesah* animal on the lintel and sides of the doors to their homes.[39] This biblical event is said to have taken place on 14 Abib, yet in modern rabbinical tradition the Passover occurs one day later on 15 Nisan, meant originally to coincide with the nearest full moon to the spring equinox.[40] The feast heralds the commencement of a week of celebrations, including the Feast of the Unleavened Bread, which occurs on 16 Nisan.

From its description in the book of Exodus, the origin of the *Pesah* feast clearly evolved from a much more archaic Semitic religious custom, adhered to by the pre-Mosaic Hebrews. The animals to be sacrificed, usually lambs in their first year, but originally also kid goats,[41] were taken from among the flocks. Instructions are given in the book of Exodus as to how the animal should be prepared: 'Eat not of it raw, nor sodden at all with water, but roast it with fire',[42] and 'neither shall ye break a bone thereof'.[43] These are curious instructions, and have implied to some Hebrew scholars that occasionally the victims were eaten raw, and their bones ground up and consumed.[44] This was because in early Semitic belief the life force was seen to reside in the blood and the bones of an animal.

Since the *Pesah* feast was a night celebration, which began at sunset, culminated at dawn and was conducted in the presence of the deity, he can have been identified only with the full moon. Curiously enough, 'the face of Yahweh' and the 'glory of Yahweh' are old designations for the full moon, which appears on the fifteenth day of the month as a visible sign of the presence of the deity.[45] In addition to this, it is a fact that at 'Arabian, Jewish and Samaritan festivals worship does not begin till after the setting of the sun and the appearance of the new moon'.[46]

So what is the meaning of the word *Pesah*, the name of the feast, which is generally translated into English as 'paschal', as in the 'paschal lamb', a symbol of the Passion in Christian Easter celebrations, which coincide with the original time of the Passover feast?[47] Although in Hebrew the word *pāsah* means 'pass (over)' while *pesah* means 'protection', this is not thought to be the true origin of the name. More likely is that it derives either from *pašāhu*, which in the East Semitic language of Akkadian means 'to be appeased' (with the adjective *pašhu* meaning 'appeased'),[48] or the Syrian root *psh*, meaning 'rejoice'. Clearly, these are more appropriate names for a feast in which the lunar deity is appeased through the sacrificial offering of newborn animals.

The principal animal sacrificed to the moon god in pre-Islamic Arabia was the bull, which was seen as a personification of the god Sin, the crescent of the new moon being its shining horns. This connection between the moon and bull worship is also reflected in the Hebrew religion, for in the book of Numbers it states that on the fifteenth day of the seventh month (the full moon coinciding with the autumn equinox) thirteen bullocks are to be given as burnt offerings to Yahweh,[49] twelve on the second day,[50] eleven on the third day[51] etc., until the seventh day, when seven are to be sacrificed.[52] Thus the greatest number of bullocks offered up in any one day coincided with the full moon, the number decreasing as it wanes – clear evidence of some form of archaic lunar devotion being at the root of this practice. In addition to this, thirteen is the number of lunar months in a year; seven days is a one-quarter cycle of the moon, while the total number of bulls sacrificed comes to seventy, the number of elders whom Moses allowed to ascend the Mountain of Yahweh (see Chapter 20).

From these various examples, we can see that there was a huge lunar influence in ancient Hebrew religious practices, which seem to have mirrored those conducted in the name of the moon god Sin by the pre-Islamic Arabs, the Semitic cousins of the Israelites. The Hebrew scholars WOE Oesterley and Theodore H Robinson concluded in this respect:

> On the analogy of the Arabs, therefore, there is every reason to believe that the new-moon feasts, and the sacrifices offered on these occasions, among the Hebrews go back to nomadic times [i.e. the age of Abraham] … It is noteworthy that these festivals are not mentioned in the Book of the Covenant nor in the Deuteronomic law, doubtless on account of their connection with lunar worship; but the observance of them was too ingrained, and they continued down to Christian times.[53]

So we can see that as late as the time of the Exodus the religious customs and practices of the Hebrews contained elements of lunar worship that clearly predated Moses' first encounter with Yahweh on the Mountain of God. Yet we know that the worship of this deity under other names went back to the age of Abraham, and thus must also have been the religion of Isaac, and his sons Jacob and Esau.

It is also worth pointing out that the Hebrews continued their association with Harran through to Jacob's day, for we read that he resided here with Laban ('white', a probable epiphet of the moon), the grandson of Nahor, Abraham's brother. Indeed, Harran was known as 'the city of Nahor'. Yet when Jacob fled from Harran all links between the two branches of the family were supposedly severed.

Josiah attempted to expunge unwanted elements of the original Yahwestic faith, as practised by the Edomites, the children of Seir, from the Pentateuch. Where their connection with events of the Bible could not be removed, they were simply denounced as enemies of Israel and blasphemers, idolaters and minions of demons and devils. Yet, as we shall see, the earliest Edomites are likely to have practised a form of Hebraic worship that more closely reflected the original religious ideals of Abraham and his descendants, such as Esau and Jacob.

MOUNTAIN OF THE MOON

The Mandaean name Sira, or Sera, as the name of the moon is phonetically so similar to Seir, the local god who gave his name to the valley and mountain range north of the Gulf of Aqaba, that it cannot be coincidence. This supposition is strengthened in the knowledge that both the Mountain of Yahweh and the wilderness in which the Israelites wandered bore names that reflect the moon god Sin. As Sinai means simply 'of Sin', it shows that 'the wilderness of Sin' and the 'wilderness of Sinai' were quite obviously one and the same place (we shall deal with a third variant, the 'wilderness of Zin', shortly).

Supporting a link between Sira, Sin and Seir is the fact that both the Harranians and the Mandaeans were related to the Nabateans, a Semitic-speaking people of Aramaean origin who inhabited Seir from the sixth century BC through to Roman times.[54] Moreover, Mandaean script is thought to derive from a Nabatean original,[55] demonstrating how the place name Seir may well have been a corruption of the Mandaean 'sira', or 'sera', or vice versa, thus making Mount Seir, like Mount Sinai, the 'mountain of the moon'.

IN THE WILDERNESS

In the book of Exodus Moses leads the Israelites into the wilderness of Sin, where they encamp by Mount Sinai for one whole year. No more is mentioned about their travels until we reach the book of Numbers. In the first chapter they are still pitched in 'the wilderness of Sinai'[56], as they are at the beginning of Chapter 9.[57] Yet then the children of Israel set forth 'according to their journeys out of the wilderness of Sinai; and the cloud abode in the wilderness of Paran'.[58] Bible scholars conclude from this statement that they had entered a region known as the wilderness of Paran, although to the authors the two places seem to be synonymous. More than this, 'the cloud abode in the wilderness of Paran' seems to imply a mountainous region, which can only be the Seir range once more. This seems to be confirmed almost immediately afterwards, as we are told that the Israelites 'set forward from the mount', armed with the mysterious Ark of the Covenant, on a three-day journey in order to seek out 'a new resting place for them'.[59] Confirmation, it would seem, that they were still encamped in the vicinity of the Mountain of Yahweh, and implying also that the wilderness of Sinai and the wilderness of Paran were one and the same. Paran is usually taken to be the desert tract that lies between Arabah on the east and the wilderness of Shur on the west, identified today with Bâdiet et-Tih, although this seems most unlikely given the evidence presented within these pages.[60]

Thereafter the Israelites come upon Hazeroth[61], which they make their 'abode'. Afterwards, Moses sends out twelve spies unto Canaan 'that went up, and spied out the land from the wilderness of Zin unto Rehob, to the entering in the Hamath'[62] in northern Canaan, implying that the Wilderness of Zin was also close to Mount Sinai, and might also have been synonymous with the Wilderness of Paran and the Wilderness of Sin. Afterwards, they return to Moses and Aaron, 'and to all the congregation of the children of Israel' in 'the wilderness of Paran, to Kadesh'.[63]

Confusing as this all might seem, it provides us with further evidence that, during their first two years in the wilderness, the Israelites wandered only a very limited distance from the Mountain of Yahweh. In addition to this, we can see that the different names given to the wilderness – Sin, Sinai, Paran and Zin – seem to refer to the very same region. Moreover, they seem to have bordered a mountainous terrain, which can only have been the Seir range. Proof of this is relatively easy, for Kadesh, the final location we are introduced to in the narrative, provides us with what will turn out to be a most crucial clue to the whereabouts of the Mountain of God.

20. THE CASE FOR THE HIGH PLACE

It is to Kadesh, in the wilderness of Paran, that the twelve spies sent out by Moses return following their clandestine sortie into Canaan. Yet they give such evil reports of the Canaanites that the Israelites give up any hope of entering the Promised Land. As punishment, the Bible tells us, Yahweh makes them remain in the wilderness for another 38 years, until that entire generation has completely died out, save for the likes of Moses, Aaron and the military commander Joshua, son of Nun, who was one of the original spies. Afterwards, we find Israel settled once more in Kadesh, which was said to be 'a city in the uttermost of thy border',[1] an allusion to the mythical king of Edom, who refuses to allow the Israelites to use the King's Highway, the royal road that cut through his kingdom. It is here at Kadesh that Miriam, Moses' sister, dies and is buried, and the lawgiver conducts a very remarkable act.

Chided by the murmurings of the Israelites, who constantly complained that they were thirsty, Moses 'smote the rock with his rod twice'[2] instead of speaking 'unto the rock before their eyes',[3] as had been commanded by Yahweh. Although water gushed forth 'abundantly and the congregation drank, and their cattle',[4] the deity cursed not only Moses but also his brother Aaron, and both were now destined never to enter the Promised Land themselves.[5] The name afterwards applied to this place was 'Meribah',[6] meaning 'quarrel' or 'strife',[7] or 'Meribah of Kadesh' as it appears in its longer form.[8]

THE SPRING OF MOSES

Although we have no need to accept this miracle as historical reality, it does parallel the manner in which holy wells and springs are said to appear miraculously in legends found throughout the world. So does the story relate to an actual location where such a spring might be found? If we examine the folklore and legends of the Bible lands, three sites emerge that all claim to be Ain Mûsa – the Spring of Moses, where Moses smote the rock with his rod. One is on the eastern shores of the Gulf of Suez, close to Jebel Mûsa in southern Sinai.[9] A second exists in the vicinity of Mount Nebo, the site of Moses' death, northeast of the Dead Sea, and the third is located on a hillside at the entrance to Wadi Mûsa, the Valley of Moses, a little over 100 kilometres northeast of Aqaba. Since we have dismissed Jebel Mûsa as the site of Mount Sinai, and there is no direct connection between the Mountain of God and Mount Nebo, only the Ain Mûsa situated in Wadi Mûsa makes any sense of the biblical narrative. Here local legend asserts that it was originally one of twelve sacred springs produced by Moses, a tradition borrowed from the Exodus story presented in the Koran, the holy book of the Muslim religion. It tells how Moses struck the rock and twelve springs gushed forth, one each for the twelve tribes of Israel.[10]

According to Arabian history, the Marmaluke sultan named Baibars came upon the Spring of Moses in Wadi Mûsa when in 1276 he travelled from Cairo to the castle of Kerak, situated on the King's Highway, south of Amman, the modern capital of Jordan, in order to quell an insurrection. It is said that en route he entered the village of el-Odma (a corruption of the word 'Edom'), situated between ancient Petra and the Wadi el-Madarah, where the holy spring was to be found. Here, it was said, 'Moses, son of Umran, peace unto him, struck with his rod that which once flowed with blood. He called on it to change by command of God unto fresh water and lo! it changed unto crystal-clear water, sweet and cool.'[11] This is the oldest known reference to this particular Ain Mûsa, although quite clearly the legend is considerably older. The reference to the spring as having originally run with blood is quite curious and does not feature in the story presented in either the Bible or the Koran. Yet since Edom means 'red', the chances are that the blood was really red silt of a type common to the deep red sandstone of Wadi Mûsa. Moreover, the name Odma, the supposed name of the village, can additionally be translated as meaning 'return to water', implying that it is also linked with the presence there of the spring.[12]

The site of Wadi Mûsa's Spring of Moses would seem to have shifted slightly over the years. Today it is identified with a fine spring that flows from beneath a dome-shaped rock located just seven kilometres east of the legendary city of Petra. It is still a site of local devotion, since its waters are considered to have curative properties, and in recent years it has been housed, rock and all, within a small whitewashed shrine. Yet this Ain Mûsa has a lesser-known rival three kilometres nearer to Petra. Known as el-Odmal, or al-Udma, it is thought to be a more likely candidate for the miraculous spring visited by Sultan Baibars in the thirteenth century.[13]

Regardless of the true identify of Wadi Mûsa's Spring of Moses, both sites bring us into an area of the Transjordan that now becomes the key to unravelling the whereabouts not only of biblical Kadesh, but also the true location of the Mountain of Yahweh.

PHARAOH'S TREASURY

In ancient times the springs of Wadi Mûsa flowed through the valley and provided vital water sources for the inhabitants of the nearby city of Petra, a Greek word meaning 'the rock'. For the most part, it is a huge necropolis that encompasses an entire valley enclosed on all sides by a ring of tall peaks which form part of the Seir mountain range. It contains around 800 ancient monuments, most of them tombs with ornate rock-cut façades in either an Assyrian or classical style. They date mostly from the second century BC to the second century AD, and were constructed by a relatively unknown Arabian culture known as the Nabateans, who were the relatives, and perhaps even the ancestors, of the Harranians and Mandaeans. They are thought to have taken up residence in the southern Transjordan after the Edomites moved westwards to fill the Palestinian territories left uninhabited when the Jews were exiled in Babylon around the middle of the sixth century BC. The first-century Jewish historian

Flavius Josephus, in his *Antiquities of the Jews,* speaks of the inhabitants of 'Nabatene', a country which stretched from the Red Sea to the Euphrates river, as the descendants of Ismael, the son of Abraham by his wife Sarah's handmaiden Hagar.[14]

Sometime around the fourth century BC the Nabateans are thought to have begun their long occupation of Petra. Here they thrived, developing a rich trade in frankincense, myrrh, perfumes, spices, gold and silver, by taking advantage of existing caravan routes that radiated outwards to all parts of the ancient world, including Afghanistan, Egypt, India and China. Having initially been able to resist Roman invasion through adequate bribes and peace offerings, Petra finally fell under Roman control following the death of the last Nabatean king in AD 106. Yet the city continued to exist as a major centre of trade and commerce through until AD 363, when a major earthquake devastated the region. Thereafter Petra lost its importance, and was finally overrun by the advancing Muslim armies in the first half of the seventh century AD. The last person to see the deserted city prior to more modern times was Sultan Baibars, who witnessed its 'most marvellous caves, the façades sculpted into the very rock face' on his journey between Cairo and Kerak in 1276.[15] From then onwards until the time of its rediscovery by the Swiss traveller and adventurer Johann Ludwig Burckhardt in 1812, the Nabatean and Roman ruins of Petra became the haunt of local Bedouin tribes who took every precaution to make sure its whereabouts remained a secret.

The best known of Petra's great tombs is the Khasneh al-Faroun, or Pharaoh's Treasury, famously featured in the action film *Indiana Jones and the Last Crusade* (1989). Its façade is 39.6 metres high, and it lies immediately opposite the entrance to a spectacular, narrow ravine, over 1.75 kilometres in length, known as the Bab al-Siq. This provides the only access to the rock city from the east, where the modern town of Wadi Mûsa is situated. The Treasury gained its curious name because the local Bedouin believed it to be the repository of treasure belonging to the daughter of Pharaoh, the unnamed Egyptian king who in both biblical and Koranic tradition pursued Moses and the Israelites following the Exodus from Egypt. According to local tradition, the rock-cut urn, 3.3 metres in height and located above the central tholos on the Treasury's second level, contained a hoard of gold coins. For hundreds of years, this provided Arab and Turkish marksmen with an ample excuse to pepper it with holes in the hope that it would release its cache of treasure.

Although the story of Pharaoh's daughter and her gold is simply the creation of Bedouin ignorant as to the origin of the tomb structure, it does provide an interesting link between the story of Moses and the Nabatean city of Petra. Indeed, according to the legend, when he deposited the gold Pharaoh was said to have 'assumed the guise of the greatest black magician of all time', while Moses was seen as 'the great white magician'.[16] What is more, other monuments in and around Petra are also linked with the Pharaoh of the Exodus. For example, there is the Faroun Pillar, a free-standing column, one of two of uncertain function (the second having fallen long ago), which stands in front of a Nabatean temple to the west of the main 'Street of Façades', as the main valley of tombs and monuments

Fig. 17. Line drawing of Petra's Khasneh al-Faroun, or Pharaoh's Treasury. Note the Bedouin marksmen taking pot shots at the urn above the Tholos.

is known today. The Bedouin once referred to this monument as Zibb Faroun, the Phallus of Pharaoh, even though it has nothing whatsoever to do with Egypt. Then there is the Qasr el-Bint Faroun, the Castle of Pharaoh's Daughter, usually abbreviated to Qasr el-Bint, a Nabatean temple complex also located to the west of the main Street of Façades.

Where might this connection with the Pharaoh of the Exodus have originated? Was it linked to the existence nearby not only of Ain Mûsa, located in Wadi Mûsa, the Valley of Moses, but also the ominous presence of Jebel Harûn, which stands just five kilometres southeast of Petra? This twin-peaked mountain has long been identified as the site of the biblical Mount Hor, where Moses' brother Aaron is said to have died and was buried, and his supposed tomb exists to this day (see Chapter 21). There are, however, even firmer reasons to suggest that Petra and its environs are important to the early history of the Israelite peoples. For instance, the narrow ravine, or Siq (Arabic for 'cleft'), that forms the main entrance into the city is known as the 'Cleft of Moses'.[17] It gained this name because the waters of Ain Mûsa once flowed through the Siq, and according to local tradition this occurred when Moses struck the rock with his rod and 'brought the stream through into the valley beyond'.[18]

More tellingly, al-Nuwairi (1279–1332), a Marmaluke historian who chronicled Sultan Baibars' journey from Egypt to Kerak, speaks of Petra in the account as 'the cities of the Children of Israel'[19] These facts alone appear to indicate that Petra has a long association with events associated with both the biblical Exodus and the Israelites' 40 years of wandering in the wilderness.

THE ROCK

In addition to this, Petra would seem to have been synonymous with a location named in the Bible as *ha-Sela,* Hebrew for 'the rock'. According to tradition, Sela lay at the southern end of the land of Edom, and in the ninth century Amaziah, king of Judah, launched a major offensive against the 'children of Seir' in Edom. He was said to have taken Sela 'by war', and apparently slaughtered 10,000 individuals in the 'Valley of Salt', located at the southern end of the Dead Sea. An equal number were thrown to their deaths from 'the top of the rock', which Amaziah named Joktheel in honour of his great victory.[20] It was from here, almost certainly, that Amaziah removed 'the gods of the children of Seir, and set them up to be his gods' in the Temple of Solomon.

Although the biblical account of Amaziah's slaughter of the inhabitants of Sela is likely to be much exaggerated (the Hebrew word for 'thousands', *alaf,* can also be translated as 'families', 'clans' or 'tents'), it is popularly believed that the story refers to a jutting mountain that dominates Petra's western horizon. Known as Umm al-Biyara, it was the site of an Edomite settlement occupied during the seventh and sixth centuries BC, before being abandoned following a conflagration. Before her death in 1987, the British archaeologist Crystal-M Bennett extensively excavated the site under the sponsorship of the British School of Archaeology in Jerusalem. Since she failed to find evidence of an Edomite presence here prior to the seventh century BC, it calls into question the view that Umm al-Biyara really is the *ha-Sela* of the Bible.[21] However, all the indications are that the place name Sela is indeed synonymous with Petra, and thus it is likely to be located somewhere in this area, even though most modern scholars like to identify it with El-Sela, a natural rock fortress north of Buseirah, on the road to Tafileh in Jordan.

Certainly we can say that Umm al-Biyara was an important Edomite settlement for the clay seal impression of an Edomite king named Qaush-gaber, who ruled during the first quarter of the seventh century BC,[22] was found on the site. Originally, the seal would have been attached to a letter or proclamation addressed to the inhabitants of the rock. Exactly what the relationship might have been between these Edomite peoples of the Iron Age and the much earlier Shasu is unclear. Yet they must have inherited at least some aspects of their culture and religion from those who occupied the same region in the Late Bronze Age, c. 1550-1200 BC, when the Exodus is thought to have taken place.

THE WATERS OF MERIBAH

That the Greek and Hebrew names of Petra both mean 'the rock' seems to connect it directly with the story of Moses striking the rock and bringing forth the waters of Meribah at Kadesh. Generally, Kadesh is identified with Ein el-Qudeirat, a village in the Negev, just under a hundred kilometres west-northwest of Petra. Here the name Kadesh appears to have been preserved in the name of a local spring called Ein Qadis. A small occupational mound exists here, and this has produced evidence of a Late Iron Age fort, c. 900–500 BC, hundreds of years after the age of the Exodus. Yet, as the minimalist Bible scholars Israel Finkelstein and Neil Silberman point out, '... repeated excavations and surveys throughout the entire area have not provided even the slightest evidence for activity in the Late Bronze Age [1500–1200 BC], not even a single sherd left by a tiny fleeing band of frightened refugees'.[23] The chances are, therefore, that the archaeologists have been digging in the wrong place, for the biblical 'city' of Kadesh can be identified with Petra, a conclusion drawn as early as 1881 by the British writer and traveller Arthur Penryn Stanley.[24]

In Hebrew Talmadic lore Kadesh, or Kadesh-barnea, as it was also called, was known as Rekem-Giah,[25] which in the Hebrew Targum, or commentary, on the book of Deuteronomy is said to have been where the Israelites encamped when in the wilderness.[26] Rekem, also spelled Arke and Arce, is Petra, a fact attested not only in ancient textual accounts of both Jewish and early Christian origin,[27] but also in Nabatean inscriptions recently discovered at the entrance to the Siq.[28] Moreover, Rekem-Giah, or Rekem gea, actually translates as 'of the ravine', a reference most surely to the Siq itself,[29] which played a prominent role in the religious beliefs of the Petra Nabateans.

Flavius Josephus, in his *Antiquities of the Jews,* gives an account of how Moses led the Israelites unto the borders of Idumea, the name by which Seir-Edom was known in his own day.[30] Here, he tells us, Moses' sister Miriam died in the fortieth year after Israel's departure from Egypt.[31] Josephus tells us that, after a public funeral, she was 'buried upon a certain mountain, which they called *Sin*'.[32] This seems to be the surest reference by far to demonstrate that Mount Sinai was in this region, even though Josephus erroneously assumes that this mountain 'called *Sin*' is a different place altogether.

Yet Josephus then has the Israelite army leaving their camp and marching through 'the wilderness of Arabia' until they come upon a place that 'the Arabians esteem their metropolis, which was formerly called Arce, but has now the name of Petra ... [and] was encompassed with high mountains'.[33] St Jerome (AD 333–420), the venerated church father, visited Petra, which he identified with '*Cades Barnea*', i.e. Kadesh, and spoke of seeing here the tomb of Miriam, Moses' sister.[34] Thus in the knowledge that the Bible tells us that she died and was buried in Kadesh,[35] then this has to be Petra, ancient Rekem. More importantly, since Josephus states that Miriam was buried on a mountain 'called *Sin*', then it implies that Mount Sinai was to be found in the proximity of Petra. This realisation thus makes it easy to conclude that Bedouin legends connecting the rock city with Pharaoh's daughter were based on even earlier traditions regarding the presence there of the tomb of Miriam. Remember, it was she who proposed to Pharaoh's daughter that the newborn Hebrew child she had plucked out of the water should be cared for by one of its kind, enabling the young Moses to be brought up by his own mother.

If Petra was ancient Kadesh, one of the key stations where the Israelites camped, then we must also conclude that it was here that the story concerning Moses striking the rock to bring forth water originated, just as the legend of Ain Mûsa implies. Perhaps the story emerged originally to help explain the extraordinary geological nature of the Siq, which is surely one of nature's great wonders of the ancient world. Having established this fact, we can go on to make the connection now between Petra and Mount Horeb, the alternative name for Mount Sinai.

And the Lord said unto Moses, behold, I will stand before thee there upon the rock in Horeb, and thou shalt smite the rock, and there shall come water out of it, that the people may drink. And Moses did so in the sight of the Elders of Israel. Exodus Chap. XVII . Ver: VI . —

page 123

Fig. 18. The book of Exodus tells us that Moses struck the 'rock in Horeb' and brought forth water. The same story is told in the book of Numbers, although the location is given as Kadesh.

THE ROCK IN HOREB

As we saw in Chapter 18, after the children of Israel entered the wilderness of Sin, the book of Exodus tells us that they pitched their tents at Rephidim, where there was no water to drink.[36] The constant murmurings caused Moses to plead with Yahweh to produce a miracle, since his people were ready to stone him if they did not drink soon, to which the deity replied:

> Behold, I will stand before thee there upon the rock in Horeb: and thou shalt smite the rock, and there shall come water out of it, that the people may drink. And Moses did so in the sight of the elders of Israel. And he called the name of the place Massah, and Meribah, because of the striving of the children of Israel, and because they tempted the Lord, saying, Is the Lord among us, or not?[37]

Bible scholars have always assumed that the two accounts in which Moses brings forth the waters of Massah and Meribah refer to completely different incidents – one that took place at Horeb in the wilderness of Sin, and another that occurred at Kadesh in the wilderness of Paran. They point out that the word used for 'rock' on the first occasion is *tzur*, while in the second instance it is *sela*.[38] Yet it seems quite plain from the two narratives that they relate to one incident alone, recorded in two different books of the Pentateuch – initially in Exodus and then again in Numbers. Should this be the case, then it means that Horeb and Kadesh are one and the same place, and that both are to be identified with Petra, where the search for the Mountain of God reaches its climax. Thus having examined the various possible candidates for the Mountain of Yahweh in the landscape around the city of rock, it is the authors' opinion that Sinai, or Horeb, has only two possible candidates. They are Jebel Harûn, which lies to the southeast of the ring of peaks surrounding Petra, and Jebel al-Madhbah, immediately west of the rock city.

THE CASE FOR JEBEL AL-MADHBAH

Let us look first at the case for Jebel al-Madhbah, a peak that rises to a height of 1,035 metres, and is accessed most easily from the Street of Façades, or Outer Siq, situated some 190 metres below its summit. It is unquestionably the site of the most significant sanctuary in Petra, and is more commonly known as the High Place (al-Madhbah in Arabic). To reach it the visitor must climb a series of steps cut into the western cliff face, close to a Nabatean amphitheatre carved out of the rock. They lead up a jagged ravine and end eventually in front of a huge rock-cut platform on which are two enormous stone obelisks, oriented east–west of each other and set some 30 metres apart. The westernmost example is positioned on the very edge of the cliff face and is a maximum of 3.5 by 2.2 metres in width, while its easterly counterpart is 2.2 by 1.95 metres at its base. Both taper towards their apexes, and, although today they are a little over six metres in height, it is estimated that they were originally around nine metres tall.

What is most amazing about the obelisks is that they are carved out of the solid bedrock, meaning that in order to create them the entire mountainside had

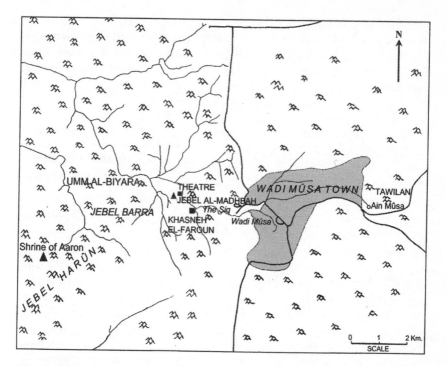

Fig. 19. Map of Petra.

to be removed. This extraordinary engineering feat was achieved by cutting away huge rectangular blocks of sandstone in a manner similar to the removal of stone blocks from the quarries on Egypt's Giza Plateau. A series of long, horizontal troughs were first cut downwards at right angles to each other, before the resulting blocks were cut away from the bedrock, leaving the whole platform, which is around 40 by 20 metres in size, looking like a massive noughts-and-crosses board.[39]

The obelisks are simply breathtaking and unique in the ancient world. Owing to the similarity between the diagonal hatching on their stone surfaces and the similar rock-carving techniques used to fashion certain monuments in the Street of Façades, the pillars are considered to be of Nabatean construction, thus no earlier than the third century BC. However, this conclusion is by no means certain, as there is every likelihood that the Nabateans inherited their rock-carving skills from the earlier Edomite communities, who are known to have cut two water cisterns into the summit of Umm al-Biyara,[40] which means Mother of Cisterns. Moreover, the British historical writer Iain Browning in his definitive work on Petra states that the obelisks of Obelisk Ridge, as it is known, are unlike any other Nabatean monument, leading him to comment, 'One must ask what was their significance to merit such herculean exertion'.[41]

In local Bedouin tradition Obelisk Ridge is known as Zibb Attûf, the Merciful Phallus, or the Phallus of Mercy. This is an interesting name, prompting Browning to declare that its 'very unusualness must denote an inheritance from the past',[42] thus 'enabling us to believe that these obelisks were originally representations of fertility deities'.[43]

Yet there may be another explanation for the name Zibb Attûf. In the Koran we find that Allah is repeatedly referred to as 'the Forgiving One, the Merciful', implying that the Bedouin title for the pillars derives from the Koran, and relates specifically to Allah in some way.[44] Furthermore, it seems more likely that the twin obelisks functioned as a cyclopean gateway on to the highest level, or realm, of the mountain, reached easily by following another stairway cut into the rock face on the northwestern side of Zibb Attûf. On ascending these steps the visitor first passes the precarious stone walls of a 'fort', dated tentatively to the Crusader period.[45] Yet beyond these, on the mountain's exposed summit, is a quite extraordinary sight.

THE HIGH PLACE OF SACRIFICE

Al-Madhbah, the High Place, is an oval-shaped platform some 64 by 20 metres in extent. On its western edge is an altar hewn out of a bank of rock, 2.72 by 1.87 metres in size and with a height of 98 centimetres. It is approached by three stone steps, and on its left-hand side is a circular basin carved into the upper surface of the rock, with a drain that leads down into a piscina. This too is approached by three hewn-out steps. Unquestionably, its purpose was to catch the blood of sacrificed animals offered up at the High Place, even though many written sources adopt the more conservative view that it is a water basin.[46]

If the hewn-out basin served to collect the blood of sacrificial animals, then it echoes the story of how on the occasion that Moses received the holy laws on Mount Sinai he 'sent young men of the children of Israel', who 'offered burnt offerings, and sacrificed peace offerings of oxen unto the Lord'.[47] Afterwards, Moses then 'took half of the blood, and put it in basons [sic]; and half of the blood he sprinkled on the altar', constructed that same morning 'under the mount' of God.[48] Might these 'basons' have served a similar function?

Immediately behind the high altar is a sunken rectangular area, 'a form of shallow courtyard'[49] which measures 14.6 by 6.4 metres in extent. Close to the centre of this levelled floor is a raised rectangular dais, 150 by 81 centimetres in size and aligned on to the altar. Browning describes this as the sanctuary's 'Mensa Sacra ... exactly the equivalent to the shewbread table on which the bloodless offerings were made in Israelite temples'.[50]

Some 10 metres south of the sunken rectangular area is a rock-cut pool, 3 metres in length, 2.3 metres in width and with a depth of 0.9 metres. Its function would seem to have been the immersion of either the officiating priests or attendees for purification purposes, something similar to the ritual ablutions or baptisms that was the style of the Mandaeans ,who originated in this same region.

The question of who was responsible for the construction of the High Place is, like the obelisks at the slightly lower level, a matter of pure speculation, with

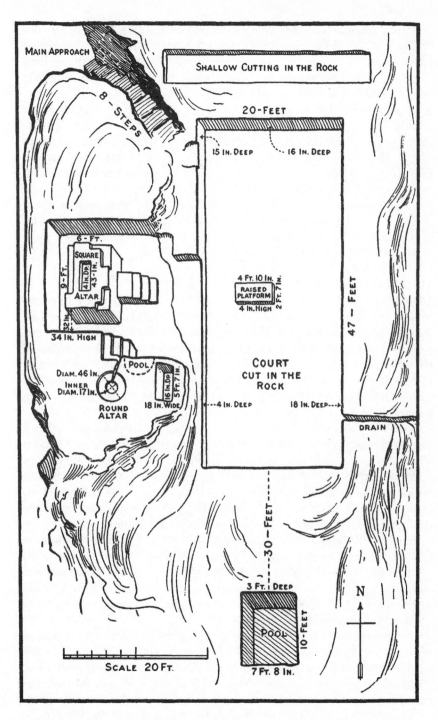

Fig. 20. Groundplan of the high place on the summit of Jebel al-Madhbah.

most scholars happy to accept that it is Nabatean in origin. Yet its proximity to Umm al-Biyara in the west, the site of a major Edomite settlement, could argue otherwise, especially in the knowledge that the Nabateans might well have inherited their rock-cutting techniques from the Edomites. This is the opinion offered by Browning, who writes concerning the High Place:

> No date can be given to this sanctuary but it is believed to be Nabatean work entirely on the strength of the high quality of the stone working. Its origins could, however, be earlier, for the Edomites are believed to have worshipped in High Places. This site may, in fact, be of very great antiquity as a place of worship even though the present setting-out was a comparatively late development.[51]

Of equal significance is the High Place's alignment, for its stone altar and stone steps are oriented at an angle of 255 degrees from north. This aims it directly at the northernmost peak of Jebel Harûn, which can be seen rising up beyond a mountain ridge named Jebel al-Barra, which acts as the southernmost tip of Umm al-Biyara.

One of the authors, Andrew Collins, was fortunate enough to be able to visit the High Place during the preparation of this book. He observed that at sunset on the spring equinox 2002 the sun rolled down the northern side of a distant peak south of Umm al-Biyara, before disappearing completely from view just a few degrees north of the altar's west-southwesterly alignment. Moreover, at precisely this moment the moon, which reached first quarter the next day, seemed to hang directly over the High Place. It was a quite breathtaking spectacle which showed that, for those who first constructed the High Place, both the proximity of Jebel Harûn and the significance of solar and lunar alignments determined its placement and orientation.

In 1927 Dr Ditlef Nielsen, a Danish professor of religious history, journeyed to Petra and spent some time on Jebel al-Madhbah in an attempt to determine the dates most associated with the mountain's westerly orientation. What he found surprised him, for on 8 April that year he observed the moon in its first quarter descend into a saddleback indentation within a wall of rock, horizontal with the eye, located on a ridge in the vicinity of Umm al-Biyara. What made this sight more extraordinary was the fact that, because the half-moon's straight surface was upright, it seemed to fill the semicircular impression, or cleft, a spectacle that was meant to be viewed only from the High Place.

WILDERNESS OF THE MOON

The date on which this lunar alignment took place is also interesting, for it occurred in the lead-up to the first full moon following the spring equinox. This hints at the alignment's greater significance, for in Israelite tradition the Passover feast coincided with the first full moon after the spring equinox. The fact that this feast almost certainly derived from an early Semitic rite in which newborn animals were offered as sacrifices to the moon makes this realisation doubly significant. Was the High Place a prehistoric sanctuary where the local inhabitants of a distant age conducted some kind of prototype Passover feast?

Were animals ritually slaughtered at the high altar, and was their blood afterwards smeared over its sides? Furthermore, was the carcass, or indeed were other 'bloodless offerings', then placed on the Mensa Sacra, the raised offerings table located in the sunken rectangular area behind the altar? This last idea is not as wild as it might seem for, as we have seen, Iain Browning has noted the obvious similarities between the rock-cut form of the High Place and the layout of Israelite sanctuaries, which were always oriented towards the west.

More evidence of moon veneration at the High Place was noted by Nielsen just below its northwestern edge. Here he found a betyl, or shrine, carved into the rock face on a ledge, just above head height. Its centrepiece was a rectangular god-block (see below), and on either side of it were half-columns surmounted by crescent moons, their tips facing upwards.[52] On examining this shrine in March 2002, Andrew Collins determined that it was Nabatean in origin and aligned, like the High Place itself,[53] on the distant peak of Jebel Harûn, further confirming the significance this mountain played in Nabatean religious tradition.

The day after he witnessed the moon set within a saddleback indentation in the vicinity of Umm al-Biyara, Nielsen explored the location in question. He climbed a ravine and found there a large 'natural auditorium', as well as an elevated 'natural pulpit in a square block of the rock'.[54] Like the altar on the High Place, it had 'a madbah, an offering place, oriented towards the new moon in the sky and the rocky new moon above'.[55] Also like Jebel al-Madhbah, it possessed 'a water basin', and, although seemingly of lesser importance, this offering place had obviously once served a similar function.[56]

LORD OF THE SHARA MOUNTAINS

Beyond the natural auditorium and pulpit on the slopes of Umm al-Biyara, Nielsen also came across graffiti carved on to the rock face. Most of it was illegible, but what he could make out was 'a triangular bull's head with the half moon above it',[57] which he said resembled examples found on ancient Arabian monuments.[58] What did it signify, and was it Edomite or Nabatean in origin?

The Nabateans' chief deity was Dhushara, which means 'Lord of the Shara Mountains', with Shara being the Aramaic name for the Seir mountain range. Initially, he was represented only in abstract form as an 'unhewn, four-cornered black stone'[59], or more generally a rectangular block, with eyes and a nose, and today these are known as god-blocks. Never was he depicted with a mouth, since it was deemed impossible to communicate directly with the god; this was achieved only via an intermediary, either a priest or his consort al-Uzza (see below).[60] During Roman times Dhushara took on an anthropomorphic form, which can also be seen in a few rock-cut shrines in and around Petra.

In his form as the god-block, the Nabatean god is found carved within the niches of betyls, classical shrines hewn out of the rock (as in the example at the High Place). The word betyl (beth-el in Hebrew), means 'House of God', and would originally have been a shrine that included free-standing stones or pillars called massēbōth.[61] For Semitic-speaking peoples of the Near East, including the early Israelites, these formed personal representations of the spirit, or *genius loci*, of high places, such as al-Madhbah.

What might be another variation on the god-block theme is to be found in the Siq, the narrow ravine leading into the rock city, which in the past might well have been seen as a macrocosmic representation of the female uterus with the totally enclosed rock city as the womb.[62] Among a series of niches containing either god-blocks or much later anthropomorphic forms of the Nabatean gods is one filled with a huge hemispherical god-block, looking like an *omphalos*, the Greek for 'navel stone'. Very likely it signifies the mound of first creation which in many ancient world cosmologies emerged out of the primeval waters at the dawn of time. However, its counterpart in the macrocosm would have been the sacred mountain of the high god, making the hemispherical god-block a further form of Dhushara.

Iain Browning believes that yet another form of Dhushara is the obelisk, like those found on Obelisk Ridge, just beneath the High Place. In his opinion, this was the natural progression from the more personalised god-block found in the niches of holy shrines. It can be seen, he feels, in the four carved stone obelisks six metres high that stand in front of the upper level of the façade on the so-called Obelisk Tomb, found on the road leading down into the Siq and dating to the first century AD.[63] However, in this case the influence could purely have been decorative, influenced by Graeco-Roman trends in architectural design originating in Egypt. These particular obelisks, which are known as *nefesh*-pyramids, bear no obvious relationship with those on Obelisk Ridge.

Much more significant is the presence around Petra of crude carvings that take the form of isosceles triangles, their points facing upwards. All of them are surmounted by decorative symbols usually consisting of trefoils, hemispheres and, more significantly, crescents. Some of the triangles are surrounded by radiating lines, giving the impression that they are shining, and most compelling of all is the fact that either side of their upright point are two bored holes, clearly meant to represent eyes. There seems little doubt that these triangular carvings represent Dhushara as the personification of the mountains, while the presence of the crescents above their apexes appears to show that both the deity and the mountains were associated directly with the moon. This is despite the fact that scholars consider that Dhushara was a sun god without any hard evidence whatsoever.

Similar to Yahweh, Sin and other Semitic moon gods, Dhushara was also connected with the bull of heaven, whose body was the holy mountain and whose horns were the crescent moon. Thus the abstract carving of a bull's head surmounted by a crescent moon examined by Ditlef Nielsen in the vicinity of Umm al-Biyara in 1927 is likely to have been an expression of the spirit of the Shara mountains, most probably Dhushara himself.

Thus we can see that the Nabatean god of the mountains had much in common with Yahweh, the deity of the Israelites, who, as we have seen, would appear to have been the *genius loci* of Mount Horeb, or Mount Sinai, the Mountain of the Moon. Was Dhushara therefore simply a much later form of Yahweh worshipped a thousand years after the age of the Exodus? To answer this question we must examine what little is known about the religion of the Iron Age Edomites, the intermediaries between the Shasu of Edom and the later Nabateans.

THE STAR AND CRESCENT

The principal deity of the Edomites was Qos, or Qaush, pronounced *cow-ûs*. His name appears as the prefix to the personal names of at least two Edomite kings – Qaush-malak (*melek* means 'king'), who reigned coincident to Tiglath-Pileser IV, king of Assyria, c. 747 BC, and Qaush-gaber, whose seal impression was found during excavations at the Edomite settlement of Umm al-Biyara. He reigned during the first quarter of the seventh century BC, coincident to Esarhaddon of Assyria. His name also appears in the personal names of many other Edomite individuals found in inscriptions dating from this same period. It is even possible that the root of the place name Kadesh (*qdš*, 'holy'), may well have derived from Qos.

In addition to this, an Aramaic inscription on a horned Edomite stela found near Petra refers to Qos-allah, or 'Qos is god', while a carved stone scarab found by Crystal-M Bennett at an Edomite site named Tawilan, located on a hill directly above Ain Mûsa in Wadi Mûsa, is thought to be an abstract representation of Qaush as the moon god (see pic. 37 of picture section).[64] It shows a star within a crescent on top of a pillar, mounted upon a rectangular or trapezoid structure, with cross-hatching, which could be either the roof of a building or, more likely, some kind of altar. To its left is a diamond shape above a horizontal line and an upward arrow, which could represent an elevated table for burnt offerings, while to the right of the star and crescent is an isosceles triangle, point upwards, above two horizontal lines and another, slightly larger arrow. It would be tempting to see this triangle as representing a holy mountain.

If this scarab does show an abstract form of Qaush, as scholars believe, then he must have possessed outright lunar qualities and was represented by the star and crescent, which later rose in prominence among Arabian cultures to become the outright symbol of the Muslim religion. This is borne out by local tradition in and around Petra, which suggests that Qaush was a god of the new moon.[65] Since the columns surmounted by crescent moons on the shrine just below the High Place at Petra also link Dhushara with the moon, it seems certain that he assimilated some aspects of the Edomite god Qaush, including his known connection with the bull and the moon. Indeed, Iain Browning cites Qaush as being a Nabatean god in his own right.[66]

Thus we can see that there appears to be a direct line of transmission between Yahweh, the god of the Shasu and Israelites, Qaush, the god of the Iron Age Edomites, and Dhushara, the high god of the Nabateans. All of them seem to have been connected with the moon, bulls, pillars (or god-blocks) and holy mountains. In addition to this, we can say that Shara, the mountain abode of Dhushara, is a later form of Seir, the ancestor god of the children of Seir. This we can see from the fact that the Aramaean Shara (*šr*) is phonetically the same as the Mandaean word Sera, or Sira, meaning 'the moon'. Remember, Mandaean script derives from a Nabatean original,[67] confirming that 'Shara' and, as we have already seen, Seir, and Sinai, all mean, simply, 'moon', or 'of the moon'.

THE WORSHIP OF VENUS

Dhushara's consort is remembered in Petra under her pre-Islamic Arab name of al-Uzza, who is represented by a god-block in a betyl that has eyes, a nose *and* a mouth (for direct communication is possible with her, as it is with the Virgin Mary in Roman Catholic tradition). She was the personification of the planet Venus, the name given to this goddess in classical tradition. Although scholars interpret al-Uzza's name as meaning 'the strong one', it may originally have derived from the Akkadian *uz*, meaning a 'goat'. This was the chief animal sacrificed to the various forms of Venus throughout the Near East, where in addition to al-Uzza she was known as Allat, Astarte, Atargatis, Ishtar and *rabbat al-thill*, 'Mistress of the Herd'.[68] Ishtar-Venus' symbol was a seven-pointed star contained in a circle, and this has been found on two sculpted stelae unearthed at Harran,[69] while in Greek art a form of Venus (or Aphrodite) is depicted riding a goat,[70] showing her link both with fertility and sexual promiscuity. Indeed, in early Christian tradition Ishtar-Venus evolved into the Whore of Babylon, who in the book of Revelation holds the cup of abominations and rides the seven-headed beast of apocalypse.[71] Brass statues of al-Uzza, or Allat, holding a cup are still sold to tourists in Petra today.

In addition to this, there seems to be a direct relationship between the worship of al-Uzza and the scapegoat that Aaron sent to Azazel on Mount Seir in order that the Israelites might atone for their sins. As mentioned in Chapter 18, Azazel also took his name from the Akkadian *uz*, meaning 'goat'. Since other forms of his name are Azza, Ouza and Uzza, the scapegoat ritual might well be a confused recollection of goat sacrifices made to an early form of al-Uzza perhaps connected with the scholarly belief that Yahweh had a consort named Asherah, who was simply another form of Allat or Astarte. Jews today celebrate *Yom Kippur*, the Day of Atonement, on the night of 10 Tisri (ancient Ethanim), the seventh month, around the time of the autumn equinox when the moon is in its first quarter.

In his book *The site of the biblical Mount Sinai: A claim for Petra,* published in 1928, Ditlef Nielsen noted that due west of Petra, beyond the Wadi Arabah, which divides the Transjordan with Palestine, is a mountain called Jebel Hilal. This he took to be another indication of Petra's lunar significance, for in Arabic *hilal* means 'new moon'.[72] In conclusion, he proposed that the landscape between Petra and Jebel Hilal was the original location of the wilderness of Sin, while Petra's Jebel al-Madhbah was the 'moon-mountain', thus the true location of Mount Sinai.[73] No modern Bible scholar appears to have taken his theories seriously, despite the overwhelming evidence to show that Petra was ancient Kadesh, where the Israelites would seem to have spent a considerable amount of time while in the wilderness. Yet had Nielsen been correct in his assumptions? Had he really pinpointed the actual location where Moses received the Ten Commandments and conversed on a one-to-one level with God himself? The case for Jebel al-Madhbah is strong, but what about Jebel Harûn, the traditional site of the Bible's Mount Hor and a site of veneration for Christians and Muslims for nearly 2,000 years. Might that turn out to be an even better candidate for the title Mountain of God?

21. THE HOUSE OF GOD

Five years after the discovery of Tutankhmun's tomb, Dr Ditlef Nielsen, the brilliant Danish professor of religion, visited Petra and concluded that Jebel al-Madhbah, the High Place, was the true location of Mount Sinai, a theory he had been developing since at least 1904.[1] Yet he chose this site in favour of Jebel Harûn (1,350 metres), the traditional site of Mount Hor, the holy mountain said to have been reached by the Israelites after they left Kadesh.[2] Because he and his brother had rebelled against the word of the deity at the 'waters of Meribah', Yahweh ordered Moses to take Aaron on to Mount Hor and there strip him of his priestly garments, which were afterwards to be placed on Aaron's son Eleazar. Moses carried out the deity's command, and once this had been done Aaron promptly expired on the spot.[3] So was Jebel Harûn really the biblical Mount Hor, and had Nielsen been right to ignore it as a candidate for Mount Sinai?

THE MOUNT OF ST AARON

As previously mentioned, Petra's High Place and the nearby betyl dedicated to Dhushara are both aimed directly at Jebel Harûn, the holiest mountain in the vicinity of the Nabatean rock city. Although no Edomite remains have been found here, it is thought to have been occupied during Nabatean times, since two water cisterns on its northern peak have been attributed to this period. When exactly the prophet Aaron, Nabi Harûn in Muslim tradition, first became associated with the mountain is unclear.

As outlined in Chapter 20, the first-century Jewish historian Flavius Josephus tells us that Moses led the Israelite army unto the borders of Idumea (Edom), where his sister Miriam died. Thereafter they came upon the city of Petra, ancient Arce, supposedly named after a Midianite king named Rekem and 'encompassed with high mountains'.[4] Here, Josephus tells us, Aaron 'went up one of them in the sight of the whole army' and thereafter 'put off his pontifical garments, and delivered them to Eleazar his son, to whom the high priesthood belonged' and afterwards died on the spot.[5] Rightly or wrongly, this mountain, the biblical Mount Hor (with *hor* simply meaning 'mountain'), came to be identified with Jebel Harûn, which lies five kilometres east-southeast of Petra. The mountain takes its name from Nabi Harûn, the Arabic name for Aaron, the Hebrew Aharon (Aramaic Haroun), translated as *har-on*, meaning 'lofty, exalted', or 'mountain of strength', suggesting that Moses' brother derived his own name from the mountain itself. Curiously enough, the Yiddish pet name of the Hebrew Aharon is Arke, the ancient name of Petra, a coincidence that cannot be ignored.

According to the book of Deuteronomy, Aaron's life expired on Mount Hor because both he and Moses showed the same impatience as the Israelites when Moses struck the rock with his rod in order to bring forth water when they were encamped at Meribah of Kadesh. Because of this act both prophets were now destined to be tortured into witnessing the Promised Land, but without ever being allowed to set foot in it.[6] Before his death, Moses was forced to witness the land of the Israelites' inheritance from the top of Mount Nebo at the peak of Pisgah in the land of Moab, before expiring on the spot.[7] Earlier, Aaron had suffered the same fate after he gazed out at the Promised Land from the top of Mount Hor.[8] Thus in the knowledge that from the summit of Jebel Harûn there is an uninterrupted view across the Wadi Arabah to modern Israel and Palestine, an identification with Mount Hor makes perfect sense.

Aaron's connection with Jebel Harûn is attested from at least the fifth century AD, when a Byzantine monastery and shrine was founded here. A partial inscription found during recent excavations on the site of the monastery by the Finnish Archaeological Project in Petra, led by Professor Jaakko Frösén of Helsinki University, mentions the name Aaron. In addition to this, charred papyri dating to AD 513, found even more recently in an excavated church in Petra, refer to a monastery on the 'Mount of St Aaron', a reference most surely to the monastery on Jebel Harûn. It must have been around this same time that the site became a place of pilgrimage, for its summit seems covered with pottery shards dating from Byzantine times, although no examples were found which predate this period.

The Byzantine monastery on Jebel Harûn was eventually to vanish without trace, although the site of Aaron's tomb was not lost. In the thirteenth century, a Muslim shrine, or weli, was constructed on the site by Es-Shimani Ibn Mohammed Qalawun at the command of Sultan Baibars, following his own visit to Petra. Within its walls were placed column drums belonging to an earlier building of uncertain origin, and these can be seen today beneath thick coatings of mortar and whitewash. From that time onwards Aaron's tomb became a major site of pilgrimage for Muslims. Indeed, it was on the excuse of visiting Jebel Harûn that the Swiss traveller Johann Burckhardt, dressed as a Bedouin, was able to view the monuments of Petra for the first time in 1812. Unable to reach the mountain's summit, he offered up a goat at its base in a manner that was obviously usual for the time. In 1927, when Ditlef Nielsen visited Petra, the site still held a special significance to the local Bedouin. According to him they made regular pilgrimages

> to the top of Jebel Harûn … and on certain days the local 'prophet' (*Nabi Harûn*) is worshipped by the sacrificing of lambs. The place is so holy that profane foreigners are not admitted: no local guide would accompany me there; and the local English commandant requested me not to go there alone.[9]

Until just recently non-Muslims were rarely allowed access to the summit of Jebel Harûn, and even today it is accessible only after a three-hour ride on the back of a camel across barren terrain. Fortunately, Andrew Collins was able to reach Jebel Harûn during his trip to Petra in March 2002. An elderly Bedouin guardian, who wore a long, curved, silver dagger in his belt and carried a gigantic metal key and wooden staff, allowed him and his wife Sue entry into the revered holy shrine. After removing their shoes, they stepped down into the underground cave where the tomb is set in a niche behind a pair of wrought-iron gates. Although viewed only in dim candlelight, it seemed to take the form of a round-edged stone box tomb, thick with whitewash. There was no clear indication that it was hollow, and it appeared too narrow to contain a human body laid out fully. Rumour has it that the true tomb is located in an even deeper crypt somewhere beneath the present one, although this could simply be an excuse why the visible tomb is quite obviously inadequate to explain the presence here of such a great prophet.

While in the area, Andrew Collins was related an age-old legend concerning the presence of the prophet's tomb on Jebel Harûn. Accordingly, Nabi Harûn came from Egypt on a flying green horse! Each time that his steed's feet had tried to set foot on the summit of any other mountain it collapsed under the weight. This happened six times until finally the horse and its rider came upon Jebel Harûn, where the animal was finally able to land without problem.[10] Thereafter the prophet made the mountain a sacred place.

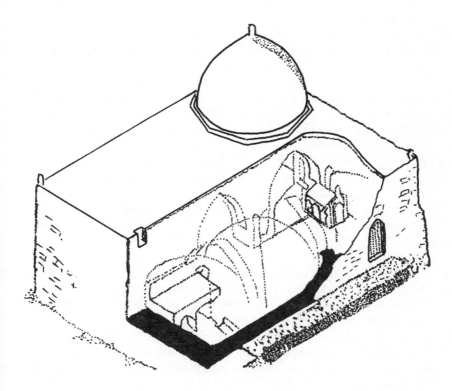

Fig. 21. Plan of Aaron's shrine on the summit of Jebel Harûn (after Chrysanthos Kanellopoulos).

Clearly the tale is pure fantasy, and yet its extraordinary deviation from the traditional story of Moses and Aaron as found in the Bible and Koran, suggests some kind of independent origin. The flying green horse, its attempts to set foot on mountain tops and the fact that Jebel Harûn was seen as the seventh mountain (seven being an important number in Near Eastern cosmology, where it is linked with Venus and the colour green) tend to suggest that the legend did not originally concern Aaron at all. More likely is that it related to a pagan deity of great antiquity who became confused with the figure of Aaron at a much later date. Once again this implies that Jebel Harûn played an important role in the religions of both the Nabateans and, very possibly, the Edomites. However, since it is clearly identified as the biblical Mount Hor, there seems to be no good reason to conclude that it was also Mount Sinai, or Mount Horeb. On the other hand, its connection with Petra's High Place shows that there must have been a sacred interplay between these two key sites, which seems to have been crucial in the emergence of the cult of Yahweh, the God of Israel, in 'the land of the Shasu'.

The authors feel that Ditlef Nielsen did get it right, and that Mount Sinai, or Horeb, the Mountain of Yahweh, is indeed Jebel el-Madhbah, which is by far the most sacred place in Petra itself. On the other hand the true location of Mount Seir, or Mount Shara, the abode of Dhushara, is more difficult to define with any sort of precision. Clearly, the entire ring of mountains that enclose Petra were seen as the abode of the high god. Yet if one mountain more than any other stands out as a possible candidate for Mount Seir it is Jebel Harûn, the biblical Mount Hor, which seems certain to have been venerated as a holy mountain by those who fashioned the High Place in its final form. Yet we cannot be certain whether Jebel Harûn was also Mount Shara, since the Nabatean temple at Petra known as the Qasr el-Bint, and thought to have been dedicated to Dhushara, has a northerly orientation towards modern Jebel esh-Shara, 'the mountain of which he was Lord'.[11] Could this have been the original Mount Shara, or is it simply a much later impostor? All the authors feel certain about is that the Mountain of God, where Moses received the Ten Commandments and conversed with Yahweh, matches very well Petra's Jebel al-Madhbah, the High Place, while Mount Hor and Mount Seir, where the scapegoat ritual took place, are almost certainly Jebel Harûn.

THE FEET OF GOD

According to the book of Exodus Moses is said to have allowed his brother Aaron, Aaron's two eldest sons, Nadab and Abihu, and seventy elders, to climb the 'mount' of Yahweh.[12] It is said that on reaching a certain level of the mountain, they saw 'the God of Israel; and there was under his feet as it were a paved work of sapphire stone, and as it were the very heaven for clearness'.[13] That this event occurred on Mount Sinai is confirmed by the fact that afterwards Moses ascended, or 'went up', the same 'mount' on the occasion that he obtained the Tablets of the Law.[14]

Bible scholars have long been perplexed by this reference to the feet of the God of Israel. Surely, there is some lost, or at least confused, meaning behind this statement. Yet a knowledge of Bedouin folklore throws considerable light on the matter, for even until fairly recent times local tradition asserted that Dhushara had stood with his feet on the highest mountain peaks.[15] Perhaps this curious legend was created to explain the low clouds that even to this day suddenly envelop the misty peaks of the Shara mountains, usually just before a rainstorm. Moreover, there seems little question that the legend connecting the feet of Dhushara with the local mountain range goes back beyond the Nabatean occupation of the region.

In Little Petra's so-called Secret Valley, where more Nabatean monuments are to be found, pairs of feet have been carved into rock faces, usually at the base of mountains. Their large size, and the fact that they are always shown in an ascending position, strongly implies that they are meant to represent the feet of gods, or a single god, who was seen to have inhabited the region.[16] To the Bedouin the carvings are a sign that the site is holy and that they should remove their shoes before proceeding any further, as is the custom in mosques (the carved feet are additionally thought to denote the presence of water sources and are treated as signs of good fortune).[17] This reminds us of how, on ascending Mount Horeb for the first time, Moses, according to the book of Exodus, was told to 'Draw not nigh hither: put off thy shoes from off thy feet, for the place whereon thou standest is holy ground'.[18]

A significant factor about the giant feet found carved on rocks around Petra is that some of them may be infinitely older than the Nabatean period. One pair to be seen on a rock face in Wadi Rum, north of Aqaba, is placed among Neolithic carvings of an ibex pursued by hunters, which predate the age of the Shasu and Edomites by thousands of years. Thus we come back to the reference in the book of Exodus to the 'paved work of sapphire stone' witnessed by Aaron, his sons and the Israelite elders beneath the 'feet' of the God of Israel. Might it be that this passage alludes to carved feet that once marked the entrance to a high place or sanctuary on a holy mountain? Unfortunately, there are no such carved feet on either of the paths that lead up to Petra's High Place, or at the base of Jebel Harûn, although this does not mean that they might not have been represented in some way in the past.

The historical writer Graham Phillips, whose book *The Moses Legacy* was published as this book went to press, has proposed that the Zibb Attûf pillars were themselves construed by the early Israelites as the feet of God resting on Mount Sinai, the Mountain of God.[19] Whatever their significance, there is powerful evidence to hint at the fact that the twin obelisks of Zibb Attûf played an important role in the foundations of the Israelite religion.

JACHIN AND BOAZ

Iain Browning, the noted writer on Petra's history, compared the layout of Petra's High Place with the design of early Israelite temples, especially its 'Mensa Sacra' or shewbread table on which either burnt or bloodless offerings were probably placed. Yet the presence at a slightly lower level of the two obelisks led him to ask whether there was a relationship between them and Jachin and Boaz, the two bronze pillars that stood on a platform either side of the steps to Solomon's Temple. As he says, 'the Edomites must have known of them. They may even have adopted them into their own mysterious pantheon, which raises, of course, the whole question of Edomite influence on Nabatean religion, to which there is regrettably at present no answer.'[20]

Browning additionally draws attention to Petra's Faroun Pillar, mentioned in Chapter 20, which was one of two that stood in a courtyard in front of a temple on raised ground behind the Qasr el-Bint temple. They are much larger than the other pillars associated with the ruins, and seem unconnected with the building's own architecture. So similar was their placement to the design of Solomon's Temple that Browning saw these obelisks as serving a similar function to Jachin and Boaz.[21] As he points out, a model of the First Temple in the Louvre shows these pillars as free-standing obelisks, which parallels their position not only in relation to the Faroun ruins, but also with respect to the stone obelisks of Zibb Attûf.

Yet Browning had not been the first scholar to make the link between the design of Solomon's Temple and Petra's Jebel al-Madhbah. In 1928 Nielsen pointed out that the High Place matched the plan of Jerusalem's fabled Temple in that it faced west, with two entrance pillars situated in the east.[22] Thus when sacrifices were offered up to Yahweh the priest faced towards the west, which he saw as the direction of the moon, as well as the setting sun. He therefore proposed that Solomon's Temple – remember, the place of residence of the Israelite god – was in fact a sanctuary dedicated to the moon god, modelled after Petra's High Place.[23]

Was it possible that Jebel al-Madhbah, with its twin-obelisks in the southeast, somehow echoed the design of Solomon's Temple, the House of Yahweh, in which the deity was deemed to dwell? A full answer to this question cannot be made until the age of both the High Place in its final form and the Zibb Attûf pillars can be properly determined. Yet if they are pre-Nabatean, as seems likely, and Jebel el-Madhbah is the true site of Mount Sinai and Mount Horeb, the original abode of the God of Israel, then it could be that it was the original Beth-el, or House of God, the antecedent of Solomon's Temple. If so, then surely it is the shrine, seat or throne of Yahweh referred to in the following lines from the Song of the Sea, found in the book of Exodus:

May you bring them [i.e. Israel] and plant them in your property mountain,
The firm seat for your sitting/throne/dwelling you devised, Yahweh,
The sanctum, my Lordship, your hands founded [authors' italics].[24]

More than this, it seems probable that the High Place is the sanctuary, or shrine, of Yahweh thought by the Near Eastern scholar Raphael Giveon to be behind the Egyptian toponym 'Yahweh in the land of the Shasu'.[25] It is worth recalling that he also suggested that the existence of this place name hinted that Seir, the homeland of the Shasu, or Edomites, must have been extremely important to the development of the religion of Israel, and in particular its connection with sacred mountains.[26] It appears as if he might have hit the nail firmly on the head in this respect.

THE HATRED OF TEMAN

There is one more piece of evidence that links Petra with the Mountain of Yahweh, and helps demonstrate the animosity that the Israelites held towards the Edomites, the descendants of Esau. The Old Testament's book of Habakkuk states, 'God came from Teman, And the Holy One from mount Paran'.[27] The Revised Version takes Paran to be Sela, while Teman was said to have been a grandson of Esau, and one of the 'dukes of Esau', or Edom.[28] That Teman was to be found in the vicinity of Petra is confirmed in the book of Amos, where we read, 'I will send a fire upon Teman, and it shall devour the palaces of Bozrah'.[29] Bozrah means 'enclosure' or 'fortress', and is thought to be modern-day el-Busseireh, which lies in the mountain district of Petra, some 32 kilometres south of the Dead Sea.[30] There is no question that Teman was a city situated in the land of Edom, and almost certainly Petra itself.[31] Moreover, we find Teman linked not only with 'mount Paran', but also with 'the mount of Esau':

> Shall I not in that day, saith the Lord, destroy the wise men out of Edom, and understanding out of the mount of Esau? And thy mighty men, O Teman, shall be dismayed, to the end that every one may be cut off from the mount of Esau by slaughter.[32]

The animosity directed at the peoples of Edom by these early Jewish prophets defies rational explanation. As already suggested, it can only have stemmed from resentment over the fact that Moses gained the holy laws of Israel from a holy mountain in the land of Edom, which must also have been known as 'mount Paran', or 'the mount of Esau'. So who exactly was Esau?

THE ORIGINS OF ESAU

After the conquest of Canaan the Bible is almost entirely silent about the Mountain of Yahweh. Most probably this was because the strict religious laws implemented by later Israelite and Judaean kings found no place for the archaic form of Hebraic worship practised by their brothers, the Edomites, the descendants of Edom, or Esau. As we saw in Chapter 18, Edom means, simply, 'red', which in all probability derives, not from the red lentil pottage with which Esau was tricked out of his birthright by Jacob, but from the predominantly red colour of the sandstone cliffs of Petra and its environs. Thus Esau, or Edom, was simply another name for the city's *genius loci*, or 'spirit of the place'. Thus in all probability 'mount Paran' and 'the mount of Esau' were simply alternative names for Mount Sinai, in other words Jebel al-Madhbah.

Esau would seem also to have been synonymous with an ancestor god of the human race called Usous,[33] alluded to in the writings of Philo, a historian from Byblos on the Levant coast, who lived in the reign of Hadrian, emperor of Rome, thus c. AD 120–140. He quotes from a book entitled *The Theology of the Phoenicians* by a Phoenician historian named Sanchoniatho, who was said to have lived prior to the Trojan wars, c. 1200 BC. According to Philo, Sanchoniatho claimed that Usous was 'the inventor of clothing for the body which he made of skins of the wild beasts which he could catch'.[34] In this respect we should recall that Esau's name in Hebrew means 'hairy', for we are told that he was born 'red, all over like an hairy garment',[35] and because he grew up to become 'a cunning hunter'.[36]

Although Philo tells us that Sanchoniatho saw Usous as a native of Tyre on the Levant coast, who was the first god to make a boat and 'venture on the sea'[37] (and thus a form of the Phoenician god Melqart, the Greek Hercules) it was also said of him that

> ... he consecrated two pillars to Fire and Wind, and worshipped them, and poured out upon them the blood of the wild beasts he took in hunting: and when these men [i.e. Usous and his brother Hypsuranius] were dead, those that remained consecrated to them rods, ... worshipped the pillars, and held anniversary feasts in honour of them.[38]

In view of Esau's integral relationship with Petra and 'mount Paran', or the 'mount of Esau', can we see in Philo's account of the twin pillars of 'Fire and Wind' a further echo of the two great obelisks of Zibb Attûf? Is the reference to 'the blood of the wild beasts' being 'poured out upon them' a memory of the animal sacrifices which unquestionably took place here?

FROM EGYPT TO PETRA

In the opinion of the authors, Petra holds the key to uncovering the true location of the Mountain of Yahweh, and thus the origins of the Israelite peoples. Graeco-Egyptian, and later Graeco-Roman accounts of the Exodus, as well as ample textual evidence, show us that a plague ravaged Egypt and the Near East during the age of Tutankhamun and his successors. It was seen as divine retribution for the country abandoning the old gods during the reign of the boy-king's half-brother Akhenaten, who forced the Egyptian people to worship one god alone, the Aten or sun-disc. As a consequence, the fallen priests and followers of the Aten, along with a large number of Asiatic followers, were expelled from Egypt in an attempt to appease the gods and rid the country of the plague, since they were seen as its root cause.

The 'polluted' priests and followers of the Aten retained a firm belief in the monotheistic principles of the Aten. This, the authors believe, they attempted to impose on the Shasu and the Asiatic 'foreigners' who were forced out of Egypt's Eastern Delta, but whose original homeland was the mountains of Seir, the land of Edom. This must have caused considerable consternation among certain elements of the tribal confederacy, which still adhered to polytheistic, and thus idolatrous, forms of worship. The story of the golden calf being made in the absence of Moses as the Israelites camped beneath Mount Sinai is perhaps a good example of the animosity towards those who erred from the faith.

Yet something unique happened when the Israelites encamped at Petra, beneath the Mountain of Yahweh. Somehow the principles of the Aten would seem to have been blended with key aspects of the local mountain god, venerated by the native Shasu, or proto-Edomites, whose chief clan was almost certainly known as 'Israel'. Unquestionably, this was the reason why, instead of leading the Israelites directly into Palestine, Moses brought them to Petra, ancient Kadesh, perhaps because many of the Asiatic/Arabic peoples who accompanied him on his journey were actually Shasu from this region. Remember too that Moses had probably been introduced to the mountain god Yahweh during his forty years in the land of the Midianites, perhaps through his father-in-law Jethro, who is described in the Bible as the priest of Midian.[39] In the opinion of the authors this is how the Mosaic religion came into existence sometime around 1300–1200 BC. The whole thing was a fusion of ideas and beliefs from peoples of different cultural and ethnic backgrounds. Moreover, the genesis of these events occurred in the vicinity of the ancient rock city of Petra, both at Jebel el-Madhbah, the High Place, the most obvious location of 'Yahweh in the land of the Shasu', and at nearby Jebel Harûn, the biblical Mount Hor. Yet what happened next? What happened when the Israelites departed Kadesh and ventured forward into the land of their inheritance? We must look now at the Bible's account of the conquest of Canaan in an attempt to determine its relationship to the origins of the Israelite race and the foundation of the modern Jewish state of Israel.

22. THE CONQUEST OF CANAAN

According to the detailed accounts contained in the book of Numbers and the book of Joshua, it was after the death of Aaron on Mount Hor that Israel's campaign against the peoples of Canaan and the Transjordan truly began. Yet, to try to piece together exactly what happened during the conquest of Canaan under the leadership of Joshua, Moses' chosen successor, we will have to suspend, temporarily at least, any belief in the historical reality of these accounts. Israel's first opponents on their journey towards the Promised Land were said to have been the armies of the kings of Hormah[1] and Arad,[2] two small kingdoms in the Negeb region of northern Sinai.[3] At this time Moses and the Israelites are said to have journeyed via the Red Sea (*yam-sûp,* 'Reed Sea', although definitely not the Bitter Lakes of the book of Exodus) in order to 'compass', or go around, the land of Edom.[4] They pitched their tents at a place called Oboth, before reaching Iye-Abarim, which was 'in the wilderness … before Moab, toward the sun-rising'.[5] Moab was the Transjordan kingdom beyond the northern limits of Edom, east of the Dead Sea, which, although mentioned in the context of the conquest of Canaan by the Israelites, is not thought to have been established until the tenth century BC.[6] Prior to this time the Transjordan plateau is said to have been sparsely populated, which in the minds of minimalist Bible scholars (see below) brings into question not only the existence of Moab, but also the biblical kingdoms of Edom and Ammon as well.[7]

IN THE LAND OF MOAB

Yet the route taken by the Israelites makes perfect sense of their departing Kadesh, modern-day Petra, on the borders with Edom, and then heading south via Mount Hor to Elim, modern Eilat, on the Gulf of Aqaba, referred to in the book of Numbers as 'the Red Sea'.[8] From here they would seem to have journeyed northwards along the Wadi Arabah, with the land of Moab, 'toward the sun-rising',[9] i.e. on their right-hand side. Finally, they would have reached the southern shoreline of the Dead Sea, where could be found the Valley of Salt. Here, we shall recall, in the ninth century BC Amaziah, king of Judah, massacred the 'children of Seir' from *ha-sela,* 'the rock'.

According to the book of Numbers, Moses then led the Israelites along the edge of the territories under the control of the king of Moab, suggesting that they had skirted the bottom of the Dead Sea and were now moving northwards parallel to its eastern shoreline.

Afraid of the Israelites advancing into his territory, Balak, the king of Moab, established on the summit of Mount Pisgah seven altars on which seven bullocks and seven rams were to be sacrificed as burnt offerings in order to persuade Balaam, a soothsayer, to curse the Israelites.[10] Yet, after hearing the voice of

Yahweh, he decided against this action, and instead blessed them. Both Balak and Balaam have name prefixes that denote the Canaanite fertility and vegetation god Baal, which simply means 'lord'. His symbol was the bull, and as the storm god Hadad he wore a helmet crowned with bull's horns. Furthermore, like Yahweh, Quash, Dhushara and Sin, the high god of the Canaanites was associated with mountains, while the chief animal sacrificed in his honour was the bull. Some

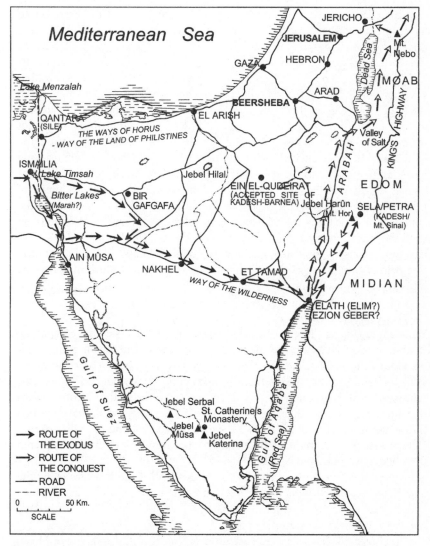

Fig. 22. Map showing the suggested routes of the exodus from Egypt to Kadesh, modern Petra, via the gulf of Aqaba, and the route of the Israelites from Kadesh via Wadi Arabah to Mount Nebo.

kind of interrelationship between this array of key Semitic gods, venerated in Syria-Palestine and the TransJordan seems certain.

Having entered the land of the Moabites, east of the Dead Sea, the Israelites finally came upon Mount Pisgah, which was said to look out over the desert. Once they had pitched their tents, the book of Deuteronomy tells us that Moses ascended 'mount Nebo, to the top of Pisgah, that is over against Jericho' and was shown the Promised Land by Yahweh.[11] With Aaron already dead, it was now the turn of Moses, who promptly expired on the spot.[12] He was buried in the land of Moab 'over against Beth-peor; but no man knoweth of his sepulchre unto this day'.[13]

Beth-peor is an odd choice for the burial place of Israel's great lawgiver, for it means 'house' or 'sanctuary' of Peor, or Baal-peor, the 'lord of the opening'. He was a god of the Moabites, supplicated through obscene rites and licentious orgies.[14] Even Israel was lured into his worship through the temptation of the daughters of Moab, and because of which 'the chiefs of the people' were hung up 'unto the Lord before the sun' in order to curtail the anger of Yahweh. Through their actions a curse fell on Israel as many more of its number fell victim to the plague.[15] According to the book of Numbers, 'those that died by the plague were twenty and four thousand'.[16] Yet this was not a plague of the body, as was the case with the first-born of the Egyptians, but one of the mind, i.e. a form of delusion or madness.

THE FALL OF CANAAN

It was at this time that the army of the Israelites split in two. One half headed north to Gilead[17] and Bashan,[18] and came against the Midianites, who had formed an allegiance with Balak, the king of Moab.[19] The other crossed the Jordan and advanced into the central highlands, north of Jerusalem, to Gibeon, where the sun was said to have stood still in the sky for a whole day.[20] One column then took the southern highlands and coastal lowlands[21] while a second advanced north, taking the northern highlands. Gradually the kings and chiefs were defeated, and their towns, cities and territories occupied or destroyed. Among those said to have fallen were Midian,[22] Heshbon,[23] Edrei,[24] Jericho,[25] 'Ai[26] and finally Hazor,[27] for here

> ... they smote all the souls that were therein with the edge of the sword, utterly destroying them: there was none left that breathed: and he burnt Hazor with fire. And all the cities of those kings, and all the kings of them, did Joshua take, and he smote them with the edge of the sword, and utterly destroyed them; as Moses the servant of the Lord commanded. But as for the cities that stood on their mounds, Israel burned none of them, save Hazor only; that did Joshua burn.[28]

From even a cursory glance, the victories attributed to Joshua seem difficult to justify in historical terms, given that the Bible tells us that Israel was little more than a displaced people who had only just emerged after forty years in the wilderness. For instance, Hazor was a fortified Canaanite stronghold in the

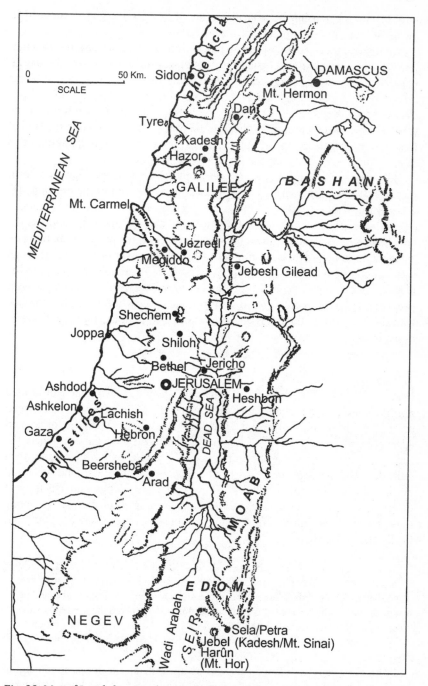

Fig. 23. Map of Israel showing the principal sites of the Israelites from the time of the conquest of Canaan through to the establishment of the united monarchy (some Arabic names are included).

mountains, while the city of Lachish, which in Hebrew means 'impregnable',[29] is said to have been taken in just two days.[30] Are we to believe that the indigenous inhabitants of Canaan were defeated and replaced by an entirely different race of quite different cultural and ethnic origin? What evidence is there that any of these events actually took place?

ARCHAEOLOGY AND THE BIBLE

In the late nineteenth and early twentieth centuries, biblical scholars were in no doubt that the Israelite armies did indeed conquer Canaan. By assuming that Rameses II was the Pharaoh of the Oppression, and/or the Pharaoh of the Exodus, biblical chronology provided a time frame for Joshua's campaign sometime between 1250 and 1200 BC, the very end of the Late Bronze Age. Thus in an attempt to confirm the validity of the Bible, people like the American archaeologist William Foxwell Albright travelled to Palestine and began excavating Bronze Age occupational mounds, thought to mark the site of key Canaanite towns and cities taken by Joshua.[31] Between 1920 and 1929 he explored several such mounds, including Hazor and Lachish, which produced startling evidence that they were occupied during the period in question and, more importantly, had suffered massive conflagrations. Clearly, these Canaanite fortresses, ruled by regional kings and petty princes, had been razed during some kind of military conflict, and, not unnaturally, this was seen as proof of the Israelite conquest. This was despite the fact that the Old Testament tells us that only Hazor was reduced to ashes; others were simply overrun and their inhabitants massacred.

PEOPLES OF THE SEA

Yet assumptions of the sort made by Albright, we now know, were somewhat premature, for it is clear that it was not the Israelites who overran many of these cities but the Peoples of the Sea.[32] They were a mixed-race, tribal confederacy generally considered to have been of mostly Aegean-Anatolian origin, and usually identified with the Philistines, traditional enemies of the Israelites, who are said to have inhabited Canaan's coastal plain. From bases in cities such as Ashdod, Gaza and Ashkelon, the Sea Peoples made repeated attacks on Egypt's northern empire, before being repelled by the forces of Merneptah in c. 1219 BC, and finally routed by the army of Rameses III in c. 1170 BC. So if the Israelite army had not razed places such as Hazor and Lachish, how can the biblical conquest of Canaan be historically confirmed? The true answer is that it can't, although Bible scholars have repeatedly found new models to explain at least some aspects of the biblical narrative.

THE PEACEFUL-INFILTRATION MODEL

For instance, in the 1920s a German biblical scholar and professor at Leipzig University named Albrecht Alt, along with a colleague, Martin Noth, came up with a very different theory regarding the origins of the Israelite race.[33] He proposed that the conquest of Canaan was a national myth created centuries after the events described in the Bible. Alt and Noth examined the evidence available and concluded that the reoccupation of Late Bronze Age sites in the Canaanite highlands, after their original abandonment, was by seminomadic peoples who set up temporary settlements sometime around 1200 BC. Moreover, they could be distinguished from the earlier Canaanite inhabitants, who had lived a relatively sophisticated lifestyle, by their use of a much cruder form of pottery.

Alt and Noth believed that at first the newcomers lived peacefully alongside the indigenous peoples as simple farmers, herding their animals, clearing forests and growing crops. Yet then, very gradually, their numbers increased to such a degree that disputes arose between the two sides, mostly over land and water rights. It was these conflicts that were recorded as the sometimes violent clashes between the incoming Israelites and the peoples of Canaan in the book of Judges, which describes the era that follows the somewhat more genocidal events of the book of Numbers and the book of Joshua.

Thus Alt and Noth's 'peaceful-infiltration' model, as it became known, saw the Israelites as pastoralists, sheep or goat herders, who 'slowly filtered into the settled land from the desert and, after a long period of uneasy coexistence with the population of Canaan, overran and destroyed the Canaanite city-states'.[34] This, then, constituted the gradual emergence of the Israelite race from the Late Bronze Age through to the time of the united monarchy under David and Solomon. But did Alt and Noth get it right any more than fundamental archaeologists such as Albright in the 1920s?

THE PEASANTS' REVOLT THEORY

In 1962, following increased criticism of Alt and Noth's peaceful-infiltration model of Israelite settlement in Canaan, the Bible scholar George Mendenhall of the University of Michigan published what he termed the 'peasants' revolt' theory to explain the origins of the Israelite people. He proposed that they were originally seminomadic pastoralists who opted out of existing political regimes centred on city systems of the coastal lowlands. Having broken the bonds imposed on them by feudal headmen and Egyptian authorities, they migrated to the highlands, where they established themselves as an independent community with self-rule. Here they were able to develop their own unique ethnicity.[35] By grouping themselves together as a tribal confederacy they were successfully able 'to challenge and defeat the dysfunctional complex of cities that dominated the whole of Palestine and Syria at the end of the Bronze Age'.[36] Thus, in his opinion,

> ... there was no statistically important invasion of Palestine at the beginning of the twelve tribe system in Israel. There was no radical displacement of population, there was no genocide, there was no large scale driving out of population, only of royal administrators (of necessity!). In summary, there was no real conquest of Palestine at all; what happened may be termed, from the point of view of the secular historian interested only in socio-political processes, a peasant's revolt against the network of interlocking Canaanite city states.[37]

Mendenhall's vision of the origins of the Israelite tribes and the conquest of Canaan, supported and expanded during the 1970s by Professor Norman K Gottwald,[38] was seen as revolutionary for its time. Moreover, it explained, quite admirably, why there was next to no archaeological evidence to substantiate the historical reality of either the Exodus or the forty years the Israelites are said to have spent in the wilderness. More significantly, Mendenhall concluded that the instigators of his peasants' revolt must have included a 'group of slave-labor captives' who had 'succeeded in escaping an intolerable situation in Egypt'.[39] Pondering more deeply on their plight, he speculated that:

> Without any other community upon which they could rely for protection and support, they established a relationship with a deity, Yahweh, who had no antecedents except in human traditions about ways in which God manifested Himself to human beings.[40]

Thus having pledged their loyalty to 'a single Overlord' with a single commonality that gave the community a unique identity, others, who were themselves 'under the burden of subjection to the monopoly of power which they had no part in creating', began swelling its ranks.[41] In the end,

> … entire groups having a clan or 'tribal' organization joined the newly-formed community, identified themselves with the oppressed in Egypt, received deliverance from bondage, and the original historic events with which all groups identified themselves took precedence over and eventually excluded the detailed historical traditions of particular groups who had joined later.[42]

What Mendenhall seems to have been implying here is that the earliest Israelite communities included Egyptian refugees whose stories of bondage and struggle in their homeland, along with their subsequent flight to freedom, eventually eclipsed more indigenous folk memories. The potency of the Exodus had the result of overriding all other localised myths until the tribal community united under one common foundation, which became the focus of their religious aspirations, regardless of the ethnic or cultural roots of other elements of the confederacy.

So who exactly were these deposed Egyptians? Incredibly, Mendenhall would seem to have seen them in terms of former worshippers of the Aten, or certainly this is what his commentators have assumed. As the leading minimalist authors Israel Finkelstein and Neil Asher Silberman put it so beautifully in their remarkable work *The Bible Unearthed*, published in 2001,

> This group [proposed by Mendenhall] may have been influenced by unorthodox Egyptian ideas on religion, like those that stimulated the monotheistic revolution of Akhenaten in the fourteenth century BCE [Before the Common Era]. This new group would therefore have been the nucleus around which the new settlers in the highlands crystallized. The rise of early Israel was therefore a social revolution of the underprivileged against their feudal lords, energized by the arrival of a visionary new ideology.[43]

In the 1960s and 1970s when the peasants' revolt theory was first proposed, it offered an entirely new alternative to the accepted views on the conquest of Canaan by the Israelites. However, the 1980s and 1990s saw the rise of the so-called minimalist theory regarding the creation of Israelite society. Using the very latest archaeological findings it attempts to demonstrate that the Exodus did not take place and Canaan was never conquered during the Late Bronze Age. Minimalist scholars consider that the Israelite nation evolved gradually out of the indigenous population of the southern and central highlands at the commencement of the period known as Iron Age I, c. 1200–900 BC. Evidence from up to 250 sites suggests that the ancestors of David and Solomon were nomadic and seminomadic herdsmen who lapsed into sedentary lifestyles, creating more permanent settlements and raising cattle, sheep and goats. Moreover, the discovery at these same sites of various sickle blades, as well as pollen-seed analysis, has demonstrated that the 'proto-Israelites', as they are now known, became farmers who grew their own wheat and barley.

PROTO-ISRAELITES

Yet were these Iron Age peoples, who lived in the very region of the globe where the Old Testament tells us the Israelites settled after the conquest of Canaan, really the first Israelites? Sadly, very little is known about their cultural and ethnic background. It is all guesswork, even for the experts. Finkelstein and Silberman cite a bronze bull discovered at a hilltop shrine near Tilfit in the hill country as proto-Israelite in origin.[44] Yet, as we have seen, this is a beast strongly associated not only with the worship of Yahweh, but also with the moon god Sin and the Canaanite god Hadad or Baal. Indeed, one fresco from the ruins of Mari, a city of the Semitic-speaking Amorites situated on the Syria–Iraq border and standing on the west bank of the Euphrates river, shows Baal as a bull 'striding on top of mountains', expressing the powerful connection between the bull of heaven and mountains.[45] Finkelstein and Silberman also cite an 'unusual stone structure' found on Mount Ebal, which is seen as 'an early Israelite altar'.[46] Whether or not this is the case is difficult to ascertain, particularly as hilltop shrines of this type were common throughout Palestine.

The only factor demarcating the early Iron Age I settlements in the central and southern highlands as special is the lack of pig bones among the domesticated-animal remains retrieved from their waste pits. This is despite the fact that they are present in contemporary sites in the coastal lowlands, the land of the Philistines, traditional enemies of the Israelites, and in the Transjordan, the homeland of 'non-Israelite' tribes such as the Moabites and Ammonites.[47] Not unnaturally, minimalist scholars have seized on these findings to demonstrate that pork abstinence among Jews and Muslims originated with these Iron Age communities, who must therefore be seen as the ancestors of the earliest Israelites.[48] Yet the authors can demonstrate equally well that the absence of pig bones at these sites may well have stemmed from a fusion of religious customs and beliefs among Asiatics and Egyptians living in the Eastern Delta prior to the time of the Exodus (see Appendix II – 'Pork Abstinence and the Worship of Set').

According to Finkelstein and Silberman, it was not until the seventh century BC, during the reign of Josiah, king of Judah, that much of what became the sacred history presented in the Pentateuch and the subsequent books of the Old Testament was committed to writing.[49] So any legends and tales concerning the events we now define as the Exodus and Joshua's conquest of Canaan must be seen as severely influenced, if not created, by the political background to this particular period of Jewish history. This was the origin of the Israelites, not a mass exodus from Egypt followed by forty years in the wilderness and a military onslaught against the Canaanite peoples of Palestine. Such stories are to be seen merely as rousing folk tales that helped provide the peoples of Judah with an ethnic identity. More importantly, the covenant made between Jacob and Yahweh can be viewed as little more than Israel's political justification for occupying Canaan, created by those involved in the original authorship of the Old Testament. These are the opinions of the minimalists, which typify the most radical approach to the origins of Israelite ethnicity and culture.

THE REAL ISRAEL

Yet the evidence presented in this book indicates that the indigenous peoples of Seir-Edom, the Shasu, the forerunners of the Edomites of the Bible, may hold the key to explaining the development of the Israelite race around the end of the Late Bronze Age. They would appear to have been the original worshippers of Yahweh, who was primarily a mountain god with bovine and lunar qualities, venerated by a tribal confederacy brought together by a core of Egyptian individuals, most plausibly former priests and followers of the Aten.

The Israel of the Victory Stela is almost certainly the chief clan of the Shasu, named perhaps after their first ancestor who might just have been Jacob, the grandson of Abraham. Should this prove to be correct, then the gradual spread of the Israelites into the Palestinian highlands during this same period can be seen as a memory of the migration of Shasu tribes into these very same regions, as recorded in Egyptian textual inscriptions of the Nineteenth Dynasty, c. 1308–1194 BC.

Minimalist scholars assert that there is no evidence of the Exodus or the conquest of Canaan. Yet a re-examination of the Exodus account from Egyptian, Graeco-Egyptian and Graeco-Roman textual sources tells us otherwise. They imply a whole different story altogether and suggest that the number of people involved was infinitely smaller than the 600,000 'men, beside children' said to have departed Egypt according to the book of Exodus.[50] The number could even have been as low as a few thousand, or even a few hundred, individuals of mixed Egyptian and Asiatic origin. This is one reason why archaeologists have never found any hard evidence of their presence in the wilderness, while another is the fact that they have only ever searched at locations associated with the Israelites in local tradition. As we have seen in the cases of Jebel Mûsa, the proposed site of Mount Sinai in southern Sinai, and Ein el-Qudeirat, the archaeologists' preferred site of ancient Kadesh in the Negev, folklore can be very misleading indeed.

As the authors have attempted to demonstrate, the biblical account of the wanderings of the Israelites in the wilderness leads us directly to Petra via Elim, modern Eilat, on the Gulf of Aqaba. Moreover, the Israelites' departure from Kadesh, their long perambulation of the Seir mountain range to 'compass' the King's Highway in Edom, and their passage along the Wadi Arabah to reach the Dead Sea and the land of the Moabites all makes good geographical sense. If there was no Exodus and no period in the wilderness, whatever its duration, why create such a precise picture of the Israelites' wanderings during this period? We are not suggesting that the biblical account is fundamentally correct, as it clearly is not. However, there is every reason to assume some kind of historical basis behind the construction of these stories in the context of which they were being used to explain the origins of the Israelite race.

Until recently, Bible scholars have always assumed that the Israelites' special relationship with God provided them with a unique outlook on life. This too may have led to somewhat misconceived notions about how to recognise the presence of Israelites at archaeological sites in Palestine. In the opinion of the authors, they would be better served looking for evidence of the spread and influence of seminomadic peoples from the Seir mountain range. And the evidence is already there, for the earliest proto-Israelite sites identified by minimalist scholars such as Finkelstein and Silberman seem to have been created by a people who had been nomads before settling into sedentary lifestyles. This is evidenced from the appearance of their settlements, a number of which are oval-shaped, with a central enclosure where domesticated animals were able to roam free. They reflect almost exactly the design of Bedouin encampments whereby the flocks and herds are contained for the duration of the stay in a central area ringed by a circle of tents.[51]

Since the Shasu were the principal nomadic peoples mentioned as having inhabited not only Edom, but also areas of Palestine and Sinai, surely they become the most likely ancestors of the many Iron Age settlements now thought to be proto-Israelite in origin. We must also not forget that the Shasu were not simply roving shepherds, leading a migratory lifestyle, or indeed vagabonds waiting in the desert passes to ambush caravans. Many settled temporarily, and even had their own towns in 'the land of the Shasu'. Thus their gradual settlement makes sense of what we know about their history, and the fact that the Israelites would appear to have occupied the sites of many former Canaanite cities.

LAND OF THEIR INHERITANCE

Clearly, there is very little evidence for the conquest of Canaan as described in the book of Numbers and the book of Joshua. In all probability these stories were, as the minimalists suggest, composed from the memory of battles and conquests undertaken by the antecedents of the Israelites in order to justify its nation's divine right to Palestine. Furthermore, there is little question that during much later times the significant role played in the establishment of Israel and the religion of Yahweh by the above-mentioned Asiatic confederacy, which included the Shasu of Transjordan, was whitewashed completely. Thus the importance surrounding the Israelites' chief sanctuaries, such as Petra's Mountain of Yahweh, was expunged from the collective memory of the Jewish people, particularly after the division between Israel and Judah following the death of King Solomon around 976 BC. We must also not forget that the Old Testament is the history only from the perspective of the kingdom of Judah. It is not that of the ten tribes that constituted the northern kingdom of Israel, formulated after the schism. They, of course, were carted off to Assyria in 721 BC, and never returned to tell the tale.

Israel's greatest achievement came during the age of David and Solomon in the eleventh and tenth centuries BC, with the establishment of an Israelite kingdom under a united monarchy. Yet there is next to no extrabiblical evidence of their reigns, and next to nothing relating to the 'House of David', from which later kings of Israel and Judah were said to have been descended.[52] The earliest known reference to the Davidic line is included within an inscription that celebrates the victories of a king of Aram-Damascus, identified as Hazael, over Jehoram, king of the northern kingdom of Israel. It dates to c. 897–883 BC and appears on a commemorative stone found in 1993 at the site of the biblical city of Dan in northern Palestine. In full it reads:

> [I killed Jeho]ram son of [Ahab] king of Israel, and [I] killed [Ahaz]iahu son of [Jehoram kin]g of the House of David. And I set [their towns into ruins and turned] their land into [desolation].[53]

After the fall of Israel to Assyria in the eighth century BC, individuals such as Josiah, king of Judah, attempted to re-establish a more strict form of the Mosaic religion as he felt it had been in the days of King David. Out of this new orthodoxy, Judaism was born and, as the books of the Bible testify, it survived through to the sack of Jerusalem and the destruction in AD 70 of the Temple by Titus (AD 40–81), the commander of the Roman legions and future emperor.

The Jewish historian Flavius Josephus records that during the long war against Rome no fewer than 97,000 Jews were carried off as captives, while another 1,100,000 died either through famine or by the sword.[54] Moreover, it was not just the inhabitants of Jerusalem who perished during the destruction, but Jews from all over Judaea. They had descended on the holy city for the week-long series of celebrations that accompany the Passover feast. Thereafter the Jews, the descendants of the tribe of Judah, had no homeland and no national place of worship, and thus began the Diaspora and period of Exile, when they were dispersed throughout the countries of Europe, Africa and the Middle East. For 1,800 years their ancestors kept alive their unique cultural traditions and religious beliefs, and vowed that one day they would return to Jerusalem. That opportunity came eventually in 1917, and only by leaping forward now to examine the climax of the Jews' long struggle to return to Zion, the ancient name for Jerusalem, can we begin to understand the full significance of the Exodus papyri removed from the tomb of Tutankhamun in 1922.

PART FIVE
ZION

23. THE RETURN TO ZION

His Majesty's Government view with favour the establishment in Palestine of a national home for the Jewish people, and will use their best endeavours to facilitate the achievement of this object, it being clearly understood that nothing shall be done which may prejudice the civil and religious rights of existing non-Jewish communities in Palestine, or the rights and political status enjoyed by Jews in any other country.

These are the key words in an historic document addressed to Baron Lionel Walter de Rothschild, 'the most important Jew in England',[1] and signed on behalf of the British government by the Foreign Secretary, the Rt Hon. Arthur James, Lord Balfour (1848–1930), on 2 November 1917. The Balfour Declaration, as it became known, was the crowning glory of sensitive negotiations between prominent Jewish supporters of the so-called Zionist cause and certain British statesmen. Their joint vision was to see the return of the Jews to the Holy Land so that, after some 1,800 years in exile, they might begin to rebuild the Jewish commonwealth.

How and why the British government came to issue such a declaration, at the height of World War One and one month before even the fall of Jerusalem, under the commander-in-chief of the Allies, General Sir Edmund Allenby, must be explored in depth. For the matter now becomes essential to understanding why Howard Carter marched into the British Consulate in Cairo in spring 1924 and threatened to make public the contents of papyrus documents found in the tomb of Tutankhamun, which revealed the 'true account ... of the exodus of the Jews from Egypt'. Remember, at the time there was growing concern in Cairo over the League of Nations' decision two years beforehand to ratify Britain's mandate over Palestine, agreed on the basis that the British government were committed to the establishment of the Jewish National Home. Since Egyptian nationalism was quite obviously pro-Arab, the whole matter was becoming a considerable headache for British diplomats working in Egypt. So where did it all begin? How did a small group of senior British statesmen come to engineer the signing of the Balfour Declaration, which paved the way for the establishment of the modern Jewish state of Israel on 14 May 1948?

THE DAY OF RECKONING
Britain's unerring interest in what would later become known as Zionism stretched back over 300 years to Puritan times. Every God-fearing Christian had to be prepared for the final days, when the souls of the righteous would ascend to God's kingdom in heaven. It would also be the time of the Second Coming of Christ, when God's only begotten son would return to complete his ministry on earth. These apocalyptic events, outlined in the book of Revelation, influenced

Christian teaching, especially among evangelical churches of the eighteenth century such as the Presbyterians and Methodists. To them the Day of Judgment was at hand, and all Christians were expected to prepare for that great day. Such sentiments, fuelled by sermons full of fire and brimstone about the ills of man and the wages of sin, must have had a lasting effect on those of a deeply religious nature.

Yet, as a prelude to the coming Day of Reckoning, the Holy Scriptures were understood to foretell the return of the Jews to Zion, an idea inspired to some degree by a prophecy to be found in Luke 21: 24, which states:

> And they [the Jews] shall fall by the edge of the sword, and shall be led captive into all the nations: and Jerusalem shall be trodden down of the Gentiles, until the times of the Gentiles be fulfilled.

The prediction goes on to say that at this time 'signs in [the] sun and moon and stars' shall be seen, and on earth there will be the 'distress of nations'.[2] Men will be 'fainting for fear, and for expectation of things which are coming on the world: for the powers of the heavens shall be shaken.' Then when humanity's final 'redemption' is at hand, the 'Son of man' shall appear on a cloud in all his glory.[3]

Obviously, the Jews *did* 'fall by the edge of the sword' when Rome sacked Jerusalem in AD 70, and they *were* 'led captive into all the nations' through the persecution they received at the hands of all nations during the exile. Lastly, Zion, or Jerusalem, *had* been 'trodden down of the Gentiles', by the Romans, the Arabs and the Crusaders. So to Christian fundamental mentality, only when 'the times of the Gentiles' had been 'fulfilled', and the Jews returned to Zion, would the 'Son of man' appear on earth. Thus we can understand why in the nineteenth century certain religiously inspired aristocrats, politicians and businessmen actively encouraged the return of the Jews to Palestine.

THE JEWS' SOCIETY

Such ideas were promoted initially by a powerful Christian group named the London Society for Promoting Christianity amongst the Jews, or the Jews' Society for short.[4] Their principal mission was to convert British Jews to the Christian faith before their final restoration to the Holy Land. In their opinion, only by introducing them to Christian worship and a greater understanding of Christ would the ancient prophecies be fulfilled; there seems to have been little respect for Jewish beliefs and ritual, which were seen as crude and archaic survivals of a bygone age.

The organisation's list of members included such eminent dignitaries as the Archbishops of Canterbury and York, as well as a large number of bishops. Yet its period of greatest growth was under the patronage of Anthony Ashley Cooper, seventh Earl of Shaftesbury (1801–85), the great Victorian reformer and statesman. From the abolition of slavery to the working conditions of children and the treatment of lunatics and prisoners, he embraced them all. He was also president of such organisations as the British and Foreign Bible Society, the Pastoral Aid Society and the Society for Conversion of the Jews. However, his greatest passion was to see the return of the Jews to Zion, a cause he did not waver from throughout his life. Indeed, through his friendship with the Prime Minister, Lord Palmerston (1784–1869), he was able to establish a British consul in Jerusalem charged with the protection of Jewish settlers arriving in the Holy Land, whatever their nationality. Although Lord Shaftesbury's ideals were clearly religious in basis, he was not slow to point out to sympathetic ministers the advantages of a Jewish homeland under the control of the British Empire. In the words of author John Michell,

> That policy, he urged, would be effective in bringing stability to a strategically important area on the trade routes between Europe and Asia, while adding to the British Empire a new province which Jewish skills and industry would soon make prosperous. With such rational-sounding justifications as these, but prompted on a deeper level by the enduring belief among the English of their special relationship with the Jews and Israel, British governments from Shaftesbury's time constantly aided or permitted the restoration of the Jews to their homeland.[5]

Foreign missions founded by the society sprang up all over the world – indeed, everywhere there were Jews to convert to Christianity. Some succumbed to the temptation, and in 1842 Lord Shaftesbury managed to have appointed as the Anglican Bishop of Jerusalem, the Rev. Michael Solomon Alexander, a Jewish professor of Hebrew and Arabic. Yet in most cases Jews simply went along with the whole idea of conversion – which involved reading Bible tracts and listening to ex-rabbis preaching the Christian faith – simply to gain free education for their children. Apparently, 'whenever the subject of their conversion was raised, the missionaries reported that their Jewish guests tended to become evasive'.[6] This was even after it was proposed that they be paid money for this privilege, something that Shaftesbury was strictly against. Reported successes were few, and eventually it dawned on the Christians that perhaps the Jews did not want to turn away from ethnic traditions thousands of years old, and so the Society for Promoting Christianity amongst the Jews faded into obscurity. Yet there is no question that Britain's obsession with scriptural prophecy from Puritan times through to the end of the Victorian age had a profound effect on the British government's policies concerning the restoration of the Jews to the Holy Land.

ERETZ ISRAEL
During the 1880s thousands of European Jews – coming mostly from Russia, where they were suffering severe hardship and oppression – began settling in Palestine, which they saw as Eretz Israel, the land of Israel, their ancestral homeland. Each year more and more colonists began to arrive in ever increasing waves. Very few of them would have considered their return to Zion as fulfilling an ancient Christian prophecy. They were simply being forced out of their native

countries as refugees who, with nowhere else to go, had made the decision to journey to the land of their forefathers, where they could begin to rebuild their lives anew, free from persecution.

It was in 1896 that national Zionism really began with the publication of an important book entitled *Der Judenstaat* ('The Jewish State'),[7] written by Theodor (Binyamin Ze'ev) Herzl (1860–1904), a journalist, writer and playwright from Budapest, who was the founder of the World Zionist Organisation. It outlined the plight of the Jews, the nature of anti-Semitism and Herzl's vision of a future Jewish state. Among his proposals was that rich Jews should give money to the Sultan of Turkey in order that poor Jews be allowed to settle in Palestine. The book inspired a generation, especially those Jews who were forced to lead intolerable lifestyles in Russia and Eastern Europe. There is no question that Herzl's book had a profound influence on the rise of Zionist ideals among Jews worldwide, many of whom had previously been reluctant to support the cause, feeling that they were better off in their countries of adoption.

Yet the Jewish settlers in Palestine, many of whom were probably unconvinced by Herzl's vision of a Jewish state, were by now struggling to keep alive. The colonies, which had mainly adopted communal agricultural lifestyles, were on the verge of collapse. They were suffering from a distinct lack of funds and sponsors, and already expansion programmes into new territories were under threat. The matter was discussed in 1897 at the First Zionist Congress, which took place at Basel in Switzerland, and it was Baron Edmond de Rothschild (1845–1934), the head of the French branch of the House of Rothschild, who decided to bail them out. Along with key Jewish bankers, he established the Jewish Colonial Trust, the first Zionist funded bank, through which he started purchasing extensive territories in Palestine and allotting them to new settlers as they arrived in the Promised Land.

Yet, even by the beginning of the twentieth century, the intended location of a Jewish national home was by no means fixed. In 1902 Neville Chamberlain, the Colonial Secretary, offered Jews in Britain the chance to make a homeland in Uganda, then part of British East Africa. It was an option that was discussed and finally rejected at the Sixth Zionist Congress the following year. The Zionists insisted that their only home was Zion, modern Jerusalem, where King David had established the seat of the kingdom of Israel, and his son Solomon had built the First Temple, nearly 3,000 years beforehand. The well-known Jewish saying 'If I forget thee, O Jerusalem, let my right hand forget her cunning',[8] taken from Psalm 137, would ensure that they could never accept anything less than the return of their rightful inheritance, the land of Palestine. From here their forefathers had been dispersed far and wide, following the sack of Jerusalem and the destruction of the Second Temple by the Romans in AD 70.

THE FIRST MEETING

At the time, the Conservative Prime Minister, Lord Balfour, had been moved by the Zionists' refusal to accept the offer of a homeland in Uganda, and became determined to learn more about their plight and aspirations. Although he had no formal contact with the Jewish community in Britain, Charles Dreyfus, the chairman of the Conservative Party in Manchester, was also the chairman of the Manchester Zionist Society. He recommended that Lord Balfour take up the matter with Chaim Weizmann (1874–1952), a leading Russian Zionist who had recently settled in Manchester and now held a post as a lecturer in organic chemistry at Manchester University. This led in 1906, after the fall of the Balfour government, to the first meeting between the two great men, who in the years to come would become key players in the establishment of the Jewish National Home.

In broken English, Mr Weizmann informed the British statesman of the dreadful atrocities that had been committed against his people in Russia by Tsarist troops, acts that had forced Jewish leaders to set their sights on regaining their ancient homeland. He went on to express the spiritual conviction of all Jews that one day they would once again make contact with the soil of Palestine, motivations that prevented them from accepting as settlement any other country.

Weizmann went on to express the matter in the clearest possible terms. 'Mr Balfour,' he started, 'if you were offered Paris instead of London, would you take it? Would you take Paris instead of London!' Surprised, and unable to comprehend the meaning of the analogy, Balfour is said to have replied, 'But London is our own!' To which Weizmann responded, 'Jerusalem was our own when London was a marsh'.[9] It was with these words that Lord Balfour became convinced of the Zionist cause. Yet, even though he was not to see Weizmann again until 1916, the impact of that first meeting remained in his mind and was unquestionably instrumental in the events that led eventually to the signing of the Balfour Declaration.

JEWISH SETTLEMENT

Weizmann was surprised, and warmed, by the cordial reception he had received from Lord Balfour, a senior British statesman, even though he realised that nothing could be done by the British government since Palestine was firmly under Turkish control, as it had been for the past four hundred years. Even so, this did not stop the gradual settlement of many more Jewish colonists, who made their homes in areas such as Jerusalem, Hebron, Tiberias, Safed, Jaffa and Haifa.

By 1907 there were 80,000 Jewish settlers in Palestine, with the number increasing to around 100,000 by the outbreak of World War One.[10] This achievement was due mainly to the impetus of Baron Edmond de Rothschild, who had consistently funded colonisation. As he was to remind Weizmann during a meeting in 1914, 'Without me the Zionists could have done nothing, but without the Zionists my work would have been dead'.[11]

Also in the year that war broke out Chaim Weizmann was introduced, through the intercession of Herbert Samuel, a leading Zionist Jew in the British government, to David Lloyd George (1863–1945), at the time Chancellor of the Exchequer. The meeting was cordial, but once again it was emphasised that Britain could do little to further Zionist aspirations since Turkey remained a neutral country. It was not until November 1914 that the Sultan agreed finally to join the Central Powers (Germany and Austria-Hungary) in their fight against the Allied coalition. According to Weizmann, Lloyd George's advocacy of a Jewish National Home long predated his eventual premiership in December 1916, a fact that led to several meetings in the intervening years.[12]

A CHRISTIAN BACKGROUND

The commitment of such eminent British statesmen to the Zionist cause must be questioned. What was it that drove them to support the aims of Zionist Jews, most of them from Russia, who wanted so desperately to settle in the land of their forefathers? The answer seems to lie in their strong religious backgrounds, which were tied in closely with a fundamental belief in the historicity and messianic potency of the Bible.

In this knowledge, we might better understand why senior British statesmen such as Lloyd George and Lord Balfour were so keen to encourage debate on a future Jewish state, and why during World War One they threw their full weight behind its establishment. Both of these men came from strict religious backgrounds – Lloyd George in his native Wales and Lord Balfour in Scotland. Indeed, according to the latter's biographer, his niece Blanche Dugdale, 'Balfour's interest in the Jews and their history was lifelong' and 'originated in the Old Testament training of his mother'.[13] Moreover, in childhood he was impressed with the view 'that Christian religion and civilisation owes to Judaism an immeasurable debt, shamefully ill repaid'.[14]

That the deep religious views of key British statesmen were instrumental in bringing about the Zionist dream is beyond doubt. In the words of Chaim Weizmann, for such people 'the return of the Jewish people to Palestine was a reality, so that we Zionists represented to them a great tradition for which they had enormous respect'.[15] For them too the Holy Land was the rightful inheritance of the Jewish race, and so Britain's place in ensuring their return seemed a forgone conclusion.

THE ACETONE PROBLEM

By the end of 1915 it was becoming clear that the war in Europe and the Mediterranean needed new impetus. This seemed especially so after the humiliating fiasco that was Gallipoli, where 250,000 Allied soldiers lost their lives trying to land on Turkish beaches in an attempt to take Constantinople that summer. More importantly, the war machine in Europe was grinding to a halt. The demand in British industry for acetone, the solvent necessary for making cordite used as an explosive in cannon shells, was becoming so great that there was now a serious shortage. Normal methods of production were considered too slow, and the British Admiralty needed some means whereby the process could be speeded up, otherwise the big naval guns that relied on cordite explosives would have to be completely reconditioned, a prospect that no one dared contemplate. It was then that Lloyd George, who had been appointed head of the Ministry of Munitions in May 1915 (he went on to become War Minister after

Lord Kitchener's death in June 1916), recalled Chaim Weizmann who, as a scientist working in the field of organic chemistry, had already pledged his support to the war effort. Convinced that he could come up with a solution to the acetone problem, he was summoned to the British Admiralty. Weizmann very quickly devised a new means of producing acetone, which enabled the supply over the next year of tens of thousands of tons' worth of raw material used to make cordite.

There is little question that Chaim Weizmann's liaison with the British Admiralty, then headed by the Rt Hon. Winston L Spencer Churchill (1874–1965), helped secure the British government's support for the Zionist cause. Indeed, it has been suggested that the issuing of the Balfour Declaration was the reward given to Weizmann for services rendered following Lloyd George's election as Prime Minister.[16] In answer to this claim, Weizmann says in his autobiography, 'I almost wish that it had been as simple as that, and that I had never known the heartbreaks, the drudgery and the uncertainties which preceded the Declaration'.[17]

The truth of the matter is that the acetone problem merely helped cement a firm bond among Chaim Weizmann, Lloyd George, Lord Balfour and Winston Churchill, and acted as a smokescreen for the real reasons behind the eventual issue of the declaration. For there is now overwhelming evidence to show that British interests in the establishment of a Jewish National Home in Palestine were linked integrally to the role Zionist Jews played in persuading the American President Woodrow Wilson (1856–1924) to enter the war on the side of the Allies.

THE US CONNECTION

At the commencement of World War One the United States of America made the decision to remain a neutral country. Then on 7 May 1915 a German U-boat sank the Lusitania, a gigantic Cunard passenger liner, en route from England to New York. The vessel was within sight of the Irish coast when the torpedo hit, but, because it quickly rolled on its side, very few lifeboats were launched, resulting in the loss of 1,198 lives, including those of 124 American citizens. The Germans, who at first heralded the strike a great triumph, quickly backtracked and issued an apology when they realised the anti-German feeling that was being whipped up in the American popular press over this appalling tragedy. Yet still President Wilson chose not to join the war effort.

The following March a French cross-Channel ferry, the Sussex, was also torpedoed by a German U-boat, killing fifty people, including a number of US citizens. Once again, President Wilson could not be persuaded to shift his stance, and merely issued an ultimatum to the Germans – either stop unrestricted attacks on vessels carrying US citizens, or risk retaliation. The Germans dutifully complied, and announced that their U-boats would henceforth desist from targeting passenger vessels and make sure that only Allied merchant ships carrying munitions would be subject to attacks.

In November 1916, following his first term in office, President Wilson came up for re-election. He fought the campaign on home issues, but decided to use the slogan 'he kept us out of the war' in order to win over the antiwar element of American society. Woodrow Wilson was re-elected by a narrow margin, and on 18 December he issued a Peace Note to all belligerent nations requesting that they make their positions clear as a prelude to any ceasefire discussions. It was to have little impact on the world scene, especially as only six days beforehand the Germans had issued their own peace offer. Finally, in early 1917, President Wilson spoke optimistically of hostilities ending soon in 'peace without victory'.[18]

Morale on the battlefields in France and Belgium was at an all-time low, and little progress was being made in the oceans. The British government knew that America's entry into the conflict would have an enormous psychological impact on the Central Powers, while at the same time reviving the fighting spirit of the Allied armed forces. But how could this be achieved, especially in view of President Wilson's rigid neutrality stance?

THE JAMES MALCOLM INITIATIVE

It was then that a relatively unknown figure entered the British political scene and offered a solution to the problem. He was James A Malcolm, an Oxford-educated Armenian Russian, who at the beginning of 1916 had been appointed by the Armenian Patriarch as a member of the Armenian National Delegation to Britain. Having become an adviser on eastern affairs to the British government, he found himself in frequent contact with members of the War Cabinet, the Foreign Office and the French Embassy. He was passionately committed to the Allied cause since his Armenian countrymen were being massacred on a regular basis by the Turks, and this could only end when the Central Powers were defeated.

It was during the late autumn of 1916 that Malcolm was introduced to Col. Sir Mark Sykes (1880–1919) of the Foreign Office, who in May that year had finalised the so-called Sykes–Picot Agreement, working with his French counterpart François Georges Picot of the French Embassy. Under the terms of this agreement when hostilities ceased the territories of the Turkish Ottoman Empire – expected eventually to fall, after its entry into the war in November 1914 – were to be divided among the Allied powers. France was to be allotted the Levant region from Cicilia in southeast Asia Minor right down to the Sea of Galilee in northern Palestine, including the whole of Syria and Lebanon. Britain would take charge of Mesopotamia (modern-day Iraq), and exercise economic control over Palestine and full control over the Haifa-Akko Bay area in the north of the country. The rest of Palestine, including the ancient holy sites in the city of Jerusalem, would be placed under the regulation of an international administration. Russia, on the other hand, would be given control of Armenia and Kurdistan (eastern Turkey, northern Syria and northwestern Iran). Only some parts of Arabia (mainly what became South Arabia) would be granted autonomous rule.

Yet now, several months later, Sykes was openly despondent about the future of the war, and saw no way to a quick victory. Malcolm, on the other hand, was optimistic about an Allied success, and saw the entry into the war of the United States as the key to turning the whole course of the conflict. Sykes agreed, but emphasised that everything the War Cabinet had done to persuade the American people to rally to the Allies' cause had always failed. Malcolm advised that the British government was going about it the wrong way. He proposed that gaining the support of the most prominent Jews in the United States, many of whom were top bankers and financiers already more or less financing the Allied cause, was Britain's only real option. More pertinently, he advised: 'You can win the sympathy of certain politically-minded Jews everywhere, and especially in the United States, in one way only, and that is, by offering to try and secure Palestine for them.'[19]

Sykes pointed out that any negotiations regarding Palestine would be impossible under the terms of the Sykes–Picot Agreement. Yet Malcolm advised strongly that Sykes find a way round the problem, perhaps through negotiations with Georges Picot at the French Embassy. He further advised that the most direct route to President Wilson was via Louis D Brandeis, America's leading Zionist, who had been inducted as Associate Justice of the Supreme Court earlier that year.[20] Already he was chief adviser to the President on Jewish affairs, and it was known that the President had shown sympathies towards the Zionist cause as early as 1911.[21] More than this, Brandeis also had a hold over him because of a certain indiscretion when Woodrow Wilson was president of Princeton. Apparently, he had been blackmailed over a series of letters written by him to the wife of a neighbour. He did not have the money being asked by the blackmailers, and so Samuel Untermeyer of the law firm Guggenheim, Untermeyer and Marshall said the company would bail him out and get back the letters provided that at the next vacancy in the Supreme Court the President appoint a candidate of their choosing. That nominee was Louis D Brandeis.[22]

A GENTLEMAN'S AGREEMENT

Thus Sir Mark Sykes entered into secret negotiations with Chaim Weizmann and another leading Zionist named Samuel Landman, a London journalist who was at the time the solicitor and secretary of the Zionist Organisation.[23] These meetings took place at Weizmann's London residence, with the full approval of the Secretary of the War Cabinet, Sir Maurice Hankey.[24] The plan was for influential Zionist Jews in America to apply pressure on the President to commit the United States to the war effort, and in exchange a 'gentleman's agreement' would be reached with Chaim Weizmann over the future of Palestine. This involved a 'Programme for a New Administration of Palestine in Accordance with the Aspirations of the Zionist Movement',[25] submitted to the Foreign Office for discussion and comment. However, the programme was not discussed at Cabinet level, simply because the Prime Minister, Herbert Henry Asquith (1852–1928), had little sympathy for the Zionist cause. Moreover, any meetings between Sykes, the Foreign Office and members of the Zionist committee had for the time being to be seen as 'off the record'. Quite obviously, this situation infuriated not only pro-Zionists such as Lloyd George, Lord Balfour, Winston Churchill and Mark

Sykes, but also the Zionists themselves. Only when Asquith was ousted from power could the 'gentleman's agreement' be put into action, although thankfully his days as Prime Minister were already numbered.

COUP D'ÉTAT

In December 1916 the inability of Asquith's War Cabinet to impose socioeconomic policies at home, while at the same time dictating policy to the Imperial Chief of Staff, General Sir William Robertson (1860–1933), led to its downfall. In a carefully orchestrated *coup d'état,* Asquith was made to resign. This resulted in a Liberal–Conservative coalition government with Lloyd George at the helm, and Lord Balfour accepting the position of Foreign Secretary. They convened a streamlined War Cabinet, and brought in leading businessmen to head new ministries, all in the hope that the government could convince the media and public of its policy of 'war to the finish'. Everything was in place, and there was now nothing standing in the way of the British government ironing out a deal with the Zionist Jews over Palestine.

At a private meeting with the Zionist committee on 7 February 1917, Sykes outlined the problems he would have to overcome to ensure that Britain, on behalf of the Jewish nation, gained control of Palestine after the war.[26] These included objections from the Arab world as well as France's claim over northern Palestine. There was, however, no immediate solution to the first problem, other than assurances that the rights of the native Palestinian Arabs be upheld at all times. The second problem could be dealt with in time. James de Rothschild was present at this meeting, as was Nahum Sokolow, an international Zionist leader, and at the end of the session the following list of Zionist objectives were put forward:

> I. International recognition of Jewish right to Palestine; II. Juridical nationhood for the Jewish community in Palestine; III. The creation of a Jewish chartered company in Palestine with rights to acquire land; IV. Union and one administration for Palestine; and V. Extra-territorial status for the holy places.[27]

Samuel Landman tells us that the 'gentleman's agreement' made between Sir Mark Sykes and the Zionist committee was done in order to secure the complete loyalty of the Zionist Jews in Britain and America. Once achieved, it was promptly authorised by the War Cabinet and Foreign Office and made known to other Zionist leaders, who, according to Landman, were encouraged to

> communicate the glad tidings to their friends and organisations in America and elsewhere, and the change in official and public opinion as reflected in the American press in favour of joining the Allies in the War, was as gratifying as it was surprisingly rapid.[28]

It was left up to Mr Justice Brandeis, and Col. Edward Mandel House, Woodrow Wilson's closest adviser, to persuade the President of the greater advantages of America's entering the war.[29] Thereafter, Landman records, that 'at the insistence of the Zionist leaders', and with the authorisation of France, the Sykes–Picot Agreement was later 'amended so that the Jewish National Home should comprise the whole of Palestine', and that the French relinquish any claim to northern Palestine.[30] 'The main consideration given by the Jewish people (represented at the time by the leaders of the Zionist Organisation),' Landman asserts with respect to Britain's outright support for the Zionist cause, 'was their [i.e. the Zionist Jews'] help in bringing President Wilson to the aid of the Allies'.[31]

AMERICA ENTERS THE WAR

As history records, Berlin's decision to recommence indiscriminate U-boat attacks at the end of January 1917, prompted the United States to break off diplomatic relations with Germany on 4 February. Yet it was not until March 1917 that the President finally asked Congress for $100 million to arm its merchant ships, and only on 2 April did the Senate vote on entering the war. It approved by 82 votes to 6, and two days later the House of Representatives gave its consent by voting 373 to 50 in favour of declaring war against the German government, but not its subjects. Thus inside six months of the Malcolm initiative, which advised that Britain secure the support of the Zionists in return for the promise of Palestine, the United States of America had joined the war effort. How exactly this came about might never be known, but it is certain that Louis D Brandeis and Col. House's heavy influence on the President contributed greatly to his decision to abandon his country's neutrality.

BUILD-UP TO THE BALFOUR DECLARATION

When in March 1917 it became clear that the League of Nations (the forerunner of the United Nations) might vote in favour of France, and not Britain, administering Palestine after hostilities ceased, an urgent round of talks began between Weizmann and Lord Balfour. Then on 25 April James de Rothschild cabled Brandeis to say that Lord Balfour was coming to the United States, and urged that American Jewry fully support 'a Jewish Palestine under British protection'.[32] Brandeis unquestionably met him on this occasion, for he cabled one of the British branch of the Rothschild family, saying, 'Have had a satisfactory talk with Mr. Balfour, also with our president. This is not for publication'.[33]

Over the next two to three months top Zionist lawyers both in Britain and the United States worked constantly on the first draft of the Balfour Declaration. It was Baron Lionel Walter de Rothschild, a senior spokesman for Jewish interests, who submitted it finally for consideration by the British government on 18 July.[34] After various suggested changes in wording it was at last ready for signing, but first the Zionists needed to gain America's support for the declaration, which was achieved finally through the help of Mr Justice Brandeis, and forwarded on 16 October 1917 by Col. House on behalf of President Wilson. This recognition of the document by the US government was seen by Lloyd George and his colleagues as a decisive factor behind the War Cabinet's final decision to issue the Declaration. Until this time certain of its members had been reluctant to support the idea of a Jewish commonwealth until the future of the Palestinian Arabs had been guaranteed.[35] Another decisive factor in its issue at this time was the belief that Germany, with Turkish help, would support a Jewish Palestine, something that both the British and US governments felt might lead to the Zionists swapping allegiance if they did not move quickly.

The Balfour Declaration was signed on 2 November 1917, confirming to all the world Britain's commitment to the establishment of a Jewish National Home. More importantly, Britain saw the document as the basis for a mandate over its future control of Palestine. It would, of course, have to be ratified by the League of Nations, but this seemed arbitrary.

To mark the signing of the document, a huge celebration was held at the Covent Garden Opera House on 2 December. One after another, key British statesmen and leading Zionist Jews offered their vision of a future Jewish commonwealth. It was a portentous event, for just one week later Jerusalem fell to the British forces under General Allenby, bringing considerable relief to Zionists worldwide, who now looked towards Chaim Weizmann as their undisputed leader and Britain as their protector.

Yet the same sentiments were not shared by the leaders of the Arab Revolt, who looked on with growing disdain at the actions of the British government, especially when the contents of the Sykes–Picot agreement became known the following year. For helping to ensure an Allied victory in the Middle East, the British had promised to back the establishment of an Arabian state that was to have included Palestine and the Transjordan, but now this seemed unlikely to materialise. Quite clearly, the Palestinian Arabs were greatly angered at the thought of losing their country, and it was only a matter of time before their vexed frustration would erupt on to the streets.

24. THE SWORD OF DAMOCLES

In an attempt to offer a hand of friendship to Palestinian Arabs in the wake of the Allies' conquest of Palestine, Chaim Weizmann, the undisputed figurehead of the Zionist Jews, travelled to Amman in the Transjordan in June 1918. He was there to meet Feisal ibn Hussein (1885–1933), the Hashemite emir of the Hejaz region of Arabia and the military leader of the Arab Revolt. Already Weizmann had met with British officials in both Egypt and Palestine, including the commander-in-chief of British forces, General Allenby, who had established a military ruling administration in Palestine, known as the Occupied Enemy Territory Administration (OETA), which upheld existing Turkish-Ottoman law.

Present at the meeting between Weizmann and Feisal was Thomas Edward 'TE' Lawrence (1888–1935), 'Lawrence of Arabia', the British liaison officer for the Arab Revolt 1916–1918,[1] who is said to have been in favour of a Jewish National Home in Palestine. Weizmann outlined his mission to the heir of the Hashemite dynasty and attempted to allay any fears concerning a future Jewish commonwealth, which at the time was to include the Transjordan.

For two hours the Arab emir shared tea with the world's most influential Zionist Jew. Feisal, it seems, was greatly sympathetic to the Zionist cause, and stated openly that he was eager to see Arab and Jew working together in harmony during the Peace Conference, which would take place once hostilities ceased. According to Weizmann, Feisal considered that 'the destiny of the two peoples was linked with the Middle East and must depend on the good will of the Great Powers'.[2] It was a remarkable meeting between two great men of their time, and one that both sides believed, quite genuinely, would bring lasting peace between the Arab and Jewish worlds. How sadly they were to be proved wrong in this respect.

The Arab Revolt against Turkish occupation in the Near and Middle East from June 1916 till the end of the war ably demonstrated the support of the Arab tribal alliance united under the leadership of Feisal's father Hussein ibn Ali of Mecca (1854–1931), the elderly sharif of the Hashemites. However, the Allied powers seemed now to be dithering over their commitment to the establishment of an independent Arab state, negotiated originally in 1915 through the intercession of the British High Commissioner to Egypt, Sir Henry McMahon (1862–1949). With the official sanction of the Foreign Office, McMahon had pledged British support to the Arab cause in the event of an uprising among the Arabian tribes as well as recognition of an independent Arabia once the war was over.[3] Unfortunately, the agreement had been vague, and was superseded, in the minds of the British government at least, by the Sykes–Picot Agreement of 1916, and, of course, the Balfour Declaration of 1917.

Despite the British government's perceived abandonment of the promises made to Feisal's father, there were still handshakes and smiles all round as the emir of the Hejaz signed an agreement with Weizmann on a future Jewish commonwealth in Palestine. It is quite clear that at this stage Feisal fully believed that at the upcoming Peace Conference the stalwart efforts of his people in creating an Allied victory in the Near and Middle East would be rewarded to everyone's satisfaction.

PARIS PEACE CONFERENCE

November 1918 saw the collapse of the Central Powers, after four years of conflict across Europe and the Middle East, and the acceptance of a general armistice from the German and Austro-Hungarian monarchs, who as a result were forced to abdicate. Allied navies occupied Constantinople, bringing an end to Turkish control over its former empire, victories reflected in the re-election of Lloyd George's coalition government that same month.

The Peace Conference finally opened in Paris on 12 January 1919, with the matter of the Jewish National Home high on the agenda. Representing the Arab world was Feisal ibn Hussein, who had flown into the French capital with TE Lawrence. The emir, there obviously to negotiate a suitable deal for Arab concerns in the Near and Middle East, was to be sadly disappointed by its outcome. When the conference finally wound up in January 1920, Feisal had failed to gain any real satisfaction from its delegates. Thus with a growing fear that France was about to seize Palestine in contradiction to the Sykes–Picot Agreement, he returned to Amman and, in March that year, proclaimed himself king of Syria and Palestine. Yet his reign was to be short-lived, for just three months later French forces moved in to crush his regime.

In view of the British government's open support for the Zionist cause, and the manner in which they had failed Feisal's father, the whole matter was seen as particularly embarrassing for them. As a consequence, Britain promptly offered Feisal the throne of Mesopotamia, which was by then under British control. The position was duly accepted by the deposed Arab emir, who from 1921 ruled the country as King Feisal I of Iraq. In 1923 Transjordan was to become a semi-independent emirate under Abdullah ibn Hussein, Feisal's brother, whilst still remaining a British mandated territory. It remained this way until 1946 when, having aided the Allies to victory in the Second World War, the mandate was formally terminated and Abdullah took the title of King of the Hashemite Kingdom of Jordan.

THE JERUSALEM POGROM

With one flashpoint alleviated, temporarily at least, another of equal embarrassment brewed in Jerusalem. In March 1920 rumours abounded that civil unrest among the Palestinian Arabs was imminent in the holy city. It was to begin on the Feast of the Passover, set to coincide that year with both the Christian Easter festival and Nabi Mûsa, an Arab festival whereby pilgrimages are made to the reputed site of Moses' tomb, situated on a height close to the Dead Sea.

There had been growing agitation among Palestinian Arabs regarding the increasing power and influence of Jewish settlers, as well as the continued presence of British troops on the streets. All this came at a time when friction was mounting daily between France and Britain over the former's occupation of neighbouring Syria and Lebanon. Already lawlessness was breaking out in the northern hill country, and it looked set to hit the streets of Jerusalem and other parts of Palestine in a matter of days.

Chaim Weizmann was very much aware of the problem, and in an attempt to defuse the tension being vented on Jewish settlers by Palestinian Arabs, visited General Allenby, whom he found living in a former German hospice on the Mount of Olives. Weizmann, who had himself travelled to Palestine in order to spend Passover with his mother at Haifa, was told bluntly that there was nothing he could do, and that the British troops had orders to quell any trouble occurring on the streets. Realising that he was wasting his time, Weizmann left the old city with an eerie sense that a pogrom, an organised demonstration, was now inevitable.

Passover came and went, and still no news reached Haifa of the situation in Jerusalem. Indeed, there was nothing but silence, which disturbed Weizmann greatly. That something dreadful had happened he was sure, and so he made his way once more to the holy city. The sight that greeted him on his arrival was one of deserted streets, which worried him still further. On enquiring, he found that a curfew had been imposed after rioting had made it necessary to restrict the movement of anyone other than police and military patrols. Apparently, Palestinians had gathered at the Mosque of Omar, listening to speeches inciting violence. This had fired up demonstrators to such a degree that they had begun to run through the streets, chanting and attacking any Jew they came across. When a group of vigilantes emerged from the Jewish quarter in order to defend their families and property, the leader, one Captain Jabotinsky, was promptly arrested. In the trial that followed in a military court, he was sentenced to fifteen years' hard labour, later quashed on appeal.[4]

With six Jews dead and many others injured, serious questions were now being asked about the cause of the Jerusalem pogrom. How could it have happened? Who was really to blame, and what would happen next? There were no easy answers, although it was quite clear that anti-Zionism had been to blame. It was even reported that some of the British officers on duty that day had incited violence against the Jews.[5] Indeed, British officials in Jerusalem were accused of having virtually turned a blind eye to the violence, a fact displayed by 'the unwillingness of the soldiers to adopt an "unmistakable and active pro-Zionist attitude"'.[6] That a riot of this nature could occur in a British-administered Palestine two and a half years after the signing of the Balfour Agreement was the biggest concern to both Palestinian Jews and Zionists worldwide. How could the British have simply stood by and let this happen?

THE SAN REMO AGREEMENT

Just a few weeks after the Jerusalem pogrom, the Allied powers met at San Remo in Northern Italy to finally decide the fate of the former territories of the Turkish-Ottoman Empire. There is no question that the Balfour Declaration played a crucial role in the League of Nations' issuing of a draft mandate in support of Britain's commitment to a Jewish National Home in the disposition of Palestine, against the recommendations of the Sykes–Picot Agreement of 1916. Thus it was agreed that Palestine should become a British protectorate, with a civil administration in operation. Britain would be responsible for implementing the Balfour Declaration through negotiations with the appropriate Jewish agency, encouraging but also regulating settlement of Jewish colonisers. From July 1920 to May 1948, British administration in Palestine would come under the charge of a series of seven high commissioners, the first of whom was Sir Herbert Samuel (1870–1963), a British Jew and confirmed Zionist, who had introduced Weizmann to Lloyd George back in 1914.

Most important of all was the fact that the Mandate recognised the historical connection of the Jewish people with Palestine, something that was deemed necessary to justify the location of the Jewish National Home. This helped allay Zionist fears that the recent unrest in Jerusalem would lead to a change in policy by the British with respect to Palestine's future. The Mandate had still to be ratified by the League of Nations, and this would not take place for another two years. Until that time any changes in the situation could lead to Palestine being annexed from British control, something that would have had grave consequences for the Zionist cause.

THE JAFFA RIOTS

As the World Zionist Organisation, under the leadership of Chaim Weizmann, geared itself up for the immigration of thousands more settlers applying for Palestinian citizenship, disaster struck the new Jewish homeland. In May 1921 major riots, far worse and more widespread than those in Jerusalem the previous year, broke out in Jaffa, leading Sir Herbert Samuel instantly to suspend further immigration. Although the move was only temporary, it shocked Weizmann and his colleagues. He knew full well that there were elements in the British government fiercely against Britain's commitment to the Jewish National Home. The Jaffa riots were not what the Zionists needed at this time, and there were even greater problems on the horizon.

That summer saw the arrival in London of a Palestinian Arab delegation, with the express wish to highlight its people's plight at the hands of the pro-Zionist British administration and the rising threat of a Jewish National Home consuming their homeland. Under the leadership of one Mūsa Kazim Pasha, it lobbied Parliament, released information through the popular press and spread what Weizmann referred to as 'fantastic stories'.[7] Although the delegation did no major damage, it raised murmurs among anti-Zionist spokesmen, who called for a reduction of British interests in overseas commitments. It was even suggested that Palestine had become 'a serious liability, a country where Jews rode roughshod over "the poor Arabs", and charged the British taxpayer several shillings in the pound for doing it'.[8]

MORE PROBLEMS

In addition to these uncomfortable complications, the High Commissioner to Palestine, Sir Herbert Samuel, initiated his own investigation into the cause of the Jaffa riots, which was published in November 1921. Among the findings of the Haycraft Commission, as it became known, was that the Arab population had indeed been responsible for the organised pogrom in Jaffa. Yet it established also that the source of the trouble lay in Britain's continued pro-Zionist stance. Furthermore, it stated that 'the Zionist desire to dominate in Palestine might provide further ground for Arab resentment'.[9] As Weizmann was to write in his biography, 'the Haycraft Report contained the germ of very many of our main troubles'.[10]

Compounding the problem still further were the findings of Lord Northcliffe, who visited Palestine in the wake of the Jaffa riots. He returned to London with the opinion 'that Jewish settlers in Palestine were mostly Communists and/or Bolshevists – and arrogant, aggressive types into the bargain', and thus a danger to the British Empire.[11] He further emphasised that it was 'lunacy to upset the fifty million Muslims for the sake of the five hundred thousand Jews' already in residence there, a statement that prompted the British press to launch a campaign against further Zionist settlement.[12] This in turn led again to calls for the annulment of the Balfour Declaration and the scrapping of British policy in Palestine.[13]

At the same time an Arab lawyer named Wadi Bustani championed a claim by Bedouin tribesmen over land rights in the Beisan area of Palestine. For a nominal fee they were granted 400,000 dunams (100,000 acres) of land, another blow for the settlers, which led Weizmann to comment, 'One of the most important and most potentially fertile districts of Palestine (and one of the very few such districts which were "State lands") was thus condemned from the outset to stagnation and sterility'.[14]

FOREIGN OPPOSITION

Opposition to the establishment of a Jewish National Home came from outside Britain as well. On the way to London the aforementioned Palestinian Arab delegation had stopped off in Rome and Paris in order to present its case to the respective governments. They, of course, were incensed by the actions of the British and called for other Allied governments to unite in condemning Britain's pro-Zionist stance, even though they themselves had endorsed the Balfour Agreement and voted in support of the British Mandate for Palestine. Around the same time, the Latin Patriarch in Jerusalem voiced his opinion on the unsatisfactory state of affairs regarding the future of its holy places. This was despite the fact that the Zionist Jews had made it clear that they held no real interest in them, advocating that it was a matter to be settled by Christian powers and the Vatican.[15] Weizmann claimed that the only holy place that Palestinian Jews laid claim to was the reputed site of Rachel's Tomb. At that time the Wailing Wall, part of the reconstructed temple built by Herod the Great, ruler of Judaea, around c. 6 BC, was outside Jewish jurisdiction.[16]

THE PALESTINE MANDATE

Weizmann's vision of a future Jewish state was beginning to look shaky. So with a campaign mounting in Britain against the British Mandate for Palestine, he spent his time travelling between London, Paris, Rome and Geneva, attempting to dispel international fears and gaining the support of potential allies. For some time before the Mandate was ratified finally in July 1922, drafts were proposed, debated and rejected by Lord Curzon, who had replaced Lord Balfour in the Foreign Office after the fall of Lloyd George's government earlier that year. This process went on for month after month, with various key lines becoming major sticking points. For instance, the final version states that the League of Nations recognises 'the historical connection of the Jews with Palestine'. However, the Zionists insisted that it should read that the League of Nations recognises 'the historic *rights* of the Jews to Palestine [authors' italics]',[17] which has an altogether different connotation. The former simply acknowledges the Jews' assumed historical link with Palestine, while the latter deems to accept that the Jews were entitled to inherit the Holy Land by virtue of the divine right of God, a statement more emotive by far.

Adding to the problem were French claims over the disputed northern frontier to Palestine, a legacy of the Sykes–Picot Agreement. They seemed to regard the country simply as 'southern Syria', and thus under their control. To the French government Zionism was 'nothing more than camouflage for British imperialism'.[18]

Then came another potential problem for Weizmann and his colleagues. An attack in the House of Lords against Britain's pro-Zionist policy in Palestine, fielded by Lord Islington, Lord Raglan and Lord Sydenham, led to a motion asking for a complete repeal of the Balfour Declaration. It was won by a substantial majority, but luckily a similar vote in the House of Commons went in favour of the Zionists. Led by the likes of Sir Winston Churchill and Major Ormsby-Gore (Lord Harlech), the motion was defeated. Despite this respite, these were nail-biting days for the Zionists, who knew that the future of the Jewish state hung in the balance, and could be decided by a handful of British politicians and aristocrats who knew very little about the real situation in Palestine. With their hands firmly tied, Weizmann and his associates held their breath as the findings of yet another White Paper were published.

THE CHURCHILL WHITE PAPER

The Churchill White Paper, as it was known, took into account all the grievances of the Arab population of Palestine and examined the probable impact of wide-scale Jewish settlement. The investigation – which despite its connection with Churchill's name was commissioned by the British High Commissioner in Palestine, Sir Herbert Samuel – found that the main problem among the Arab population was that the Jews exist, and desire to exist, in Palestine. It also foresaw further problems in both the immigration and nationalisation of foreign Jews – whether it related to a few hundred settlers or tens of thousands, it made no difference whatsoever.

By far the greatest disappointment in the White Paper of 1922 was the removal of the Transjordan from the provisions for the establishment of the Jewish National Home. Up until then the Zionists had expected to take control not only of Palestine, but also those areas of the Sinai, Transjordan and Lebanon that were seen as having once formed part of the Israelite Empire, established under King David. Now they were to be denied the vast region east of the Jordan river, which constituted the loss of no less than three-quarters of the territory originally covered by the Mandate. Despite these findings, the White Paper confirmed the right of Jewish settlement, yet stipulated that it must not exceed the absorptive capacity of the country.

Zionists viewed the Churchill White Paper as a serious whittling down of the Balfour Declaration, but despite such disappointing setbacks the Mandate still came up for ratification in July 1922 at a members' council of the League of Nations in London. Yet even then the Zionists were made to sweat, for the matter was not discussed until the eleventh hour of the final day, 24 July, and even then uncertainty still surrounded the outcome. Finally, Lord Balfour was himself allowed to introduce the subject of the ratification of the Palestine Mandate. As Weizmann noted at the time with a huge sigh of relief and reserved sense of jubilation, 'Everything went off smoothly, and with the unanimous vote of ratification there ended the first chapter of our long political struggle'.[19]

THE ZIONIST COMMISSION

Yet it was not all plain sailing for the pro-Zionist Jews of Palestine, even after the ratification of the British Mandate. In March 1918 a governing body known as the Zionist Commission was established to oversee Jewish communal organisations, until that time under the control of the rabbis, many of whom did not fully support the Zionist cause. Incensed at being outmanoeuvred, the Jewish religious leaders set up their own assembly, which would regularly petition the British administration in Palestine to request separate representation.

Nothing was resolved, and in the British press the spokesman for the anti-Zionist assembly, which included many prominent rabbis, was one Jacob de Haan, a Dutch lawyer, ex-socialist, ex-Zionist, described as a 'born-again orthodox Jew, and homosexual'.[20] Somehow he managed to become Public Enemy Number One in the eyes of the pro-Zionists, owing to his repeated attacks on 'the godless Zionists' initially in the Daily Telegraph in 1919 and then later in The Times during the early 1920s. Eventually, however, his accusations went too far, and in 1924 he was assassinated by two members of a Jewish militia, apparently at the orders of the Zionist Labour Movement.[21] According to the historian Naomi Shepherd in 1999, 'The background of the killing has never been clear, but given the importance the Zionist movement attributed to its image in the British press, silencing de Haan may well have been a priority.'[22]

AND THEN A TOMB WAS UNCOVERED ...

Such was the political situation in Palestine when, on the morning of Saturday, 4 November 1922, workmen clearing away sand and spoil from an area beneath the tomb of Rameses VI in Egypt's Valley of the Kings uncovered the steps to a previously unknown tomb of a forgotten pharaoh. In a matter of a few brief months the discovery of the resting place of the boy-king Tutankhamun became the biggest news story since the end of the war. It was the archaeological find of the century. The whole world was held transfixed by the daily news reports on developments in the Valley, while its discoverers, the British Egyptologist Howard Carter and his sponsor Lord Carnarvon, were everywhere hailed as heroes.

The tomb's Antechamber was entered in late November 1922, its Burial Chamber, officially at least, three months later. The removal of the gilded shrines that surrounded the stone sarcophagus in which were the series of coffins containing the mummified king took place during the winter season of 1923–4. Just as the huge granite lid was hoisted above its carved stone coffer, Carter's long dispute with Egypt's Antiquities Service, and its ruling body the Ministry of Public Works, reached its climax, leading his archaeological team to down tools and go on strike. Soon afterwards Lady Carnarvon's concession to dig in the Valley was withdrawn, leaving Carter out of work and in a state of despair.

Perplexed by the British government's blank refusal to put pressure on the Egyptian government to reissue the concession and allow him back into the tomb, Carter went into action. He stormed into the offices of the British High Consul in Cairo and insisted that 'unless he received complete satisfaction and justice, he would publish for the whole world to read the documents that he found in the tomb giving the true account according to the Egyptian Government'[23] of the exodus of the Jews from Egypt'.[24]

This much we know only too well, but can we now better understand exactly what was going on inside Carter's head when he delivered this loaded statement to the British diplomat? From the evidence of the Exodus account presented within these pages, we can be pretty certain that his words were no idle threat. He would seem to have believed that he possessed highly controversial information regarding the biblical story of the Exodus. So much so that he considered that its implications would bring into question the very rudiments of the biblical story so crucial to the foundation not only of ancient Israel, but also, by virtue of this fact, the establishment of a modern Jewish state on the same soil. He knew that, if he so desired, his high profile in the world media could enable him to deliver his findings to the widest possible audience.

THE CONTENTS OF THE EXODUS PAPYRI

Yet how do we know this might have been Carter's objective that day in the offices of the British High Consul? First, we can now say with some certainty that the Exodus occurred either during or directly after the Amarna age, most probably in the reign of Horemheb. In all likelihood it began during the co-regency between Amenhotep III and Akhenaten, when the deposed priesthoods and the Egyptian people as a whole became scared that in abandoning the old gods there would be a terrible price to pay. Deities needed to be appeased on a regular basis with ritual offerings and sacrifices and, as the Hittite king Mursilis

II came to believe, failing to do so would result in some form of divine retribution.

Thus when a plague began sweeping across Egypt's northern empire towards the end of Akhenaten's reign it was deemed just punishment for Egypt having not supplicated the gods for some thirteen years. Yet nothing was done until after control of the country had been transferred from Akhenaten's city at Tell el-Amarna to either Memphis or Thebes, which did not occur until the reign of the boy-king Tutankhamun. By this time the plague had taken the life of Queen Tiye and was obviously still devastating Egypt's vassal kingdoms in the Near East.

Under Tutankhamun, control of the empire was placed in the hands of Aye, the priest and vizier, and Horemheb, the king's Deputy and Regent, who was in charge of all military affairs. Through the influence of the latter some effort would appear to have been made to convince the king that the only way to rid the land of the plague was to round up those responsible and expel them from the Two Lands. This meant the 'polluted' priests and followers of the Aten. Yet also targeted, it would seem, were the Asiatic peoples that had settled in border areas, such as the Eastern Nile Delta. They too were blamed for the presence of the plague, perhaps because they were seen as having introduced it into Egypt from Syria-Palestine during the reign of Akhenaten.

In all probability, the decision to rid the country of these undesirable elements was taken originally by Tutankhamun under the advice of both Horemheb and the newly reformed Amun priesthood. Yet the final expulsions of both the Egyptians and the Asiatic peoples almost certainly occurred during Horemheb's own reign, when we know the plague was still rife in the land of the Hittites. This then is the view of the Exodus on offer from a re-examination of the Graeco-Egyptian and Graeco-Roman historical sources on the life of Moses and the Exodus from Egypt. Thus it is likely that some semblance of the early stages of these events was contained in the Exodus papyri removed from Tutankhamun's tomb.

So, having refrained from revealing the contents of the Exodus papyri at the time of their discovery, Carter allowed his anger to get the better of him when he realised that not only had the Egyptian government turned its back on him, but now Egypt's British administration wanted to do the same. Being prepared for this eventuality, he delivered his calculated bombshell knowing that it would spur the British officials in the consulate to jump into action. He knew full well what he was doing, and we can see this from Lee Keedick's typewritten account of exactly what happened during that all-important meeting in Cairo. After recounting how Carter had threatened to reveal the contents of the papyri documents found in the tomb, he tells us,

> Realising the potentialities of such a threat, when Great Britain was having such trouble on account of the Balfour promises to both the Jews and the Arabs, the Vice Royal lost his temper completely and let fly at Carter's head an ink well that stood on his desk that was half full of ink … Eventually cooler heads prevailed and an adjustment was made so that Carter was silenced and the threat never materialised.[25]

Such a threat on Carter's part must have come like a shot out of the blue for the British official he confronted. If the disgruntled, and highly volatile archaeologist was right in what he claimed, then making public such explosive revelations would provide the Palestinian Arabs with enough ammunition to call into question the Zionist Jews' historical right to settle on their soil. Indeed, if it could be effectively shown that the whole basis for the biblical account of the Exodus and the conquest of Canaan was seriously flawed, it would have left it open for Palestinian Arabs to call for the annulment of both the Balfour Declaration and the British Mandate for Palestine.

The British knew full well that the mounting opposition to the Jewish National Home, not just in Palestine but also among the Arab population of Egypt, was a serious problem. Egypt was itself like a tinderbox waiting to explode. The Jaffa riots of 1921 had taken the British administration by surprise, and it was now feared that the pro-nationalist Zaghlul government, sympathetic to the Palestinian cause, could stir up even further hatred against British occupation in Egypt. Having backed the establishment of a Jewish commonwealth, Britain realised that it was in a somewhat precarious position, which could be deliberately ignited at any time.

If allowed to reach the public domain, Carter's claims could have catalysed a major political crisis, which would have caused untold damage to British policy in the Near and Middle East. It might even have incited the heirs to the Hashemite dynasty, including King Feisal of Iraq and Abdullah, the emir of Jordan, to raise a new revolt against British occupation in Palestine. Although they now ruled their own countries, the Hussein family obviously despised the British government for having broken their promises regarding the establishment of the intended Arab state in the Hussein–McMahon correspondence of 1915.

FEARS OF PARTITIONING

What consequences all this might have had for the future Jewish commonwealth would have been incalculable. By denying the historical validity of the biblical account of the Exodus and the conquest of Canaan, Palestinian Arabs could have called into question Jewish claims over key territories in their native land. Even though the Mandate had been ratified two years beforehand, there was growing concern among Weizmann and his colleagues that the geographical extent of the intended Jewish commonwealth might be whittled down by the League of Nations in order to satisfy mounting opposition from Palestinian Arabs. This would have seriously weakened its potential as a Middle Eastern state of economic and strategic importance able to compete on the world stage. Already the Transjordan had been annexed from any future negotiations in the Churchill White Paper of 1922, even though this constituted three-quarters of the territory originally designated in the draft for the British Mandate for Palestine. If it could now be shown that Joshua and the armies of the Israelites had never conquered Canaan, then this too would have weakened the Zionists' historical connection with the country. Clearly, this could not be allowed to happen as it would undermine the political and economic value of the future Jewish state.

THE QUESTION OF AQABA

The fear of further partitioning hung like a Sword of Damocles over the future success of Eretz Israel. Moreover, it was to remain a threat right through until November 1947, when its territorial status came up for final review at a meeting of the United Nations, the successor of the League of Nations. Representatives of its member countries voted to remove from the outlined Jewish state the southern half of the Negev in the south of the country, which was to be designated Palestinian Arab territory under the control of the Hashemite Republic of Jordan. This effectively deprived the future state of Israel of the coastal lowlands, including the key town of Gaza. Infinitely more distressing was the fact that this partitioning also denied the Jews access to the Gulf of Aqaba, the eastern arm of the Red Sea.

At the time Weizmann described the head of the Gulf of Aqaba as little more than a 'useless bay'.[26] Yet his intention was to develop the coast around Eilat, ancient Elim, west of the Jordanian port of Aqaba, into a thriving city, providing access for ships departing from the Red Sea bound for the Persian Gulf and Indian Ocean. Yet, without access to Eilat, it meant that any vessel wishing to make the same journey would first have to depart from a Mediterranean port and then travel via Port Said and the Suez Canal to reach the Red Sea, adding considerably to the sailing time.

The whole idea was seen as unacceptable to the Zionists, and in an attempt to block the decision, Chaim Weizmann – who in May 1948 was chosen to be Israel's first President – flew to Washington to seek the assistance of Harry S Truman (1884–1972), the American President. Having promised that under Jewish administration the Negev in Northern Sinai would be transformed from a barren desert into a centre for international trade and commerce, he was able to convince the President of his case. A compromise was reached whereby instead of the Negev being divided horizontally through its geographical centre, it was split vertically, with the eastern half going to Israel, thus allowing them access to the Gulf of Aqaba. This left the western half of the Negev, including the towns of Gaza and the coastal plain, in the hands of the Palestinian Arabs, hence what we know today as the Gaza Strip. In addition to this, an extensive region from the northern highlands right down to the southern highlands, including key towns such as Jenin, Nablus, Ramallah, Jericho, Bethlehem, Hebron and Beersheba, were also to remain Palestinian territories under Jordanian control. Today they form part of the West Bank, due to their location west of the Jordan river. Jerusalem was itself to be partitioned, with one half going to Israel and the other half to Jordan. After the Arab-Israeli war of 1967, when an alliance of Arab states, principally Syria, Egypt and Jordan, entered eastern Palestine and were beaten back by Israeli forces, all Arab Palestinian territories, including the Jordanian half of Jerusalem, have come under Israeli control.

The problem of further partitioning with respect to the national borders of the future state of Israel did not occur until November 1947, just six months before Israel's proclamation of a state of independence on 14 May 1948, and the termination of the British Mandate to Palestine at midnight that night. However,

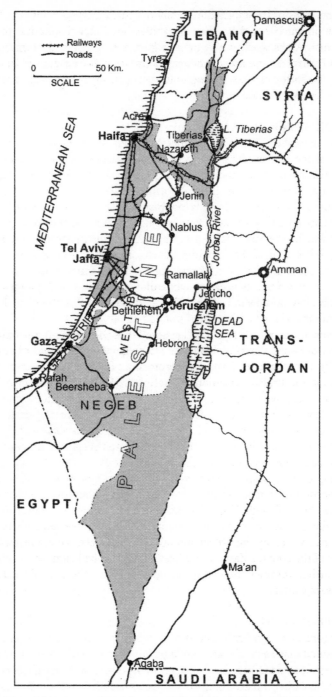

Fig. 24. Map of the proposed Jewish state of Israel (shaded) as of 1948, the year of its declaration of independence.

with the Transjordan annexed from any negotiations even before the Mandate's ratification in 1922, there was every likelihood that continued protests by Palestinian Arabs would result in even greater anti-Zionist feelings both in the British Parliament and among the member states of the League of Nations. Thus during the spring of 1924 the fear of further partitioning remained a real one for Zionist Jews worldwide.

AN ADJUSTMENT WAS MADE …

According to Lee Keedick, after Carter had made his outrageous outburst in the offices of the British High Consul in Cairo, 'an adjustment was made so that Carter was silenced and the threat never materialised'. So we must assume that the matter was nipped in the bud before it was allowed to go any further. Afterwards, Carter went off on his highly successful tour of the United States and Canada organised by Keedick, and the whole matter was dropped. He returned to London in the summer of 1924 and sat it out as Sir John Maxwell, the principal executor of the Carnarvon estate, attempted to formulate a new deal with the Minister of Public Works, Morcos Bey Hanna, on behalf of Almina, Countess of Carnarvon. It was an arduous business and progress seemed painfully slow. So slow in fact, that, just as Morcos Bey was about to allow Carter back into the tomb, he was ousted from office.

Events in the outside world had eclipsed those occurring in the offices of the Ministry of Public Works as finally the British government found its opportunity to rid Egypt of the hated Zaghlul government. It followed the death of Sir Oliver Lee Stack, the British Governor-General of the Sudan and Commander of the Egyptian Army, who was second only in command to the High Commissioner. On 19 November 1924 he and his Australian driver were driving through the streets of Cairo in a motorcade when they were gunned down by Wafdist terrorists, thought to be linked with Zaghlul's nationalist party. Britain demanded a personal apology for the assassination from the Prime Minister, along with the bringing to justice of the perpetrators, an indemnity payment of £500,000, and the imposition of martial law, including a ban of meetings of five or more persons. Even though Zaghlul condemned the murder, denouncing it as a despicable act of terrorism, his attempts to call for some kind of compromise went unanswered by the British authorities, who seized the opportunity to take control of the country. Zaghlul and his Cabinet resigned, and were replaced by a pro-British government headed by one Ahmad Pasha Ziwar, an old acquaintance of Howard Carter.

NEW BEGINNINGS

Finding the new Egyptian Prime Minister sympathetic towards his plight, Carter was assured that a suitable deal would be ironed out soon enough. He found also that the mood had changed dramatically in the offices of the High Consul, which, despite his earlier threats to expose the contents of the Exodus papyri, were now seemingly working in his favour. Even General Allenby, who had become the Egyptian High Commissioner after the war, was now disposed to finding some kind of final solution in the dispute between Almina, Countess of Carnarvon, and the Ministry of Public Works. He realised that there was much to gain from the reopening of the tomb, which would bring with it considerable benefits both in a political sense and in public relations, in that it might help dispel any criticism surrounding Britain's decision to once again seize control of Egypt.

Provided that Carter and Lady Carnarvon renounced formally their claims over any of the treasures from the tomb, a new concession covering its final clearance could be granted. Carter was unhappy about this arrangement, seeing the many years that he and Lord Carnarvon had laboured in the Valley without any kind of financial remuneration. However, there was little else he could do other than to make an official protest. So on 13 January 1925, some eleven months after he and his colleagues had downed tools and gone on strike, Mahmoud Bey Sidky, the new Minister of Public Works, issued a one-year concession to Carter as archaeological agent acting on behalf of Almina, Countess of Carnarvon. Although it was deemed that the Egyptian government had full right to the entire contents of the tomb, it did promise to provide at its discretion

a choice of duplicates as representative as possible of the discovery provided that such duplicates may be separated from the whole without damage to science.[27]

Carter returned to his job as chief excavator of the tomb of Tutankhamun, where he worked for seven more years to complete its clearance, the concession being renewed annually. During this time five successive governments came and went in Egypt. They culminated in 1930 with the return of the Nationalists, and one of the first acts of this so-called 'People's Government' was to pass a law forbidding any art treasure discovered in a tomb from leaving Egypt – and this applied equally to originals and duplicates. It did not matter what the nature of the items was, or how they were found, the rules would remain the same. Thus Almina, Countess of Carnarvon, failed to gain, officially at least, any prize objects from the tomb. Yet she did not go away completely empty-handed, for in the autumn of 1930 the Egyptian government sent her a sum of £36,000, an amount equivalent to a group of duplicate items from the tomb identified by Carter and independently assessed and valued by the Belgian Egyptologist Jean Capart. It also just happened to be the exact figure proposed as a final settlement of the cost of seventeen years of excavations in the Valley of the Kings.

Thus ended Howard Carter and the Carnarvon Estates' working relationship with Egypt, even though the British Egyptologist would not finish clearing the tomb of its treasures until the spring of 1932. Other than in private conversations with Lee Keedick in the spring of 1924, Carter would never again allude to the discovery in the tomb of the Exodus papyri. However, if during that fateful meeting with the British diplomat in Cairo in February–March 1924 'an adjustment was made so that Carter was silenced' then we can understand why he might have kept quiet about the subject for the rest of his life.

MORE AT STAKE?

Exactly what kind of 'adjustment' was made with Mr Carter and how it might have brought about his complete silence in the affair remains unclear. Can it simply have been a pledge by the High Consul to support his fight against the Zaghlul regime, or had there been more at stake? Money perhaps, or top-secret information that predicted the fall of the Nationalists in a matter of months, allowing Carter to restart his negotiations with a new Minister of Public Works, who he was assured would look more favourably on his predicament? The truth of the matter is that we do not know. It could have been any of these proposed options, or perhaps none of them.

Yet we cannot leave the matter there. By accepting that Carter's verbal assault on the British diplomat was preplanned, and concerned historical matters that he must have been privy to for some time, we must ask ourselves whether he acted alone or was working in collusion with others.

It is all too easy to forget that less than a year beforehand Carter's friend and sponsor, the fifth Earl of Carnarvon had died unexpectedly under somewhat baffling circumstances. Remember too that it was the fifth earl who nonchalantly announced to the world that papyrus documents had been found in the tomb within days of its discovery, a fact confirmed in the national press by his close colleague, the philologist Alan H Gardiner. Is it possible that before his death Lord Carnarvon was aware of Carter's plan to use the Exodus papyri to blackmail the British authorities in Cairo or, indeed, any other interested party that might have had something to lose if their contents became publicly known? More pressingly, what, if anything, did any of this have to do with his lordship's untimely death?

25. THE FATE OF THE MISSING PAPYRI

When George Edward Stanhope Molyneux Herbert, the fifth Earl of Carnarvon, passed away in his bed at the Grand Continental Hotel, Cairo, during the early hours of 5 April 1923, he took with him to the grave certain secrets, shared in life only by his closest friends and associates. We can be pretty certain that they included his and Howard Carter's clandestine forays into the tomb of Tutankhamun, along with their illegal removal of art treasures. If these antics had become more widely known, then there is no question that it would have meant ruin for Lord Carnarvon's reputation and the end of Carter's career as a respected archaeologist.

Yet did the Earl of Carnarvon take with him to the grave other more dangerous secrets, shared only by him and Carter? There can be little doubt that, although Carter's decision to try to blackmail a British diplomat in Cairo with the contents of the Exodus papyri in February–March 1924 might have been spontaneous, there was much more behind this outrageous threat. Its nature was calculated and meant to cause the greatest possible reaction, which it indeed appears to have done. Yet as we have seen, eventually 'cooler heads prevailed and an adjustment was made so that Carter was silenced and the threat never materialised'.[1]

TRANSLATED IN SECRET?

Yet the question remains: was this the only occasion that Howard Carter intended to use the explosive material contained in the papyri? More importantly, did the fifth Earl of Carnarvon become embroiled in this dangerous affair before his untimely death? Indeed, was the whole plot hatched not by Carter acting alone, but by Carnarvon and Carter working together in the wake of the discovery of the tomb?

If it might be considered possible that the missing papyri were spirited out of the tomb in the same manner as a number of other art treasures found therein, then their contents must have been translated in secret. There is no evidence that the philologist and Egyptologist Alan H Gardiner was involved in this fiasco. Yet, he being a close friend of Lord Carnarvon, we know he was asked in December 1922 to translate any papyri found in the tomb, and this might well have included the Exodus text.

Perhaps Carnarvon and Carter at first intended fully to record the existence of the papyri, hence the mention of them in letters sent out by his lordship and in various newspaper accounts of the time. Yet after the translations had been done, the highly sensitive nature of their contents now made it impossible for them to be recorded officially. If, as Keedick records, they did contain 'a true account' of the Exodus which was explosive in nature, then maybe Carnarvon and Carter conceived of a plan to approach certain individuals who, for their own reasons, might have wished to ensure that their contents did *not* reach the public domain. To understand more fully this line of thought, it will be necessary to delve a little more deeply into the private life of the fifth Earl of Carnarvon.

ALMINA, COUNTESS OF CARNARVON

On 26 June 1895, at the age of 29, the fifth earl married Almina Victoria Marie Alexandra Wombwell, the nineteen-year-old daughter of Marie ('Mina') Felice Wombwell, née Boyer, a woman said to have been of mixed French and Spanish extraction. Despite being the wife of an Englishman named George Wombwell, Marie is known to have had a lengthy affair with Alfred de Rothschild (1842–1918),[2] a grandson of the founder of the British branch of the House of Rothschild, the wealthiest and most powerful Jewish family in Europe. He was born in London on 20 July 1842 and died on 31 January 1918; and, even though his close relationship with Marie Wombwell, a staunch Catholic, is not in dispute, the couple never married, owing, most probably, to their religious differences.

The fact that Almina – whose name is a combination of 'Al' and 'Mina', abbreviations of her parents' first names – was an illegitimate daughter of Alfred Rothschild is also something which has not been denied by the Carnarvon family. For example, Almina's parentage is recorded in the memoirs of the sixth Earl of Carnarvon.[3] It is acknowledged even in the guidebook to the Carnarvon family home at Highclere Castle,[4] while a framed photograph of Alfred remains on display in one of the rooms open to the public.[5]

It is no secret either that prior to his wedding to Almina, which took place with full pomp and ceremony in St Margaret's Chapel, Westminster Abbey, the fifth earl was in serious financial trouble. With the family fortunes exhausted, his lordship approached the exorbitantly rich Alfred de Rothschild and demanded that if he was to marry his daughter then he would require £150,000 to cover his existing debts. In addition to this, a payment of half a million pounds was to be divided between himself and his wife as part of a marriage dowry.[6] Furthermore, a covenant was to be entered into, by which the happy couple would be guaranteed financial security for as long as they remained together. In this way, they could enter married life with a clean sheet and peace of mind, while Almina would be able to look forward to a secure future as a member of the British aristocracy.

In 1898 Almina bore the fifth earl a son, Henry George Alfred Marius Herbert, who, as heir to the Carnarvon estate, was given the hereditary title Lord Porchester. This he bore until the death of his father in April 1923, when he became the sixth Earl of Carnarvon. Yet the fact that his third name was Alfred is another clear indication that the Carnarvon family did not deny Almina's illegitimacy. Three years after the birth of Lord Porchester, Almina bore her husband a daughter, Evelyn, who, in contrast with their son, would became a constant companion to her father in his later years.

Long after her marriage to the fifth Earl of Carnarvon, Almina remained in constant touch with her father, who kept his part of the bargain and ensured that she and her husband never went short of money. Every so often she would meet with Alfred at NM Rothschild and Sons, the powerful and very influential merchant bank founded by the British branch of the House of Rothschild, to ask for large sums of money. She was never refused, and often the amount provided would be thousands of pounds at a time, for as the sixth earl recalls in his memoirs:

> Almina was in the very happy position of being able to go to her father and ask for five, ten or twenty thousand pounds, to which he would gently reply, 'Oh, puss-cat, I gave you ten thousand pounds only last week. Whatever have you done with it, my darling child?'[7]

Indeed, the sixth earl reminisces on his own visits to see his 'godfather' Alfred de Rothschild at his offices 'for equally mercenary reasons'. According to him, 'we usually found three Rothschilds sitting at their desks: Nathan, Leo and Alfred [who] were always delighted to see me and very spoiling'.[8]

As we know, the fifth earl suffered a debilitating motorcar accident in Germany around 1901, leaving him with breathing problems. His physician, Dr Marcus Johnson, persuaded him to take seasonal holidays in Egypt, where the dry air would benefit his frail health. Yet, after a few brief years, he grew tired of the constant round of social life and dusty streets in Cairo, and transferred his attentions to Luxor where he became interested in the subject of Egyptology and, in particular, the acquisition of antiquities. This, of course, led eventually to his own excavations on the Theban west bank from 1907 onwards, many of which were unquestionably funded from money supplied to Lady Carnarvon by Alfred de Rothschild. She would accompany her husband on some of his Egyptian expeditions, but increasingly she remained behind in England, with her place being taken in later years by the couple's teenage daughter Evelyn. Indeed, it becomes clear that from the outset her parents' marriage was one more of convenience than love, since the couple, who had little in common, barely experienced the closeness and intimacy expected of a relationship today.

As history records, Almina did not accompany her husband to Egypt when he received news of Carter's 'wonderful discovery' of 'a magnificent tomb with seals intact' on 6 November 1922. Neither did she accompany him out to the Valley of the Kings for the official opening of the Burial Chamber in February 1923, and she had been difficult to locate when the fifth earl fell terminally ill in March that year. Only on being alerted to her husband's worsening condition at the end of that month did she decide to join him in Cairo.

The principal reason for Almina's absence from her husband's side throughout the final years of his life was her role as the founding light of various convalescence and nursing homes, the first of which was established at Highclere during World War One for soldiers wounded in action. Her interests in this field were kindled shortly before the hostilities started, when, at a dinner thrown at Highclere Castle in the presence of Field Marshal Horatio, Lord Kitchener, the fifth earl consented to the use of his home as a hospital. Dr Marcus Johnson agreed to take charge of the venture, although so much did Almina throw her heart and soul into the work that she went on to establish another nursing home for soldiers at Bryanston Square, London, where she would spend nearly all of her time. The last of its patients left in 1919, and afterwards she founded another private hospital, called Alfred House, named after her father, in the Mayfair district of London. It was seen as the *crème de la crème* of nursing homes, and during its heyday it attracted a long list of well-to-do patients, including George V's son, Henry, Duke of Gloucester, and even Noël Coward.

Quite obviously Almina's strong commitment to her nursing homes, in which she took the role of governess, took up a considerable amount of her time and, having little or no interest in Egyptology, she was given an amiable excuse not to accompany her husband on his expeditions to Egypt. Indeed, the last time that she visited Egypt before her husband's fatal illness was during the 1919–20 winter season. Yet it is clear that there were now other reasons for her staying away from her husband.

TIGER DENNISTOUN

Sometime before the death of Lord Carnarvon, Lady Carnarvon had befriended a woman named Dorothy Dennistoun, the wife of Lt Col. Ian Onslow 'Tiger' Dennistoun, a retired Grenadier Guard. Although the couple were divorced, Dorothy still kept in touch with her husband, who now lived in Paris. Then one day in 1921, she learned that Almina was about to make one of her regular trips to the French capital. Since she would be staying at the Ritz Hotel, where Dorothy's husband had a small apartment, she asked Almina whether she would be a darling and collect some articles of hers that were still in his possession. She accepted the proposal, and on her arrival in Paris Almina made contact with Dennistoun. Yet she was shocked by what she found, for according to her he was living in 'an attic that not one of my servants would be seen in. There was no fireplace, no hot or cold water, only a very small window overlooking a courtyard.'[9] She was also horrified by his appearance: 'He looked like death. A thin, emaciated, poor creature. His clothes were shiny, and he looked as though he had not had food enough to keep body and soul together.'[10] So overcome was she with pity that Almina ordered him immediately to buy a new wardrobe and move into her suite in order that she might better take care of him.

Despite his poor health (he suffered from acute asthma), Almina was instantly attracted to Tiger Dennistoun, and very soon the couple became inseparable. They were married eventually in a register office on 19 December 1923, just eight months after the fifth earl's death. Yet just two years later Almina's name was dragged through the dirt in the most public of fashions during a celebrated legal case in which Dorothy Dennistoun attempted to sue her former husband for alimony. The matter of exactly when Almina had begun her relationship with Col. Dennistoun was broached when Dorothy took the witness box, although mercifully she claimed that she did not know, allowing everyone to breathe a sigh of relief. The case was won by neither plaintiff nor defendant, although unquestionably it went in favour of the latter, due mainly to the dynamic opening and closing speeches of Mr Norman Birkett KC.[11] Almina spent the next decade caring for Tiger Dennistoun, initially in Scotland, and then, after moving around a while, at Hove, near Brighton in West Sussex, where he ended his days.

Although the sixth earl implies in his memoirs that Almina was no more than a friend to Tiger Dennistoun before the death of his father, this is untrue. It is now known that the couple were romantically involved even before the fifth earl's death. Moreover, the fifth earl 'definitely knew Almina was having an affair with the Colonel'.[12] Indeed, it would seem that he actually encouraged the affair, making it clear that their own relationship was long dead.[13]

We come now to the testimony of Tony Leadbetter, a surviving godson of Almina. His mother Anne had been her close companion until 1969, when the once wealthy countess passed away at the age of 93, having spent her final years virtually penniless, living in an end-terraced house in Bristol. Leadbetter has made it clear to the authors that when Lord Carnarvon fell ill Almina was in Paris with Tiger Dennistoun. She did not feel inclined to leave his side, and did so only after it became clear that her husband was terminally ill. According to him:

> The impression I got was that she arrived late and that it was all a terrible pain and a waste of time and money and the sooner it was over and done with the better. I don't think she grieved over him at all.[14]

This statement is backed up by *The Egyptian Gazette* of Friday 30 March 1923, which reports that 'Lady Carnarvon has arrived in Cairo and has joined Lord Carnarvon and Lady Evelyn Herbert at the Continental-Savoy'. Given that the paper would have gone to press during the night hours, this places Almina in Cairo no earlier than Thursday, 29 March, just one week before his lordship passed away.[15]

INHERITANCE

As we have seen, during their married years, the fifth earl and Lady Almina relied heavily on the good will of Alfred de Rothschild. When he died in 1918 at the age of 76, Alfred left his daughter and their children a large proportion of his estimated £1.5 million estate, including his London home at Seymour Place.[16] Yet we know that before the commencement of the 1922–3 winter season, Lord Carnarvon was once more suffering financial difficulties, and was extremely reluctant to sponsor Carter for another year of excavations in the Valley of the Kings. This situation must have been compounded still further when, on discovering the tomb, Carnarvon realised that he was now looking at another five seasons of excavation to ensure the full clearance of the tomb (it in fact took ten years!).

Faced with such a daunting prospect, and aggrieved by the vast fortune that Almina and his children had been left by her father, is it possible that Carnarvon's financial frustration led him to concoct some kind of plan? Did it involve the papyrus documents found in the tomb? From Carter's outburst in the offices of the British High Consul in Cairo we know that the contents of the supposed papyri found in the tomb exploded the accepted version of the Exodus story, and thus would have been of extreme embarrassment to Zionists worldwide. Is it possible therefore that the Earl of Carnarvon intended to try to persuade certain leading Zionist Jews that he had at his disposal ancient Egyptian documents that, owing to their highly sensitive nature, were best kept private? Thus in order to ensure that they never reached the public domain, and to compensate for the archaeological irregularities on the parts of himself and Howard Carter, did he suggest some kind of financial remuneration? The plan could have been as simple as that, and if this was the case then to whom might it have been directed?

THE HOUSE OF ROTHSCHILD

There is, it must be stated, no real evidence that any such blackmail attempt was ever carried out. Yet if it was, then the most obvious candidates to whom it might have been directed was of course Alfred's immediate family, the Rothschilds. Their origins go back to the five sons of one Baron Mayer Amshel Rothschild (1744–1812), the celebrated Jewish banker and financier from Frankfurt in Germany. His third son, Nathan Mayer (1777–1836), settled in England and became the founder of the merchant bank NM Rothschild and Sons, located at New Court, St Swithin's Lane, in the City of London. He went on to finance the Duke of Wellington's Peninsular campaign in Spain, and provided enough gold bullion through French banking contacts to finance Britain's European allies in the anti-Napoleon coalition. In 1812, his younger brother James (1792–1868) settled in Paris in order to coordinate these complex transactions, and from his financial empire sprang the French branch of the family. It is said that after Napoleon's defeat by Wellington at the Battle of Waterloo in 1815, Nathan de Rothschild, as its financier, was the first man in England to receive notification of Britain's triumph.[17]

Afterwards, the House of Rothschild rose to power as Europe's leading banking family, consolidating its wealth and influence in European society, expressed by their uniting emblem of five arrows clenched in a fist. Mayer Amshel died in his ghetto home in Frankfurt in 1812. Yet beforehand he had told his sons always to work together and trust one another, something that was always upheld and helped no doubt by constant interfamily marriages. Each of the five sons established themselves in different European cities, and quickly they became multimillionaires. As we saw, Nathan Mayer set up shop in London, while his younger brother, James, settled in Paris where he founded Rothschild Frères, which in just twenty years became France's leading bank.

BARON EDMOND DE ROTHSCHILD

James's fourth son, Baron Edmond de Rothschild (1845–1934), was to play a powerful role in the establishment of the Jewish National Home. As we have seen, he financed Jewish settlements in Palestine from the early 1880s onwards, including the pioneering Rishon le-Zion community, founded by Russian immigrants. Edmond gave the settlers 30,000 francs, and thus began a lifelong passion for the Zionist cause.

In 1897 Baron Edmond established the Jewish Colonial Trust, the first Zionist-funded bank, which helped aid the purchase of extensive territories in Palestine for incoming Jewish settlers. He continued to plough money into the colonies through to the end of the nineteenth century, when he handed over administration, along with substantial funds, to the Jewish Colonization Association, which helped extend the Jewish farming villages in Palestine into towns. In 1924 he vested all his holdings in Palestine in a company called the Palestine Jewish Colonization Association, and set up his son James (1878–1957) as its first president. The revenues generated by PICA were enough to fund various industrial enterprises, including the Palestine Electric Corporation, as well as other projects involving higher education, hospitals and research.

James de Rothschild (1878–1957) settled in England and became a British citizen, even serving as a captain in the army during World War One. However, he shared his father's passion for Zionism, and in the lead-up to the signing of the Balfour Declaration worked alongside Chaim Weizmann and key British statesmen, such as Sir Mark Sykes and Lord Balfour.

THE BRITISH BRANCH

As for the British branch of the family, allegiances with the Zionist cause are more difficult to define. Following the death of Nathan Mayer de Rothschild in 1836, his place in the banking empire was taken by Lionel Nathan de Rothschild (1808–79). Over the next forty years NM Rothschild and Sons became involved in some of the most crucial financial deals undertaken by the British government. They included loans connected with the emancipation of the slaves, the Irish famine of 1847, the Crimean War and the purchase of shares in the Suez Canal from the khedive of Egypt, Ismail Pasha, in 1875. This last transaction was of enormous political and strategic importance to Britain, and was made possible only by an on-the-spot loan of 4 million pounds to the government of Benjamin Disraeli (1804–81), who was himself the country's first Jewish Prime Minister.

Following Lionel's death in 1879, his eldest son Nathaniel 'Natty' Mayer de Rothschild (1840–1915) took control of NM Rothschild and Sons. Through the intervention of his friend and colleague Benjamin Disraeli, with whom he liaised regarding the purchase of shares in the Suez Canal, Queen Victoria consented to grant him a peerage, thus he became the first Lord Rothschild. Natty was for forty years a leading Anglo-Jewish lay preacher, as well as the director of the Bank of England. He was also a Liberal MP and, as a member of the Royal Commission on Alien Immigration, fought hard to keep the gates open for Russian Jewish asylum seekers entering Britain. However, Natty was no Zionist, and made it clear that he would 'view with horror the establishment of a Jewish Colony [in Palestine] pure and simple'.[18]

ALFRED AND LEOPOLD DE ROTHSCHILD

Nathaniel had two brothers, Leopold, the youngest, and Alfred, the father of Lady Almina, Countess of Carnarvon. Alfred remained unmarried, presumably because of his long-term love affair with Marie Wombwell. Even though he was a partner of NM Rothschild and Sons, he was more interested in the artistic, social and sporting life, and by all accounts was an aesthete and dandy. Alfred's lavish banquets at Seymour Place and Halton, his country estate in Buckinghamshire, were legendary in society circles. Moreover, he kept his own private orchestra and circus, for which he was famous. Apparently, his party piece was to stop traffic in the street by driving a coach drawn by four zebras![19] Along with his younger brother Leopold, he also owned and raced horses, which would sport the blue and amber colours of the Rothschilds.

Neither Alfred nor Leopold would seem to have had any strong convictions towards the Zionist cause. However, the same cannot be said for Nathaniel's eldest son, Lionel Walter (1868–1937), who, despite wanting to be a naturalist, was persuaded by his father to enter a life of banking, commerce and politics. Only afterwards was he allowed to pursue his other, more scientific, interests, and on the death of his father in 1915 he became the second Lord Rothschild.

As history records, it was Lionel Walter de Rothschild to whom the Balfour Declaration was addressed. He was a Zionist through and through, and worked closely alongside Chaim Weizmann in the lead-up to the signing of this historic document. At the celebration of this great event at the Covent Garden Opera House on 2 December 1917 both Walter and James, the son of Baron Edmond de Rothschild, delivered poignant speeches. Walter told the audience that it was 'the greatest event that has occurred in Jewish history for the last eighteen hundred years', while James declared that the 'British government had ratified the Zionist scheme'.[20]

In spite of Walter's importance in Zionist history, it was his younger brother Nathaniel Charles (1877–1923) who took control of NM Rothschild and Sons. Although he was not destined to play an active role in the Zionist cause, because he suffered from melancholy and shunned London life, he did meet with Weizmann and was sympathetic to the cause. Nathan's wife Rozsika ('Jessica') was much more actively involved in Zionism, and played an important role in helping Weizmann and his colleagues to meet and put their views to Englishmen of influence.[21]

According to Chaim Weizmann the House of Rothschild 'perhaps were the most famous family in Jewish exilic history',[22] even though they were much divided on the issue of Zionism. Yet from the involvement of Baron Edmond de Rothschild and his son James, to the part played in this affair by his British counterpart Lionel Walter de Rothschild, the family staked much on the success of Zionism. There is no question that through the influence of its international banking system the House of Rothschild stood to benefit financially and politically from the achievement of its ultimate goal – the establishment of a Jewish National Home in Palestine. The same has to be said of the British government, which staked its reputation on achieving the British Mandate for Palestine through its signing of the Balfour Declaration. With the ultimate establishment of the Jewish state, it could look forward to a strong partner who would help bring stability to the Middle East, and also tender its interests in the oil fields of Iraq and Arabia, while at the same time securing its trade routes to India. Any attempts at derailing the British government's long-term aims in this area would have been seen as a major threat to its foreign policies in the Near and Middle East.

WHAT HAPPENED TO THE MISSING PAPYRI?

If Lord Carnarvon had been in league with Carter with respect to his intended exploitation of the Exodus papyri, then it is possible that he utilised this ploy to threaten those who had the most to lose by the derailment of the planned Jewish National Home. Whether or not this is correct may never be known. All we do know is that, if Carter had been allowed to release details of the contents of the documents to the world media, then it would have seriously derailed Zionist aspirations. As such, he agreed not to do so, and the matter was quietly forgotten. Thereafter, Carter would no longer have posed any real threat to any interested parties. Since he was a respected Egyptologist, it is unlikely that at some later point he would ever have broken his silence and admitted having removed from the tomb papyrus documents that had not been catalogued or recorded in the first place. Unquestionably, it would have meant the end of his career as a greatly respected Egyptologist, successful author, public lecturer and speaker at after-dinner functions. There was no way that he was ever going to put all this at risk, especially as his digging career was effectively over by the spring of 1932. No, his outburst in the offices of the British High Consul in Cairo must be seen as a one-off, never to be repeated.

At the end of the day we have no absolute proof that the Exodus papyri actually existed, but neither can it be proved that they did *not* exist. Yet if they did, then what became of them? Did Carter destroy them in the belief that they might eventually fall into the wrong hands? Are they languishing in some forgotten drawer of a museum, tucked underneath dozens of other more insignificant papyri? Or were they passed on to a third party with a vested interest in their contents, who either destroyed them or placed the documents in a safety-deposit box, where they remain out of reach of prying eyes? Unfortunately, there are no answers. We can only but hope that in the years to come some evidence of their final fate emerges on to the Egyptological scene, just as much as a clearer picture has now emerged of the events surrounding the opening of the tomb in the decades following its discovery.

RARE-METAL POISONING

And what about the death of the fifth Earl of Carnarvon? Might this have been linked in some way with the explosive contents of the Exodus papyri? As we know, he died under somewhat curious circumstances on 5 April 1923, having contracted pneumonia after his immune system had been weakened by septicaemia, which set in after he was infected by a mosquito bite sustained some five weeks earlier. This much is true. Yet there seems to be compelling evidence to suggest that even before this time his physical health was deteriorating rapidly. As Thomas Hoving records, 'Every few days one of his teeth chipped or just fell out. He did not realize it at the time, but this was one symptom of a deep infection exacting a terrible toll upon his body'.[23]

So something else was making the British aristocrat ill and all the indications are that it was the result of some form of rare-metal poisoning, most probably caused by the unwitting ingestion of mercury. His colleague Arthur Mace also became ill around the same time, and there is every reason to believe that he too suffered from rare-metal poisoning, although in his case it was diagnosed as having been caused by arsenic. It is realised that these are feeble pointers towards some kind of primary cause behind the death of Lord Carnarvon. Yet, if the suspected poisoning did not stem from contact with a substance already present in any Egyptian tomb, we must ask ourselves whether or not the British aristocrat – and, of course, Arthur Mace – might have been exposed to a rare-metal poison through some other means?

It is known that Carnarvon and Mace were together on a Nile cruise that his lordship and Lady Evelyn took to Aswan at the end of February 1923. Shortly afterwards, both men's health began to deteriorate. Is it possible that they might have come into contact with some form of toxic substance during their short break? Unfortunately, this seems unlikely for two reasons. First, Mace was ill before he embarked on the cruise, and, secondly, the effects both of arsenic and mercury poisoning come as a result of long-term contamination over many weeks, possibly even months or years. This is unless large quantities of the substance are introduced to the body in an extremely short space of time, and no evidence of this possibility has emerged in the cases of either Carnarvon or Mace.

The only possible means of establishing further clues regarding the precise cause of death in both instances is, as the chemist and historian Michael Carmichael has suggested, by examining their earthly remains and extracting hair samples for a so-called hair-shaft test. This is standard practice for toxicologists wishing to determine whether or not a person has absorbed drugs into his or her system. It works equally well on live or dead hair cells, for they both retain traces of the drug even after death. In the case of Lord Carnarvon, an examination of his remains might help solve this great mystery, although it is highly unlikely that the Carnarvon estate would ever grant permission for the body of the fifth earl to be exhumed for this purpose. Despite this, the authors feel that this is the only way to settle the matter one way or another.

Carter's own actions with respect to the alleged Exodus papyri make it very probable that there is more behind the cause of Lord Carnarvon's death than has previously been recognised by historians working in this field. Because of this, we cannot remove Lord Carnarvon's name from some involvement in the misuse of the missing papyri found in Tutankhamun's tomb until we have all the answers. Neither can we deny the fact that, if George Edward Stanhope Molyneux Herbert, the fifth Earl of Carnarvon, did succumb to a form of rare-metal poisoning, then it can never be totally ruled out that his death was not the result of foul play by persons unknown with a vested interest in keeping the contents of the papyri secret.

APPENDIX I
THE DEATH OF TUTANKHAMUN

In his international bestseller *The Murder of Tutankhamun*, first published in 1998, the paleopathologist Bob Brier accuses Aye, Tutankhamun's vizier and administrator, of assassinating the boy-king. This conclusion was reached after he examined forensic evidence derived from the pathological studies of Tutankhamun's remains conducted by Professor Ronald G Harrison of the University of Liverpool.

After scholarly requests to examine the mummified body, Harrison was finally granted permission by the Egyptian authorities to X-ray the boy-king in 1968. Since its earlier examination by Dr Douglas E Derry, professor of anatomy at the Egyptian University, Cairo, in 1925,[1] the skeleton had rested in one of the gilded coffins reinterred inside the great quartzite sarcophagus left *in situ* within the tomb.

Working alongside a specialised team which included experienced radiologists, physicians, dentists and Egyptologists, Harrison was allowed to expose the pathetic remains of the king for just two days only. What they found shocked them, for there was considerable damage to the skeleton never officially recorded by Carter and Derry. Harrison even found that the body had been sawn in half in order to free it from the innermost coffin. Yet this realisation simply enabled Harrison to carry the head, and other body parts, over to the machine and photograph them individually. The team were allowed to carry out their work only in daylight hours, and the X-rays taken were carefully transported back to Luxor, where they were developed in one of the rooms of the Winter Palace Hotel, rented for this purpose.

When published for the first time, the X-rays taken of the skull caused a sensation, for they showed that a small fragment of bone was lodged within its interior, fuelling the theory that Tutankhamun might have died from a blow to the head, received either accidentally or as a result of foul play. Harrison attempted to play down the significance of the tiny bone by pointing out that it had probably become dislodged from the base of the nose during the postmortem embalming process. Yet Bob Brier doubted this solution, pointing out that a nasal bone of the sort indicated by Harrison was porous and splintered when broken, while the one inside Tutankhamun's skull was more substantial in size. Brier went on to conclude that it had broken away from the inside of the skull during Carter and Derry's quite violent stripping of the mummy back in 1925.[2] This was important, for a number of Egyptologists had continually cited the mistaken way in which some speculative writers wrongly used the presence of the small bone as evidence of Tutankhamun's cause of death. Yet, as Brier pointed out, the bone fragment was a 'red herring', diverting the eyes away from the real evidence that the boy-king had suffered severe internal injuries after a major blow to the head.[3]

WAS IT MURDER?

Bob Brier's initial clue that foul play might have been involved in the death of the pharaoh came as he watched a BBC documentary in which Professor Harrison was asked to comment on his findings concerning the X-rayed skull of Tutankhamun. During the interview, he pointed out the presence at the base of the head, close to the neck, of an inexplicable 'density', or dark area, before adding that in his opinion,

This is within the normal limits [of skull growth], but in fact, it could have been caused by a hemorrhage under the membranes overlaying the brain in this region. And this could have been caused by a blow to the back of the head and this in turn could have been responsible for death.[4]

What exactly was this dark area, or 'density', at the bottom of the skull, and how might it have been the result of 'a blow to the back of the head'? Among those consulted by Brier in an attempt to find some answers was Dr Gerald Irwin, medical director of the Radiologic Technology Program at the CW Post Campus of Long Island University, and an expert on the X-rays of head-trauma patients. Having been shown the Harrison video, Dr Irwin examined an X-ray photograph of Tutankhamun's skull sent to Brier by one of Harrison's former colleagues at Liverpool University, who has since died. In conclusion, Irwin agreed that the dark area (as well as a thinning of the skull at this point) could easily have been the result of a blow to the back of the head.[5] Furthermore, he speculated that this type of trauma, or effect, was, as Harrison had hinted, strong evidence of a haematoma, the accumulation of blood beneath the skin. The density could thus be explained in terms of a calcified membrane that had grown over a blood clot, something physicians refer to as chronic subdural haematoma, a swelling caused by blood.

Irwin commented also on the strange position of the trauma that was at the base of the head, where the neck joins the skull.[6] If Tutankhamun had been struck purposefully then it must have occurred when he was either lying on his stomach or on his side.[7] Brier concluded that, although the evidence presented by the X-ray was not proof of foul play, it added up to what the police might argue was an 'indication of suspicious circumstances'.[8]

So is this what happened to Tutankhamun? Was he perhaps bludgeoned while asleep in bed, leaving him to die a slow painful death as he lay in a delirious state waiting for the end to come? Certainly, this is what Bob Brier believes, and he could well be right, for the evidence suggesting that the boy-king did indeed die from a blow to the head is very powerful indeed. But was it foul play? Was somebody *responsible* for his death?

The true answer is that nobody knows. The only evidence we have for the involvement of foul play in the boy-king's death derives from personal interpretations of the Harrison X-ray made in 1968 and what little we know about the life of Tutankhamun. It is just as likely that he sustained his wound through accidental means. For example, falling backwards awkwardly can result very easily in blows to the base of the skull. Thus he could easily have been thrown backwards out of his chariot and knocked his head on a rock, or some other similar such protrusion. There is no reason to assume murder took place just because of the peculiar positioning of the trauma. Then there is the problem of why the would-be assassin did not complete the job. If he, or she, had bludgeoned the king while he was asleep, why not finish him off there and then, either with repeated blows or by strangling him while he lay unconscious? Surely, the person, or persons, responsible would not have assumed that the king was dead simply by giving him one single blow to the head. Logically, this makes no sense whatsoever.

Even if murder is the answer, Bob Brier's choice of Aye as the murderer seems totally illogical. According to him, the only other candidate was Horemheb, the king's Deputy and Regent, who took charge of military and political affairs from Memphis, Egypt's administrative centre; and, if he had done the dirty deed, then nothing would have prevented him from seizing the throne of Egypt. Thus by default the only other possible candidate was Aye who, as we know, succeeded Tutankhamun as king of Egypt. In the opinion of the authors, this theory is baffling in the extreme, for the evidence weighs heavily against it.

Following Tutankhamun's sudden and presumably unexpected death, it was Aye, the old family retainer, who was left to make the arrangements for the funeral. This we know is correct because Aye is depicted on the wall of the tomb wearing the leopard skin of the *sem*-priest. He stands before the mummified body of Tutankhamun in his guise as Osiris, god of the underworld, holding an adze and carrying out the Opening of the Mouth ceremony. In this capacity Aye takes the role of Horus, the 'son' of Osiris, reviving his spiritual 'father', an act conducted *only* by the heir apparent. This mural demonstrates also that Aye was decreed honorary heir to the throne of Egypt, and thus was responsible for conducting the various rites of passage that would enable the boy-king to enter the next world.

WORSHIP OF THE ATEN

Then we come to the presence in the tomb of various personal items that either depict the Aten sun-disc in all its glory or bear inscriptions that include the name of the Aten, some nine years after Tutankhamun is supposed to have abandoned all interest in Akhenaten's hated religion. By far the best example is the famous gilded throne chair found in the Antechamber. On the inside of the backrest we see the king seated, with his young queen standing before him, equal in height. In her left hand she holds an offering cup of balm, or oil, and with the other she is seen touching his shoulder in a most tender fashion. Both king and queen are portrayed in typical Amarna style, but more significantly we see the Aten sun-disc, with its rays ending in hands that offer life in the form of *ankhs*, directly above the young couple. Moreover, the name of the king appears both in its later form of Tutankhamun *and* its Amarna form of Tutankhaten.

Since this beautiful work of art was deemed suitable to accompany the pharaoh on his journey into the next world, it seems clear that Tutankhamun, as well as his wife Ankhesenamun, must have remained sympathetic towards the outlawed religion, even at the very end of his reign. Moreover, since we know that Aye was almost certainly responsible for making the king's funeral arrangements, he would have been aware that various items of Amarna art were being placed in the tomb, demonstrating that he too retained at least some sympathies towards the Aten. This realisation implies very strongly that Ankhesenamun and Aye were working in concert, and were not opposed to each other's religious or political ideals.

Having established these facts, we come now to a matter crucial to this debate, the correspondence between Ankhesenamun and Suppiluliumas, the king of the Hittites, following the death of Tutankhamun.[9] In the knowledge that there was no heir to the throne, she feared a military coup, an uprising, from those who sought to take away her power and influence. It forced her into a decision unprecedented in Egyptian history. In order to try to find a suitable partner, who would rule the kingdom with an iron fist comparable with that of the greatest of pharaohs, she sent a letter to Suppiluliumas beseeching him to send her a son so that he might become her husband. At first he was suspicious of the request, but eventually he relented and dispatched a young prince named Zannanza, who was mysteriously murdered en route from the land of Hatti, i.e. Turkey, to Egypt.[10]

In her original message to Suppiluliumas, she tells him, 'Never shall I pick out a servant of mine and make him my husband!'[11] Whom exactly might she have been referring to when she made this powerful statement? Aye had been an important member of the royal court at Amarna during Akhenaten's reign. He took the title Master of the Horse, which in effect meant that he was a military adviser and vizier to the king. Yet in inscriptions he also styled himself 'Father of the God', a title he kept from the reign of Akhenaten through to his own brief four-year reign. By 'God' he meant god-king, or pharaoh, implying that he was a relative, or in-law, of Akhenaten. The same title, 'Father of the God', was used by Yuya, the *father* of Tiye, the Great Royal Wife of Amenhotep III, Akhenaten's father.[12] Thus Aye was most probably related to the heretic king, and it has been proposed that he was probably the father of Nefertiti.[13] Since Aye was regarded therefore as a member of the royal household, Ankhesenamun can hardly have been referring to him as a 'servant of mine', in other words a commoner.

So to whom had she been referring in the plea to the Hittite king?

Ankhesenamun's statement refers most likely to Horemheb, who was devoid of any royal blood, or royal connections. He is the only other suspect in the hunt to find the hypothetical killer of Tutankhamun. As a military genius he had quite obviously set his sights on becoming king at a very early stage in the Amarna heresy, and quite probably he worked in concert with the disbanded Amun priesthood, as well as other army officials, to achieve his aims. If this is correct, then the sheer fact that Horemheb did not ascend to the throne after the death of Tutankhamun makes it even more unlikely that the boy-king was assassinated. For, if Horemheb was responsible for his murder, then Aye would never have become king; it is as simple as that.

With these thoughts as a backdrop to the death of Tutankhamun, we can now better understand why Ankhesenamun dispatched a message to the Hittite king asking him for a husband. Quite obviously, she had been faced with the prospect that, since the couple had produced no heir, there was no one to succeed her husband to the throne. She therefore feared that Horemheb was plotting to seize the throne by initiating a military coup and forcing her to marry him in order to legitimise his reign. In fear, she pleaded with the Hittite king to send her a son, only to find that the young prince was assassinated on his way to Egypt. With time running out for the frightened queen, she honoured Aye with the title of king of Egypt in order to block Horemheb's intentions.

A HUNTING ACCIDENT?

So how exactly did Tutankhamun die? Since it is noted that the boy-king was a keen hunter,[14] there is every possibility that, while on a hunting expedition, he fell awkwardly from his chariot and sustained a blow to the head that eventually proved fatal. Remember, he was only around eighteen years of age when he died, and may not have been as experienced in this pursuit as he might have thought. We must also not confine the accident to a hunting expedition, for it could have occurred at any time that he was in motion on a chariot.

When his skull was examined originally by Carter and Derry in 1925 it was found to have been shaved, an uncommon practice for a dead king. Can we imagine, therefore, the physicians of the royal court removing the king's hair in order to determine the nature of the swelling that would have occurred in the weeks that followed the initial blow to the head? Thus having found no external evidence of a wound, they could have done little to alleviate the swelling, leaving the king to suffer ever-worsening headaches and blackouts as the haematoma gained ground. Finally, he would have fallen into a coma before losing his fight for life. Since calcification occurred around the swelling, it points towards the fact that Tutankhamun must have lived for a minimum of two months after the blow, and conceivably up to several months before death eventually overcame him.[15]

PHARAOH'S FALL

Where does this vivid picture of the dramatic events that would seem to have occurred at the end of Tutankhamun's reign leave us with respect to the relationship between the

Amarna period and the biblical Exodus, which seems so obviously linked with the Amarna aftermath?

The answer is this: as early as 1923, even before Carter and Derry's examination of the mummified remains of Tutankhamun, the British Egyptologist Arthur Weigall, in his book *Tutankhamen And Other Essays*, highlighted a curious story in the Talmud, the literary corpus containing the folklore of the Jews. It echoes the violent manner in which Tutankhamun seems to have died, and yet concerns the fate of the pharaoh said to have ruled Egypt at the time when Moses left Goshen for the land of Midian, having slain an Egyptian official whom he found maltreating an Israelite. According to the legend, at this time Pharaoh was struck down with leprosy (an allusion, perhaps, to the fact that he was infected by the much shunned Aten heresy). Moreover:

> While he was in this agony [with leprosy], the report was brought to him that the children of Israel in Goshen were careless and idle in their forced labor. The news aggravated his suffering, and he said: 'Now that I am ill, they turn and scoff at me. Harness my chariot, and I will betake myself to Goshen, and see the derision wherewith the children of Israel deride me.' And they took and put him upon a horse, for he was not able to mount it himself. When he and his men had come to the border between Egypt and Goshen, the king's steed passed into a narrow place. The other horses, running rapidly through the pass, pressed upon each other until the king's horse fell while he sate upon it, and when it fell, the chariot turned over on his face, and also the horse lay upon him. The king's flesh was torn from him … [and his] servants carried him upon their shoulders, brought him back to Egypt, and placed him on his bed.
>
> He knew that his end was come to die, and the queen Alfar'anit and his nobles gathered about his bed, and they wept a great weeping with him.[16]

Could it be possible that preserved among the folklore of the Jews is a dim recollection of the fall that led to the death of Tutankhamun? Although there are elements in the Talmud legend that do not make sense of what we know about the boy-king, a connection with the reign of Tutankhamun cannot be ruled out. Weigall himself was of the opinion that the pharaoh in question was none other than Akhenaten,[17] owing to the clear relationship between the Amarna regime and Manetho's Osarsiph-Moses story and the fact that the Talmud asserts that the king produced so many offspring ('He had three sons and two daughters by the queen Alfar'anit, besides children from concubines'[18]). However, Weigall would surely have switched his focus of attention to Tutankhamun if he had lived to see the X-ray of the boy-king's skull produced in 1968 by Professor Harrison. Such evidence weighs heavily against Bob Brier's belief that Tutankhamun was murdered in his sleep by the orders of Aye, a theory that holds no weight whatsoever.

APPENDIX II
PORK ABSTINENCE AND THE WORSHIP OF SET

In recent years, anthropologists and archaeo-zoologists have accumulated a wealth of new material regarding the nature and spread of animal husbandry in the Near East during the Bronze Age and Iron Age. This alone has led to fresh ideas regarding the ethnicity of proto-Israelite sites in the Palestinian central highlands, based on the absence among the faunal assemblages of pig bones. For instance, sites from the early highland settlements in the Late Bronze Age, c. 1550–1200 BC, do contain the remains of pigs, reared and probably eaten as part of a staple diet, but those that thrived during the Iron Age, c. 1200–585 BC, contain almost none at all. As Brian Hesse of the Department of Anthropology at the University of Alabama at Birmingham admits in this respect, 'Iron Age sites in Palestine present a picture of mostly pigless deposits ... Expanding the search for pig remains to later phases of the Iron Age as well as samples not well defined chronologically within the Iron Age just produces more negative results'.[1]

Since pork abstinence forms such a major role in the religious customs of Jews and Muslims today, minimalist scholars such as Israel Finkelstein and Neil Asher Silberman have proposed that the absence of pig bones among Iron Age communities in the central highlands defines their inhabitants as proto-Israelites, emerging for the first time with their own individual ethnicity.[2] They point out that 'pigs were not cooked or eaten, or even raised' at these sites.[3] Moreover, at the same time Iron Age sites in surrounding regions, which were the territories of Israel's traditional enemies, pig bones are found in abundance.[4] Such statistics have led Finkelstein and Silberman to conclude:

> Perhaps the proto-Israelites stopped eating pork merely because the surrounding peoples – their adversaries – did eat it, and they had begun to see themselves as different. Distinctive culinary practices and dietary customs are two of the ways in which ethnic boundaries are formed. Monotheism and the traditions of Exodus and covenant apparently came much later. Half a millennium before the composition of the biblical text, with its detailed laws and dietary regulations, the Israelites chose – for reasons that are not entirely clear – not to eat pork. When modern Jews do the same, they are continuing the oldest archaeologically attested cultural practice of the people of Israel.[5]

Does this new understanding of pigless Iron Age sites in the central highlands really indicate the presence here of early Israelite communities developing their own unique form of ethnicity? Religious rules forbidding the eating of pork are to be found in the Pentateuch.[6] Within the regulations for governing the relationship between Israel and Yahweh in the book of Leviticus, Chapter 11, it states, 'And the swine, because he parteth the hoof, and is clovenfooted, but cheweth not the cud, he is unclean unto you. Of their flesh ye shall not eat, and their carcases ye shall not touch; they are unclean unto you.'[7] The same basic rule is repeated in Deuteronomy, Chapter 14.[8]

Although these regulations probably date only to the seventh century BC, when sweeping religious reforms were made in order to standardise the worship of Yahweh, they must reflect an older tradition of pork abstinence that reaches back to a time when the first Israelites settled in the central highlands. Indeed, according to biblical archaeologist Roland de Vaux,

The most likely answer is that the prohibition is pre-Israelite in origin and that it was preserved in Israel after its religious origins were forgotten. After all, Jews and Muslims of today abstain from eating pork without knowing why, except that it is forbidden by the Torah and by the Koran. And it is quite possible that this revulsion for the pig, which became second nature to the Israelites, was reinforced by the ritual usage which they saw made of it in certain pagan rites.[9]

Scholars are generally of the opinion that the origins of pork abstinence among the early Israelites were derived from reasons of health, placement, distribution, religion and politics.[10] Yet in the main, proto-Jewish pig taboos emerged because of reasons of hygiene. Pigs were considered unclean, uncouth animals, used on rubbish dumps to dispose of waste materials, and were often riddled with tapeworms. Thus there was always the naïve belief that diseases, such as leprosy, could be transmitted, simply by making contact with pigs or by drinking their milk. It was these health considerations that were the primary motivation behind the Israelite elders forbidding the consumption of pork, and in so doing they set themselves apart from neighbouring tribes, such as the Philistines, Moabites and Ammonites, who were less worldly-wise.[11]

Although these considerations make perfect sense, and unquestionably played a role in the development of religious rules concerning the prohibition of pork among the Israelite tribes, it is possible that this tradition reflects ideas that stem originally not from Palestine but from ancient Egypt. Moreover, the absence of pig bones from assumed proto-Israelite sites in the central highlands is more likely to provide evidence of a strange fusion of the ancient Egyptians' fear and loathing of the pig, and the animal's association with the trickster god Set.

THE UNCLEAN ANIMAL

Herodotus, the Greek historian and traveller of the fifth century BC, spent some considerable time in Egypt recording its customs and traditions. He noted that Egyptians considered the pig 'an unclean animal, so much so that if a man in passing accidentally touch a pig, he instantly hurries to the river, and plunges in with all his clothes on'.[12] He further states:

> ... the swineherds, notwithstanding that they are of pure Egyptian blood, are forbidden to enter into any of the temples, which are open to all other Egyptians; and further, no one will give his daughter in marriage to a swineherd, or take a wife from among them, so that the swineherds are forced to intermarry among themselves. They do not offer swine in sacrifice to any of their gods, excepting Bacchus [Osiris] and the Moon, whom they honour in this way at the same time, sacrificing pigs to both of them at the same full moon, and afterwards eating of their flesh.[13]

Herodotus also says with respect to a pig sacrificed at the full moon that 'the tip of the tail, the spleen, and the caul [a membrane enveloping the intestines] are put together, and having been covered with all the fat that has been found in the animal's belly, are straightway burnt'.[14] What remains of the victim is eaten the same day, and 'at any other time they would not so much as taste it. The poorer sort, who cannot afford live pigs, form pigs of dough, which they bake and offer in sacrifice'.[15] In the case of rites to Osiris, whom the Hellenic Greeks identified with Bacchus, the animal was sacrificed at the door of his temple, before being carried away by the swineherd from 'whom it was furnished'.[16] In the first century AD the Roman biographer and moralist Plutarch also recounts how in Egypt, although the pig was seen as an impure animal, it was offered up once a year as a sacrifice to the moon goddess Selene.[17]

In addition to these observations on pig taboos and sacrifice in ancient Egypt, the second-century Roman naturalist and historian Aelian had much to say about the pig in this country. According to him, the beast 'in sheer gluttony does not spare even its own young', and if it 'comes across a man's body it does not refrain from eating it'.[18] For these reasons, the Egyptians detested 'the animal as polluted and omnivorous'.[19] He cites Manetho also as having said 'that one who has tasted of sow's milk becomes covered with leprosy and scaly eruptions'.[20] As a consequence, Aelian observed:

> ... the Egyptians are convinced that the Sow is an abomination to the sun and the moon. Accordingly when they hold the festival of the moon they sacrifice Pigs to her once a year, but at no other seasons are they willing to sacrifice them either to her or to any other god ...[21]

Finally, Aelian tells us that, according to the Greek astronomer and physician Eudoxus of Cnidus (d. 355 BC), Egyptians refrained from sacrificing pigs because, once the corn was sown, herds of them trod and pressed the seeds in order that they remained fertile and were not consumed by birds.[22]

THE BLACK PIG

Such were the customs associated with the pig in ancient Egypt: on the one hand it was reviled as an unclean animal, and on the other it was treated as sacred and offered up in sacrifice once a year at the time of the full moon. Although its revulsion may stem from considerations of hygiene and cleanliness, the pig's place in Egyptian society was connected directly with rites and rituals surrounding Set (or Seth, the Greek Typhon), the god of chaos and disorder, who was the ruler of the burning desert wastes.

One story that confirms Set's form as a pig is the myth concerning the coming into being of that powerful Egyptian symbol the Eye of Horus. In the 112th chapter of the Book of the Dead it speaks of how one day the sun god Re said to Horus, 'Let me see what is coming to pass in thine eye.' On looking, Re tells Horus, 'Look at that black pig', at which the falcon god sustained immediately an injury to his eye. The text goes on to relate how the injurer was none other than Set, who had transformed himself into a black pig.[23] As a consequence of his actions, the god Re ordered that henceforth the pig was to be cast out as an abominable creature.

More importantly, Set appears as a pig also in the myth of Osiris, the god of the underworld, which expresses the eternal process of death and resurrection. After Osiris has been slain by his evil brother Set, Osiris' widow Isis flees to the Nile Delta in order to ensure the safety of their son Horus. Here she takes on the form of a kite, and 'keeps watch for the rampaging monster Set, the wild pig' as her son Horus, the falcon, remains concealed in the nest.[24] Another tale, and one that seems to reflect an earlier tradition in which Osiris was slain by Set in the form a pig, or wild boar,[25] tells of how 'Typhon was hunting a boar when he discovered the mangled and slain body of Osiris, and that for this reason pigs were sacrificed once a year'.[26]

The sacrifice was thus an act of vengeance, inflicted on the slayer of Osiris, who took the form of a black pig, or boar. In his classic work The Golden Bough, first published in 1922, the British anthropologist Sir James George Frazer (1854–1941) argued that originally the pig sacrificed in the name of Osiris was the god himself, in his guise as the spirit of the corn.[27] The clear connection between pigs and corn is expressed in Eudoxus' account of how, after the fields were sown each year, swine were sent out to trample down the seeds in order that the birds did not eat them. Only during much later times, so Frazer believed, was the animal seen as a subject of abhorrence and repulsion, fit only to represent the trickster god of chaos and disorder.

THE WORSHIP OF SET

Even though Set's form as a pig, or boar, is not in dispute, in ancient Egyptian art and literature he was portrayed more commonly as a mythical beast referred to as the *set*-animal, or *fenekh*, a hybrid form of the desert fox, and also as a hippopotamus. In addition to this, he was depicted with a human body and the head of the *set*-animal, carrying a spear in one hand. Through the association with his son Sobek, a crocodile-headed god, Set was venerated also in the form of a crocodile, particularly at the Temple of Kom Ombos in southern Egypt. Often he was shown in the company of Horus, his eventual slayer, standing over him (very possibly the origin of Christian iconography in which St Michael is shown spearing Satan in the form of a dragon). Through the predominance of the cult of Sobek in the Eastern Delta, Set of Ombos was also venerated with great passion here. For instance, at temples in the area of Tell ed-Dab'a, ancient Avaris and Pi-Ramesse (Raamses of the Bible), the god was worshipped by successive kings of the Thirteenth Dynasty, c. 1786–1700 BC, some of whom bore names honouring Sobek.

The Thirteenth Dynasty ran concurrently with the Fourteenth, and constituted the first half of the Second Intermediate Period of Egyptian history, c. 1786–1575 BC. These two dynasties were brought to a close when the Hyksos warlords overran Egypt around 1730–1650 BC and established their capital city at Tell ed-Dab'a. Since this was the cult centre of Sobek, and his father Set, the god of borderlands or frontiers and 'divine stranger',[28] he became synonymous with the attributes of the Hyksos' own god Baal.[29] Henceforth, this new, composite, deity was venerated under the name of Sutekh (a Babylonian rendering of Set), and even after the departure of the Hyksos from Egypt his cult thrived in the Eastern Delta.

Although the worship of Set had to go underground during Akhenaten's Amarna regime, it was revived in the reign of Horemheb, particularly within the Eastern Delta. For instance, he commissioned the construction of an enormous temple of Set at Tell ed-Dab'a, directly over a much earlier cult site. Here the Egyptian female ruler Sobek-nofru, or Sobekkare, c. 1789–1786 BC, had been venerated as a deity during the Thirteenth Dynasty, just prior to the arrival of the Hyksos.[30] Indeed, it would seem that Horemheb's temple was built on the same axis as an Asiatic temple built also on the same site, showing a continuity through from the Thirteenth to late Eighteenth Dynasty, a period of over 400 years.

Another place in the Eastern Delta that became a centre for the worship of Set was the border town of Sile. Rameses I, who reigned for just over a year following the death of Horemheb, c. 1308 BC, had been the mayor here during the reign of his predecessor. Like his father Sethos, who governed the town during the time of Amenhotep III, Rameses is known to have been a devotee of Set. The tradition was continued by Rameses' son Seti I, and afterwards by Seti's own son Rameses II, who some time after Year 34 of his reign set up a commemorative stone known as the '400 years stela', which was found at Tanis. It shows the king paying homage to Set in his Semitic form as Baal, or Sutekh, complete with a human body and conical-shaped crown.[31] The god's distinctive facial features depict him as an Asiatic, and thus he appears in his guise as ruler of foreign territories.[32]

The '400 years stela' proclaims the veneration of Set by the king's immediate ancestors, including his great-grandfather Sethos, who also features in Manetho's story of Osarsiph-Moses. It also marks the 400th year of Set's reign in the Eastern Delta, which the Austrian Egyptologist Manfred Bietak believes began at ancient Avaris, modern-day Tell ed-Dab'a, during the age of a Thirteenth Dynasty king named Nehesy, who ruled c. 1720–1705 BC.[33] However, as previously mentioned, the kings of this dynasty venerated the female ruler Sobek-nofru, a devotee of Sobek, at the very spot in Tell ed-Dab'a where a major Hyksos temple had almost certainly been dedicated to Sutekh (see below). This was likewise replaced during the reign of Horemheb by a huge stone temple also dedicated to Set. Thus there seems to be every reason to conclude that it was in fact she who introduced the worship of Sobek and Set into the Eastern Delta, and not any king of the Thirteenth Dynasty.

LINE OF TRANSMISSION

Since the Hyksos embraced the worship of Set most fully when at Avaris, it seems likely that they would have made sacrifices to the god. Indeed, this is attested in one account dating back to the Ramesside period and relating to the Hyksos king Apophis, c. 1608–1575 BC. He is said to have made Set his personal god, and to have served no other in the land except him. A fine temple was built for the god, situated next door to the 'House of Apophis' and here the king 'appeared [every] day to make daily sacrifice to Seth'.[34] There is, however, no indication that any of these sacrifices were of pigs. Indeed, at the site of Tell ed-Dab'a's main Hyksos temple, which has been compared in style to one found at Hazor in the northern highlands of Palestine, evidence has come to light which indicates that pigs were never sacrificed there.

Within the building's hollow mud-brick altar, known as a *bamah* (c. 3 × 2 metres in size), as well as in nearby refuge pits, a mass of ashes and charred bones have been found, the product of countless sacrificial burnt offerings over a period of many years. Many of the bones belonged to cattle or, to a lesser degree, sheep, but no pig bones were found at all among the charred remains, even though there is ample evidence that the pig was used as a food offering in Hyksos tombs.[35] As Bietak has commented with respect to these findings, 'It looks as if, for offerings to the gods, pigs were already considered as taboo.'[36] Thus it is possible that the Hyksos adopted these religious practices from the native Egyptians. Yet before this statement might be justified it must be pointed out that the pig is thought to have been venerated in Palestine as early as Palaeolithic times, pre-8,000 BC,[37] through to the Early Bronze Age, c. 3500–2200 BC, and Middle Bronze Age, c. 2000–1550 BC.[38] Indeed, the pig, or wild boar, which seems to have become associated both with the high god Baal[39] *and* chthonic,[40] or underworld, deities, would seem to have been 'the sacrificial animal par excellence' in later ages.[41] More significantly, it is known that there was widespread abstinence of pig meat among the Phoenicians of Syria and the Lebanon, the inhabitants of Cyprus (which included a major Phoenician colony), the pre-Islamic Arabs and many other Semitic-speaking peoples of the ancient world.[42]

Despite this knowledge, there is no evidence of pork abstinence among the Late Bronze Age sites excavated anywhere in Palestine, implying a different line of transmission for the earliest Iron Age I communities of the central highlands. It is the authors' belief that this tradition originated in Egypt's Eastern Delta at the time of the Hyksos, had been adopted by later Asiatic settlers in the post-Hyksos period and was carried out of Egypt into the central highlands of Palestine in the wake of the collapse of the Amarna period. This, of course, was the time frame of the Exodus as suggested by various ancient writers such as Manetho and Apion. Although the earliest Iron Age I settlements date back no earlier than 1200–1100 BC, a period of perhaps a hundred years should be allowed for the migration and settlement of these peoples.

If pork abstinence among the proto-Israelite communities really did stem from Egypt, then it could be argued that it came about through the presence in Palestine of a strong Egyptian military presence, particularly during the reigns of Merneptah and his father Rameses II in the thirteenth century BC. However, outside of strategic garrison sites such as Jerusalem (see Chapter 18), Egyptian fortifications were to be found only along the coastal trade route between Egypt and Syria. This makes no sense whatsoever of the pigless Iron Age sites reported extensively in the central highlands, and not in the coastal lowlands where you might expect them to be found if an Egyptian presence was responsible for the introduction of pork abstinence.

The only contradiction to the pattern is Tell Jemmeh, a site on the south coast of Palestine where only 0.3 per cent of the bone assemblage unearthed from its Late Bronze Age refuge pits represents the pig. This has led Hesse to suppose that the evidence 'may reflect the establishment of dietary behaviour and perhaps food rules based on Egyptian social stratification'.[43] In other words, the settlement of Egyptians in the area gave rise to an aversion of the pig at Tell Jemmeh.

Much more likely is that the biblical and Graeco-Egyptian and Graeco-Roman traditions of the expulsion of Egyptian and Asiatic peoples from the Egypt Nile Delta to Palestine in the wake of the Amarna age provides us with a more obvious line of transmission of pig taboos among the earliest Israelites. If nothing more, the powerful new evidence of pork abstinence among the bone assemblages at Iron Age I sites in the central highlands argues for an Exodus hundreds of years after the expulsion of the Hyksos.

APPENDIX III
EGYPTIAN NAMES AMONG THE LEVITES

After Sigmund Freud made the link between the Amarna age and the life of Moses during the late 1930s, the subject was destined to be ignored by the Egyptological community until the publication in 1990 of a book entitled *Moses: Pharaoh of Egypt*, by the Egyptian-born historian Ahmad Osman. He went further than Freud, and Arthur Weigall before him, by stating boldly that Akhenaten and Moses *were one and the same person*. Osman attempted to make a case for Akhenaten's abandoning the throne of Egypt in Year 17 of his reign. According to him, the heretic king then exiled himself to the Sinai peninsula, where he remained for forty years, before returning to demand the release of the imprisoned followers of the Aten in Year 1 of Rameses I's brief reign, c. 1308–1307 BC. Despite the fact that there is no clear indication that Akhenaten might have survived after Year 17, Osman's book brought the idea of a relationship between the collapse of the Amarna regime and the historical origins of Moses and the Exodus into the modern era.

Osman has also demonstrated that some of the most important Israelites who left Egypt at the time of the Exodus bore Egyptian names. For example, Moses has always been thought to derive his name from the Hebrew *Mōše(h)*, 'to draw', or 'drawn', as in 'I drew him out of the water'.[1] More likely, however, is that it comes from the Egyptian *moše*, meaning '(is) born', or more simply 'son', as in Thut*mose*, 'son of the god Thoth', or Ra*meses*, 'son of the sun-god Re'.[2]

In addition to this, Merari, the youngest son of Levi,[3] who became the eponymous ancestor of the Merarites,[4] one of the three branches of the Levite priesthood,[5] is traditionally thought to derive his name from the Hebrew/Canaanite word meaning 'bitter'.[6] However, it is more likely that it comes from the Egyptian *mrry/mrri*, meaning 'to love', or 'beloved'.[7] Curiously enough, there was a Mery-re II, a high priest of the Aten, who lived during the reign of Akhenaten and whose empty rock-cut tomb is situated in the cliffs beyond the site of Akhenaten's city at Tell el-Amarna in Middle Egypt.[8]

Then there is Phinehas, the son of Eleazar, the high priest and chief of the Levites,[9] who was the grandson of Aaron.[10] He played an active role during Israel's forty years of wandering in the wilderness, and went on to become the ancestor of the Zadok priesthood.[11] The Hebrew meaning of his name is 'mouth of brass',[12] but it quite clearly derives from the Egyptian *p3-nhsy*, meaning 'the Nubian', denoting a person with dark skin or a true Nubian.[13] Strangely enough, there was also a Pinehesy, a Chief Servitor of the Aten, who lived during the reign of Akhenaten. Like that of Mery-re II, his empty tomb can be found in the cliffs beyond the site of Akhenaten's city.

Osman has attempted to demonstrate that Merari and Phinehas were indeed the two historical figures of similar-sounding names who served Akhenaten at Amarna, and then took flight with the pharaoh when he departed for Sinai after abandoning the throne.[14] Whereas Osman might well be right in this respect, there is no real evidence to prove this theory one way or another, especially as the names Mery-re and Pinehesy were probably not unique to Akhenaten's reign.

THE LEVITE PRIESTHOOD
Even so, Osman certainly seems to have been on to something, for there appears to be a pattern in the distribution of the Egyptian personal names found among the Israelites. For

instance, the grandmother of Phinehas is given as Putiel,[15] a hybrid name derived from the Hebrew/Canaanite *el*, 'of God', and the Egyptian *p3 dy*, meaning 'the given'.[16] While Assir (Izhir), a son of Korah, the Levite, and grandson of Izhar, the brother of Amram, Moses' father,[17] would seem to have derived his name from *asar*, or Osiris, the Egyptian god of the underworld.[18]

Lastly, there is Hur, a companion of Moses and Aaron, whose name in Hebrew means 'a hole', as of a snake.[19] Yet it is more likely to derive from the Egyptian *hr*, 'Horus',[20] the falcon-headed god whom the pharaoh embodied during his lifetime. The book of Exodus tells us that, in the company of Moses and Aaron, Hur ascended the 'mountain head' at Rephidim, plausibly Horeb[21], although perhaps Mount Hor, on the occasion that the Israelites under Joshua went to battle against the Amalekites when they were encamped in the wilderness of Sin.[22] With Yahweh's rod in his hand, Moses would lift up his arm and the battle would go in Israel's favour, but when it dropped through exhaustion the Amalekites would prevail.[23] As Moses became more weary, and the Amalekites started to gain the upper hand, Aaron and Hur placed a stone beneath him and held up each of his arms until 'the going down of the sun'[24] ('until the sun's entry' in earlier versions[25]). Eventually, Joshua and the Israelite army were victorious. Thereafter, Moses built an altar on the 'mountain head' which was called ' "Yahweh Is My Flag(Pole)", and he said, "For an arm (is?) on Yah[weh]'s *kēs*." '[26]

Quite obviously, an explanation of this final line is in order before we can go any further. Yahweh's flagpole or arm, and Moses' rod would seem to refer to a 'memorial pillar' of some sort,[27] established by an altar on the 'mountain head'. Furthermore, the word *kēs* is thought to mean 'seat', thus implying 'an arm (is) on Yahweh's seat', indicating that the altar is a 'memorial [pillar] on Yahweh's throne', i.e. the mountain.[28] Should the authors be correct in their identification of Horeb or Sinai, the Mountain of Yahweh, as Petra, and this is indeed what is being alluded to in the account, then these expressions might well relate to the twin pillars and altar upon Jebel al-Madhbah (see Chapter 20).

We read about Hur again on the occasion when Moses allowed Aaron, his two eldest sons Nadab and Abihu, and seventy elders to ascend to the first level on the Mountain of Yahweh. Just as Moses and Joshua are about to ascend still further, the lawgiver asks the elders to 'Tarry [i.e. wait] ye here for us, until we come again unto you: and, behold, Aaron and Hur are with you'.[29] Even though Hur is never mentioned again in the Bible, his close connection with both Moses and Aaron on the Mountain of Yahweh strongly suggests that he was both a blood relation and a member of a priestly caste.

If this assumption proves correct, then it would mean that each and every one of the Israelites shown to have Egyptian personal names, i.e. Moses, Merari, Phinehas, Assir and, almost certainly, Putiel and Hur, were Levites, or their immediate family belonged to the tribe of Levi, who was the third son of Jacob. According to the Bible, it was from Levi's three sons – Gershon, Kohath, the grandfather of Moses and Aaron, and Merari, whom we have already encountered – that the three branches of Levites stemmed. Each one took on priestly duties on behalf of the Israelites right down until the time of King Solomon, when they became the jurisdiction of the Zadok priesthood alone.[30]

The book of Numbers records that the role of high priest of the Levites was conferred originally on Aaron and his four sons by Moses, and after the death of his eldest sons, Nadab and Abihu, it was shared jointly by Eleazar and his younger brother Ithamar.[31] Yet later we read how Aaron and Eleazar were requested to accompany Moses on to Mount Hor, where Aaron was stripped of his priestly garments, which were then given to Eleazar as his successor, making him chief among the Levite leaders.[32] According to the account, 'And Eleazar the son of Aaron the priest shall be prince of the princes of the Levites, *and have* the oversight of them that keep the charge of the sanctuary [of Yahweh]'.[33] Eleazar's son Phinehas, who was placed in the service of the Ark of the Covenant, succeeded his father.[34] As we have seen, he was destined also to become the ancestor of the Zadok priesthood.

In the book of Deuteronomy the Levites are charged with carrying the Ark of the Covenant, serving Yahweh and blessing the people.[35] It is also the Levites who proved themselves particularly zealous on the occasion that, when encamped at Mount Sinai, the Israelites began worshipping the golden calf in Moses' absence. It is said that they rounded up some three thousand individuals and put them to death.[36] Levites from later periods also bore Egyptian names. For example, Hophi and Phinehas, the sons of Eli, were the priests of the sanctuary at Shiloh[37] and accompanied the ark on its travels during the war with the Philistines,[38] thus c. 1200–1150 BC. The name Phinehas we know already, but Hophni we find has been thought to derive from the Egyptian *hfn(r)*, meaning a 'tadpole'![39] More likely is that it comes from the root *hfn*, meaning 'to fear' or 'to be humble'.[40]

Such a profusion of Egyptian personal names among the Levites is difficult to explain, especially as none appear among any of the other tribes. Either it indicates that the family began using Egyptian names simply because of their long association with Egypt, or they really were Egyptians, or certainly descendants of Egyptians. If so, then could they have originally been followers of Akhenaten's monotheistic religion as Osman proposed in the cases of Merari and Phinehas? Might they themselves have had Asiatic connections? Certainly, Akhenaten is known to have employed the services of high-ranking Asiatics at his royal court. For example, in 1988 the Belgian archaeologist Alain Zivie found in the Memphite necropolis at Saqqara the intact tomb of a hitherto unknown chief minister of the heretic king named Aper-el (or Abd-el), 'servant of El', a name of clear Asiatic derivation.[41]

If nothing else, this evidence for the presence of Egyptian names among the Levites and their families is a further indication that at the core of the Israelite tribes was a priestly elite. Although its origin remains obscure, the chances are that it was Egyptian in origin, or it contained Asiatics who had become Egyptianised through generations of settlement in Egypt's Eastern Delta. Either way, it helps allay any doubts regarding the historical validity of the Exodus account.

POSTSCRIPT

Tutankhamun: The Exodus Conspiracy is one of the new genre of scholarly works that are now challenging our accepted views of the past. If, through reading this book, it has inspired you to begin you own investigations into the mysteries of Tutankhamun, ancient Egypt and the search for the roots of the Bible, or if it simply makes you question our current understanding of history, then it has achieved its aim.

If you wish to take these matters further, may we suggest you review the recommended book-list and bibliography. Almost all of the titles are available through the library Interloan system. Ask your local librarian for details.

Should you feel that you can add to our understanding of the subjects under discussion in this book, and/or you wish to be kept informed of future publications, conferences, tour expeditions, or simply new developments in the field of ancient history, write to Andrew Collins and Chris Ogilvie-Herald at PO Box 189, Leigh-on-Sea, Essex SS9 1NF. Also why not visit Eden – the Andrew Collins website at www.andrewcollins.net for exclusive articles, new material and further insights into *Tutankhamun: The Exodus Conspiracy* and other related topics.

RECOMMENDED BOOKLIST

Aldred, Cyril, *Akhenaten: King of Egypt,* 1988.

Carter, Howard, and A C Mace, *The Tomb of Tut.ankh.Amen,* vol. I, 1923; Howard Carter, vol. II, 1927; Howard Carter, vol. III, 1933.

Evans, Lorraine, *Kingdom of the Ark,* 2000.

Finkelstein, Israel, and Neil Asher Silberman, *The Bible Unearthed,* 2001.

Frayling, Christopher, *The Face of Tutankhamun,* 1992.

Har-el, Menashe, *The Sinai Journeys: The Route of the Exodus,* 1968.

Hoving, Thomas, *Tutankhamun – The Untold Story,* 1978.

James, T.G.H., *Howard Carter: the Path to Tutankhamun,*1992.

Laughlin, John C H, *Archaeology and the Bible,* 2000.

Nielsen, Dr. Ditlef, *The Site of the Biblical Mount Sinai: A claim for Petra,*1928.

Osman, Ahmed, *Moses Pharaoh of Egypt,*1990.

Phillips, Graham, *The Moses Legacy,* 2002.

Redford, Donald B, *Egypt, Canaan, and Israel in Ancient Times,*1992.

Reeves, Nicholas, *The Complete Tutankhamun,*1995.

Weigall, Arthur, *Tutankhamen And Other Essays,*1923.

For full publications details see the Bibliography.

NOTES

PRELUDE

1 This account of the death of the fifth Earl of Carnarvon and the sixth earl's journey from India to be at his father's bedside is taken from Carnarvon, *No Regrets: The Memoirs of the Earl of Carnarvon*, pp. 118–22.
2 Ibid., p. 119.
3 Ibid., p. 124.

PART ONE: TUTANKHAMUN

CHAPTER 1: THE KING IS DEAD

1 All dates for the reign of Egyptian kings are taken from Sir Alan Gardiner, *Egypt of the Pharaohs*.
2 Brier, *The Murder of Tutankhamen: A 3000-year-old Murder Mystery*, p. 8.
3 Ibid.

CHAPTER 2: MYSTERY IN THE VALLEY

1 For a discussion on the names inscribed originally on the magic bricks see Fairman, 'Once again the so-called coffin of Akhenaten', *JEA* 47 (1960), p. 37.
2 However, for an argument that the coffin was prepared originally for Meritaten, see ibid., pp. 30–2.
3 See Aldred and Sandison, 'The Pharaoh Akhenaten: a problem in Egyptology and pathology', *BHM* 36 (1962), p. 301.
4 See Davis, *The Tomb of Queen Tiyi: The Discovery of the Tomb*, 1910.
5 In 1910 Smith wrote a paper for Theodore M Davis' book *The Tomb of Queen Tiyi* reassessing the age of the remains, originally cited in 1907–8 as 25 to 26 years at death, after he had been repeatedly asked whether the bones could be those of a much older man of, say, 28 to 30 years, i.e. the youngest possible age of Akhenaten at the time of death. Since the skull of the individual, in his opinion, showed signs of hydrocephalus, i.e. water on the brain (a fact later dismissed by Dr Douglas E Derry after his own examination of the remains – see below), he concluded that 'the bones, therefore, cannot be regarded as those of a perfectly normal person', thus allowing him to propose that the process of ossification might have been delayed. He was therefore persuaded to admit that the person could have been 28 to 30 years of age, but this clearly went against his own better judgment for, in his final opinion, 'I still maintain the opinion mentioned above: – that the skeleton is that of a man twenty-five or twenty-six years of age, without excluding the possibility that he may have been several years older'. See Smith, 'Note of the estimate of the age attained by the person whose skeleton was found in the tomb', pp. xxiii–xxiv. See also Smith, *The Royal Mummies*, p. 54, in which he reasserts the age of the person as 25 or 26 years, but now adds, 'no anatomist would be justified in refusing to admit that this individual may have been several years younger or older than the above estimate, which after all is based upon averages'.
6 Harrison, 'An Anatomical Examination of Pharaonic Remains Purported to be Akhenaten', *JEA* 52 (1966), pp 95–119.
7 Ibid., p. 111.
8 Ibid.
9 Derry, 'Note on the skeleton hitherto believed to be that of King Akhenaten, *ASAE* 31 (1931), pp. 115–19. See also Engelbach, 'Material for a revision of the history of the heresy period of the XVIIIth Dynasty', *ASAE* 40 (1940), p. 151.
10 Filer, 'The KV 55 body: the facts', *EA* 17 (Autumn 2000), pp. 13–14.
11 See Note 17 for a fuller account of the controversy over the age of the body found in KV 55.
12 Derry, pp. 116–17.
13 Filer, p. 14: 'A comparison was made between the X-rays of the KV 55 skull and those of the

skull of Tutankhamun. They are strikingly similar in size and shape, hinting at some familial relationship'.

14 Harrison, pp. 113–14.
15 Welsh, *Tutankhamun's Egypt*, p. 54.
16 Engelbach, 'The so-called coffin of Akhenaten', *ASAE* 31 (1931), pp. 98–114; Engelbach, 1940, p. 152.
17 For the theory that Smenkhkare was Nefertiti see, for instance, Samson, *Nefertiti and Cleopatra: Queen-Monarchs of Ancient Egypt*, pp. 86–9, 95–7, and Reeves, *Akhenaten: Egypt's False Prophet*, 2001, pp. 170–3, after the work of John R Harris in 1973. For strong arguments against this conclusion, see Allen, 'Nefertiti and Smenkh-ka-re', *GM* 141 (1994), pp. 7–17. There are so many reasons why Smenkhkare cannot possibly have been Nefertiti. First, the main confusion comes from the assumption that the co-regent using the names Nefernefruaten and Ankhkheperure was one and the same person. However, it makes better sense to conclude that, as Allen suggests, there were in fact two co-regents – one Nefertiti and the other Smenkhkare, the latter having been given the same throne name by Akhenaten, seemingly after the former's departure from the scene. Secondly, there are various depictions of Smenkhkare, some of them in the company of Akhenaten. For a round-up of these see Engelbach, 1931, p. 105. Thirdly, Smenkhkare married, or at least took as his consort, Meritaten, Akhenaten's eldest daughter. For example, their two names were inscribed in cartouches accompanying an unfinished wall relief of a royal couple originally intended to represent Akhenaten and Nefertiti in the rock tomb of Meryre II at el-Amarna. See Davies, *The Rock Tombs of El Amarna: Part II – The tombs of Panehesy and Meryra II*, pp. 43–4, pl. xli. If Smenkhkare was really Nefertiti, then why should a woman go through the motions of taking a royal wife? In the opinion of the authors this makes no sense whatsoever.

Then, of course, there is the problem of the identity of the body in KV 55, which according to the anatomical examinations by Smith (1912), Derry (1931) and Harrison (1966), and most recently by Filer (2000), is that of a young man between 20 and 25–6 years of age, making it unlikely to be Akhenaten. Only one royal male fits the picture, and this is Smenkhkare. The high-profile Amarna expert Nicholas Reeves, who argues in his books and on TV documentaries that Smenkhkare is Nefertiti and the body in KV 55 is Akhenaten, refuses to accept the results of these anatomical examinations and instead cites the findings of Fawsia Hussein and John R Harris, who in 1988 decided that the body belonged to a mature man in his mid-thirties, due to sinus ageing. See Reeves, 2001, pp. 83–4. However, Hussein and Harris have been criticised for their procedures, and their findings are rarely quoted or accepted by Egyptologists. Yet to ensure that Akhenaten *was* found in KV 55, the body has to be seen as at least 35 years of age, and if his body *has* been found, and Smenkhkare *is* Nefertiti, then this provides the perfect opportunity for the search for Nefertiti's tomb in the Valley of the Kings. This is the current aim of the Amarna Royal Tombs Project, founded in 1998 by Nicholas Reeves, after permission was given by Egypt's Supreme Council of Antiquities for a British team to begin exploration of the Valley. This is the first time that a digging concession of this kind has been granted since the days of Howard Carter.

18 Harris, 'Akhenaten and Nefernefruaten in the Tomb of Tut'ankhamûn', in Reeves, *After Tut'ankhamûn: Research and excavation in the Royal Necropolis at Thebes*, 1992, pp. 55–62.
19 Eaton-Krauss, 'The Sarcophagus in the Tomb of Tut'ankhamûn', in Reeves, 1992, pp. 85–90.
20 Welsh, *Tutankhamun's Egypt*, p. 8.
21 For a more recent case for the body from KV 55 being that of Smenkhkare see Rose, 'Who's in Tomb 55', *Archaeology* 55:2 (March/April 2002), pp. 22–7; Filer, 'Anatomy of a Mummy', *Archaeology* 55:2, (March/April 2002), pp. 26–9.
22 See, for example, Reeves, 2001, pp. 81–4, 173–4.
23 Fairman, 'Once again the so-called coffin of Akhenaten', *JEA* 47 (1960), pp. 25–40.
24 Harrison, pp. 115–16.
25 Davis, *Excavations: Bibân el Molûk: The Tombs of Harmhabi and Touatânkhamanou*, 1912, p. 2.
26 Ibid., pp. 3, 125.
27 Ibid., p. 127.
28 Ibid., p. 128.
29 Ibid.; Carter and Mace, *The Tomb of Tut.ankh.Amen*, I, pp. 77–8; Welsh, *Tutankhamun's Egypt*, pp. 9–10.
30 Hoving, *Tutankhamun – The Untold Story*, pp. 61–2.
31 Davis, 1912, p.3.

CHAPTER 3: CARTER'S QUEST

1 Mahdy, *Tutankhamun: The Life and Death of a Boy King*, pp. 54–5.
2 Harris, 'How long was the Reign of Horemheb?' *JEA* 54 (1968), p. 97; Aldred and Sandison, 'The Pharaoh Akhenaten: a problem in Egyptology and pathology', *BHM* 36 (1962), pp. 298–9.
3 Vandenberg, *The Forgotten Pharaoh: The Discovery of Tutankhamun*, p. 21.
4 Ibid.
5 Ibid., pp. 24–5.
6 Petrie, *Tell el Amarna*, p. 38.
7 Redford, *Akhenaten: The Heretic King*, p. 141. Another interpretation of the name Akhenaten is 'He who is useful to the Sun-disc', although this makes little sense of its intended spiritual implications. See ibid.
8 Petrie, p. 41.
9 Ibid.
10 Derry, 'Note on the skeleton hitherto believed to be that of King Akhenaten, *ASAE* 31 (1931), p. 116.
11 See, for instance, Aldred and Sandison, pp. 305–15.
12 Burridge, 'Akhenaten: A New Perspective. Evidence of a Genetic Disorder in the Royal Family of 18th Dynasty Egypt', *JSSEA* 23 (1993), p. 65.
13 Ibid.
14 Phillips, *Act of God: Tutankhamun, Moses and the Myth of Atlantis*, p. 68.
15 Burridge, p. 65.
16 Burridge, pp. 63–74; Burridge, 'Did Akhenaten Suffer from Marfan's Syndrome?', *BA* 59:2 (June 1996), pp. 127–8.
17 Filer, 'The KV 55 body: the facts', *EA* 17 (Autumn 2000), p. 14.
18 See Collins, *Gods of Eden*, Ch. 11.
19 See Stecchini, `Notes on the Relation of Ancient Measures to the Great Pyramid', in Tompkins, *Secrets of the Great Pyramid*, pp. 287–382.
20 Molleson & Campbell, 'Deformed Skulls at Tell Arpachiyah: the Social Context', in Campbell & Green (eds), *The Archaeology of Death in the Ancient Near East,* Oxbow Monograph No. 51, 1995, pp. 45–55.
21 Hoving, *Tutankhamun – The Untold Story*, p. 27.
22 The permit or 'Authorization to Excavate' issued to Carnarvon was renewable annually, the details of which can be found in James, *Howard Carter: The Path to Tutankhamun*, Appendix II, pp. 413–15, and Carter, *Tut.Ankh.Amen: The Politics of Discovery*, pp. 3–6. The latter work also gives the dates when the permit was renewed and, following Carnarvon's death, the change from 'excavation' rights to 'clearance' rights issued to his widow, Almina, Countess of Carnarvon.
23 Whether or not Carter had been issued a temporary permit during the interim period between Davis' giving up his own concession and the issuing of an official permit to the fifth earl in 1915, is not known. But, given that World War One had begun just a few months beforehand, this might well have been an oversight by the Department of Antiquities. In any case, Carter's activities in Upper Egypt, official or otherwise, would have been of little importance to the British and Egyptian officials based in Cairo. Their attentions would have been focused most fully on the initial stages of the conflict, and whether or not the Turks now intended to seize control of the Suez Canal, Britain's vital artery between the Mediterranean Sea and the Indian Ocean.

CHAPTER 4: THE SEARCH COMMENCES

1 Reeves, *The Complete Tutankhamun*, p. 44.
2 Burghclere, 'Introduction', in Carter and Mace, *The Tomb of Tut.ankh.Amen*, I, p. 27.
3 A modern translation of the Greek word *hyksos* is given as 'rulers of foreign lands'. See Laughlin, *Archaeology and the Bible*, p. 72.
4 Carnarvon and Carter, *Five Years' Explorations at Thebes: A record of work done 1907–1911.*
5 Winstone, *Howard Carter and the Discovery of the Tomb of Tutankhamun*, p. 114.
6 Carter and Mace, I, p. 80.
7 Ibid., I, p. 81.
8 Ibid.
9 Ibid. I, p. 82.
10 Ibid.
11 Breasted, *Pioneer to the Past: The Story of James Henry Breasted Archaeologist*, p. 328.

12 Carter and Mace, I, p. 82.
13 Ibid., I, p. 83.
14 Ibid., I, p. 85.
15 Breasted, p. 328.
16 Ibid.
17 Carter and Mace, I, p. 85.
18 Hoving, *Tutankhamun – The Untold Story*, p. 73.
19 Ibid.

CHAPTER 5: DEATH OF THE GOLDEN BIRD

1 Carter and Mace, *The Tomb of Tut.ankh.Amen*, I, p. 90.
2 Gardiner, *My Working Years*, p. 37.
3 Carter and Mace, I, p. 87.
4 Breasted, *Pioneer to the Past: The Story of James Henry Breasted Archaeologist*, p. 332.
5 Carter and Mace, I, p. 88.
6 Ibid., I, p. 89.
7 See, for example, James, *Howard Carter: the Path to Tutankhamun*. Background information on Arthur J Callender is severely lacking but both James and Dawson and Uphill's *Who was who in Egyptology* does provide us with some biographical material.
8 Hoving, *Tutankhamun – The Untold Story*, p. 81.
9 A letter from Herbert E Winlock, assistant curator of Egyptology at the Metropolitan Museum, New York, to its director Edward Robinson, dated 28 March 1923, quoted in Hoving, p. 82. See also James, p. 218, who quotes the first paragraph.
10 Breasted, p. 342.
11 Letter from Winlock to Robinson, 28 March 1923, op. cit.
12 Ibid.
13 Breasted, p. 342.
14 Letter from Winlock to Robinson, 28 March 1923, op. cit.
15 Ibid.
16 Ibid.
17 Hoving, p. 52.
18 Breasted, p. 342.
19 For instance, TGH James takes a sceptical approach to the incident by questioning 'how a cobra could have got through the bars of the cage' and if they were so widely set 'surely the canary could have got out'. See James, p. 306. Yet during the filming for the TV series *The Face of Tutankhamun*, which accompanied the publication of Christopher Frayling's book of the same title, an opportunity presented itself to test the validity of the story. A live cobra was set before a birdcage containing a canary on the steps of 'Castle Carter' at the head of the Valley of the Kings. All present watched in amazement as the snake reduced itself to the necessary width and began sliding through the bars, prompting the film crew to stop the poor bird from being consumed. See Frayling, *The Face of Tutankhamun*, pp. 55–6.
20 Carter, Lett's No. 46 Indian and Colonial Rough Diary 1922, entry for Friday 24 November, the Griffith Institute, Ashmolean Museum, Oxford.
21 James, p. 305.
22 Carter, Lett's No. 46 Indian and Colonial Rough Diary 1922, entry for Friday 24 November, the Griffith Institute, Ashmolean Museum, Oxford.
23 See, for instance, Alan H Gardiner's account of events quoted in his daughter Margaret Gardiner's *A Scatter of Memories*, p. 98: 'On November 23rd Carnarvon arrived at Luxor with his daughter Evelyn'.
24 Carter and Mace, I, p. 92.
25 Ibid.
26 Ibid., I, p. 93 n. 1.
27 Ibid., I, p. 94.
28 Ibid., I, p. 96.
29 Ibid., I, p. 96.
30 Carter, MSS. Notebook 1, the Griffith Institute, Ashmolean Museum, Oxford. The notebook contains extended entries, some sketches and newspaper cuttings relating to the discovery. According to a spokesperson from the Griffith Institute, it 'is clear that this is not a diary which was written at the end of each day'. Indeed, it is unlikely that there ever was one. Rather, it is a

reconstruction of events using Carter's appointments diaries and his (and Mace's?) recollections. It is clear that this notebook was written up at a much later date than the entries therein. As such, it is likely that they do not always give us an accurate account of events.

31 Ibid.
32 Carter and Mace, I, p. 100.
33 Ibid.
34 Ibid., I, p. 101.

CHAPTER 6: UNOFFICIAL OPENING

1 Carter and Mace, *The Tomb of Tut.ankh.Amen*, I, p. 98.
2 Carter, Lett's No. 46 Indian and Colonial Rough Diary 1922, entry for Sunday, 26 November, the Griffith Institute, Ashmolean Museum, Oxford.
3 Carnarvon, typewritten draft article dated 10 December 1922, quoted in Reeves and Taylor, *Howard Carter before Tutankhamun*, pp. 140–1. At the time of publication of Reeves and Taylor's book this letter formed part of a collection owned by Reeves, but it is now held by the Department of Egyptian Antiquities at the British Museum.
4 Carnarvon, 'The Egyptian treasure: story of the discovery', *The Times*, 11 December 1922, pp. 13–14.
5 Typewritten draft article written by Lord Carnarvon, 10 December 1922, quoted in Reeves, *Howard Carter before Tutankhamun*, pp. 140–1.
6 Ibid.
7 Ibid.
8 Ibid.
9 Carter, *Tut.Ankh.Amen: The Politics of Discovery*, p. 4.
10 Carter and Mace, I, p. 93.
11 Hoving, *Tutankhamun – The Untold Story*, pp. 84–5.
12 Carter, p.4.
13 Hoving, p. 85.
14 Carter and Mace, I, p. 101.
15 Hoving, pp. 90–103.
16 Ibid., p. 91.
17 Carter and Mace, I, p. 97.
18 Carter and Mace, I, p. 104.
19 Ibid., I, p. 178.
20 Wynne, *Behind the Mask of Tutankhamen*, pp. 114–16.
21 Herbert, Mervyn, diary 1917–23 (an earlier diary covers the period 1912–17 but is not referenced in this work), Private Papers Collection, Middle East Centre, St Antony's College, Oxford, GB165–0144. Permission to quote from the diary was kindly given by Janet Powell and Martin Argles.
22 Ibid.
23 Ibid.
24 Ibid.
25 Carter and Mace, I, 101–2.
26 Lucas, 'Notes on Some of the Objects from the Tomb of Tut-ankhamun', *ASAE* 41 (1942), pp. 135–47.
27 Ibid., p. 136.
28 Ibid.
29 Ibid.
30 Lucas, 'Notes on Some of the Objects from the Tomb of Tut-ankhamun', *ASAE* 45 (1947), pp. 133–4.
31 Ibid.
32 Herbert, George, account of discovery of Tutankhamun's tomb (copy), c. 1922–23, British Library Manuscript Collection, RP 17991. The account is undated and while the British Library reference gives a broad period within which it could have been written, the authors believe that it was probably composed sometime between 26–30 November 1922, when the events described in the text were still fresh in Carnarvon's mind. According to staff at the British Library the original papers have been exported yet the copies were deposited at the library as per legal requirements for historical documents. No further information was forthcoming but it is more

than likely that the originals were either sold as part of a private transaction or bought at auction. The current province of Carnarvon's original account is unknown and we have been unable to trace its present owner.

33 Ibid., pp. 5–6, 9.
34 Letter from Lord Carnarvon to Alan H Gardiner, 28 November 1922, quoted in Reeves and Taylor, *Howard Carter Before Tutankhamun*, pp. 141–2. This letter forms part of a collection of Gardiner papers archived at the Griffith Institute, Ashmolean Museum, Oxford.

CHAPTER 7: THE TREASURE OF TUTANKHAMUN

1 The Turin papyrus of Rameses IV's tomb, Museo Egizio, Turin. See Carter and Gardiner, 'The tomb of Ramesses IV and the Turin plan of a royal tomb', *JEA* 4 (1917), pp. 130–58. See also Desroches-Noblecourt, *Tutankhamen: Life and Death of a Pharaoh*, p. 259 and pl. 165.
2 In his book Carter claimed that the rope tie between the handles of the double-door had been broken in antiquity by tomb plunderers. But, given that there is little evidence of the robbers' activities in the Burial Chamber and Treasury (see Chapter 13), it may well have been Carter and company who broke the seal in their desire to see what lay beyond the first door of the shrine. See Carter and Mace, *The Tomb of Tut.ankh.Amen*, I, p. 183.
3 Ibid., I, p. 184. The authors recognise that the quotations from Carter and Mace's first volume of *The Tomb of Tut.ankh.Amen* and used to accompany the text of this chapter supposedly relate to Carter and company's official entry into the Burial Chamber and Treasury on Friday 16 February 1923. However, it is clear that Carter's words (with the help of Mace) are mainly expressing his initial feelings when he first entered these same chambers some three months beforehand in November 1922.
4 Ibid.
5 Ibid., I, p. 185.
6 The evidence for Carter's resealing the hole, and also stamping the wet mortar with his own prefabricated seal of the necropolis, can be seen in Burton's photograph (Plate 11) of the wall between the Antechamber and the Burial Chamber before it was dismantled in February 1923. Since Burton did not join Carter's team until mid-December 1922, just a few weeks *after* Carter et al. had breached the wall, the photograph cannot be misinterpreted as showing a record of a resealing in antiquity. Burton, Harry, Griffith Institute, Oxford, photograph GB7 282.
7 Herbert, account of discovery of Tutankhamun's tomb (copy), c. 1922–23, British Library Manuscript Collection, RP 17991, pp. 1–10.
8 Gardiner, *My Working Years*, pp. 37–8.
9 Dawson to Robbins, Memorandum, 'Informing him of Lord Carnarvon's offer of exclusive news on the opening of Tutankhamun's' tomb', 14 November 1922, TNL Archive at the Archives and Records Office of the News International Group, GR/3/19/3.

CHAPTER 8: SIX WEEKS TO LIVE

1 Rapp, unpublished memoirs (GB165–0234), Private Papers Collection, Middle East Centre, Oxford.
2 Letter from James Henry Breasted to his son Charles Breasted, dated 12 March 1923, quoted in Breasted, *Pioneer to the Past*, p. 347.
3 Breasted, p. 347.
4 James, *Howard Carter: The Path to Tutankhamun*, p. 254.
5 Letter from Lord Carnarvon to Howard Carter, 23 February 1923?, in the Carter archives of the Metropolitan Museum of Art, New York, and quoted in James, p. 254 and Hoving, *Tutankhamun – The Untold Story*, pp. 222–3.
6 Hoving, p. 222.
7 For instance, see Reeves and Taylor, *Howard Carter before Tutankhamun*, pp. 156–7.
8 Merton, 'Ld. Carnarvon's Death. 16 Years' Work in Egypt', *The Times*, 6 April 1923, p. 11.
9 Brackman, *The Search for the Gold of Tutankhamen*, p. 106.
10 Merton, op. cit.
11 Breasted, p. 347.
12 Reeves, *The Complete Tutankhamun*, p. 62.
13 James, pp. 256–7.
14 Ibid., p. 257.
15 Gardiner, *My Working Years*, p. 40.

16 Merton, op. cit.
17 Letter from Lady Evelyn Herbert to Howard Carter, 18 March 1923, in the Carter archives of the Metropolitan Museum of Art and quoted in James, pp. 257–8.
18 Letter from Albert Lythgoe to Howard Carter, 20 March 1923, held by the Egyptology Department of the Metropolitan Museum of Art and quoted in Hoving, pp. 223–4.
19 Merton, op. cit.
20 Letter from the Hon. Richard Bethell to Howard Carter, 26 March 1923, held by the Egyptology Department of the Metropolitan Museum of Art and quoted in Hoving, p. 224.
21 Merton, op. cit.
22 Ibid.
23 Carnarvon, *No Regrets: Memoirs of the Earl of Carnarvon*, pp. 120, 124.
24 Letter from Alan Gardiner to his wife, dated 1 April 1923, quoted by Margaret Gardiner in *A Scatter of Memoirs*, pp. 107–8.
25 Merton, op. cit.
26 Ibid.
27 'Lord Carnarvon's last hours: sudden failure of hotel lights', *Daily Express*, 6 April 1923, p. 1.
28 Merton, op. cit. Merton incorrectly states that his death occurred at 2.30 a.m.
29 Ibid.
30 Ibid.
31 *Daily Express*, 6 April 1923, p. 1.
32 This appears to have been Algernon Maudslay (1873–1948), a public servant, although the authors have been unable to verify this fact.
33 Gardiner, pp. 39–40.
34 Reeves, p. 62.
35 Hoving, p. 221.
36 Letter from Lord Carnarvon to Howard Carter, December 1922–January 1923, source unknown, quoted in Hoving, p. 153.
37 Weigall, *Tutankhamen And Other Essays*, p. 96.
38 Ibid., p. 89.

PART TWO: THE CURSE

CHAPTER 9: THE CURSE OF CARNARVON

1 Brackman, *The Search for the Gold of Tutankhamen*, p. 114.
2 From a conversation between Anthony Leadbetter, a surviving godson of Almina, Countess of Carnarvon, and the authors on 3 August 2001.
3 Carnarvon, *Ermin Tales: More Memoirs of the Earl of Carnarvon*, 1980, p. 16.
4 Ibid.
5 Ibid.
6 Ibid.
7 Ibid.
8 Ibid.
9 Ibid.
10 From a conversation between Anthony Leadbetter and the authors on 3 August 2001.
11 'Cheiro' (Hamon), *Confessions: memoirs of a modern seer*, 1932, p. 38; 'Cheiro' (Hamon), *Real Life Stories: A Collection of Sensational Personal Experiences*, 1934, p. 29.
12 'Cheiro' (Hamon), 1932, Mark Twain, p. 168; Sarah Bernhardt, p. 147; Austin Chamberlain, pp. 123–4; Oscar Wilde, p. 152; Mata Hari, pp. 248–57.
13 Ibid., p. 132.
14 Ibid., pp. 97–100.
15 Ibid., pp. 108–9.
16 Ibid., pp. 113–16.
17 Ibid., pp. 39–42.
18 Ibid., p. 62.
19 Ibid., p. 66.
20 Ibid., p. 68.
21 Wynne, *Behind the Mask of Tutankhamen*, p. 51.
22 'Cheiro' (Hamon), 1932, pp. 135–44.

23 Ibid., pp. 142, 144.
24 'Cheiro' (Hamon), 1934, p. 45.
25 Ibid., pp. 19–26, 35–47. See also Nelson, *Out of the Silence*, pp. 31–2.
26 'Cheiro' (Hamon), 1934, p. 45.
27 Ibid., p. 46.
28 Ibid., p. 47.
29 Ibid.
30 Carnarvon, *No Regrets: Memoirs of the Earl of Carnarvon*, 1976, p. 120.
31 Lee, ... *the grand piano came by camel: Arthur C Mace, the neglected Egyptologist*, p. 111.
32 Carter, *The Tomb of Tut.ankh.Amen*, II, p. xxv.
33 Ibid.
34 'Lord Carnarvon's last hours: sudden failure of hotel lights', *Daily Express*, 6 April 1923, p. 1.
35 Rapp, unpublished memoirs (GB165–0234), Private Papers Collection, Middle East Centre, Oxford.
36 Weigall, *Tutankhamen And Other Essays*, p. 137.
37 Ibid., pp. 137–8.
38 Wynne, p. 95.
39 Ibid., pp. 95–6.
40 Ibid., p. 96.
41 Ibid., p. 96.
42 Ibid.
43 Ibid.
44 Ibid., p. 103.
45 Ibid.
46 Ibid., p. 104.
47 Ibid.
48 Ibid.
49 Carnarvon, 1976, pp. 120–2. It is, however, recognised by the authors that large sections of this book were taken wholesale out of Barry Wynne's own book *Behind the Mask of Tutankhamen*, published in 1972, particularly in areas dealing with the death of the fifth Earl of Carnarvon and his contact with Count Louis Hamon and Velma. Indeed, it seems likely that Wynne may well have had a hand in significantly contributing to the writing of the sixth earl's memoirs.
50 See Coates and Bell, *Marie Corelli: The Writer & the Woman*.
51 Reeves, *The Complete Tutankhamun*, p. 62 and Mahdy, *Tutankhamun: The Life and Death of a Boy King*, p. 129, the latter of whom states that Corelli said the old Egyptian book contained the classic curse line, 'Death comes on [swift] wings to him who enters the tomb of a Pharaoh'.
52 Keys, 'Curse (& Revenge) of the Mummy Invented by Victorian Writers', *The Independent*, 31 December 2000.
53 Ibid.
54 LMA (Louisa May Alcott), 'Lost in a Pyramid' *The New World*, vol. 1, no. 1, 1869, p. 8. Periodicals collection, Library of Congress, Washington DC, Cat. No. AP2 N6273. The authors would like to thank Fred Bauman, manuscript reference specialist, at the Library of Congress for his help in obtaining the reference details for this item. See also Montserrat, 'Louisa May Alcott and the Mummy's Curse', *KMT* 9:2 (Summer 1998), pp. 70–5.
55 See Stoker, *The Jewel of Seven Stars*. By far the best film to be based on Stoker's book is *The Awakening* (1980), starring Charlton Heston.
56 A letter from Herbert E Winlock, assistant curator of Egyptology at the Metropolitan Museum, New York, to its director Edward Robinson, 28 March 1923, quoted in Hoving, *Tutankhamun – The Untold Story*, p. 82. See also James, *Howard Carter: The Path to Tutankhamun*, p. 218, who quotes the first paragraph.
57 Vandenberg, *The Forgotten Pharaoh: The discovery of Tutankhamun*, p. 158.
58 Ibid.
59 Weigall, pp. 137–8.
60 Wynne, p. 200.

CHAPTER 10: A SENTENCE OF DEATH

1 Carnarvon, *No Regrets: Memoirs of the Earl of Carnarvon*, p. 124.
2 Ibid.
3 Ibid.

4   'Lord Carnarvon's last hours: sudden failure of hotel lights', *Daily Express*, 6 April 1923, p. 1.
5   Winstone, *Howard Carter and the Discovery of the Tomb of Tutankhamun*, p. 189.
6   *Daily Express*, 6 April 1923, p. 1.
7   For instance, see Vandenberg, *The Forgotten Pharaoh: The Discovery of Tutankhamun*, 1978, p. 160.
8   For instance, see Carnarvon, p. 126; Wynne, *Behind the Mask of Tutankhamen*, p. 134.
9   *Daily Express*, 6 April 1923, p. 1.
10 For those readers who possess a copy of Nicholas Reeves's superb book *The Complete Tutankhamun*, a photograph of the death certificate (currently on display at Highclere Castle) appears in a plate on Page 63, and the time of death is clearly visible.
11 Mahdy, *Tutankhamun: The Life and Death of a Boy King*, p. 130.
12 Vandenberg, 1978, p. 161.
13 Ibid.
14 Carnarvon, p. 127.
15 Ibid.
16 'Egyptian collectors in a panic: Sudden rush to hand over their treasures to museums: Groundless fears', *Daily Express*, 7 April 1923, p. 1.
17 Ibid.
18 Ibid.
19 Brackman, p. 113.
20 Ibid.
21 Ibid., p. 114.
22 Hoving, *Tutankhamun – The Untold Story*, p. 227.
23 Ibid.
24 Ibid.
25 Vandenberg, *The Curse of the Pharaohs*, 1973, p. 19.
26 Ibid.
27 Ibid.
28 A letter from Herbert E Winlock, assistant curator of Egyptology at the Metropolitan Museum, New York, to its director Edward Robinson, 28 March 1923, quoted in Hoving, *Tutankhamun – The Untold Story*, p. 82. See also James, *Howard Carter: The Path to Tutankhamun*, p. 218, who quotes the first paragraph.
29 Carter, *The Tomb of Tut.ankh.Amen*, II, p. xxv.
30 See Lucas, 'The Chemistry of the Tomb', in Carter, II, pp. 162–88.
31 Ibid., II, p. 165.
32 Ibid., II, pp. 165–6.
33 Ibid., II, p. 166.
34 Vandenberg, 1973, p. 157.
35 Ibid.
36 Ibid.
37 NBC television report, no screening date, c. 1990s.
38 Hoving, p. 221.

CHAPTER 11: THE PRESENCE OF POISON

1   Quoted in Brackman, *The Search for the Gold of Tutankhamen*, p. 114.
2   Morton, 'Tragedy of Lord Carnarvon', *Daily Express*, 6 April 1923, p. 4.
3   A number of Internet news sites posted articles on the discovery. For example see http://www.egyptvoyager.com/drhawass_findingthetomb_2.htm.
4   Posted on various Internet news sites. For example see: http://abcnews.go.com/sections/science/DailyNews/egyptmayor000523.html.
5   Email from Michael Carmichael to Andrew Collins, dated 11 January 2002.
6   Ibid.
7   Letter from Arthur C Mace to his wife Winifred, dated 4 March 1923, quoted in Lee, … *the grand piano came by camel: Arthur C Mace, the neglected Egyptologist*, p. 109.
8   Letter from Arthur C Mace to his wife Winifred, dated 4 March 1923, quoted in James, *Howard Carter: The Path to Tutankhamun*, p. 253.
9   Letter from Arthur C Mace to Albert Lythgoe, dated 14 January 1927, from the Mace file at the Metropolitan Museum of Art, New York, quoted in Lee, p. 138.
10 Ibid.

11 Ibid., pp. 139–40.
12 Letter from Arthur C Mace to Albert Lythgoe, dated 14 January 1927, from the Mace file at the Metropolitan Museum of Art, New York, quoted in ibid., p. 140.
13 Letter from Arthur C Mace to Albert Lythgoe, dated 7 August 1927, from the Mace file at the Metropolitan Museum of Art, New York, quoted in ibid.
14 Ibid.
15 Chris Ogilvie-Herald spoke at length with Christopher C Lee, the curator of the Paisley Museum in Scotland, during July 2001, who was unable to elaborate any further on the cause of Mace's arsenic poisoning.
16 Email from Dorothy Arnold to Andrew Collins, dated 12 March 2002.
17 Pearce, 'Bangladesh's arsenic poisoning – who is to blame?' UNESCO Courier, January 2001.
18 F Hoefear, Histoire de la chimie, 1842, I, p. 226, quoted in Lucas, 'Poisons in Ancient Egypt', JEA 24 (1938), pp. 198–9.
19 Pliny, Natural History, XV, xiii, 45.
20 Lucas, p. 198.
21 Ibid., p. 199.
22 Ibid., p. 199.
23 Email from Michael Carmichael to Andrew Collins, dated 11 January 2002.
24 See Davis, The Serpent and the Rainbow.
25 For further information on arsenic sulphate visit www.sis.gov.eg/pharo/html/immort03.htm.
26 See Lucas, op. cit.
27 Harmon, 'Oakland arsenic fears resurface', Detroit News, 12 March 1997.
28 Hoving, Tutankhamun – The Untold Story, p. 221.
29 Email from Michael Carmichael to Andrew Collins, dated 11 January 2002.

CHAPTER 12: LOCKOUT!
1 Carter, Tut.Ankh.Amen, The Politics of Discovery, pp. 10–12.
2 Ibid., p. 69
3 Ibid., p. 5.
4 Ibid.
5 Ibid., Appendix I, p. 133.
6 Ibid.
7 Ibid., p. 134.
8 Carter and Mace, The Tomb of Tut.ankh.Amen, II, p. 51.
9 Ibid., II, p. 53.
10 Carter, p. 99.
11 Hoving, Tutankhamun – The Untold Story, p. 325.

CHAPTER 13: TOMB ROBBERS
1 Lucas, 'Notes on Some of the Objects from the Tomb of Tut-ankhamun', ASAE 41 (1942) p. 136.
2 Carter, The Tomb of Tut.ankh.Amen, II, pp. 89–90.
3 Ibid., II, p. 90.
4 Lucas, p. 137.
5 Ibid.
6 Ibid., pp. 137–8.
7 Hoving, Tutankhamun – The Untold Story, p. 350.
8 Ibid.
9 Ibid.
10 Ibid., pp. 350–1.
11 Ibid., p. 351.
12 Ibid.
13 Ibid.
14 Ibid., p. 354.
15 Ibid.
16 Ibid., pp. 352–3.
17 Ibid.
18 Ibid., p. 350.
19 Ibid., p. 352.

20 Ibid.
21 Ibid., p. 351.
22 Ibid.
23 Ibid., p. 356.
24 See Harris, 'Akhenaten and Nefernefruaten in the Tomb of Tut'ankhamûn,' in Reeves, *After Tut'ankhamûn: Research and excavation in the Royal Necropolis at Thebes*, p. 60. For information online concerning the Nelson-Atkins sequins go to http://echoesofeternity.umkc.edu/ Sequins.htm
25 Harris, p. 60
26 Hoving, p. 356.
27 Ibid., p. 355.
28 Reeves, *The Complete Tutankhamun*, pp. 96–7.
29 Carter, III, p. 34.
30 Hoving, p. 357.
31 Ibid. The authors made every attempt to trace the current whereabouts of the rings inherited by Phyllis Walker through an intermediary. Initially they were informed that these items were stored in the basement of the Egyptian Museum in Cairo, along with the other objects bequeathed by Farouk. They were told also that the 'rings are felt to be fakes by all who have had a chance to study them'. Yet, later, they were advised that the former curator of the museum, who had catalogued the Farouk material, claimed that there were no rings in the collection. There is obviously an element of confusion here and one that the authors have been unable to resolve. For the moment at least the location of the rings remains a mystery.
32 Lee, ... *the grand piano came by camel: Arthur C Mace, the neglected Egyptologist*, p. 100, from a conversation with Margaret Orr.
33 'Cheiro' (Hamon), *Real Life Stories: A Collection of Sensational Personal Experiences*, p. 47.
34 Ibid., pp. 49–50.
35 'Tragedy of the Hon. R Bethell. Death at his club. Tut-ankh.amen curse recalled', *Daily Mail*, 16 November 1929, p. 11.
36 'Cheiro' (Hamon), p. 52, cf. Universal News Service press release on the death of Lord Westbury, February 1930.
37 Ibid., p. 49.
38 Ibid., p. 51.
39 *Daily Mail*, 16 November 1929, p. 11.
40 'Tragedy of Lord Westbury. "I cannot stand any more horrors." Pharaoh's curse', *Daily Express*, 22 February 1930, pp. 1–2.
41 Ibid., p. 1.
42 For instance, the shadowy role played by Howard Carter and Lord Carnarvon in the purchase, on behalf of the Metropolitan Museum of Art, of the collection of some 225 items that came to be known as the Treasure of the Three Princesses, which went on display for the first time in 1926. See Hoving, pp. 127–37.
43 Letter from Arthur Weigall to Howard Carter, dated 25 January 1923, to be found in the Carter Files, Department of Egyptian Art, Metropolitan Museum of Art, New York, and quoted in James, *Howard Carter: the Path to Tutankhamun*, p. 242.
44 James, pp. 242–3.

CHAPTER 14: A SCANDALOUS ACCOUNT

1 Carter's confrontation with a British official in Cairo has come down to us through the memoirs of Lee Keedick, president of the Keedick Lecture Bureau and Carter's lecture agent in the US, yet the identity of the official is not at all clear. Keedick records Carter as having said that he confronted the 'British Vice Royal of Egypt', but after Egypt's independence in 1922 that office no longer existed. This fact seems to have been acknowledged by Thomas Hoving, for, in his book *Tutankhamun – The Untold Story*, he draws upon Keedick's memoirs but states that the official with whom Carter had his row was the vice-consul. Quite how Hoving reaches this conclusion seems unclear. While on the other hand TGH James in his book *Howard Carter: The Path to Tutankhamun* says it was General Sir Edmund Allenby, who served as Egypt's High Commissioner from 1919 until his retirement in 1925. Yet there is nothing in Keedick's notes to indicate that this was indeed the case.

According to the 'Foreign Office List and Diplomatic and Consular Year Book' for 1924, the vice-consul during the spring of 1924 was a Captain TC Rapp. The authors have identified him as Sir Thomas Cecil Rapp (1893–1984), who spent most of his life as a diplomat in various postings around the world. Rapp's own memoirs, from 1920–52, are located in the Private Papers Collection of the Middle East Centre at St Antony's College, Oxford. The authors could find no reference in them to the reported meeting with Howard Carter during this period. However, Rapp's memoirs relating to his term in Cairo amount to no more than seventeen or so pages and one would not expect, in so short an account, for the confrontation to have been recorded. Although, not within the above context, Rapp does mention meeting Carter shortly after Carnarvon's death when he was attending to the 'formalities for the transfer of his body to England'. It is possible that Keedick, not being a man of politics, misunderstood the intricacies of the British forms of political office, but until further research can shed more light on with whom exactly Carter had his confrontation, the official's identity remains a mystery. Thus for the purpose of this book the authors will refer to the unknown person as the 'British official'.

2 The reference here to the 'Egyptian Government' does not, of course, mean the Zaghlul government of 1924, but the one officiating in Tutankhamun's day.

3 Taken from a two-page extract of Lee Keedick's memoirs, headed 'Howard Carter', which include notes on the British Egyptologist. Although undated, they were probably written down in 1924 during Carter's lecture tour of the United States and Canada. The copies used by the authors were kindly supplied by TGH James.

The authors attempted to track down more extensive information, which Lee Keedick may have recorded about Carter, by attempting to trace his son Robert Keedick. Sadly, Robert died on 1 November 2000 in Florida and his surviving relatives, wife Mable and son Ted, were not in a position to help us with our enquiries, but were kind enough to respond to our queries as best they could.

4 Keedick, op. cit.

5 The exact date of the exchange is not recorded in Keedick's memoirs. However, from the authors' knowledge of the situation with respect to the 'lock out' at the tomb, the subsequent court case and the cancellation of the concession it would seem to have occurred around February/March 1924. Carter's diary notes that on 3 March 1924 he had an appointment at 08.30 at 'The Residency' in Cairo, where the offices of the High Commissioner and the High Consul were located. Plausibly it was during this meeting that the exchange occurred, since no other appointment at the Residency is recorded in his diary between January 1924 and 21 March 1924 when Carter left for England via Venice to prepare for his spring tour of North America.

6 Hoving, *Tutankhamun – The Untold Story*, p. 311.

7 Letter from Lord Carnarvon to Alan H Gardiner, dated 28 November 1922, quoted in Reeves and Taylor, *Howard Carter: Before Tutankhamun*, p. 141.

8 Budge, *Tutānkhamen: Amenism, Atenism, and Egyptian Monotheism etc.*, pp. xviii–xix.

9 Merton, 'An Egyptian treasure: Great find at Thebes: Lord Carnarvon's long quest'; 'Doctor Petrie's views: Unique finds', *The Times*, 30 November 1922, p. 13.

10 'The Egyptian find: Lord Carnarvon's hopes: Difficulties of photography: The unopened chamber', *The Times*, 18 December 1922, p. 14.

11 Telegram from Howard Carter to Alan H Gardiner, date unknown, c. early December 1922, quoted in Vandenberg, *The Forgotten Pharaoh*, p. 125. The authors have been unable to track down this item, but have no reason to doubt its existence.

12 'The Egyptian treasure: The importance of the find: Dr. A Gardiner's views', *The Times*, 4 December 1922, p. 7.

13 Carter and Mace, *The Tomb of Tut.ankh.Amen*, I, p. viii. It is a fact, however, that papyrus fragments were indeed found in boxes deposited in the Antechamber. For instance, the online 'Tutankhamun: Anatomy of an Excavation' resource at http://www.ashmol.ox.ac.uk/gri/4tut.html records that the items found in Box. No. 101y(1) included 'Piece of dried papyrus about 45 mm long. From a mat? Not kept.' While the contents of Box No. 102 likewise included 'Piece of papyrus', presumably also not kept.

14 Carter and Mace, I, p. viii.

15 Herbert, account of discovery of Tutankhamun's tomb (copy), c. 1922–3, British Library Manuscript Collection, RP 17991.

16 Reeves, 'Tutankhamūn and his Papyri', *GS* 88 (1985), pp. 39–45.

17 Ibid., p. 39.

18 Ibid.

19 Belzoni, *Narrative*, p. 235 f.; cf. Belzoni, *Description of the Egyptian Tomb*, 1821, 10, quoted in ibid., p. 40.

20 *List of Egyptian Antiquities belonging to Hy. Salt Esqr. forwarded to the British Museum,* one of two MSS in the Department of Egyptian Antiquities, the British Museum, quoted in ibid., p. 40.
21 Ibid., p. 40, cf. Arundale, Bonomi and Birch, Gallery, 47.
22 Ibid., pp. 40–1. The item in question is British Museum No. EA882.
23 Ibid, pp. 40, 44 n. 14.
24 Ibid.
25 Reeves and Taylor, *Howard Carter before Tutankhamun,* p. 18.
26 Reeves, 1985, p. 41.
27 Reeves, *The Complete Tutankhamun,* 1995, p. 129.
28 Budge, p. xii.
29 Brackman, *The Search for the Gold of Tutankhamen,* p. 180.
30 Hoving, p. 311.
31 Keedick, op. cit.

PART THREE: MOSES

CHAPTER 15: AGE OF THE EXODUS

1 Ex. 1: 8. All biblical quotations and references are taken from the Revised King James Bible, unless otherwise indicated.
2 Ex. 1: 11.
3 Ex. 1: 12.
4 Ex. 1: 14.
5 Ex. 2: 1.
6 Ex. 2: 3.
7 Ex. 2: 10.
8 Acts 7: 22.
9 Josephus, *Antiquities of the Jews,* II, x, 1–2.
10 Ex. 3: 1.
11 Ex. 3: 2–3.
12 Ex. 3: 7–8.
13 Ex. 3: 14.
14 Ex. 3: 14–15.
15 Ex. 14: 21.
16 Ex. 16: 1.
17 Ex. 19: 11.
18 Ex. 33: 6.
19 Ex. 32: 4.
20 Deut. 34: 1.
21 Deut. 34: 6.
22 Keedick, 'Howard Carter', unpublished memoirs, c. 1924.
23 Easton, *The Illustrated Bible Dictionary, s.v.* 'Pharaoh', pp. 538–42, which describes Rameses II as Pharaoh of the Oppression.
24 Gen. 45: 10; 46: 28, 29, 34.
25 Gen. 47: 11.
26 Num. 13: 22
27 Ps. 78: 12, 43.
28 Easton, *s.v.* 'Zo'an', pp. 713–14.
29 Bietak, 'Avaris and Piramesse: Archaeological Exploration in the Eastern Nile Delta', *PBA* 65 (1979), pp. 228–9.
30 Adam, 'Recent discoveries in the Eastern Delta', *ASAE* 55 (1958), pp. 306, 318–20.
31 Ibid., p. 320.
32 Ibid., p. 323; Habachi, 'Khata'na-Qantir, Importance', *ASAE* 52 (1952), p. 443.
33 See Adam, pp. 322–4.
34 Habachi, pp. 443–4.
35 Van Seters, *The Hyksos: a new investigation,* pp. 127–51.
36 Naville, 'The Geography of the Exodus', *JEA* 10 (1924), pp. 28–32.
37 Van Seters, pp. 148–9.
38 Bietak, pp. 247–53.

39 Ibid., p. 269.
40 Ibid., p. 273.
41 Ibid., p. 279.
42 Easton, s.v. 'Pharaoh', pp. 538–42.
43 Pritchard, Ancient Near Eastern Texts Relating to the Old Testament, 'Hymn of Victory of Mer-ne-Ptah (The "Israel Stela")', pp. 376–8.
44 Ibid., p. 378.
45 Lichtheim, Ancient Egyptian Literature, pp. 57–73.
46 Pritchard, p. 378 n. 19.
47 Lichtheim, pp. 77.
48 P Anastasi VI, 4: 11–5:5, in Redford, Egypt, Canaan, and Israel in Ancient Times, p. 228.
49 Naville, The Store-city of Pithom and the Route of the Exodus, pp. 4–5.
50 Ibid.
51 Ibid., p. 4.
52 Ibid., pp. 13–14, 28.
53 Ibid, pp. 4, 10, 12–13.
54 Ibid., pp. 12–13.
55 Ibid., pp. 11–12. See Ex. 5: 7–8.
56 Holladay, Cities of the Delta, pt. III: Tell el Maskhuta: Preliminary Report on the Wadi Tumilat Project 1978–1979, pp. 10–27.
57 Millard, 'How Reliable Is Exodus?', BAR 24:4 (July/August 2000), p. 55.
58 All dates for biblical events are taken from Easton, The Illustrated Bible Dictionary, Appendix I – Chronological tables, pp. 715–27. However, Wright, The Illustrated Bible Treasury, p. 173, gives 973 BC as the date for the foundation of Solomon's Temple.
59 Ex. 12: 40.
60 Bimson, 'A Chronology for the Middle Kingdom and Israel's Egyptian Bondage', SISR 3 (1979), pp. 64–9.
61 Ibid.
62 Wilson, The Exodus Enigma, p. 20.
63 Ibid.

CHAPTER 16: MOSES THE EGYPTIAN

1 Weigall, The Life and Times of Akhenaten.
2 Weigall, Tutankhamen And Other Essays, p. 100.
3 Ibid., pp. 101–2.
4 See Manetho, trans. Waddell, p. xiv.
5 Weigall, p. 107.
6 Manetho, Aegyptiaca, quoted in Josephus, Flavius Josephus Against Apion, trans. Whiston, I, 26.
7 Ibid.
8 Ibid.
9 Ibid.
10 Ibid.
11 Ibid.
12 Ibid.
13 Manetho, trans. Waddell, fr. 54, l. 237.
14 Manetho, trans. Whiston, I, 26.
15 Ibid., Osarsiph, or Osarsêph in Manetho, trans. Waddell, fr. 54, l. 238, seems to be derived from the names of two deities, Asar, or Osiris, god of the underworld, and Sêph, a Hebrew variation of the name Set, god of the burning desert wastes, venerated at Avaris by the Hyksos Asiatic kings under the name Sutekh (see Appendix II – 'Pork Abstinence and the Worship of Set'). In Egyptian mythology, Set governed the northern sky, the place of darkness, while in Jewish tradition the region of darkness is called Sêphôn, a name connected with the word Sâphôn, 'north'. See Budge, The Gods of the Egyptians, II, p. 249. However, the Jews would have seen in the name Osarsiph a form of the Hebrew name Joseph, which might itself have derived from the same word root. See Manetho, trans. Waddell, p. 125 n. 3.
16 Manetho, trans. Whiston, I, 26.
17 Ibid. I, 14.
18 Manetho, trans. Waddell, fr. 54, l. 246.

19 Manetho, trans. Whiston, I, 26.
20 Ibid.
21 Ibid. It is 'grandfather Rapsês' in Manetho, trans. Waddell, fr. 54, l. 245.
22 Manetho, trans. Whiston, I, 27.
23 Weigall, pp. 108–9.
24 Ibid., p. 109.
25 Ibid., p. 110.
26 Ibid., p. 111.
27 Ibid.
28 Ibid., p. 112.
29 Ibid.
30 See Greenberg, The Hab/piru, and Na'aman, 'Habiru and Hebrews: the transfer of a social term to the literary sphere', JNES 45:4 (1986), pp. 271–88; Rowton, 'Dimorphic structure and the problem of the 'Apirū-'Ibrîm', JNES 35:1 (1976), pp. 13–20.
31 Weigall, pp. 115–16.
32 It is acknowledged by the authors that Eduard Meyer identified characters in Manetho's account of Osarsiph-Moses with Amenhotep III and Akhenaten. See Meyer, Geschichte des Altertums, ii, pp. 421, 424–5. However, he connected the main events surrounding the expulsion from Egypt of 'the lepers', 'impure people' and Asiatics with the reigns of Rameses II and Merneptah. See ibid., pp. 420–6 and Meyer, Aegyptische Chronologie, pp. 92–5.
33 Budge, Tutānkhamen, Amenism, Atenism and Egyptian Monotheism etc., p. xiii.
34 Freud, Moses and Monotheism, pp. 97–8.
35 Ibid., p. 42.
36 Ex. 12: 12.
37 Weigall, p. 111.
38 Hecataeus of Abdera, quoted in Diodorus Siculus, Bibliotheca Historica, 40, 1–8.
39 Ibid., 40, 1.
40 Ibid., 40, 3.
41 Apion, Aegyptiaca, quoted in Josephus, II, 2.
42 Redford, Akhenaten: the Heretic King, p. 152.
43 Weigall, p. 110.
44 Budge, Gods of the Egyptians, I, p. 471; II, p. 361.
45 Aldred, Akhenaten – King of Egypt, pp. 43, 260; Redford, p. 149.
46 Redford, pp. 146–7.
47 Aldred, pp. 87, 273.
48 Apion, in Josephus, II, 2.
49 Like for instance, the reign of Ahmose, the first king of the Eighteenth Dynasty, who reigned c. 1575–1550 BC, and under whom the Hyksos Asiatic kings were expelled from Egypt. This last case is argued by Ralph Ellis in Tempest and Exodus, who cites the rainstorms and accompanying period of darkness described in the so-called Tempest Stela, dating from Year 1 of Ahmose's reign, to prove that both the Thera eruption and the biblical plagues occurred at this time. A connection between the aftermath of the Thera eruption and the plagues of Egypt is also posited by Ian Wilson in his 1985 book The Exodus Enigma, although he places this event during the reigns of Hatshepsut, c. 1490–1468 BC, and Thutmose III, c. 1490–1436 BC, the time frame of the Exodus offered by a literal interpretation of biblical chronology. A connection between the Tempest Stela and the Thera eruption is offered by Polinger Foster and Ritner in 'Texts, Storms, and the Thera Eruption', JNES 55:1 (1996), pp. 1–14. However, their arguments are persuasively demolished by Wiener and Allen in 'Separate Lives: The Ahmose Tempest Stela and the Theran Eruption', JNES 57:1 (1998), pp. 1–28. There is no question that the aftermath of the Thera eruption was felt in Egypt and might well have influenced the narrative of the book of Exodus. However, the problem comes from the dating of the event, with most scholars today opting for a high date in the range of 1628 BC based on dendrochronology and recalibrated Carbon-14 dates of organic materials from Akrotiri. For a general view of the Theran eruption and its effects on the Aegean and the Mediterranean see McCoy and Heiken, 'Anatomy of an Eruption: How a Terrifying Series of Explosions Reshaped the Minoan Island of Thera', Archaeology 43:3 (1990), pp. 42–9. Another school has proposed a lower date in the range of 1520 BC, while many historians continue to hold on to the traditional date of c. 1450 BC, based on stratigraphic evidence from the Minoan culture of Crete and Akrotiri on Thera/Santorini, and from contemporary cultures in other regions of the Mediterranean. For a full account of the problems regarding the dating of the Thera eruption see Manning, A Test of Time: the volcano of

Thera and the chronology and history of the Aegean and east Mediterranean in the mid second millennium BC. Whichever date best fits the evidence, none of them correspond with the reign of Ahmose and so it is extremely unlikely that the Exodus was connected in any way with activities during his reign, including the expulsion of the Hyksos, an idea originally derived from Josephus in *Contra Apionem*, quoting Manetho, who believed that the Asiatics were synonymous with Joseph and his brethren. See Manetho, trans. Whiston, I, 14. In Josephus' opinion, Manetho had *implied* that the Shepherds were synonymous with the 'Captives', or Hebrews enslaved in Egypt during the time of the Oppression, as contained in the 'sacred books' of the Jews. This fact seems to be affirmed by an earlier statement to the effect that the Hyksos had built Jerusalem, even though the Old Testament tells us that the holy city did not rise to any kind of prominence until the time of the united monarchy under David and Solomon. Perhaps inevitably, Josephus seized this statement to demonstrate how Manetho had preserved a record of the departure from Egypt of the Israelite nation at the time of the Exodus.

CHAPTER 17: DIVINE RETRIBUTION

1 Manetho, *Aegyptiaca*, quoted in Josephus, '*Flavius Josephus Against Apion*', trans. Whiston, I, 26.
2 Ibid.
3 Ibid.
4 Ibid.
5 Redford, *Pharaonic King-Lists, Annals and Day-books*, 1986, p. 293.
6 Assmann, *Moses the Egyptian: The Memory of Egypt in Western Monotheism*, p. 39.
7 For an extensive discussion on the relationship between the Hyksos, the Thera eruption and the Tempest Stela see Chapter 16, Note 49. See also Redford, *Egypt, Canaan, and Israel in Ancient Times*, 1992, pp. 419–20.
8 Aldred, *Akhenaten: King of Egypt*, pp. 173–4.
9 Ibid., p. 174.
10 Pendlebury, 'Summary report on the excavations at Tell el-'Amarnah 1935–1936', *JEA* 22 (1936), p. 198.
11 Ibid.
12 This includes a broken fragment of a statue from the north entrance to the royal palace at Amarna showing a person's hands and forearms holding an offering table. Its inscription gives the names of Akhenaten, his father Amenhotep III and the Aten in the later form current only after Year 9 of Akhenaten's reign. See Pendlebury, pp. 197–8.
13 Aldred, p. 174.
14 Pendlebury, p. 198.
15 Aldred, p. 180.
16 See, for example, Reeves, *Akhenaten; Egypt's False Prophet*, pp. 75–8.
17 Assmann, p. 26.
18 See Pausanias, *Description of Greece,* I, 42.
19 Aldred, p. 164.
20 Mahdy, *Tutankhamun: The Life and Death of a Boy King*, p. 175.
21 Manetho, trans. Whiston, I, 26.
22 Aldred, p. 164.
23 Manetho, trans. Whiston, I, 26.
24 Manetho, trans. Waddell, fr. 54, l. 232.
25 Ibid., fr. 50, l. 96, from Josephus, *Contra Apionem*, who gives the reign of Ôrus as 36 years 5 months; fr. 51, from Theophilus, *Ad Autolyc.*, iii. 19, who gives 36 years 5 months; fr. 52, from Syncellus, according to Africanus, who gives 37 years; fr. 53 (a), from Syncellus, according to Eusebius, who gives 36 years (38 years in another copy); 53 (b) Armenian version of Eusebius, which gives 28 years.
26 Ibid., fr. 50, l. 96, from Josephus, *Contra Apionem*, who gives the reign of Amenophis as 30 years 10 months; fr. 51, from Theophilus, *Ad Autolyc.*, iii. 19, who gives 30 years 10 months; fr. 52, from Syncellus, according to Africanus, who gives 31 years; fr. 53 (a), from Syncellus, according to Eusebius, who gives 31 years; 53 (b) Armenian version of Eusebius, which gives 31 years.
27 Ibid., fr. 50, l. 96, from Josephus, *Contra Apionem*, who gives the names of 18 kings of the Eighteenth Dynasty; fr. 51, from Theophilus, *Ad Autolyc.*, iii. 19, who gives 18 kings; fr. 52, from Syncellus, according to Africanus, who gives 16 kings; fr. 53 (a), from Syncellus, according to Eusebius, who gives 14 kings (but Syncellus elsewhere says he leaves out two kings); 53 (b) Armenian version of Eusebius, which gives 14 kings.

28 Ibid., fr. 52, from Syncellus, according to Africanus; fr. 53 (a), from Syncellus, according to Eusebius; fr. 53 (b), Armenian version of Eusebius: 'This is the king who was reputed to be Memnon, a speaking stone'.
29 Manetho, trans. Waddell, fr. 50, l. 96, from Josephus, *Contra Apionem,* who gives the reign of Acenchêrês as 12 years 1 month; fr. 51, from Theophilus, *Ad Autolyc., iii.* 19, who gives the reign of Acenchêrês as 12 years 1 month; fr. 52, from Syncellus, according to Africanus, who gives the reign of Acherrês as 12 years; fr. 53 (a), from Syncellus, according to Eusebius, who gives the reign of Achenchersês as 12 years; 53 (b), Armenian version of Eusebius, which gives the reign of Achencheres as 16 years.
30 Ibid., fr. 50, from Josephus, *Contra Apionem;* fr. 51, from Theophilus, *Ad Autolyc., iii.* 19.
31 Ibid., fr. 50, from Josephus *Contra Apionem;* fr. 51, from Theophilus, *Ad Autolyc., iii.* 19.
32 Ibid., fr. 52, from Syncellus, according to Africanus.
33 Ibid., fr. 53 (a), from Syncellus, according to Eusebius; fr. 53 (b), Armenian version of Eusebius.
34 Ibid., fr. 50, l. 96, from Josephus, *Contra Apionem,* who gives the reign of Ramessês as 1 year 4 months; fr. 51, from Theophilus, *Ad Autolyc., iii.* 19, who gives him 1 year 4 months; fr. 52, from Syncellus, according to Africanus, who gives him 1 year; fr. 53 (a), from Syncellus, according to Eusebius, who gives him 68 years; 53 (b), Armenian version of Eusebius, which gives him 68 years.
35 Ibid., fr. 50, l. 96, from Josephus, *Contra Apionem,* who gives the reign of Harmaïs as 4 years 1 month; fr. 51, from Theophilus, *Ad Autolyc., iii.* 19, who gives the reign of Harmaïs as 4 years 1 month; fr. 52, from Syncellus, according to Africanus, who gives the reign of Armesis as 5 years; fr. 53 (a), from Syncellus, according to Eusebius, who gives the reign of 'Armaïs, also called Danaus' as 5 years; 53 (b), Armenian version of Eusebius, which gives the reign of 'Armaïs, also called Danaus' as 5 years.
36 Ibid., fr. 53 (a), from Syncellus, according to Eusebius.
37 Ibid., fr. 53 (b), Armenian version of Eusebius.
38 Ibid., fr. 53 (a), Syncellus's additional note to Eusebius's text.
39 Indeed, the principal of them, Josephus in *Contra Apionem,* who includes a version of Manetho's *Epitome,* believed that the expulsion of the Hyksos from Egypt was a distorted memory of the Exodus, so would have chosen to ignore any contrary claim by Manetho regarding its suggested time frame in the Amarna Age. Moreover, it was from Josephus that another source of Manetho's *Epitome,* the *Ad Autolucus* of Theophilus (d. c. AD 181–6), the saint and Greek ecclesiastical writer, was derived. It is for this reason alone that before his entry for 'Tethmôsis', or Ahmose, the founder of the Eighteenth Dynasty, Theophilus writes:

Moses was the leader of the Jews … when they had been expelled from Egypt by King Pharaôh whose name was Tethmôsis. After the expulsion of the people, this king, it is said, reigned for 25 years 4 months, according to Manetho's reckoning. (See Manetho, trans. Waddell, fr. 51, from Theophilus, Ad Autolyc. iii. 19.)

A third source that fails to link the reign of Acenchêrês with the time frame of the Exodus was the *Pentabiblon Chronologicon* of Sextus Julius Africanus (d. c. AD 232), a Greek Christian historian. Although his work is no longer extant, sections from it, including Manetho's *Epitome,* are quoted by Syncellus. His entry for Ahmose, or Amôs as he calls him, states that in his reign:

Moses went forth from Egypt, as I [Africanus] here declare; but, according to the convincing evidence of the present calculation [put forward by me, Syncellus] it follows that in this reign Moses was still young'. (See Manetho, trans. Waddell, fr. 52, from Africanus)

Clearly, Africanus was simply quoting an earlier form of Manetho, which included the entry concerning the Exodus having occurred in the reign of Ahmose. Yet Syncellus himself obviously had contrary views on when exactly the Exodus took place, calculated perhaps using biblical chronology.

40 For a full résumé of these different Graeco-Egyptian and Graeco-Roman Exodus accounts, see Redford, 1986, pp. 282–96.
41 See, for instance, Lysimachos, *Aegyptiaca,* from Josephus, *Contra Apionem,* trans. Waddell, I, 34.
42 Ibid.
43 Ibid.
44 Ibid., I, 35.

45 Cheremon, quoted in ibid., I, 33.
46 Ibid.
47 Pompeius Trogus, quoted in Assmann, p. 36.
48 Bower, *Scotichronicon*, I, 9.
49 Ibid.
50 Ibid., I, 12.
51 Ibid., I, 14.
52 Ibid., I, 15.
53 Ibid., I, 18.
54 Ibid.
55 For the descendants of Scota colonising the Irish DílRiata, see *Lebor Gabála Erenn: The book of the taking of Ireland*, Bk. 5, VIII, 384–6. Bk. 5, VIII, 387, which states: 'Scota d. Pharao, king of Egypt, also died in that battle [of Sliab Mis against the demons and Fomoraig, that is, against the Túatha Dé Danaan] the wife of Érimón s. Míl. For Míl s. Bile went a-voyaging into Egypt, for ships' companies strong, and he took Scota to wife, and Érimón took her after him. In that night on which the sons of Míl came into Ireland, was the burst of Loch Luigdech in Iar-Mumu.' Yet Scota's ancestry is confusingly set in two different periods of history, for she is the daughter of 'Pharao', named as Chencres (see Bk. 5, VIII, 409, 424, 435) and of 'Nectanebus' (Nekhtnebef, c. 380–363 BC), see Bk. 5, VIII, 410. Both kings are seen to have been on the throne when an Irish voyage of four vessels, led by Míl s. Bile reached Egypt, although clearly these events are deemed to have taken place around the time of the Exodus. After her death, Scota was said to have been buried in 'Scota's Grave' between Sliab Mis and the sea. See Bk. 5, VIII, 420.
56 For Scota going to Scotland see the 'Pleading of Baldred Biset', 1301, as referenced in the Intro. to Bower, p. xx.
57 For Scota going straight to Ireland see 'Instructions', 1301, as referenced in the Intro to Bower, p. xx.
58 For Scota going first to Ireland and then on to Scotland see *Chron. Picts-Scots*, 106–16 and *SEHI*, 609–10, as referenced in the Intro. to Bower, p. xix. Here Scota is the wife of Nelus or Niulus, a Greek, the son of a certain Lacedaemonian Aeneas, a prince of the Choriscii.
59 See the 'Pleading of Baldred Biset', 1301, as referenced in the Intro. to Bower, p. xx.
60 Nennius, *Historia Brittonum*, 15.
61 Bower, I, 10.
62 For a very interesting thesis that Scota, Pharaoh's daughter, was in fact Meritaten, the eldest daughter of Akhenaten, see Evans, *Kingdom of the Ark*. She links her expedition with various Late Bronze Age finds in Britain and Ireland which appear to show an Egyptian influence here at this time.
63 Moran, *The Amarna Letters*, EA35, 11–15.
64 Aldred, p. 283.
65 Ibid.
66 Goetze, 'The Plague Prayers of Mursilis' in Pritchard, *Ancient Near Eastern Texts relating to the Old Testament*, KUB, xiv, 8; KUB, xxiv, 3, pp. 394–6.
67 Ibid. KUB, xiv, 8, p. 394.
68 Ibid., KUB, xiv, 8, p. 395.
69 Ibid., KUB, xxiv, 3, p. 396.
70 Kitchen, *Suppiluliuma and the Amarna Pharaohs: A Study in Relative Chronology*, p. 47.
71 Moran, EA11, 5–14.
72 Phillips, *Act of God*, pp. 301–2.
73 Ex. 11: 1.
74 Ex. 12: 29–30.
75 Phillips, pp. 302–3.
76 Gardiner, *Egypt of the Pharaohs*, pp. 244–5.
77 Redford, 1986, p. 282.

PART FOUR: YAHWEH

CHAPTER 18: THE SEARCH FOR YAHWEH

1 Giveon, 'Toponymes ouest-Asiatiques à Soleb', in *VT* 14, 1964, pp. 239–55; Giveon, *Les Bédouins Shosou des documents Égyptians*, 1971, pp. 24–8.
2 Giveon, 1964, pp. 244–5; Giveon, 1971, pp. 25–7.

3 Giveon, 1964, pp. 244–5; Giveon, 1971, p. 27.
4 Redford, *Egypt, Canaan, and Israel in Ancient Times*, p. 272 n. 70, cf. P. Harris I, 76:9 ('Se'ir with the Shasu clans').
5 Ward, 'The Shasu "Bedouin": notes on a recent publication', *JESHO* 15 (1972), pp. 50–1.
6 Ibid.
7 Grdseloff, 'Édôm, d'aprés les sources égyptiennes', *RHJE* 1 (1947), p. 74 n. 1, after Champillion and Sethe.
8 P Anastasi IV, 18, quoted in Redford, p. 228.
9 Redford, p. 203.
10 Ibid., p. 270. See also Moran, *The Amarna Letters*, EA 285: 5-6.
11 Barkay, 'What's an Egyptian Temple doing in Jerusalem?', *BAR* 26:3 (May/June 2000), pp. 48–57, 67.
12 Redford, p. 271. See also Moran, *EA* 287.
13 Redford, p. 275; Ward, p. 46.
14 Redford, p. 275.
15 Giveon, 1971, pp. 235–6.
16 Ward, p. 52, cf. P Anastasi I, 19, 1–4 and 23, 7–8.
17 Ibid., p. 53.
18 Ibid., p. 54.
19 Giveon, 'The Shosu of the Late XXth Dynasty', *JARCE* 8 (1969–70), p. 52.
20 Giveon, 1971, pp. 48–9.
21 Giveon, 1969–70, pp. 51–3.
22 Giveon, 1971, p. 28.
23 Ibid., p. 28.
24 Ibid., p. 236.
25 See Grdseloff, pp. 86, 98–9.
26 Ibid., pp. 81–2.
27 Redford, pp. 272–3.
28 Giveon, 1971, pp. 74–7; Grdseloff, pp. 79–83.
29 Gen. 32: 38.
30 See Greenberg, *The Hab/piru*, and Na'aman, 'Habiru and Hebrews: the transfer of a social term to the literary sphere', *JNES* 45:4 (1986), pp. 271–88; Rowton, 'Dimorphic structure and the problem of the 'Apirû-'Ibrîm', *JNES* 35:1 (1976), pp. 13–20.
31 Ex. 3: 1.
32 Easton, *The Illustrated Bible Dictionary, s.v.* 'Horeb', p. 336.
33 Ex. 3: 14.
34 Ex. 3: 15, trans. Propp. *Exodus 1–18: A New Translation with Introduction and Commentary*, p. 6.
35 Propp, p. 204.
36 Ex. 6: 3.
37 Gen. 33: 20.
38 Ex. 15: 17.
39 Ex. 15: 17, trans. Propp, p. 22.
40 Ex. 3: 5.
41 Ex. 19: 11, 18, 20, 23.
42 Ex. 33: 6.
43 Ex. 32: 15.
44 I Kings 19: 8.
45 1 Kings 19: 9.
46 1 Kings 19: 3.
47 Har-el, *The Sinai Journeys: The Route of the Exodus*, p. 181.
48 Ibid.
49 Ibid.
50 Ibid.
51 Ibid.
52 Petrie, *Researches in Sinai*, pp. 251–2.
53 Ibid., pp. 252–3.
54 Ex. 13: 17.
55 Ex. 13: 18.
56 Propp, pp. 339, 486–7.
57 Ex. 15: 22.

58 Lucas, *The Route of the Exodus of the Israelites from Egypt*, pp. 32–3.
59 Ex. 15: 27.
60 Lucas, p. 48.
61 1 Kings 9: 26.
62 Ex. 16: 1.
63 Ex. 17: 1–6.
64 Ex. 19: 1–2.
65 Finkelstein and Silberman, *The Bible Unearthed: Archaeology's New Vision of Ancient Israel and the Origin of its Sacred Texts*, p. 13.
66 Deut. 33: 2.
67 Jud. 5: 3–5.
68 Redford, p. 272 n. 70, cf. P. Montent, Kemi 5 (1937), pl. III ('despoiler of the land of the Shasu, plunderer of the mountain of Se'ir'); Ward, pp. 50–1.
69 Redford, p. 272 n. 70, cf. P Anastasi vi. 54–56 ('clans of the Shasu of Edom'); Giveon, 1971, pp. 235–6.
70 Deut. 2: 10.
71 Deut. 2: 11.
72 Gen. 6: 4, Num. 13: 33. See Collins, *From the Ashes of Angels,* for a full account of the relationship between the Anakim, Nephilim and the Watchers of the 'Book of Enoch'.
73 Gen. 36: 20.
74 Gen. 14: 6.
75 Deut. 2: 12, 16.
76 Gen. 36: 8.
77 Gen. 36: 20.
78 Odelain and Séguineau, *Dictionary of Proper Names and Places in the Bible, s.v.* 'Horites', p. 164.
79 Pritchard, *Ancient Near Eastern Texts relating to the Old Testament,* 'Hymn of Victory of Mer-ne-Ptah (The "Israel Stela")', p. 378 n. 19.
80 Easton, *s.v.* 'Se'ir', p. 611.
81 Gen. 36: 9.
82 Gen. 36: 8.
83 Bamberger, *Fallen Angels,* p. 154.
84 Ibid.
85 Lev. 9: 3, 15; 10: 16.
86 Lev. 16: 9–10.
87 See Collins, *From the Ashes of Angels,* p. 252.
88 Bamberger, p. 154, cf. *Pirke d'R Eliezer,* ed. D Luria, Warsaw, 1852; *Bereshit Rabba,* ed. J Theodor and Ch. Albeck, Berlin, 1912–29.
89 Ibid.
90 Bamberger, p. 155.
91 Gen. 25: 30–1.
92 Gen. 36: 16; 1 Chr. 1: 36
93 Neilsen, *The Site of the Biblical Mount Sinai: A claim for Petra,* p. 11.
94 Num. 20: 14–21.

CHAPTER 19: MOUNTAIN OF THE MOON

1 Vaux, *The Bible and the Ancient Near East,* p. 152.
2 2 Kings 22: 2.
3 2 Chron. 25: 1.
4 2 Chron. 25: 14.
5 Eze. 35: 3–5.
6 Mackenzie, *The Myths of Babylonia and Assyria,* p. 52.
7 Ibid.
8 Gen. 10: 22, 11: 10, 24–7, 22: 21.
9 Gen. 11: 26.
10 1 Chron. 1: 32.
11 Gen. 11: 28, 31, 15: 7.
12 Gen. 11: 2.
13 Woolley, *Ur of the Chaldees,* p. 14.

14 Ibid.
15 Gilbert, *Magi: The quest for a secret tradition*, p. 177.
16 Ibid.
17 Ibid.
18 Gündüz, 'The Knowledge of Life', *JSS* 3 (1994), pp. 32–3, 35.
19 Gen. 12: 1–5.
20 Gen. 12: 6.
21 Gen. 12: 8.
22 Jg. 21: 19.
23 Easton, *The Illustrated Bible Dictionary, s.v.* 'Si'nai', p. 634. Some sources link the name 'Sinai' with the Hebrew *seneh*, meaning 'bush'. See Odelain and Séguineau, *Dictionary of Proper Names and Places in the Bible, s.v.* 'Sinai', pp. 354–5. However, it could be argued that the legend of the Burning Bush evolved as a result of ignorance concerning the true origin of the name Sinai.
24 Gündüz, p. 201.
25 Ibid., p. 200.
26 Ibid., p. 224.
27 Ibid.
28 Ibid., p. 44.
29 Ibid.
30 Ibid., p. 224; Drower, *The Mandaeans of Iraq and Iran*, pp. 265–9.
31 Drower, p. 266.
32 Ibid.
33 Gündüz, p. 225.
34 Ibid., p. 207.
35 Ibid.
36 Oesterley and Robinson, *Hebrew Religion: Its Origin and Development*, p. 65.
37 Ibid., p. 128. See also Nielsen, *Die altarabische Mondreligion und die mosaische Ueberlieferung*, 1904, p. 50.
38 Ibid.
39 Ex. 12: 12–28.
40 Deut. 16: 1: 'Observe the month of Abib and keep the passover unto the Lord thy God'. See also Oesterley and Robinson, p. 128; Nielsen, *Handbuch der Altarabischen Altertumskunde*, 1927, i, 244.
41 Propp, *Exodus 1–18: A New Translation with Introduction and Commentary*, p. 392.
42 Ex. 12: 9.
43 Ex. 12: 46.
44 Oesterley and Robinson, p. 131.
45 Nielsen, *The Site of the Biblical Mount Sinai: A claim for Petra*, 1928, p. 21.
46 Ibid., p. 23.
47 At the Council of Nicea in AD 325 it was decided that since the Last Supper is thought to have occurred on the feast of the Passover (most probably on the Feast of the Unleavened Bread), then Easter Day should be celebrated on the first Sunday either on or after the full moon that follows the spring equinox in the northern hemisphere. This Roman calculation of Easter Day was imposed on the Church of England at the Synod of Whitby in AD 664.
48 Propp, p. 399.
49 Num. 29: 12–13.
50 Num. 29: 17.
51 Num. 29: 20.
52 Num. 20: 32.
53 Oesterley and Robinson, pp. 128–9. For a review of the lunar cult among the Semitic peoples of the Near East see Nielsen, 1901, pp. 50 ff., and 1927, i, pp. 213–24.
54 Gündüz, pp. 2, 12, 37, 51, 119, 131.
55 Ibid., p. 83, 118–19.
56 Num. 1: 1.
57 Num. 9: 1.
58 Num. 10: 12.
59 Num. 10: 33, 35.
60 Easton, *s.v.* 'Paran', p. 521.
61 Num. 11: 35.
62 Num. 13: 21.
63 Num. 13: 26.

CHAPTER 20: THE CASE FOR THE HIGH PLACE

1 Num. 20: 16.
2 Num. 20: 11.
3 Num. 20: 8.
4 Num. 20: 11.
5 Num. 27: 14; Deut. 32: 51–2.
6 Num. 27: 14.
7 Easton, *The Illustrated Bible Dictionary, s.v.* 'Meribah', pp. 458–9.
8 Deut. 32: 51.
9 Stanley, *Sinai and Palestine in connection with their history*, p. 67.
10 *The Koran*, Sura 2: 60.
11 Zayadine, 'Caravan Routes Between Egypt and Nabataea and the Voyage of Sultan Baibars to Petra in 1276' in Hadadi, *Studies in the history and Archaeology of Jordan*, II, p. 173, quoting al-Nuwairi's MS No. 1578, Bibliothèque Nationale, Paris.
12 Ibid., p. 169
13 Ibid., p. 170. Also personal conversation between Andrew Collins and Ahmad Muammar, an archaeologist and tour guide from Wadi Mûsa in March 2002. He too feels that the el-Odmal spring is more likely to be the true site of Ain Mûsa.
14 Josephus, *Antiquities of the Jews*, I, xii, 4.
15 Zayadine, p. 173, Quoting Nuwairi.
16 Browning, *Petra*, p. 128.
17 Stanley, p. 95.
18 Stanley, p. 89, quoting Sheikh Mohammed, source unknown.
19 Zayadine, p. 173, quoting Nuwairi.
20 2 Kings 14: 7; 2 Chron. 25: 11–12.
21 Zayadine, p. 167.
22 Browning, pp. 26–7.
23 Finkelstein and Silberman, *The Bible Unearthed*, p. 63.
24 Ibid., pp. 95–6.
25 The Targums of Onkelos, Jonathan and Jerusalem refer to Kadesh-barnea as Rekem-Giah, 'of the ravine'. See Stanley, p. 94 n. 3.
26 Nielsen, *The site of the biblical Mount Sinai: A claim for Petra*, p. 9, cf. the Targum of Deut. 1: 19.
27 Rekem, or Rokan, was an ancient name for Petra, see Jerome, *De Loc. Heb voc. Petra* and *Rekem*, quoted in Stanley, p. 94 n. 3. See also Josephus, *Antiquities of the Jews*, IV, vii, 1, who states that Petra was called Arecem, after a Midianite king named Rekem. He says also that Mount Hor lay above Arke, i.e. Arecem, or Rekem.
28 Browning, p. 114.
29 Stanley, p. 94 n. 3, cf. Schwarz, pp. 23–4.
30 Josephus, IV, iv, 5.
31 Ibid., IV, iv, 6.
32 Ibid.
33 Ibid., IV, iv, 7.
34 Jerome, *De Loc. Heb. Voc. Petra* and *Rekem*, as quoted in Stanley, p. 94 n. 3 & 4.
35 Num. 20: 1.
36 Ex. 17: 1.
37 Ex. 17: 6–7.
38 Stanley, p. 95.
39 It has been suggested that there were originally four obelisks on the Obelisk Ridge, since two other rectangular stone bases are to be found in the proximity of the existing examples. However, having examined these in some detail, Andrew Collins is of the opinion that they are simply the stumps of cut blocks removed from the plateau in antiquity. For instance, the base to the west of the westerly positioned obelisk shows clear signs of horizontal sawing across its upper surface, implying that its block or pillar was removed in this manner. This makes little sense of the view that it was originally an obelisk, for it hardly seems likely that the Nabateans, or whoever, would have sawn away an existing pillar and left two others standing. The fourth stump, which lies to the west of the easterly placed obelisk is much too small to conform with the height of the existing pillars, also ruling it out as a possible obelisk.
40 Browning, p. 185. Here the author states that: 'If they [i.e. the water cisterns] are Edomite, as has been suggested, it would indicate that the Edomites were not only capable of the techniques of rock cutting but might have passed this skill on to the Nabateans'.

41 Browning, p. 211.
42 Ibid., p. 212.
43 Ibid.
44 For instance, see *The Koran*, Sura 2: 54, 28: 17.
45 Browning, p. 212.
46 Ibid., pp. 214–16.
47 Ex. 24: 5.
48 Ex. 24: 6.
49 Browning, p. 213.
50 Ibid., pp. 215–16.
51 Ibid., p. 216.
52 Nielsen, p. 16.
53 The betyl is orientated at an angle of 251 degrees from north.
54 Nielsen, p. 16.
55 Ibid.
56 Ibid.
57 Ibid.
58 Ibid. See also Nielsen,
59 Glueck, *The Other Side of the Jordan*, p. 178.
60 Personal communication between Andrew Collins and Ahmad Muammar, an archaeologist and tour guide from Wadi Mûsa, in March 2002.
61 See Robertson Smith, *The Religion of the Semites*, pp. 201–12, for a full account of the veneration of pillars among the early Semites.
62 Personal communication between Andrew Collins and Ahmad Muammar in March 2002.
63 Browning, pp. 46–7.
64 Ibid., pp. 108, 210–11.
65 Personal communication between Andrew Collins and Ahmad Muammar in March 2002.
66 Browning, p. 48.
67 Gündüz, 'The Knowledge of Life', *JSS* 3 (1994), pp. 83, 118–19.
68 Ibid., p. 154.
69 Ibid., p. 138.
70 Ibid., p. 154.
71 Rev. 17: 3–6. For the association between Venus and Babylon see Hislop, *The Two Babylons, or the papal worship proved to be the worship of Nimrud and his wife*, pp. 5–6.
72 Nielsen, p. 21. With respect to Jebel Hilal, Menashe Har-el says that it cannot have been connected with the moon because its name derives not from *hilal*, 'new moon', but *hallal*, meaning 'lawful'. See Har-el, *The Sinai Journeys: The Route of the Exodus*, p. 284. This must surely be a matter of speculation, and in the knowledge that biblical place names for the region reflect lunar connotations, there is no reason to assume that Mount Hilal does not take its name from the Arabic word for the new moon.
73 Nielsen, p. 21.

CHAPTER 21: THE HOUSE OF GOD

1 See Nielsen, *Die altarabische Mondreligion und die mosaische Ueberlieferung*, 1904, pp. 171–6. Here he is comparing Petra's al-Madhbah with the design of the Mosaic high place.
2 Num. 20: 22.
3 Num. 20: 25–29.
4 Josephus, *Antiquities of the Jews*, IV, iv, 6–7; IV, vii, 1.
5 Ibid., IV, iv, 7.
6 Deut. 32: 51–2.
7 Deut. 34: 1–5.
8 Deut. 32: 50.
9 Nielsen, *The site of the biblical Mount Sinai: A claim for Petra*, 1928, p. 19.
10 This story of Nabi Harûn was related to Andrew Collins by Mu'tasim Nawafleh, the head barman of the Petra Forum Hotel, Petra, in March 2002.
11 Browning, *Petra*, p. 172.
12 Nielsen, 1928, p. 22; Ex. 24: 9.
13 Ex. 24: 10.
14 Ex. 24: 15.

15 Personal communication between Andrew Collins and Ahmad Muammar in March 2002.
16 Ibid.
17 Ibid.
18 Ex. 3: 5.
19 Phillips, *The Moses Legacy*. As this book goes to press, neither Andrew Collins or Chris Ogilvie-Herald have been able to read Graham's book, which they hope will throw even further light on many of the subjects explored in *Tutankhamun: The Exodus Conspiracy*.
20 Browning, p. 212.
21 Ibid., pp. 196–7.
22 Nielsen, 1928, pp. 15–16.
23 Ibid., pp. 15–16, 18–19.
24 Ex. 15: 17, trans. Propp, *Exodus 1–18: A New Translation with Introduction and Commentary*, p. 22.
25 Giveon, *Les Bédouins Shosou des documents Égyptians*, p. 28.
26 Ibid., p. 236.
27 Habak. 3: 3.
28 Gen. 36: 11, 15, 42.
29 Amos 1: 12.
30 Easton, *The Illustrated Bible Dictionary*, s.v. 'Bozrah', p. 107.
31 Jer. 49: 7; Ezek. 25: 13.
32 Obad. 8–9.
33 Hastings, *Encyclopaedia of Religion and Ethics*, s.v. 'Phoenicians', ix, p. 893.
34 Sanchoniatho, in Philo, as quoted in Cory, *Ancient Fragments*, p. 4.
35 Gen. 25: 25.
36 Gen. 25: 27.
37 Sanchoniatho, in Philo, as quoted in Cory, p. 5.
38 Ibid.
39 Ex. 18: 1.

CHAPTER 22: THE CONQUEST OF CANAAN
1 Num. 14: 45, 21: 3.
2 Num. 21: 1–2.
3 Odelain and Séguineau, *Dictionary of Proper Names and Places in the Bible*, s.v. 'Arad', p. 34; s.v. 'Hormah', p. 164.
4 Num. 21: 4.
5 Num. 21: 11.
6 Finkelstein and Silberman, *The Bible Unearthed*, p. 64.
7 Ibid.
8 Num. 21: 4.
9 Num. 21: 11.
10 Num. 23: 1–6.
11 Deut. 34: 1–4.
12 Deut. 34: 5.
13 Deut. 34: 6.
14 Num. 25: 3; Josh. 22: 17–18.
15 Num. 25: 1–6, 31: 16.
16 Num. 25: 9.
17 Num. 32: 39.
18 Num. 21: 33–5.
19 Num. 22: 2, 4.
20 Jos. 9: 17–27; 10: 12–13.
21 Jos. 10: 28–39.
22 Num. 31: 1–12.
23 Num. 21: 25.
24 Num. 21: 33.
25 Jos. 5: 10–15; 6: 1–27.
26 Jos. 7: 2–5; 8: 1–29.
27 Jos. 11: 10–13.
28 Jos. 11: 11–13.

29 Easton, *The Illustrated Bible Dictionary*, s.v. 'Lachish', p. 413.
30 Jos. 10: 31–2.
31 Silberman, 'Visions of the Future: Albright in Jerusalem', *BA* 56:1 (1993), pp. 8–16.
32 See, for example, Redford, *Egypt, Canaan and Israel in Ancient Times*, p. 265.
33 See Alt, *Essays on Old Testament History and Religion*.
34 Silberman, 1992, pp. 25–6.
35 Mendenhall, 'The Hebrew Conquest of Palestine', *BA* 25:3 (1962), pp. 66–87.
36 Ibid., p. 73.
37 Ibid.
38 See Gottwald, *The Tribes of Yahweh*.
39 Mendenhall, p. 73.
40 Ibid.
41 Ibid., p. 74.
42 Ibid.
43 Finkelstein and Silberman, p. 104.
44 Mazar, 'The "Bull Site" – An Iron Age I Open Cult Place', *BASOR* 247 (1937), pp. 27–42. See also ibid., p. 109.
45 Mazar, p. 30.
46 Finkelstein and Silberman, p. 109.
47 Ibid., p. 119.
48 Ibid.
49 Ibid., pp. 43–7.
50 Ex. 12: 37
51 Finkelstein and Silberman, pp. 112–13. See also Silberman, 'Who Were the Israelites?', *Archaeology* 45:2 (1992), pp. 22–30.
52 See Whitelam, *The Invention of Ancient Israel: The Silencing of Palestinian History*, pp. 164–7.
53 See Finkelstein and Silberman, p. 129.
54 Josephus, *Wars of the Jews*, VI, ix, 3.

PART FIVE: ZION

CHAPTER 23: THE RETURN TO ZION

1 Comay, *Who's Who in Jewish History after the period of the Old Testament*, s.v. 'Rothschild family', p. 313.
2 Luke, 21: 25.
3 Luke, 21: 26–8.
4 See Gidney, *The history of the London Society for Promoting Christianity amongst the Jews from 1809 to 1908*.
5 Michell, *Eccentric Lives and Peculiar Notions*, p. 169.
6 Ibid., p. 170.
7 Herzl, *Der Judenstaat: Versuch einer modernen Losung der Judenfrage ... Dritte Auflage*.
8 Ps. 137: 5. See Weizmann, *Trial and Error: The Autobiography of Chaim Weizmann*, p. 125.
9 Dugdale, *Arthur James Balfour: First Earl of Balfour, etc.*, vol. 1, pp. 434–5.
10 Weizmann, p. 164.
11 Ibid., p. 165.
12 Ibid., p. 192.
13 Dugdale, p. 433.
14 Ibid.
15 Weizmann, p. 200.
16 Ibid., pp. 191, 224.
17 Ibid., pp. 191–2.
18 Pope and Wheal, *The Macmillan Dictionary of the First World War*, s.v. 'United States of America', p. 487.
19 John, *Behind the Balfour Declaration: The Hidden Origins of Today's Mideast Crisis*, p. 58.
20 Landman, *Great Britain, the Jews and Palestine*, p. 4.
21 John, p. 58.
22 Ibid., p. 59.
23 Landman, p. 4.

24 John, p. 60.
25 Ibid.
26 Ibid., pp. 62–3.
27 Ibid., p. 63.
28 Landman, p. 5.
29 Ibid., p. 4.
30 Ibid., p. 5, cf. the Franco-British Convention, December 1920 (Cmd. 1195).
31 Ibid.
32 John, p. 67.
33 Ibid.
34 Weizmann, p. 256.
35 Ibid., p. 266.

CHAPTER 24: THE SWORD OF DAMOCLES

1   See Graves, *Lawrence and the Arabs.*
2   Weizmann, *Trial and Error,* p. 293.
3   See Westrate, *The Arab Bureau: British Policy in the Middle East, 1916–20.*
4   Weizmann, p. 319.
5   Ibid., quoting an account from 1923 by Philip Graves, *Times* correspondent at the time of the Jerusalem pogrom.
6   Ibid., p. 320, quoting an account from 1923 by Philip Graves, *Times* correspondent at the time of the Jerusalem pogrom
7   Ibid., pp. 348–9.
8   Ibid., p. 349.
9   Ibid., pp. 350–1.
10 Ibid., p. 350.
11 Ibid., p. 351.
12 Ibid.
13 Ibid., pp. 351–2.
14 Ibid., p. 343.
15 Ibid., p. 353.
16 Ibid., p. 355.
17 Ibid., p. 348.
18 Ibid., p. 360.
19 Ibid., p. 364.
20 Shepherd, *Ploughing Sand: British Rule in Palestine 1917–1948,* p. 39.
21 Ibid.
22 Ibid.
23 The reference here to the 'Egyptian Government' does not, of course, mean the Zaghlul government of 1924, but the one officiating in Tutankhamun's day.
24 From Lee Keedick's memoirs, headed 'Howard Carter'.
25 Ibid.
26 Weizmann, p. 562.
27 Hoving, *Tutankhamun – The Untold Story,* p. 348.

CHAPTER 25: THE FATE OF THE MISSING PAPYRI

1   From Lee Keedick's memoirs, headed 'Howard Carter', c. 1924.
2   Ferguson, *The House of Rothschild: The World's Banker 1849–1998,* p. 247.
3   Carnarvon, *No Regrets,* p. 6.
4   Greenwood, *Highclere Castle,* 'Smoking Room': 'The table was probably brought to Highclere by the fifth Countess who was an illegitimate daughter of the wealthy Alfred de Rothschild'.
5   Identified by the authors during a visit to Highclere on Friday 3 August 2001.
6   Ferguson, p. 247; Carnarvon, pp. 6, 115.
7   Ibid., p. 21.
8   Ibid.
9   Hyde, *Norman Birkett: The Life of Lord Birkett of Ulverston,* p. 149.
10 Ibid.
11 Ibid., pp. 133–56.

12 Personal interview between Tony Leadbetter, a surviving godson of Almina, Countess of Carnarvon, and the authors on 3 August 2001.
13 Ibid.
14 Personal interview between Tony Leadbetter and the authors on 3 August 2001.
15 *The Egyptian Gazette*, 30 March 1923.
16 Ferguson, p. 247.
17 Comay, *SV Who's Who in Jewish History after the period of the Old Testament*, Rothshild Family, p. 307.
18 Ferguson, p. 281.
19 Comay, *SV, Rothschild Family*, p. 313.
20 Ferguson, p. 452.
21 Weizmann, *Trial and Error*, p. 205.
22 Ibid., p. 204.
23 Hoving, *Tutankhamun – The Untold Story*, p. 221. Hoving accepts that Carnarvon's decline in health began *prior* to the fatal mosquito bite that led eventually to Carnarvon's unexpected death. Email from Thomas Hoving to Chris Ogilvie-Herald dated 18 July 2001.

APPENDIX I: THE DEATH OF TUTANKHAMUN

1 See Carter, *The Tomb of Tut.ankh.Amen*, II, pp. 106–40; Derry, 'Report upon the Examination of Tut.ankh.Amen's Mummy', in Carter, II, pp. 143–61.
2 Brier, *The Murder of Tutankhamen: A 3000-year-old Murder Mystery*, pp. 166–7.
3 Ibid., p. 167.
4 RG Harrison's comments quoted in ibid., p. 165.
5 Ibid., pp. 172–3.
6 Ibid., p. 172.
7 Ibid., p. 173.
8 Ibid.
9 Güterbock, 'The Deeds of Suppiluliuma as Told by His Son Mursili II', *JCS* 10 (1965), pp. 41–130.
10 Ibid., pp. 107–8, Fragment 31, Bo 4543 and 9181.
11 Ibid., p. 94, Fragment 28, Kbo V 6, Aiii.
12 Aldred, *Akhenaten: King of Egypt*, p. 221.
13 See, for instance, Aldred, p. 221.
14 See, for instance, Mahdy, *Tutankhamun: The Life and Death of a Boy King*, p. 301.
15 Ibid., Brier, p. 174.
16 Ginzberg, *The Legends of the Jews*, II, p. 297.
17 Weigall, *Tutankhamen And Other Essays*, p. 116.
18 Ginzberg, II, p. 297.

APPENDIX II: PORK ABSTINENCE AND THE WORSHIP OF SET

1 Hesse, 'Pig Lovers and Pig Haters: Patterns of Palestinian Pork Production', *JE* 10:2 (Winter 1990), pp. 195–225. For a full distribution of Iron Age pig remains see Table 3, pp. 215–16.
2 Finkelstein and Silberman, *The Bible Unearthed*, pp. 119–20.
3 Ibid., p. 119.
4 For instance, at Mount Ebal, near Nablus (ancient Shechem), and Raddana in the highlands there were no pig bones at all in the bone assemblage, while at Shiloh just 0.1 per cent of the faunal assemblage were pig bones. These figures contrast markedly against 10.4 per cent at Ashkelon, 18 per cent at Tel Miqne and 8 per cent at Tel Batash, sites on the southern coastal plain traditionally associated with the Philistines during this period, and 4.8 per cent at Hesban in the Transjordan, south of Amman, land of the Ammonites and Moabites. See Finkelstein, 'Ethnicity and Origin of the Iron Settlers in the Highlands of Canaan,' *BA* 59:4 (December 1996), p. 206.
5 Finkelstein and Silberman, pp. 119–20.
6 See Hunn, 'The Abominations of Leviticus Revised: A Commentary on Anomaly in Symbolic Anthropology', in Ellen and Reason, eds., *Classifications in their Social Context*, 1979, pp. 103–116.
7 Lev. 11: 7–8.

8 Deut. 14: 8.
9 Vaux, *The Bible and the Ancient Near East*, p. 267.
10 See Hesse.
11 Blaisdell, 'Abominable and relatively unclean flesh: parasites and the prohibition against pork in Ancient Egypt and Israel', *Argos* 19 (1998), pp. 363–70.
12 Herodotus, *The History of Herodotus* ii, 47.
13 Ibid.
14 Ibid.
15 Ibid.
16 Ibid.
17 Plutarch, *Isis and Osiris*, 8.
18 Aelian, *On the Characteristics of Animals*, x, 16.
19 Ibid.
20 Ibid.
21 Ibid.
22 Ibid.
23 Budge, *The Gods of the Egyptians*, ii, p. 368.
24 Redford, *Egypt, Canaan, and Israel in Ancient Times*, p. 47.
25 Frazer, *The Golden Bough*, p. 475.
26 Hastings, *Encyclopaedia of Religion and Ethics*, xii, p. 133.
27 Frazer, *The Golden Bough*, pp. 472–6.
28 Te Velde, *Seth, God of Confusion*, p. 119.
29 Ibid., pp. 121–2.
30 Bietak, p. 269–70; Habachi, 'Khatâ'na-Qantîr: importance', *ASAE* 52 (1952), pp. 458–70.
31 Te Velde, pp. 124–5.
32 Ibid., p. 125.
33 Bietak, p. 270.
34 Gardiner, *Late Egyptian Stories*, pp. 85–6.
35 Bietak, 'Avaris and Piramesse: Archaeological Exploration in the Eastern Nile Delta', *PBA* 65 (1979), pp. 250–1.
36 Bietak, p. 251.
37 A jawbone of a large wild pig was found alongside human remains on Mount Carmel, while at Gezer in the coastal lowlands a number of pig bones were found in a cave later used in the Early Bronze Age as a storehouse. See Vaux, p. 253.
38 Ibid., pp. 252–4.
39 Ibid., p. 259: 'In a mythological text, eight "wild boars" (or pigs, *hnzr,*) form part of the retinue of Baal along with seven "young servants"; and in an as yet unedited text, twelve "wild boars" (or pigs, *hnzr*) must come to work at Ugarit with eleven artisans'.
40 Bones of pigs have been found in underground sanctuaries at Gezer and Tell el-Fâr'ah in Palestine. See ibid., p. 265.
41 Ibid., p. 256, quoting A Bertholet, *Kulturgeschichte Israels*, 1919, p. 23.
42 Ibid., p. 266, cf. the works of Movers and Bochart, *Hierozoicon*, 1675, col. 702–3.
43 Hesse, p. 212.

APPENDIX III: EGYPTIAN NAMES AMONG THE LEVITES

1 Ex. 2: 10; Propp, *Exodus 1–18: A New Translation with Introduction and Commentary*, p. 152.
2 Propp, p. 152.
3 Ex. 6: 16.
4 Num. 3: 33, 35; 26: 57.
5 Num. 3: 17, 1 Chron. 5: 27, 6: 1.
6 Easton, *The Illustrated Bible Dictionary, s.v.* 'Merari', pp. 457–8.
7 Osman, *Moses: Pharaoh of Egypt*, p. 185; Propp, p. 276, after Cody, 1969: 40 n. 4.
8 Osman, p. 185.
9 Num. 3: 32.
10 Ex. 6: 25.
11 1 Chron. 27: 17.
12 Easton, *s.v.* 'Phin'ehas', p. 548.
13 Propp, p. 280, after Lauth 1871: 139–40; Cody 1969:71.
14 Osman, p. 185.

15 Ex. 6: 25.
16 Propp, p. 280.
17 Ex. 6: 21.
18 Propp, p. 280.
19 Easton, s.v. 'Hur', p. 340.
20 Odelain and Séguineau, *Dictionary of Proper Names and Places of the Bible*, s.v. 'Hur', p. 166; Propp, pp. 617–8.
21 Propp, p. 617, cf. ibn Ezra; Houtman 1989: 118.
22 Ex. 17: 8–10.
23 Ex. 17: 11.
24 Ex. 17: 12.
25 Ex. 17: 12. Trans. Propp, p. 26.
26 Ex. 17: 13–15. Trans. ibid.
27 Propp, p. 620.
28 Ibid.
29 Ex. 24: 14.
30 1 Kings 2: 27, 35; 1 Chron. 29: 22.
31 Num. 3: 4.
32 Num. 20: 25–6.
33 Num. 3: 32.
34 Jg. 20: 28.
35 Deut. 10: 8, 31: 9, 25.
36 Ex. 32: 26–9.
37 I Sam. 1: 3.
38 I Sam. 4: 4, 11, 17, cf. 2: 29, 34.
39 Odelain and Séguineau, s.v. 'Hophni', p. 164.
40 Budge, *An Egyptian Hieroglyphic Dictionary,* i, 480a.
41 Osman, p. 185.

BIBLIOGRAPHY

Abbreviations: ASAE, *Annales du Service des Antiquîtes de l' Egypte,* Cairo; BA: *Biblical Archaeologist,* Atlanta, GA; BAR: *Biblical Archaeology Review,* Pitman, NJ; BASOR, *Bulletin of the American School of Oriental Research,* Atlanta, GA; BHM, *Bulletin of the History of Medicine,* Baltimore, MD: CGC, *Catalogue général du musée de Caire,* Cairo; EA: *Egyptian Archaeology: Bulletin of the Egypt Exploration Society,* London; GS: *Göttinger Miszellan,* Göttingen, Germany; JARCE: *Journal of the American Research Center in Egypt,* Cairo; JCS: *Journal of Cuneiform Studies,* Chicago, IL; JE: *Journal of Ethnobiology,* Flagstaff, AZ; JEA: *Journal of Egyptian Archaeology,* London; JESHO: *Journal of the Economic and Social History of the Orient,* EJ Brill, Leiden, Holland; JNES: *Journal of Near East Studies,* Chicago, IL; JSS: *Journal of Semitic Studies,* Oxford Univ. Press, Oxford; JSSEA, *Journal of the Society of the Study of Egyptian Antiquities,* Toronto; OUP: Oxford Univ. Press, Oxford; PBA: *Proceedings of the British Academy,* London; RHJE: *Revue de l'histoire juive en Égypte,* Cairo; SISR: *SIS Review – Journal of the Society for Interdisciplinary Studies,* London; VT: *Vetus testamentum,* Leiden, Holland.

Adam, Sheheta, 'Recent discoveries in the Eastern Delta', *ASAE* 55 (1958), pp. 301–24.

Aelien, *On the Characteristics of Animals,* with English trans. by A F Scholfield, 3 vols., Wm Heinemann, London; Harvard Univ. Press, Cambridge, MA., 1959.

Bible, The Holy, 1611, Revised, OUP, 1905.

Alcott, Louisa May, *see* LMA.

Aldred, Cyril, *Akhenaten: King of Egypt,* 1988, Thames and Hudson, London, 1991.

Aldred, Cyril, and A T Sandison, 'The Pharaoh Akhenaten: a problem in Egyptology and pathology', *BHM* 36 (1962), pp. 293–316.

Allen, James P, 'Nefertiti and Smenkh-ka-re', *GM* 141 (1994), pp. 7–17.

Alt, Albrecht, *Essays on Old Testament History and Religion,* 1953, Basil Blackwell, Oxford, 1966.

Assmann, Jan, *Moses the Egyptian: The Memory of Egypt in Western Monotheism,* 1998, Harvard Univ. Press, Cambridge, MA, 1999.

Bamberger, Bernard J, *Fallen Angels,* 1952, Barnes & Noble, New York, NY, 1995.

Barkay, Gabriel, 'What's an Egyptian Temple doing in Jerusalem?', *BAR* 26:3 (May/June 2000), pp. 48–57, 67.

Bietak, Manfred, 'Avaris and Piramesse: Archaeological Exploration in the Eastern Nile Delta', *PBA* 65 (1979), pp. 225–96.

Bimson, John J, 'A Chronology for the Middle Kingdom and Israel's Egyptian Bondage', *SISR* 3 (1979), pp. 64–9.

Blaisdell, J D, 'Abominable and relatively unclean flesh: parasites and the prohibition against pork in Ancient Egypt and Israel', *Argos* 19 (1998), pp. 363–70.

Bower, Walter, *Scotichronicon,* gen. ed. D.E.R. Watt, vol. I, Books I and II, eds. John and Winifred Macqueen, Aberdeen Univ. Press, Aberdeen, 1993.

Brackman, Arnold C, *The Search for the Gold of Tutankhamen,* Robert Hale, London, 1978.

Breasted, Charles, *Pioneer to the Past: The Story of James Henry Breasted Archaeologist,* Charles Scribner's Sons, New York, NY, 1943.

Brier, Bob, *The Murder of Tutankhamen: A 3000-year-old Murder Mystery,* Weidenfeld and Nicolson, London, 1998.

Browning, Iain, *Petra,* 3rd ed., 1989, Jordan Distribution Agency/Chatto & Windus, London, 1995.

Budge, E A Wallis, *An Egyptian Hieroglyphic Dictionary,* 2 vols., 1920, Dover, New York, NY, 1978.

Budge, E A Wallis, *The Gods of the Egyptians,* 2 vols., 1904, Dover Publications, 1969.

Budge, Sir Ernest A Wallis, *Tutānkhamen, Amenism, Atenism and Egyptian Monotheism, with hieroglyphic texts of hymns to Amen and Aten,* Martin Hopkinson, London, 1923.

Burghclere, Winifred, 'Introduction', in Carter and Mace, *The Tomb of Tut.ankh.Amen,* I, pp. 1–40.

Burridge, Alwyn L, 'Akhenaten: A New Perspective. Evidence of a Genetic Disorder in the Royal Family of 18th Dynasty Egypt', *JSSEA* 23 (1993), pp. 63–74.

Burridge, Alwyn L, 'Did Akhenaten Suffer from Marfan's Syndrome?', *BA* 59:2 (June 1996), pp. 127–8.

Campbell, S, & A Green, eds., *The Archaeology of Death in the Ancient Near East: Oxbow Monograph 51,* Oxbow Books, Oxford, 1995.

Capart, Jean, *The Tomb of Tutankhamen,* Geo. Allen and Unwin, London, 1923.

Carnarvon, The 5th Earl, *see also* Herbert, George Edward Stanhope Molyneux.

Carnarvon, Lord, typewritten draft article, dated 10 December 1922, Department of Egyptian Antiquities, British Museum, quoted in Reeves, *Howard Carter before Tutankhamun,* pp. 140–1.

Carnarvon, The 5th Earl, 'The Egyptian treasure: story of the discovery', *The Times,* 11 December 1922, pp. 13–14.

Carnarvon, [The 6th] Earl of, *Ermine Tales: More Memoirs of the Earl of Carnarvon,* Weidenfeld and Nicolson, London, 1980.

Carnarvon, [The 6th] Earl of, *No Regrets; Memoirs of the Earl of Carnarvon,* Weidenfeld and Nicolson, London, 1976.

Carter, Howard, Lett's No. 46 Indian and Colonial Rough Diary 1924, The Griffith Institute, Ashmolean Museum, Oxford.

Carter, Howard, MSS. Notebook 1, The Griffith Institute, Ashmolean Museum, Oxford.

Carter, Howard, *Tut.Ankh.Amen: The Politics of Discovery,* with an introduction by Nicholas Reeves, Libri Publications, London, 1998.

Carter, Howard, and Alan H Gardiner, 'The tomb of Ramesses IV and the Turin plan of a royal tomb', *JEA* 4 (1917), pp. 130–158.

Carter, Howard, and A C Mace, *The Tomb of Tut.ankh.Amen,* vol. I, 1923; Howard Carter, vol. II, 1927; Howard Carter, vol. III, 1933; 3 vols., Cooper Square Publishers, New York, NY, 1963.

'Cheiro', (Count Louis Hamon), *Confessions: memoirs of a modern seer,* Jarrolds, London, 1932.

'Cheiro', (Count Louis Hamon), *Real Life Stories: A Collection of Sensational Personal Experiences,* Herbert Jenkins, London, 1934.

Coates, T F G, and R S Warren Bell, *Marie Corelli, the Writer & the Woman,* Hutchinson, London, 1903.

Collins, Andrew, *From the Ashes of Angels,* Michael Joseph, London, 1996.

Collins, Andrew, *Gods of Eden,* Headline, London, 1998.

Comay, Joan, *Who's Who in Jewish History after the period of the Old Testament,* 1974, Routledge, London and New York, NY, 1995.

Cory, I C, *Ancient Fragments,* 1832, Wizards Bookshelf, Savage, MN, 1975.

Daily Express, 'Lord Carnarvon's last hours: sudden failure of hotel lights', 6 April 1923, p. 1.

Daily Express, 'Egyptian collectors in a panic: Sudden rush to hand over their treasures to museums: Groundless fears', 7 April 1923, p. 1.

Daily Express, 'Tragedy of Lord Westbury. "I cannot stand any more horrors." Pharaoh's curse.', 22 February 1930, pp. 1–2.

Daily Mail, The, 'Tragedy of the Hon. R Bethell. Death at his club. Tut-ankh.amen curse recalled.', 16 November 1929, p. 11.

Davies, N de G, *The Rock Tombs of El Amarna: Part II. – The tombs of Panehesy and Meryra II*, 1905, Egypt Exploration Fund, London, 1979.

Davis, Theodore M, *Excavations: Bibân el Molûk: The Tombs of Harmhabi and Touatânkhamanou*, with Theodore M. Davis, 'The discovery of the tombs'; Sir Gaston Maspero, 'King Harmhabi and Touatânkhamanou'; George Daressy, 'Catalogue of the objects discovered', Constable, London, 1912.

Davis, Theodore M, *The Tomb of Queen Tîyi*: with Theodore M Davis '*The Discovery of the Tomb*'; Gaston Maspero, 'Sketch of the life of Queen Tîyi'; G Elliot Smith, 'Note of the estimate of the age attained by the person whose skeleton was found in the tomb'; Edward Ayrton, 'The Excavations of 1907'; George Daressy, Catalogue of the objects discovered'; E. Harold Jones, 'Illustrations in colour', Constable, London, 1910.

Davis, Wade, *The Serpent and the Rainbow*, Wm Collins, London, 1986.

Dawson, Geoffrey, to Gordon Robbins, Memorandum, 'Informing him of Lord Carnarvon's offer of exclusive news on the opening of Tutankhamun's tomb', 14 November 1922, Archives and Records Office, News International Group, London, GR/3/19/3.

Dawson, Warren R, and Eric P Uphill, *Who was who in Egyptology*, 3rd revised ed. by M L Bierbrier, The Egypt Exploration Society, London, 1995.

Derry, D, 'Note on the skeleton hitherto believed to be that of King Akhenaten', *ASAE* 31 (1931), pp. 115–19.

Derry, Douglas E, 'Report upon the Examination of Tut.ankh.Amen's Mummy', in Carter, *The Tomb of Tut.ankh.Amen*, II, pp. 143–61.

Desroches-Noblecourt, Christine, *Tutankhamen: Life and Death of a Pharaoh*, The Connoisseur and Michael Joseph, London, 1963.

Diodorus of Sicily, with an English trans. by Francis R Walton, 12 vols., Wm Heinemann, London; Harvard Univ. Press, Cambridge, MA, 1967.

Drower, E S, *The Mandaeans of Iraq and Iran*, OUP, 1937.

Dugdale, Blanche E C, *Arthur James Balfour: First Earl of Balfour, KG, OM, FRS., etc.*, vol. 1, Hutchinson, London, 1936.

Easton, M G, *The Illustrated Bible Dictionary*, 1894, Bracken Books, London, 1989.

Eaton-Krauss, Marianne, 'The Sarcophagus in the Tomb of Tut'ankhamūn', in Reeves, 1992, pp. 85–90.

Ellen, Roy F, and David Reason, eds., *Classifications in their Social Context*, Academic Press, London; New York, NY; San Francisco, CA, 1979.

Ellis, Ralph, *Tempest & Exodus*, 2000, Edfu Books, PO Box 165, Cheshire, CW8 4WF, 2001.

Engelbach, R, 'Material for a revision of the history of the heresy period of the XVIIIth Dynasty', *ASAE* 40 (1940), pp. 133–65.

Engelbach, R, 'The so-called coffin of Akhenaten', *ASAE* 31 (1931), pp. 98–114.

The Egyptian Gazette, author unknown, gossip column, 30 March 1923.

Evans, Lorraine, *Kingdom of the Ark,* Simon and Schuster, London, 2000.

Fairman, H W, 'Once again the so-called coffin of Akhenaten', *JEA* 47 (1960), pp. 25–40.

Filer, Joyce M, 'The KV 55 body: the facts', *EA* 17 (Autumn 2000), pp. 13–14.

Filer, Joyce M, 'Anatomy of a Mummy', *Archaeology* 55:2, Archaeological Institute of America, New York (March/April 2002), pp. 26–29.

Finkelstein, Israel, 'Ethnicity and Origin of the Iron I Settlers in the Highlands of Canaan: Can the Real Israel Stand Up?', *BA* 59:4 (December 1996), pp. 198–212.

Finkelstein, Israel, and Neil Asher Silberman, *The Bible Unearthed: Archaeology's New Vision of Ancient Israel and the Origin of Its Sacred Texts,* The Free Press, New York, NY, 2001.

Frazer, Sir James George, *The Golden Bough: A Study in Magic and Religion,* abridged edition, 1922, Macmillan, London, 1941.

Frayling, Christopher, *The Face of Tutankhamun,* Faber and Faber, London, 1992.

Freud, Sigmund, *Moses and Monotheism,* Hogarth Press and the Institute of Psychoanalysis, London, 1940.

Ferguson, Niall, *The House of Rothschild: The World's Banker 1849–1998,* 1998, Penguin, London, 2000.

Gardiner, Alan H, *Egypt of the Pharaohs,* 1961, OUP, 1964.

Gardiner, Alan H, *My Working Years,* privately published, 9 July 1962.

Gardiner, Sir Alan H, *Late-Egyptian Stories,* Bibliotheca Aegyptiaca, Brussels, 1931.

Gardiner, Margaret, *A Scatter of Memories,* Free Association Books, London, 1988.

Gidney, the Rev. W T, *The history of the London Society for Promoting Christianity amongst the Jews From 1809 to 1908,* London Society for Promoting Christianity amongst the Jews, London, 1908.

Gilbert, Adrian, *Magi: The quest for a secret tradition,* Bloomsbury, London, 1996.

Ginzberg, Louis, *The Legends of the Jews,* vol. II, 1920, The Jewish Publication Society of America, New York, NY, 1969.

Giveon, Raphael, *Les Bédouins Shosou des documents Égyptians,* E J Brill, Leiden, Holland, 1971.

Giveon, Raphael, 'The Shosu of the Late XXth Dynasty', *JARCE* 8 (1969–1970), pp. 51–3.

Giveon, Raphael, 'Toponymes ouest-Asiatiques à Soleb', in *VT* 14 (1964), pp. 239–55.

Glueck, Nelson, *The Other Side of the Jordan,* 1940, American Schools of Oriental Research, New Haven, CN, 1945.

Goetze, Albrecht, 'The Plague Prayers of Mursilis' in Pritchard, *Ancient Near Eastern Texts relating to the Old Testament,* pp. 394–6.

Gottwald, Norman K, *The Tribes of Yahweh,* Orbis Books, Maryknoll, NY, 10545, 1970.

Graves, Robert, *Lawrence and the Arabs,* Jonathan Cape, London, 1927.

Grdseloff, Bernhard, 'Édôm, d'aprés les sources égyptiennes', *RHJE* 1 (1947), pp. 71–99.

Greenberg, Moshe, *The Hab/piru,* 1955, American Oriental Society, New Haven, CN, 1975.

Greenwood, Sarah, *Highclere Castle,* Norman Hudson, Upper Wardington, Banbury, Oxon., 1988.

Gündüz, Şinasi, 'The Knowledge of Life', *JSS* 3 (1994).

Güterbock, Hans Gustav, 'The Deeds of Suppiluliuma as Told by His Son Mursili II', *JCS* 10 (1965), pp. 41–130.

Habachi, Labib, 'Khatâ'na-Qantîr: importance', *ASAE* 52 (1952), pp. 443–559.

Hadidi, Dr Adnan, *Studies in the history and archaeology of Jordan,* 3 vols., Department of Antiquities, Amman, Jordan, vol. 1, 1982; vol. 2, 1985; vol. 3, 1987.

Hamon, Count Louis, *see* 'Cheiro'.

Har-el, Menashe, *The Sinai Journeys: The Route of the Exodus,* 1968, Ridgefield Publishing Company, San Diego, CA, 1983.

Harmon, Brian, 'Oakland arsenic fears resurface', *The Detroit News,* 12 March 1997.

Harris, J R, 'Akhenaten and Nefernefruaten in the Tomb of Tut'ankhamūn', in Reeves, 1992, pp. 55–72.

Harris, J R, 'How long was the Reign of Horemheb?' *JEA* 54 (1968), pp. 95–9.

Harrison, R G, 'An Anatomical Examination of Pharaonic Remains Purported to be Akhenaten', *JEA* 52 (1966), pp. 95–119.

Hastings, James, ed., *Encyclopaedia of Religion and Ethics,* 13 vols., 1915, T & T Clark, Edinburgh, 1930.

Herbert, George, 5ᵗʰ Earl of Carnarvon, account of discovery of Tutankhamun's tomb (copy), c. 1922–3, British Library Manuscript Collection, RP 17991.

Herbert, George Edward Stanhope Molyneux. 5th Earl of Carnarvon, and Howard Carter, *Five Years' Explorations at Thebes. A record of work done 1907–1911 ... With chapters by F L Griffith, George Legrain, George Möller, Percy E. Newberry and Wilhelm Spiegelberg,* Henry Frowde, London, 1912.

Herbert, Mervyn, diaries 1917–1923, Private Papers Collection, Middle East Centre, St Antony's College, Oxford, GB165–0144.

Herodotus, *The History of Herodotus,* 1910, 2 vols., J. M. Dent, London; E P Dutton, New York, NY, 1940.

Herzl, Theodor, *Der Judenstaat: Versuch einer modernen Losung der Judenfrage ... Dritte Auflage,* Breitenstein, Leipzig & Vienna, 1896.

Hesse, Brian, 'Pig Lovers and Pig Haters: Patterns of Palestinian Pork Production', *JE* 10:2 (Winter 1990), pp. 195–225.

Hislop, *The Two Babylons, or the papal worship proved to be the worship of Nimrud and his wife,* 3ʳᵈ edition, Partridge, London, 1921.

Holladay Jr., John S, *Cities of the Delta, pt. III: Tell el Maskhuta: Preliminary Report on the Wadi Tumilat Project 1978–1979,* Undena Publications, Malibu, 1982.

Hoving, Thomas, *Tutankhamun – The Untold Story,* Simon and Schuster, New York, NY, 1978.

Hunn, Eugene, 'The Abominations of Leviticus Revised: A Commentary on Anomaly in Symbolic Anthropology', in Ellen and Reason, *Classifications in their Social Context,* pp. 103–16.

Hyde, H Montgomery, *Norman Birkett: The Life of Lord Birkett of Ulverston,* Hamish Hamilton, London, 1964.

James, T G H, *Howard Carter: the Path to Tutankhamun,* Kegan Paul, London, 1992.

John, Robert, *Behind the Balfour Declaration: The Hidden Origins of Today's Mideast Crisis,* Institute for Historical Review, Costa Mesa, CA, 1988.

Josephus, Flavius, *Antiquities of the Jews, see* Flavius Josephus, *The Works of Flavius Josephus.*

Josephus, Flavius, *Flavius Josephus Against Apion, see* Flavius Josephus, *The Works of Flavius Josephus.*

Josephus, Flavius, *Wars of the Jews, see* Flavius Josephus, *The Works of Flavius Josephus.*

Josephus, Flavius, trans. Wm. Whiston, *The Works of Flavius Josephus,* Wm. P Nimmo, Edinburgh, nd. (c. 1870).

Keedick, Lee, 'Howard Carter', unpublished memoirs, c. 1924.

Keys, David, 'Curse (& Revenge) of the Mummy Invented by Victorian Writers', *The Independent,* 31 December 2000.

Kitchen, Kenneth, *Suppiluliuma and the Amarna Pharaohs: A Study in Relative Chronology,* Liverpool Univ. Press, Liverpool, 1962.

Koran, The, trans. with notes by NJ Dawood, 1956, Penguin, Harmondsworth, Middlesex, 1990.

LMA (Louisa May Alcott), 'Lost in a Pyramid' *The New World,* vol. 1, no. 1, 1869, p. 8. Periodicals collection, Library of Congress, Washington, DC, Cat. No. AP2 N6273.

Landman, Samuel, *Great Britain, the Jews and Palestine,* New Zionist Press, London, 1936.

Laughlin, John C H, *Archaeology and the Bible,* Routledge, London, 2000.

Lebor Gabála Erenn: The book of the taking of Ireland, Bk. 5, ed. and trans. with notes, etc., R A Stewart Macalister, 1956, Irish Texts Society, Dublin, 1995.

Lee, Christopher C., … *the grand piano came by camel: Arthur C Mace, the neglected Egyptologist,* Mainstream Publishing, Edinburgh, 1992.

Lichtheim, M, *Ancient Egyptian Literature* II, Univ. of California Press, Berkeley, CA, 1976.

Lucas, Alfred, 'Notes on Some of the Objects from the Tomb of Tut-ankhamun', *ASAE* 41 (1942), pp. 135–47.

Lucas, Alfred, 'Notes on Some of the Objects from the Tomb of Tut-ankhamun', *ASAE* 45 (1947), pp. 133–4.

Lucas, A, 'Poisons in Ancient Egypt', *JEA* 24 (1938), pp. 198–9.

Lucas, A, *The Route of the Exodus of the Israelites from Egypt,* Edward Arnold, London, 1938.

Mackenzie, Donald A, *Myths of Babylonia and Assyria,* Gresham Publishing, London, nd. (c. 1910).

Mahdy, Christine el, *Tutankhamun: The Life and Death of a Boy King,* Headline, London, 1999.

Manetho, with an English trans. by W G Waddell, 1940, Wm. Heinemann, London; Harvard Univ. Press, Cambridge, MA, 1964.

Manning, Stuart W, *A Test of Time: the volcano of Thera and the chronology and history of the Aegean and East Mediterranean in the mid second millennium BC,* Oxbow Books, Oxford, 1999.

Mazar, Amihai, 'The "Bull Site" – An Iron Age I Open Cult Place', *BASOR* 247 (1937), pp. 27–42.

McCoy, Floyd W, and Grant Heiken, 'Anatomy of an Eruption: How a Terrifying Series of Explosions Reshaped the Minoan Island of Thera', *Archaeology* 43:3 (1990), pp. 42–9.

Mendenhall, George E, 'The Hebrew Conquest of Palestine', *BA* 25:3 (1962), pp. 66–87.

Merton, Arthur, 'An Egyptian treasure: Great find at Thebes: Lord Carnarvon's long quest.'; 'Doctor Petrie's views: Unique finds', *The Times,* 30 November 1922, p. 13–14.

Merton, Arthur, 'Ld. Carnarvon's Death. 16 Years' Work in Egypt', *The Times,* 6 April 1923, p. 11.

Meyer, Eduard, *Aegyptische Chronologie,* Abhandlungen der Königl. Preuss. Akademie der Wissenschaften, Leipzig, 1904.

Meyer, Eduard, *Geschichte des Altertums,* 2 vols., 1907, J G Cotta'sche Buchhandlung Nachfolger, Stuttgart and Berlin, vol. 1, 1925 ; vol. 2, 1928.

Michell, John, *Eccentric Lives and Peculiar Notions,* 1984, Adventures Unlimited, Kempton, IL, 1999.

Millard, Alan, 'How Reliable Is Exodus?', *BAR* 24:4 (July/August 2000), pp. 51–7.

Molleson, Theya, & Stuart Campbell, 'Deformed Skulls at Tell Arpachiyah: the Social Context', in Campbell & Green, *The Archaeology of Death in the Ancient Near East: Oxbow Monograph 51,* pp. 45–55.

Montserrat, Dominic, 'Louise May Alcott and the Mummy's Curse, *KMT* 9:2 (Summer 1998), pp. 70–5.

Moran, William L, ed. and trans., *The Amarna Letters,* John Hopkins Univ. Press, Baltimore, 1992.

Morton, H V, 'Tragedy of Lord Carnarvon', *Daily Express,* 6 April 1923, p. 4.

Na'aman, Nadav, 'Habiru and Hebrews: the transfer of a social term to the literary sphere', *JNES* 45:4 (1986), pp. 271–88.

Naville, Edouard, 'The geography of the Exodus', *JEA* 10 (1924), pp. 18–39.

Naville, Edouard, *The Store-city of Pithom and the Route of the Exodus,* Egypt Exploration Fund, London, 1903.

Nelson, Edith Halford, *Out of the Silence,* Rider, London, nd. (c. 1945).

Nennius: British History and The Welsh Annals., ed. and trans. John Morris; 'History from the Sources', gen. ed., John Morris, Phillimore, London and Chichester, 1980.

Nennius, *Historia Brittonum,* see *Nennius: British History and The Welsh Annals.*

Nielsen, Ditlef, *Die altarabische Mondreligion und die mosaische Ueberlieferung,* Karl J Trübner, Strassburg, 1904.

Nielsen, Dr Ditlef, *The site of the biblical Mount Sinai: A claim for Petra,* Paul Geuthner, Paris; Nyt Nordisk Forlag Arnold Busck, Copenhagen; Otto Harrassowitz, Leipzig, 1928.

Nielsen, Dr Ditlef, *Handbuch der Altarabischen Altertumskunde,* vol. 1, 'Die altarabische kultur', NYT Nordisk Forlag/Arnold Busch, Copenhagen, 1927.

Odelain, O, and R Séguineau, *Dictionary of Proper Names and Places in the Bible,* 1978, Robert Hale, London, 1991

Oesterley, W O E, and Theodore H Robinson, *Hebrew Religion: Its Origin and Development,* SPCK, London, 1952.

Osman, Ahmed, *Moses Pharaoh of Egypt,* Grafton Books, London, 1990.

Pausanias, *Description of Greece,* with an English trans. by W H S Jones, 4 vols., 1918, Wm. Heinemann, London; Harvard Univ. Press, Cambridge, MA, 1964.

Pearce, Fred, 'Bangladesh's arsenic poisoning – who is to blame?' *UNESCO Courier,* Paris, January 2001.

Pendlebury, J D S, 'Summary report on the excavations at Tell el-'Amarnah 1935–1936', *JEA* 22 (1936), pp. 194–8.

Petrie, W M Flinders Petrie, *Researches in Sinai,* with chapter by C T Currelly, John Murray, London, 1906.

Petrie, Sir William Matthew Flinders, *Tell el Amarna;* with chapters by Prof. A H Sayce; ... F Ll Griffith; ... and F C J Spurrell, Methuen, London, 1894.

Phillips, Graham, *Act of God: Moses, Tutankhamun and the Myth of Atlantis,* Sidgwick & Jackson, London, 1998.

Phillips, Graham, *The Moses Legacy,* Sidgwick & Jackson, London, 2002.

Pliny, *Natural History,* English trans. H Rackham, in 10 volumes; vol. 4, 1945, Harvard Univ. Press, Cambridge, MA; Wm. Heinemann, London, 1986.

Plutarch, *Isis and Osiris,* see *Plutarch's Moralia.*

Plutarch, *Plutarch's Moralia,* `The Face of the Moon', trans. H Cherniss & W C Helmbold, Wm. Heinemann, London, 1957.

Polinger Foster, Karen, and Robert K Ritner, 'Texts, Storms, and the Thera Eruption', *JNES* 55:1 (1996), pp. 1–14.

Pope, Stephen, and Elizabeth-Anne Wheal, *The Macmillan Dictionary of the First World War,* 1995, Macmillan, London, 1997.

Pritchard, James B, ed., *Ancient Near Eastern Texts relating to the Old Testament,* 1955, Princeton Univ. Press, Princeton, NJ, 1969.

Rapp (1893–1984), T C, unpublished memoirs, Private Papers Collection, Middle East Centre, Oxford.

Redford, Donald B, *Akhenaten: The Heretic King*, 1984, Princeton Univ. Press, Princeton, NJ, 1987.

Redford, Donald B, *Egypt, Canaan, and Israel in Ancient Times,* Princeton Univ. Press, Princeton, NJ, 1992.

Redford, Donald B, *Pharaonic King-Lists, Annals and Day-books: A Contribution to the Study of the Egyptian Sense of History,* Benben Publications, Mississauga, Ontario, 1986.

Reeves, C N, 'Tutankhamūn and his Papyri', *GS* 88 (1985), pp. 39–45.

Reeves, C N ed. and intro., *After Tut'ankhamūn: Research and excavation in the Royal Necropolis at Thebes,* Kegan Paul, London 1992.

Reeves, Nicholas, *Akhenaten: Egypt's False Prophet,* Thames and Hudson, London, 2001.

Reeves, Nicholas, *The Complete Tutankhamun,* Thames and Hudson, London, 1995.

Reeves, Nicholas, and John H Taylor, *Howard Carter before Tutankhamun,* British Museum Press, London, 1992.

Robertson Smith, W, *The Religion of the Semites,* 1889, Meridian Library, New York, NY, 1957.

Rose, Mark, 'Who's in Tomb 55', *Archaeology* 55:2 Archaeological Institute of America, New York (March/April 2002), pp. 22–27.

Rowton, Michael B, 'Dimorphic structure and the problem of the 'Apirû-'Ibrîm', *JNES* 35:1 (1976), pp. 13–20.

Samson, Julia, *Nefertiti and Cleopatra: Queen-Monarchs of Ancient Egypt,* The Rubicon Press, London, 1990.

Shepherd, Naomi, *Ploughing Sand: British Rule in Palestine 1917–1948,* John Murray, London, 1999.

Silberman, Neil A, 'Visions of the Future: Albright in Jerusalem', *BA* 56:1 (1993), pp. 8–16.

Silberman, Neil Asher, 'Who Were the Israelites?', *Archaeology* 45:2 (1992), pp. 22–30.

Smith, G Elliot, 'Note of the estimate of the age attained by the person whose skeleton was found in the tomb', 1910, pp. xxiii–xxiv, see Davis, *The Tomb of Queen Tiyi.*

Smith, G Elliot, *The Royal Mummies,* L'institut français d'archéologie orientale, Cairo, 1912.

Stanley, Arthur Penrhyn, *Sinai and Palestine in connection with their history,* John Murray, London, 1881.

Stecchini, Livio Catullo, 'Notes on the Relation of Ancient Measures to the Great Pyramid', in Tompkins, *Secrets of the Great Pyramid,* pp. 287–382.

Stoker, Bram, *The Jewel of Seven Stars,* Wm. Heinemann, London, 1903.

Te Velde, Herman, *Seth, God of Confusion: A Study of his Role in Egyptian Mythology and Religion,* E J Brill, Leiden, 1967.

Times, The, 'The Egyptian find: Lord Carnarvon's hopes: Difficulties of photography: The unopened chamber, 18 December 1922, pp. 13–14.

Times, The, 'The Egyptian treasure: The importance of the find: Dr A Gardiner's views', 4 December 1922, p. 7.

Tompkins, Peter, *Secrets of the Great Pyramid,* Allen Lane, London, 1971.

Van Seters, John, *The Hyksos: a new investigation,* Yale Univ. Press, New Haven and London, 1966.

Vandenberg, Philipp, *The Curse of the Pharaohs,*1973, Coronet, Dunton Green, Sevenoaks, Kent, 1975.

Vandenberg, Philipp, *The Forgotten Pharaoh: The Discovery of Tutankhamun,* 1978, Hodder and Stoughton, London, 1980.

Vaux, Roland de, *The Bible and the Ancient Near East,* Darton, Longman and Todd, London, 1972.

Ward, William A, 'The Shasu "Bedouin": notes on a recent publication', *JESHO* 15 (1972), pp. 35–60.

Weigall, Arthur, *The Life and Times of Akhenaten*, 1910, Thornton Butterworth, London, 1923.

Weigall, Arthur, *Tutankhamen And Other Essays*, Geo. H. Doran, New York, NY, 1923.

Weizmann, Chaim, *Trial and Error: The Autobiography of Chaim Weizmann*, East and West Library, London, 1950.

Welsh, Frances, *Tutankhamun's Egypt*, Shire Egyptology, Princes Risborough, Bucks., 1993.

Westrate, Bruce, *The Arab Bureau: British Policy in the Middle East, 1916–1920*, Pennsylvania State Univ. Press, Univ. Park, PE, 1992.

Whitelam, Keith W, *The Invention of Ancient Israel: The Silencing of Palestinian History*, Routledge, London/New York, NY, 1996.

Wiener, Malcolm H, and James P. Allen, 'Separate Lives: The Ahmose Tempest Stela and the Theran Eruption', *JNES* 57:1 (1998), pp. 1–28.

Wilson, Ian, *The Exodus Enigma*, 1985, Guild Publishing, London, 1986.

Winstone, H V F, *Howard Carter and the discovery of the tomb of Tutankhamun*, Constable, London, 1991.

Woolley, C Leonard, *Ur of the Chaldees*, Ernest Benn, London, 1929.

Wright, William, ed., *The Illustrated Bible Treasury*, Thom. Nelson, London, 1897.

Wynne, Barry, *Behind the Mask of Tutankhamen*, Souvenir Press, London, 1972.

Zayadine, Fawzi, 'Caravan Routes Between Egypt and Nabataea and the Voyage of Sultan Baibars to Petra in 1276' in Hadadi, *Studies in the History and Archaeology of Jordan*, II, pp. 159–73.

Documentaries

NBC television report on fungal agents in Tutankhamun's tomb, no screening date, c. 1990s.

INDEX